THE LIFE AND THOUGHT OF SIGER OF BRABANT, THIRTEENTH-CENTURY PARISIAN PHILOSOPHER

An Examination of His Views on the Relationship of Philosophy and Theology

Tony Dodd

The Edwin Mellen Press
Lewiston•Queenston•Lampeter

Library of Congress Cataloging-in-Publication Data

This volume has been registered with the Library of Congress.

ISBN 0-7734-8477-9 (hard)

A CIP catalog record for this book is available from the British Library.

The Edwin Mellen Press
Box 450
Lewiston, New York
USA 14092-0450

The Edwin Mellen Press
Box 67
Queenston, Ontario
CANADA L0S 1L0

The Edwin Mellen Press, Ltd.
Lampeter, Ceredigion, Wales
UNITED KINGDOM SA48 8LT

Printed in the United States of America

THE LIFE AND THOUGHT OF SIGER OF BRABANT, THIRTEENTH-CENTURY PARISIAN PHILOSOPHER

This book is dedicated to my wife Claire and to my children Felicity, Juliet and Alexander for the untold and countless sacrifices which they have made over the last few years during the research and completion of this study.

TABLE OF CONTENTS

xvi

PREFACE

First of all, I wish to acknowledge the huge debt that I owe to a number of most distinguished predescessors, such as Pierre Mandonnet and above all Fernand Van Steenberghen, who have enabled Siger of Brabant to be brought to the intention of so many scholars. Without their painstaking research and that of so many others, it would have been impossible to develop this study which was successfully presented for doctoral examination at the University of Exeter in 1995.

Some explanation may also be required for more traditional sections of readership regarding the methodology of this work. Having originally studied both Scholastic Philosophy and Theology at the Pontifical Gregorian University in Rome, I have always maintained a very considerable interest in the issues raised within this book, as a result of the enthusiasm and inspiration instilled in me by so many of the professors there. Hence, much of my work as a theologian and as a teacher has centred around the relationship between what could be described as secular knowledge and religious belief, with the notions of academic freedom and legitimate religious authority never far from the surface.

Clearly all writers of any age and any religious tradition need to be fairly examined in their independent integrity rather than merely from the perspectives of particular committed viewpoints of others; nevertheless it should of course be acknowledged that the former are always to be accurately placed within their particular historical, intellectual and cultural contexts.

Consequently, I have come to believe that, without in any way superimposing any artificial conceptualisation of the ideas of different thinkers into totally inappropriate categories and compartments, the underlying processes of argument and rationalisation can often be seen to be similar or even identical, despite the apparent contrasts with regard to content. Logicians, of course, still use similar principles of argument to those espoused during the Middle Ages. Historians, furthermore, acknowledge that one of the principal aims of their discipline is to learn from the past and to identify analogous sets of circumstances to guide humankind at the present time and in the future.

A study of Siger of Brabant, the acknowledged leader of the group of independent scholars in the Faculty of Arts during the critical period of 1270-1277 in the most pre-eminent university of the Middle Ages , seemed to present a most appropriate area of research. The more I subsequently discovered of the nuances and developments in his teaching and the more I reflected upon its implications, the closer I came to sense an understanding of his persona, feeling an empathy across the centuries with his intellectual struggles. I have no doubt that there are lessons in this conflict within himself and with some of his contemporaries that are relevant and important for us today.

I acknowledge that many more traditional scholars who might justifiably describe themselves as greater medieval "purists" than myself would prefer simply to examine medieval writings independently of later thought. They will understandably feel uncomfortable with part of my approach which tries to break out from a more "two-dimensional" understanding and to open up a much broader perspective. At the same time in all the five core chapters regarding Siger's ideas and thought (Chapters Four to Eight), I have also tried to take full account of the perfectly valid point of view of this more traditional approach by analysing Siger's ideas as found in his writings within their own historical context before drawing out any further implications from this broader perspective.

It is therefore with this intention in mind that I have tried to provide a contemporary insight into the relevance of Siger of Brabant, not only in medieval context but also to intellectual thinkers today. His academic struggle does indeed deserve not only to be more widely known within the circle of medievalists but also to reach a wider knowledge and understanding of scholars of many disciplines today. I hope that, without lessening the quality of its scholarship, this book will prove of considerable interest to many such readers.

TONY DODD

ACKNOWLEDGEMENTS

The author wishes to express his deepest appreciation to:

Dr. Alastair Logan of the University of Exeter for his invaluable help and support throughout the development of this thesis;

Dr. Jacqueline Hamesse, of the College Thomas More, Louvain and Secretary of the Societé Internationale pour l'Étude de la Philosophie Médiévale for her valuable information and help at both the beginning of my research and later;

Signora Marilena Rossi Caponeri, Senior Archivist of the Commune of Orvieto, and her assistants, and also Signora Lucia Tammaro-Conti of the Biblioteca Municipale of Orvieto for the willingness and earnestness with which they guided me through a wide range of records and documents in their care;

Dr. Antonio Carol Hortensch of Pamplona for so kindly sending me a copy of his unpublished thesis which he submitted successfully to the University of Navarra to obtain his doctorate in 1990;

Dr. Stephen Brock of the Ateneo Romano della Santo Croce for kindly sending me copies of his own and two other papers delivered at a

Philosophy Conference held there in Rome on 25-26 February 1993, which I was unfortunately unable to attend;

the late Mr. Keith Donaldson, Senior Librarian of the University College, Scarborough and his assistants for their enormous interest and patience, especially in deciphering my handwriting.

THE LIFE AND THOUGHT OF SIGER OF BRABANT, THIRTEENTH-CENTURY PARISIAN PHILOSOPHER

INTRODUCTION

There have, traditionally, been two ways of looking at the problem of the relationship between medieval philosophy and theology, since serious re-examination of the philosophy of this period really began in earnest around the middle of the nineteenth century.

There have been those writers, such as Étienne Gilson, who believed that the great philosopher-theologians of the Patristic and Medieval periods were so imbued with the background of their religious faith that their philosophical teachings were only developed in the light of these beliefs. Hence, Gilson claimed that we can only speak accurately of Christian philosophers or, come to that, of Jewish or Islamic philosophers [1]. Thus, the thought of Thomas Aquinas is presented, for example, in what he sees as the natural theological order, starting from his discussion of God [2], rather than from a metaphysical or even a logical basis, as Descartes does of course. To some extent, this was the perspective of Stephen Tempier and other opponents of Siger who, as we shall see, viewed some of his positions as being irreconcilable with the neo-Augustinian thought which they tended to identify with Christian orthodox belief.

On the other hand, there have been those who have delineated a sharp distinction between the two areas, focusing on the pagan origins of Greek thought. As a result, there has been a strong emphasis on the characteristic distinctiveness of such Platonic and Aristotelian ideas from the teachings of Christian tradition.

Indeed, there were a number of rationalist thinkers, such as Bartholémy Hauréau, who saw most medieval thinkers as struggling valiantly to become free from and independent of the influence of the Church, although usually failing to do so. To some extent, even Van Steenberghen, a modern expert on Siger to whom very frequent reference is made in the course of this study, falls into this category, though for different reasons. He emphasizes what he sees as Siger's personal internal crisis to avoid falling into heresy, while trying to develop his thought independently from revelation, as, for example, when Thomas Aquinas presents objections to his positions [3]. Indeed, Van Steenberghen declares that we have much more cause to describe Thomas and others as philosophers, who happen to be Christians, rather than to speak of Christian philosophy as such [4]. A positive asset of this approach is that it should facilitate the discovery of a deeper common thread within all three of the faiths of Western Europe during the period in question, thus making dialogue between them more feasible [5].

In more recent times, there has been a growing tendency, however, to follow a third and more thematic approach to medieval philosophy, perhaps looking at one single issue from the perspective of a number of philosophers or, alternatively, considering the overall thought of a philosopher/theologian, but comparing the teaching with those of modern-day thinkers. There is some interest and attractiveness in this, especially since much of twentieth century philosophy, particularly in Great Britain and the United States, has been concerned with the analysis of language. After all, originally Logic had comprised the almost exclusive content of the Arts Faculties in the early part of the thirteenth century and still remained fundamental, as we shall see, even in the latter decades of that century, after the wider corpus of Aristotle's range of writings had been opened up for research and discussion.

A number of good examples of this modern approach can be found in modern studies on Plato and Aristotle, though it can also be noted in writers such as Kenny, who presents some of its analytical aims and presuppositions in his books on Thomas Aquinas [6] and Wyclif [7]. Such a stance makes a very valuable contribution to the task of understanding medieval thinkers today. Indeed, it will at times be adopted in the course of this study. However, it does have the drawback that most modern writers tend to focus unduly on those very issues which particularly interest them today, rather than give a fair overall consideration to the full scope of a medieval writer's thought. Some will go even further and, as a result of an identification of philosophy with twentieth century linguistic analysis and a corresponding call for meaningfulness, will positively exclude from consideration much that Siger and his contemporaries certainly did consider to be philosophy.

Nevertheless, a yet bigger problem arises, in so far as issues and problems are often lifted right out of their historical context into the twentieth century - a point well noted by Marenbon [8]. For example, it is often forgotten that almost all those areas of study, which we call scientific today, fell under the ambit of the Faculty of Arts during the period of our investigation. In addition, many modern writers often neglect to consider adequately the world-views of medieval thinkers, such as the flatness of the world, the astronomical views of Ptolemy, rather than those of Copernicus and Galileo, or the perceived animation of the stars and planets. Furthermore, because this approach is so issue-orientated, it is inclined to fail to make sufficient reference to the wider environment and historical context of the period.

To overcome such drawbacks of what is, in this respect, an almost rootless method, this study will tend to follow an approach that involves some historical analysis rather than being simply direct thematic analysis. This must not of course be confused with what, in the area of biblical scholarship, is called the historico-critical method. Here, it will indeed include a survey of the relevant Sigerian material, relating it to modern perspectives on the relationship between philosophy and theology and on other issues. However, Siger's historical, geographical, sociological, ecclesiastical and, perhaps, psychological contexts will never be far from mind.

The chosen method is, therefore, somewhat akin to that phenomenological approach strongly advocated by Ninian Smart [9] and adopted by many contemporary theologians and religious educators over the last thirty years or so of the twentieth century. While this may have some kinship, as

Lonergan complains, with existentialism, his fears, that in the area of metaphysics it creates a "highly purified empiricism", are not valid when it is considered as a general process and methodology of general and particular examination of Siger's thought and of its context [10].

It is argued that this methodology sheds insights that earlier writers - including Mandonnet and Van Steenberghen - have been unable to take on board sufficiently. To be fair, this situation may have arisen partly as a result of their Neothomist training. This would not have made it easy for them to maintain their study of Siger's teaching and wider academic role at a distance from a Thomist perspective and to provide a more neutral and objective examination.

This approach is not, however, as is often improperly assumed, merely a kind of ultra-objective view of religious thought or practice, but involves an empathetic, though impartial, grasp of a belief-system. This is accomplished with the aid of a temporary "bracketing-out" process of one's own views or even prejudices, so that it is possible to enter mentally into the psyche of a typical believer. Here, likewise, it is hoped that the reader will find himself or herself able, in this sense, to empathize with the actual situation of Siger, without also bringing too much twentieth-century baggage along. Subsequently, having understood the context of the issues, it will be possible to see that much of what Siger has to say is still relevant today.

It will be argued that much of the negative criticism directed at Siger and colleagues, such as Boethius of Dacia, in the Faculty of Arts at the University of Paris, has been unjustified over the years ever since the Condemnations of 1270 and 1277. These latter will be discussed in some depth and it will further be argued that his significance goes much deeper than the contemporary influence he may have had on others, supporters or opponents alike, in the third quarter of the thirteenth century. Indeed, this study will argue that Siger paved the way for that independence of thought and critical opposition to the ecclesiastical authoritarianism of Rome and of the Catholic Church in general which was later to come to flourish in the Renaissance and also in the Protestant Reformation.

To draw on another educational analogy, this method can also in this case be described as "process-orientated" rather than merely "content-orientated". In other words, it is the ways and processes by which Siger comes to his teachings, rather than their actual content, which will be of the greatest interest to, and have most in common with, the modern reader.

For example, the conflict of Siger and his colleagues with the Church Establishment of their day, unsought and undesired on their part as it may have been, does in some ways mirror later conflicts of far more recent Christians, such as those of Darwin and of the Catholic Modernists, in the last two centuries.

Many thirteenth century Popes and other Church leaders felt threatened by the growing independence of intellectual thought which appeared to challenge orthodox religious teaching and, perhaps more crucially, the social and political consequences which could also challenge their temporal power and worldly influence. The most critical difference, however, between the medieval period and more recent times is that they became no longer able to exert such absolute and complete control over the publication and spread of such ideas.

For example, Renan, writing as recently as 1852, had been unable to discover the works of any individual "Averroists", as he termed them, so completely had their works disappeared. He only speaks of them indirectly from the writings of others such as Bonaventure [d.1274], Albert the Great [d.1280] and Thomas Aquinas [d.1274] but, above all, the later frenzied attacks of Raymond Lull [d.1315]. Even so, he declares in the original publication of this seminal essay that he is unable to discover even the names of any of them from these other writers [11].

Furthermore, although the Index of Forbidden Books was still very much in existence even as recently as the 1960s, intended still as a tool to attempt to restrict the spread of new ideas among Church members, nevertheless, even in a pre-television age, this could not possibly have such complete success, once mass-printing had been invented. It had become impossible to destroy all copies of books of which there was official disapproval. As we shall see, however, even in

6

the thirteenth century, copies of manuscripts containing the teaching of Siger were hidden away, deliberately or otherwise, in old libraries and archives - sometimes with unclear or even disguised attribution of authorship.

From examining his fight to assert the independence of the teaching of the Faculty of Arts from that of Theology, it will be possible to discover how his perspective of the relationship between philosophical investigation and revealed theology was in many ways analogous to that of theistic scientists in later centuries, who did not necessarily seek to resolve any apparent conflict between theories and conclusions arising from their empirical research and the traditional teaching of doctrines of Christianity. It will be demonstrated that this in no way implies that Siger ever held a position akin to those accusations of "double-truth", made by Stephen Tempier, the Archbishop of Paris, in 1277. This was considered to involve the assertion that the same statement can be simultaneously true for philosophy but false for theology or vice versa:

> Dicunt enim ea esse vera secundum philosophiam, sed non secundum fidem catholicam, quasi sint duae contrariae veritates, et quasi contra veritatem sacrae Scripturae sit veritas in dictis gentilium damnatorum [12].

[Thus they state things to be true acording to philosophy, but not according to the Catholic faith, as if there are two contrary truths and as if there is a truth in the sayings of pagans in hell that is opposed to the truth of sacred scripture.]

It has been frequently stated that the so-called empirical "certainties" of science have for many people subsequently replaced the former revealed "certainties" of theology and of faith. It will be argued here that, while this may well be the case in so far as attitudes to the content of knowledge are considered, it is on the other hand the investigative method of philosophy, as found in the independent-minded Artists like Siger, that has really led to and been replaced by the processes of scientific investigation.

In the first two chapters, the historical and intellectual context of Siger will be outlined, along with a survey of earlier research and awareness about his teaching over the years. The third chapter will provide an outline of his life and career, according to the present state of knowledge, while the ninth chapter will provide an original and speculative examination of what might have happened to him during the years following his denunciation in Paris in 1277 and his murder in Orvieto a few years later.

The intervening chapters will provide, firstly, an examination of his general views on the nature of truth - to search for any hint of teaching of the "double-truth" here, whether conscious or otherwise; this will be followed by research into his writings to clarify his position over the four main issues cited by Stephen Tempier in his earlier 1270 set of thirteen Condemnations. These chapters will also examine in detail clues as to Siger's views on the relationship between philosophy and revelation and any evidence that indicates his particular relevance to issues of contemporary theology and philosophy.

Finally, the reader will be offered some additional conclusions resulting overall from the research contained in this study, which will further assess Siger's place in intellectual history.

CHAPTER ONE

THE HISTORICAL CONTEXT OF SIGER

1.0.   Introduction.

This chapter will enable the subsequent study of the life and thought of Siger to be placed within its wider historical context within the latter part of the thirteenth century.   It will then examine the early development of the University of Paris.   Finally, the particular changes taking place within the Faculty of Arts will be noted, from the opening-up of the wider study of the works of Aristotle until the major Condemnation of 1270, along with the influences of the various religious and intellectual groups of this period within the Church as a whole and within the University in particular.

1.1.   Background to the Historical Context of Thirteenth Century Intellectual Thought.

For the last decade of the eleventh century, and for much of the twelfth century, Christianity had tried to counter the challenge of Islam and Judaism by officially sanctioning and encouraging recruitment to the Crusading armies and by unofficially turning a blind eye to pogroms.   Nevertheless, we do of course find profound thinkers of considerable stature, such as Anselm of Canterbury and Peter Abelard.

However, in the space of about one hundred years from around the middle of the twelfth century, the rediscovery of a large number of Greek philosophical writings from Aristotle, Plato and others, including the Neoplatonist Proclus, was to transform the medieval approach to learning. As these became available in Latin translations by Michael Scot and others, so also there should be noted the additional influences of Islamic writers and commentators such as Ibn Sina [Avicenna] and Ibn Rushd [Averroes] and of Jewish philosophers, such as Gabirol and Maimonides.

The translations, made in those countries, such as Italy, Sicily and above all Spain, where Christians, Jews and Muslims were in close proximity and often spoke the same languages, were soon to spread through the main centres of learning in Northern Europe too [1].

This era marks the beginning of that approach to study which was to become known as Scholasticism and which was to have such a profound effect on the development of Western learning. The impact of the discovery of this range of intellectual literature outside of the sphere of the Church and of its Fathers was to have enormous repercussions. It was to provide fresh ideas and approaches, provoking the development of new types of theology, with a different style and range from the more traditional and familiar Augustinianism, and also a new dimension of philosophical speculation and investigation on the part of European thinkers.

1.2.   The Development of the University as a Thirteenth Century Institution.

The monasteries had of course managed to maintain a love of learning throughout the so-called Dark Ages but we must note that the number of those who had access to this fund of scholarship was limited to those accepted for the religious life in the traditional way.   In any case, the community life and the life of prayer had always, according to the Rule of St. Benedict, to take priority over study.

Jewish communities, on the other hand, had encouraged literacy and learning for all (even, quite frequently, for women and girls) in their "synagogue-schools", but Christianity had no real equivalents to this, although gradually the Cathedral Schools increased in importance as the secular clergy and students there were more mobile than the monks and hence able to exchange and diffuse new ideas more widely.   Some scholars were even able to visit centres of learning under Islamic influence.

However, the thirteenth century in Europe was to be the age of the founding of the "university", literally referring by its title to the whole group of masters and students residing in the same town or city.

In some case, the universities were directly founded as such (e.g. Naples in 1224), but in Paris and Oxford, which were to become by far the two most prestigious and influential seats of learning in this century, their origins can be traced back to the earlier twelfth century schools of ecclesiastical foundation [2].

Paris was thus typically constituted with four faculties: firstly that of Arts, then leading on to study in the higher ones of Theology, Law and Medicine. Other centres in Northern France, such as Chartres and Rouen, for short periods during the twelfth century, had possessed notable schools, but the pull of Paris had enabled a consistency of excellent teaching to be maintained, which had ensured an early pre-eminence in its reputation, especially in theology [3].

Bologna in Northern Italy on the one hand, and Salerno in Southern Italy on the other, were at the same time acquiring enviable reputations for Law and Medicine respectively, although these two were to be very much the least important faculties in Paris [4].

1.3.   The Origins and Early Development of the University of Paris.

The previous century had been a momentous period from the point of view of Christianity. The Western Church had been involved in the Crusades and all that they implied. The Papacy had extended its power and boldly flexed its muscles in several ways. In Italy, there had been a renewed impetus for the study of Roman law, but in Northern France it was scholasticism which was to provide the impetus for a sudden spurt in the number of masters and students coming together there in this way.

It was above all as a result of Peter Abelard, who had taught in Paris from 1102 to 1136, and whose reputation was so highly esteemed, that Paris attracted from many parts of Europe so many students, with dreams of becoming as revered for their learning and teaching as he had been.

In the second half of the twelfth century there were several schools in Paris, but it was the cathedral school of Notre Dame, where Peter Lombard (eventually to become Bishop of Paris from 1159 to 1164) took over from Abelard, that became pre-eminent for theology. The more mystical school of Saint-Victor had been revered for theology for a while but had lost its influence by 1200. There were also, however, several schools on the Mont Ste. Généviève, which certainly owed their origins to Abelard and where his disciples seemed to have maintained more of his independent spirit [5].

However, it was the ambition of many to have the ability and authority to teach, because this was the time of such heresies in Southern Europe as the Cathars and, in particular, the Albigensians in Languedoc [6], with the result that the "licentia docendi" became very highly prized. This licence was always required before permission was granted to teach and in Paris it needed the sanction and approval of the Chancellor of Notre Dame.

The Statutes of the University of Paris were granted in 1215 by Bull of Pope Innocent III, who had himself in 1208 summoned a crusade against the

Albigensians.   He had been a former Paris Master, as well as one of Bologna, while his pontificate (1198-1216) marks a high point of secular power and associated claims of the medieval papacy [7].   In fact, he may be less well-known to theologians for his approval of the new Rule for Francis of Assisi and his followers than he is for the eight month-long interdict of France and his six year-long interdict of England.   The latter was only concluded by King John making England over to the Pope and agreeing to pay him rent for the kingdom, an event which itself was to lead to the Barons forcing John to sign the Magna Carta, so prompting Papal excommunication of anyone who accepted the latter.

The Bull founding the University was carried out through his legate Robert de Courçon and included strong condemnations of earlier abuses of authority when bribes and excessive fees had been demanded down the years by Chancellors.   These statutes were also significant for being recognized not only by the Pope but also by King Philip II of France, so marking the first public decree of this kind in European education [8].

In fact, such abuses as these regarding the authority to grant the "licentia docendi" [licence to teach] had been going on for some time, as is indicated by the fact that in 1179 the Third Lateran Council had found it necessary to forbid any chancellor of any cathedral school to charge a fee for granting this licence and at the same time to refuse him permission to withhold it from any properly qualified applicant.

Here we have the roots of the principle, as upheld in universities today, of academic independence from either civil or ecclesiastical interference. However, as we shall see later in this study, the Church was to claim rights, not only in matters directly affecting the Faculty of Theology, but also those of the Faculty of Arts, in its demand for orthodoxy of belief and teaching.

It is interesting to note that, even in the 1960s, Roman Catholic priests were required to take an "Anti-Modernist" oath and to make a profession of orthodoxy in belief, before being granted the right to take their final oral examination to obtain their own "licentia docendi" or Licentiate degree at the Pontifical Gregorian University in Rome and at other ecclesiastical universities.

The question of fees for the granting of degrees is of course another matter. In fact, the Chancellor of Notre Dame, who was effectively acting as Provost of the new University, did resist for a while those pressures which were attempting to force him to grant degrees to those who could not or would not pay fees, but ultimately free-licencing did become the norm in Paris. It should be noted that students, one way or another, were responsible for their own board and lodging, quite apart from fees to their masters. This will explain why benefices and canonical stipends were so much sought after and how it must have seemed a solution to financial problems for an impecunious academic to join a religious order!

There had been, interestingly enough, an original privilege, granted earlier in 1200 by King Philip II, as a result of an attempt by the Chancellor to punish the perpetrators of a student brawl, which the King had counteracted by granting to the students certain immunities from prosecution and from loss of property [9].

The episode regarding the free granting of the Licence actually marked the first of many internal struggles within the fledgling University as it was striving in its birth throes with no real precedent to guide it. After all, the Chancellor actually had the authority also to deprive a master of his Licence, a student of his privileged status and even the power to excommunicate - which was, at that time, a very far-reaching power with many subsidiary effects for social and civil life in addition to the more obvious religious and spiritual consequences.

However, on the other hand, since he was not actually a member of the University himself, he could not compel the masters to admit to their society (which was somewhat analogous to a trade-guild in this respect) someone whom he had already licenced. In this way, they could restrict his power and make life difficult for him in his position. Indeed, they could compel a new Master to swear loyalty to their statutes in order to obtain entrance to their academic circle.

In 1212, the Chancellor had tried to get this oath made to him personally, so that he would in effect, if he had succeeded, become Head of the Masters' Guild himself. Innocent III had then intervened to prevent this from happening. It is not known whether this was for sincere reasons of supporting academic independence, as a salvo in inter-ecclesiastical strife, or perhaps simply, because, as a former Parisian Master himself, he felt nostalgia and understanding of the very real problems involved there.

The vital matter for the University, however, was that, with the assent and support of the king too, the Pope required the Chancellor to grant a Licence to all candidates approved by the various faculties. By this Bull, which was to be confirmed by subsequent ones of Innocent's successors, there also came the recognition of the right of the university to determine and to ratify its own statutes. Furthermore, both teachers and students also received the right to enjoy the revenues from ecclesiastical benefices without actually having to take up residence in them [10].

Likewise, because of this double support from kings and popes, it came about that the University became largely free from the control, not only of the Chancellor, but also effectively of the Bishop of Paris. Hence, on the Left Bank, in the area later to become known as the Latin Quarter, there developed almost a kind of autonomous republic that included both the masters and the thousands of students from many different countries. This was to mean that any interference with its independence was to cause a certain amount of bitter resentment, often of an international flavour. The Rector, who was elected as the Dean of the Arts Faculty, was practically a mini-sovereign, who governed, albeit with difficulty at times of strife or dissension, a large number of people, including all those, like innkeepers, who depended for their livelihood on the University.

However, this is not to imply that a close eye was not kept upon the events within by the Pope and by the local Archbishop, who claimed ultimate authority [11]. The University was clearly perceived as having enormous and unrivalled influence and indeed most scholars of stature, not to mention several Popes, were to spend some part of their student or teaching career in Paris.

1.4.   The "Nations" in Paris.

In Bologna, there had been in the twelfth century two large groups of students and masters; the Citramontani, consisting mainly of the Tuscans and the Lombards, and the Ultramontani, which included some thirteen or more different "nations" each preserving its distinct identity [12].   Hence the fourfold division of students in Paris into the French, Norman, Picard and English "nations" was not without precedent.   However, there it was also unfortunately to be another factor leading to strife and quite frequently to be a focus for excessive rivalry.

The German students, who in the thirteenth century were still small in number, affiliated to the English, while the Flemish joined that of the Picards, whose area stretched as far as the River Meuse.   The Italians joined their fellow-Latins in the nation of the French, who however came predominantly from the Ile-de-France.   The actual nomenclature of the four groups derived from the identity of the nationalities which predominated in them at the time of their foundation [13]. At the time of the events with which this study is concerned, the French nation was numerically about equal in size to the other three put together [14].

Each group had quite considerable independence from one another and elected its own officers and representatives, although it seems that the distinction meant much less for the three smaller faculties of Theology, Medicine and Law than it did for the first and most basic one of Arts.   In fact, for some questions which concerned the University as a whole, the decision of an assembly of representatives of the seven groups [four nations and three smaller faculties] was required [15].

This could well be the reason why it came about that the Rector (who, unlike the Chancellor, had to be an actual member of the University) came to be named always by the members of the Faculty of Arts, since their numerical majority would have enabled them to have this influence.   Moreover, matters which did solely concern this Faculty were decided on the principle of one nation-one vote, whatever the overall numbers in each nation [16].

It needs to be mentioned at this stage that the young students were directly excluded from representation in the official deliberations, for one had to be a Master to be a "member" of the Arts Faculty and a doctor (a status achieved at this period by masters following a public lecture and a banquet fairly soon afterwards!) to be able to pass on to participation in the discussions with the other three faculties.

It seems likely, however, that in some respects the relationships in practice between the different nations and between the different faculties would not be totally dissimilar to those of the modern ecclesiastical universities in Rome and some other European cities today. (Indeed, later in Paris, a number of national "colleges" came to be affiliated to the original four individual "nations" [17]).

For example, when the writer studied at the Pontifical Gregorian University in Rome in the 1960s, there were numerous colleges of national nomenclature, such as the German, the English, the Spanish and the Scots, dating from the sixteenth and the seventeenth centuries, to which other nationalities could be admitted; hence, Welsh students were usually admitted to the Collegio Inglese and Hungarians to the Germanicum.   Friendship contacts inevitably were stronger among nation-groups who had the common link of residence, language and culture, although friends were also often made within the faculty and year groups across the language-barriers too.

1.5.   The Faculty of Arts in Paris.

The basic faculty was that of Arts, for it was presupposed in the thirteenth century that all students, who were later to embark on studies in one of the other faculties, had completed at least six years of studies since enrolment in the Arts Faculty, somewhere around the age of fifteen, and had successfully obtained the degrees of Bachelor and Master of Arts [18].

In Paris, some of the early official provisions for the bachelor's degree are contained in the regulations issued in 1252 for the English Nation [19]. The first two years were spent in listening to lectures and attending disputations, followed by two years of participating in disputations under the supervision of a Master, with whom the student had enrolled. At both stages, there was considerable student dropout, whether because of failure, inability to pay the Master's fees or simply because the student did not need or want further education. In the fifth year, at a Lenten disputation, it was decided whether the Bachelor's degree could be awarded. If so, under the guidance of his Master, the Bachelor took part in further disputations and was expected to give some of the afternoon lectures. Finally, after seven or eight years, the candidate, if successful, took part in a solemn disputation and gave a formal inaugural lecture to mark his own admission as a full member of the Arts Faculty [20].

After a couple of years or so as a fully-fledged Master, most then progressed to study in another faculty, which would by no means be certain to be in theology, which was considered to be a somewhat theoretical and abstract science, although it was of course to be in Paris that theology was to see its finest teaching in Europe and to maintain a truly international flavour and reputation. Nevertheless, Law was much more popular with the ambitious who wanted to develop a civil or ecclesiastical career [21].

It should be noted that, at this time, most teaching relied on the oral lecture and oral disputation, so that the scarcity of written material in the Faculty of Arts must have been particularly acute, paticularly given the youth and relative poverty of many of the masters and students.

Traditionally, over the preceding centuries, the "Liberal Arts", ever since the time of Boethius (c.475 - c.525), had covered, firstly, what was known as the "trivium" and then the "quadrivium". The "trivium" involved the verbal disciplines of grammar, logic and rhetoric, which did not aim so much at the acquisition of knowledge as the ordering and organization of experience and at the development of basic skills, to be employed in later learning in one's life. The "quadrivium" consisted of the four mathematical sciences of arithmetic, astronomy, geometry and music [22].

Around the time of the Papal Bull establishing the University, the first two basic years of the Arts course concentrated on the areas of grammar and logic, rather than rhetoric. These were vital as a grounding for all international scholarship and at this time served as the basis from which all other areas of study in learning, within and beyond the Faculty of Arts developed, and as the fundamental methodology upon which they depended [23].

Traditionally, there had been many teachers of logic and of grammar in Paris for over a hundred years and little tradition in other areas such as physics, astronomy or metaphysics [24]. Yet another reason for there being no change in this practice during the early years of the University will be seen in the next chapter, although this situation was soon to be transformed.

1.6.   The Early Teaching of Aristotle's Works in Paris.

As early as 1210, even before the official establishment of the University had been ratified, the local Provincial Council of Paris, held in Sens, had forbidden, under pain of excommunication, both the public and the private teaching of Aristotle's writings on natural philosophy [25]. These were generally taken to refer to those on mathematics, physics and metaphysics and, under the same condemnation, there were included any commentaries on these works.

In the University Statutes of 1215, the study of Aristotle's Logic was still, as it had been for many years, sanctioned, but his Metaphysics and other books on natural philosophy were forbidden by the Papal Legate, Robert de Courçon, in his regulations for the Arts Faculty [26].

The fact that such restrictions were perceived to be necessary would seem to indicate that there must already before this time have been some considerable interest in these books of Aristotle and in their Arab Commentators, especially Ibn Sina and Ibn Rushd. However, it is not surprising that, in the real world, there would be some curiosity at what was forbidden, while the genuine desire for more knowledge made it impractical to expect people to teach and to study some of the Aristotelian literature, but to ignore the bulk of it.

Hence, even while the ban was still in force, many scholars were still reading the books privately. Perhaps, human nature being what it is, they may have sometimes used the excuse that they needed to read them in order to refute them. Certainly, in later centuries, when the Holy Office's Index of Forbidden Books was still in operation, this excuse was used by many theologians, as well as philosophers.

The strength of the motivation of curiosity directed towards whatever the powers-that-be are trying to repress is even in the modern age a common phenomenon, not only in totalitarian civil societies. In the context of the Roman Catholic Church, it is perhaps relatively recently illustrated by the astonishing success of Hans Küng's first popular book, The Council and Reunion, which was published in 1961 just before the opening of the Second Vatican Council in the following year [27]. Initially, such a book by an unknown author achieved little success until a very strong rumour swept through Rome that Cardinal Ottaviani, the Head of the Holy Office, disapproved of some of the partly-veiled attacks on the Curia and that the book was about to be put on the Index. It is arguable that it was this sequence of events that achieved for Dr. Küng the fame and notoriety that was to give him almost the status of a folk-hero and to enable him to emerge publicly ahead of a number of other equally talented young theologians. By such accidents of fate are reputations sometimes established.

Returning to our examination of the events of the first two decades of the thirteenth century, we can surmise that the fact that Aristotle's logic, the basis of his applied philosophy, was, and had for a long time been, officially acceptable, must have caused ambivalent feelings among many intelligent people. Certainly, it was considered necessary to renew the ban in 1228 [28].

It is noteworthy, incidentally, that this ban only applied to Paris, so that the teaching of Aristotle's natural philosophy was permitted not only in Oxford, but even in Toulouse, where the locals were enthusiastic in publicizing this fact, after its founding in 1229 in the wake of the Crusades against the Albigensians [29].

1.7.　　　The Effects of the Interventions of Pope Gregory IX on the Teaching within the University of Paris.

It appears that the issue regarding the teaching of the Aristotelian Corpus was far from solved for, on 13 April 1231, Pope Gregory IX revised the ban by determining that Aristotle's Physics could be taught after all, provided that, after approval by an appointed commission of three named theologians, a censored and edited version was produced [30]. Although there is little evidence to suggest that this was achieved successfully, the effect of this intervention was, however, to give yet another boost to the reading of Aristotle's writings on physics and metaphysics over the next few years.

Nevertheless, it would be fair to say that the effect of the condemnations of 1210, 1215 and 1228 and the intervention of 1231 was to slow down the public study and teaching of Aristotle. Indeed, although logic continued to be taught, there has not yet been found any written evidence of any philosophical activity in Paris in the fields of physics or metaphysics before 1240 [31]. At the same time, a general change in the intellectual climate is strongly indicated by the fact that on 20 April 1231, barely a week later, the Pope gave two senior ecclesiastics the power to lift any excommunications that had been incurred over this matter by either masters or students [32].

In fact, three years before his intervention on Aristotle's Physics on 7 July 1228, he had warned the Faculty of Theology to teach a theology "sine fermento mundanae scientiae ..... non adulterantes verbum Dei philosophorum figmentis" [avoiding the leavening of worldly knowledge and the watering down of the Word of God with ideas fabricated by philosophers] [33]. In practice, because all theologians had already studied elements of philosophy, it would have been difficult for them to ignore controversies regarding Aristotle totally. However, it would have acted as a practical reminder to them to concentrate on the exposition of Scripture and of the Book of Sentences of Peter Lombard. In the same year, the Pope appointed William of Auvergne, though still only a deacon, as Archbishop of Paris. He was the first Master in Theology to hold that post, so it may have been hoped that a respected theologian would succeed in keeping a close eye on religious orthodoxy within the University [34].

Nevertheless, the spirit of this intervention must have been successfully maintained in the Faculty of Theology, because it is hard otherwise to understand how the Faculty of Arts would have been able to be granted permission to teach all of Aristotle's works by 1255 and indeed it seems that Roger Bacon, the English Dominican, was happily lecturing on physics in the Faculty of Arts more than ten years before that [35].

However, some years ago, Professor Grabmann, to whom reference will be made in the next chapter, discovered a very important and useful manuscript in the archives of the Court of Aragon, kept in Barcelona. This had been composed around 1230-1240 and contains a kind of handbook for students in the Faculty of Arts in Paris at that time. Its author appears to be an unknown Master of the Faculty, whose purpose is to help students in their preparations for examinations [36].

This document classifies the various branches of philosophy into:
a) natural philosophy, whose nature is studied under various degrees of abstraction (physics, mathematics and metaphysics),
b) moral philosophy (which is concerned with ethics, the subject of the will) and
c) rational philosophy (which is concerned with the subject of the intellect or of reason) [37].

This then becomes even more fascinating with the discovery that the suggested questions for revision are top-heavy with topics concerned with "rational philosophy", in contrast to the fact that very few are involved with "natural philosophy", including metaphysics, while not many more deal with ethics. This would seem to suggest that, up to this date, the Faculty of Arts was mainly concerned with teaching grammar, logic and ethics.

What seems to have happened is that the 1228 and 1231 interventions of Gregory IX had the effect of distancing the two faculties of Theology and of Arts from one another. This had the consequence that, from about 1240 onwards, the latter became more and more concerned with philosophy, above all that of Aristotle and his commentators of course, rather than merely remaining the source for learning grammar and logic, simply as the basis for supposedly more advanced learning in the other faculties.

This process was to lead to the establishment and development of medieval philosophy as an academic pursuit, worthy of study for its own sake, and hence with full academic status and esteem, yet with some undefined, though integral, relationship to theology proper. Indeed, the relationship between philosophy and theology and the independent status of the former was later to lead to accusations of "double-truth" - that something could be at the same time both true for philosophy and untrue for theology (or vice versa) - as will be seen later in this study.

Thus there developed in Paris in Arts course with a strongly philosophical character, in which logic predominated for the first two years, before the three philosophies, as discussed above, then supplemented the old "quadrivium" in varying proportions [38]. This is in contrast to Oxford, where the influence of Robert Grosseteste (1175-1253), Roger Bacon (c.1210-1292) and other Englishmen was to make it the great centre for what we would understand as science today [39].

However, it should be borne in mind that at the same time there must in many cases have been personal and individual relationships between members of the two faculties. On the one hand, the theologians would in their younger years have passed through the Faculty of Arts - or, at least, undertaken a similar course for at least six years elsewhere - while, on the other hand, the active Regent Masters in the Faculty of Arts were all clerics of some sort and would be likely to have had some Christian perspective behind their world-views, however devout they may or may not have been.

1.8.   The Removal of Official Sanctions against the Works of Aristotle.

It had not proved possible to prevent the spread and growth of the appetite for the reading of Aristotle's works, which were now becoming more and more available in translation. During the 1240s, all his main areas of learning seem to have been the subject of study in the Faculty of Arts in Paris. As Knowles describes it, "by 1250-60, he was being treated in many quarters as a kind of precursor of Christ, an intellectual Baptist" [40].

It is, incidentally, during this period of transition that Robert Kilwardby was probably teaching in the Arts Faculty from about 1237-1245, before joining the Dominican Order [41]. He was later to become the Archbishop of Canterbury and was to promulgate in Oxford in 1277 a series of condemnations that mirrored those of Paris, which represent the climax of much of the conflict considered in this study.

Indeed, in the Statutes of 1252, determining the admissions within the English Nation and the conditions therein for the entry of Bachelors to study for their Masters degree ("licentia docendi"), there was already being required not only a knowledge of Aristotle's works on Logic, but also the official requirement of understanding his "De Anima" [42].

However, the crucial date in this process was 19 March 1255 when the wheel turned full-circle officially, for, with the demand for the compulsory study of all his known works, the University officially accepted Aristotelianism [43]. Undoubtedly, this would also mark a further stage in the process whereby the Faculty of Arts was to see itself less and less in a preparatory and subordinate role to the other faculties (in particular, in Paris, to that of Theology); students, bachelors and masters alike began to view the study of philosophy as a discipline worthy of research in its own right.

We have already seen that, ever since the beginning of the thirteenth century, there had been an emphasis on the need of theologians and others to follow the strict rules of logic and grammar; and with the passing of the traditional "trivium" and "quadrivium", the more charismatic styles and independence of theologians such as Peter Abelard or the classical eloquence of writers such as Bernard of Clairvaux had been replaced with a kind of uniformity of expression, of argument and even of style [44].

However, the effect of the opening-up of this huge corpus of Aristotelian literature, including the Commentaries by Jewish and Arab writers, such as Maimonides, Ibn Sina and Ibn Rushd, was to lead to a spirit of open critical investigation, such as had not previously been seen.

So, for example, the English Secular Master, John Sackville, who had in 1256 been elected Rector of the Arts Faculty - and hence of the University too - appears to have followed Aristotle and Ibn Rushd in his views on the eternity of the world and on the non-divisibility of species in non-material beings in his De Principiis Naturae [45]. Although this work is unlikely itself to predate 1263, its heterodox Aristotelianism will almost certainly be based upon Sackville's earlier ideas which, with his prominent position as Rector around the time that the subject of this study was probably arriving in Paris as a student, may be of some considerable significance [46]. Certainly, the teaching and approach of this relatively unknown scholar must, in view of his position, have been circulating around the Faculty and provided considerable food for thought and discussion by the young students and we may well be in a position to focus on one of the formative influences on the young Siger.

Certainly, the fact that Sackville, few of whose works are extant today, was in such a senior position indicates the kind of attitudes and ideas then beginning to develop in Paris. Within less than two years, however, he was forced to go to Rome with colleagues to defend the position of the Seculars in their conflict with the Orders. In any event, whether in response to threats or compulsion (or even because he felt that he had had enough of the stresses of this conflict) he is found as Secretary to the Duke of Gloucester in 1258. Although he appears to be back in Paris in 1263 - again a crucial time for Siger's development and the formation of his ideas - he seems then to have remained in England from 1265 until his death about thirty years later.

A different fact, which may also have some bearing on trends in the Arts Faculty at this time, is that the three greatest figures in the Faculty of Theology had all left by 1260. Bonaventure had been elected General of the Franciscans in 1257, while Albert the Great had been in Cologne since 1248, where Thomas Aquinas was to join him in 1259. Hence, as Copleston points out, there was now no theologian of great stature to challenge the early development of the potentially threatening ideas and approach of the Faculty of Arts in the 1260s and the path was clear that would lead to those shattering conflicts which are to be considered in this study [47].

1.9.   The Impact of the Advent of the Religious Orders on the University of Paris.

Traditionally, as we have seen, students would normally pass through the Faculty of Arts and complete a course as Bachelor and Master of Arts, including an element of teaching and disputation, before they could enter the Faculty of Theology. However, the Religious Orders, especially the new mendicant Franciscans and Dominicans, were allowed their own schools for teaching their young members as "Exempt Religious"; in practice, therefore, they would move on to study theology there without themselves having experienced Aristotelian philosophy in the Faculty of Arts.

The Dominicans had arrived in Paris in 1217 and the Franciscans only two years later, so their influence had been there almost from the very beginning of the University. Moreover, about 1236, Alexander of Hales, who had been a secular Regent Master of Theology for quite some time, joined the Franciscan Order. Thus, the Englishman gained for the order in this way a Chair in Theology which they were to claim and maintain for many years. Indeed, this event marks what was claimed to be the origin of the Franciscan school of theology in Paris [48]. At the same time, it is only fair to note that Alexander himself, who died in 1245, can be described as the first Western Christian thinker to draw on Aristotelian thought for his theological writings [49]. His own Summa Theologiae may very well have had a considerable influence on the thought of Thomas Aquinas. He also taught the Tuscan Bonaventure, who was himself later to become his successor, albeit with much more of the Augustinian ethos in his theological approach and without the Aristotelian interest to which Albert the Great and Thomas were to return and to develop much further.

Roland of Cremona, the first holder of a Dominican Chair of Theology, which he had acquired much earlier in 1229 (interestingly enough, two months after the Masters had gone on strike), also indicated some sympathy with and knowledge of Aristotle's works, despite the interventions of Gregory IX [50]. Most of his immediate successors, however, showed much less positive support, perhaps responding to some of the reservations expressed by the Pope in his 1228 and 1231 interventions [51]. However, it was undoubtedly Albert the Great, who really dedicated his life to spreading the works of Aristotle, both before and after he left Paris for Cologne in 1248. Although his approach as a theologian was to use Aristotelian philosophical thought as a tool to create a structure in the service of theological understanding, this marks a very clear and defined change of emphasis from the old Augustinian approach.

William of Auvergne, the secular Bishop of Paris from 1228 to 1249, had in fact granted a second Chair of Theology to the Dominicans and no doubt the Franciscans would have been anxious to attain parity as soon as possible. It is a matter of speculation whether the former was in any way connected with assistance that the Dominican Order, specifically founded to preach and preserve

Christian orthodoxy, may have offered William, who initiated the seizure of copies of the Talmud from the synagogues of Paris during the Lent of 1240, and, despite Jewish protests, their subsequent burning two years later [52]. Certainly, by the confirmation of the privileges of the University in its foundation and the subsequent close supervision of its teaching, the Faculty of Theology in Paris had been perceived as responsible for the official teaching of the Church [53]. We do not know the total number of Regent Masters in any of the faculties. However, the fact that Honorius III had decreed in 1218 that an extra master should be appointed to Theology [54], over and above the number of eight originally fixed by Innocent III [55], may give some indication of the kind of limits being practised, save where there were later to be appointed additional members to that faculty from the Religious Orders.

However, it can well be understood that the secular clergy, who had traditionally been at the heart of the Faculty of Theology and of the University as a whole since its very origins, now saw a threat and danger to their position of dominance. With the death of William and the imprisonment of King Louis IX in the following year, Pope Innocent IV was to accept some of the protests of the Seculars, who demanded that from 1252 no religious order should be permitted to hold more than one Chair.

More conflict was to arise the following year. There had been a general strike by masters and students against the alleged violence of the royal police against the students. The Dominicans and the Franciscans had ignored this strike and continued with their lectures, so that the Secular teachers among the University authorities attempted to impose a ban upon them. Then, in 1254, Innocent IV was to suspend the members of the mendicant orders from being able to exercise their pastoral ministry of administering the sacraments and of preaching in Paris.

However, within a few weeks the Pope was dead and all his sanctions against the orders were revoked by his successor Alexander IV, who also reinstated all their other privileges. They thus now became effectively the winners in this series of disputes and took their revenge on their former protagonist,

William of Saint-Amour (d. 1272), whom the Pope persuaded the King to banish from France.

The diocesan clergy were now on the retreat in the Faculty of Theology, while, on the wider European plane, the new Pope was flexing his muscles in pursuit of power and the growth of his influence. He continued to enlist the support of the supranational Franciscans and Dominicans, who as "Exempt Religious" were directly subject to his authority and not to that of the local bishops, in his attempt to be the unchallenged leader of Europe, superior to all kings and emperors in the temporal sphere and to all local bishops in both the temporal and spiritual spheres.

Furthermore, it must have been very tempting for many academic, impecunious, young students to try to join the Orders, thereby ensuring for themselves guaranteed material support, rather than having to be involved in the machinations and stringpulling necessary to obtain benefices and other such financial help.

Hence, we can well imagine the motives behind the founding in 1257 of the Sorbonne, named after the Chaplain of St. Louis, as a College for secular theologians, on the model of the great houses of studies of the friars and of the older monastic orders. Thus, they could gain something comparable to the relative security of the Franciscans and the Dominicans.

Another factor in this conflict may perhaps be discerned in the growth of the apocalyptic-type ideas, which had derived from the teaching of the Calabrian monk Joachim of Fiore, which, despite initial Papal support granting him permission to found a new order in 1196, had been however condemned by the Fourth Lateran Council in 1215. Nevertheless, some of his ideas found increasing favour among some members of the mendicant orders. The third phase of Divine Salvation was predicted to begin in 1260, which would usher in the coming of the Kingdom of the Third Person of the Trinity, the Holy Spirit, and see the demise of the Church - as it was then known - because of its alleged corruption. The growth of these ideas, although not officially accepted, had rubbed off on many ordinary people, who in any case were beginning to look to the Orders rather than to the Secular clergy for spiritual inspiration, no doubt to the annoyance and resentment of the latter.

It has been argued, indeed, that Bonaventure himself, while reacting intellectually against the dangers of Joachimism, was "gripped in his imagination by some aspects of it" and certainly that he saw the Franciscan Order as having a special role to play in the establishment of the final perfect order, identifying St. Francis with the Angel of the Sixth Seal in the Book of Revelation [56]. In contrast, of course, the Spiritual Franciscans were dedicated to an immediate reform of the orders and were to be persecuted for their adherence to what they saw as the strict principles of Francis. They wore patched and skimpy habits and attacked those Franciscans who were involved in building libraries, churches and other activities they considered to be too worldly.

Bonaventure also points out that the very name Order of Preachers, adopted by the Dominicans, indicates that their priority lies first with speculative thought as such and its implications, and only subsequently with devotion as such; on the other hand, he argues, the Franciscans, from the time of their founder, were primarily concerned with devotion and only subsequently with speculation [57].

The Dominicans had indeed played a major part in a further major disputation with leading Jewish Rabbis in Barcelona in 1263 [58], as well as taking on the mantle of leadership for the Inquisitorial Tribunals investigating the Southern heresies.

Thus, just as we have seen the tension between the Seculars and the Orders, so there was therefore much tension within the Orders and some genuine rivalry between the two great Mendicant Orders.

It has already been noted in this section that Albert the Great was to be a powerful catalyst for the spread of philosophy again and for a recognition of its potential to make a valuable contribution to the study of theology - after a gap of nearly seven hundred years or so since the days of Boethius. In fact, by no means all Dominicans were as enthusiastic in this respect, but it was his pupil Thomas Aquinas who was to develop the great <u>Summa contra Gentiles</u> and the <u>Summa Theologiae</u> as a framework for theology, accepting the relationship of reason and faith and the use of philosophy to help enunciate his theology.

It has been pointed out that, at this time, the development of the respective theological schools of the two orders seems to be determined by the respective activity of the two great masters: Thomas leads the Dominicans into a powerful philosophical intellectualism, while Bonaventure's influence was for some time to lead the Franciscans into a kind of mystical theology, largely based upon Augustinian theology with its emphasis on illuminative Neoplatonism [59]. This conflict of ideas was to contribute to the bitterness engendered after Thomas' death, when many of his teachings were condemned in 1277, as we shall see, by Stephen Tempier and the Franciscan Archbishop of Canterbury John Peckham.

At times, the Orders would find themselves, willingly or unwillingly, whether from similar or different perspectives, caught up in the tensions between the papacy and the King, on whose side the French secular clergy might in some respects find themselves. At other times, of course, the latter might ally themselves more with the Pope over the questions of the rights and the privileges of the clergy or of the authority of the secular power to levy taxes on them. The multinational orders, on the other hand, would tend to be more international in outlook.

This was a very big contemporary power-game, in which many sincere and many innocent people found themselves involved or even victims. Indeed, the climax of the attempts to assert the total ultimate authority of the papacy was to come with the decree "<u>Unam Sanctam</u>" of Pope Boniface VIII in 1302, which included, among other claims, that every human being should submit totally to both his spiritual and his temporal authority in order to merit salvation [60]. All this was, of course, a very complicated issue but it does need to be kept in mind when we examine the controversies opened up by Siger's thought later in this book.

Hence, it is now possible to see how all those tensions between the Seculars and the Orders, which were more about power and influence than anything else, were now to shift somewhat from the Faculty of Theology, over which more control could obviously be marshalled and imposed, to that of the Faculty of Arts and to its relationship with religious authority.

Indeed, the theologians from the second half of the thirteenth century were either in the religious orders or else in either the Maison de Sorbonne (open to the non-French) or the Maison de Navarre (open to the French Seculars). In this way, the ecclesiastical authorities were able to keep a much tighter rein on intellectual expression among the theologians, particularly important when we recall that the University had acquired a kind of independent status, somewhat akin to that of an embassy.

All this explains too the context within which some of the next generation of leaders in the Arts Faculty, such as Siger of Brabant and Boethius of Dacia, were to try to walk the tightrope of declaring that, as academics and philosophers, they were neither commenting on nor attacking the doctrines of the Church, but at the same time could claim to be loyal and devout Christians.

1.10.   The Developing Relationship and Rivalry between the Faculties of Arts and of Theology.

In 1271, Roger Bacon had lamented the lack of scholarship among the Seculars in Paris, whom he accused of forty years of laxity in not producing any work of academic importance and of being too keen on material ambition, pleasure and wealth [61]. In fact, this was probably because of the pre-eminence of Bonaventure and Albert and aggravated by all the internal tensions involved in trying to preserve the status of the Seculars in the power-struggles outlined in the previous section.

However, with the departure of both Albert and Thomas, the Faculty of Arts, during the decade of the 1260s, could only gain in esteem for its own scholarship and investigation into Aristotle, while at the same time, in the absence of the forementioned Aristotelian theologians, would find themselves being pulled further and further away from the other faculty into a potentially more isolated and more vulnerable position regarding accusations of heterodoxy.

Of course, the growing sense of independence between 1240 and 1275, quite apart from the questions of orthodoxy, was also surely seen as a threat to the dominance and ultimate authority of Theology. Perhaps, indirectly, it was also seen as a threat in some quarters to the ultimate threat and full control over learning by the Church authorities.

It should nevertheless be remembered that, though younger than the theologians, the students and masters who studied philosophy, were themselves clerics of some rank or other with some Christian background or commitment, bringing their own conscious and subconscious perspectives to the study of Aristotle.

Another important factor about philosophy, which must not be neglected in any such consideration, is that herein could be found a common language of ideas and concepts within which principles could be agreed with Muslim and Jewish thinkers and commentators, so that further theological dialogue and polemics could be conducted.

While the distinction between philosophy and theology might in practice be emphasized at times by members of the Faculty of Arts in their search for what they saw as the truth, nevertheless, as we shall see, the primary status of the "truths of revelation" was generally upheld by them and apparently not forgotten. Perhaps the dilemmas which will be encountered in this study may find a parallel in the search for truth, in the fact of apparently opposing revealed and magisterial teaching of the Christian Church by more recent Christian thinkers, such as Charles Darwin and Teilhard de Chardin, in the field of science.

Nevertheless, the intellectual links in the relationship between philosophy and theology at this time are very deep and real. Thurot affirmed that all the great philosophers of the Middle Ages were theologians [62]. This is perhaps debatable - and certainly will be challenged in the course of this study - but it must be accepted that, in some respects, philosophy and theology could not be totally separated.

At the same time, the Faculty of Theology in Paris was (with the exception of the University of Toulouse, which had almost certainly been founded with the maintenance of orthodoxy as its "raison d'etre") unique at this time and fairly represented authentic and approved theology as it was manifested during this period. For example, a number of its Masters were to become bishops of Paris and of other prominent sees. Such was the esteemed authority of the theologians indeed that, just over a century later in 1387, Pierre d'Ailly was even claiming before Pope Clement VII, in the aftermath of <u>Unam Sanctam</u>, that the Pope himself could not decide matters of dogma on his own, but needed the Masters and Professors in Theology to act as jury to decide cases of heresy [63].

On the other hand, the status of the Regent Masters in the Faculty of Arts was, at least in theory, more independent from the strictures of the Church. They could claim to be carrying out academic investigations, for example, into the thought of Aristotle, regardless of whether or not it concurred with official dogmatic orthodoxy. Hence, the Faculty was gaining a status and independence of its own. Theologians might well consider their subject to be the "queen of the sciences", but not all philosophers were going to allow their role to be restricted to giving a grounding in skills of argument to future theologians.

There seems to be little doubt that almost all writers have taken with them to their examination of the events and issues which will be considered in this study a considerable amount of intellectual baggage and personal feelings, whether conscious or unconscious, which have meant thay they have tended to gloss over or ignore many of the examples of internal conflict which have been outlined in the last few sections of this chapter. They have tended to be Roman Catholic clerical writers, often Dominicans, and have naturally tended to be somewhat defensive regarding the less salubrious aspects of ecclesiastical activity, while being happy to emphasize the sincerity and integrity of a man like Thomas Aquinas.

Furthermore, even though Thomas relied so much on Aristotle, Thomism was, for almost a hundred years following Leo XIII's Encyclical "Aeterni Patris" in 1879 [64], almost sanctified as the "Christian Philosophy" par excellence and this may have clouded impartial investigation of some of his contemporaries.

Thirdly, many writers down the years have also failed for a number of reasons, some quite understandable, to take adequate account of the surrounding historical, geographical and social context of the written word of this period, including the polemics and conflicts.   Today, we are better able to use more modern perspectives and approaches, suggested by other disciplines, as well as by psychology and the discovery of much more literature of the Middle Ages.

CHAPTER TWO

A SUMMARY OF PREVIOUS REFERENCES TO

AND RESEARCH INTO SIGER OF BRABANT

2.0.   Introduction.

This chapter examines to what extent the memory of Siger came to be lost or distorted in subsequent centuries and whether he may have had any influence on later writers.   It will then proceed to consider the scholarship surrounding his re-discovery in the nineteenth and early part of the twentieth century.

In the latter sections, it will acknowledge the major contributions made towards this by a number of academics, above all Pierre Mandonnet (1858-1936) and Fernand Van Steenberghen (1904-1995), whose extraordinary scholarship has stretched through virtually the entire twentieth century.   However, since no other writers have undertaken major examinations of his life and thought as a whole, less reference can be made in this chapter to those numerous articles written about diverse aspects of his works and teaching .   Due reference will be made to these in later chapters and full acknowledgement will be given in the bibliography.

2.1.   Dante Alighieri.

For almost six centuries, Siger of Brabant remained a somewhat shadowy enigma for both historians and theologians alike, since virtually the only known and established fact about him was his very existence and practically nothing else.

Indeed, none of his works seem to have been rediscovered during this period as they remained locked away in archives and libraries within universities, monasteries and other clerical establishments up and down Europe.

The earliest known reference to him that had been preserved throughout this time is found in six fascinating verses of La Commedia Divina of Dante Alighieri:-

> Questi onde a me ritorna il tuo riguardo
> E il lume d'uno spirto, che in pensieri
> Gravi, a morir gli parve venir tardo.
> Essa è la luce eterna di Sigieri
> Che, leggendo nel vico degli strami,
> Sillogizzò invidiosi veri.
> (Paradiso, Canto X, lines 133-138).

[This, from whom your glance returns to me, is the light of a spirit, in serious thoughts, to whom dying appears to come slowly. It is the everlasting light of Siger, who, when teaching in the Street of Straw, did not escape envy in pronouncing true arguments.]

What makes these verses so interesting is not only the implied praise in the expression referring in such a sympathetic way to the "eternal light of Siger", but also the additional fact that these laudatory words were not merely left as personal thoughts of the poet himself but were actually placed into the mouth of none other than Dante's hero Thomas Aquinas himself.

This is the context of the verses: Dante and Beatrice have reached the Fourth Heaven, which is the Sun, and is the abode of those learned in divine matters. They find themselves completely dazzled by a blinding shaft of light, which is emanating from a shining crown made up of twelve exceptional spirits. These belong to Thomas Aquinas, who has the central place, with Albert the Great on his right, (the two great Dominican friends of the mid-thirteenth century who were indeed at one time pupil and master); the great canonist Gratian and the theologian Peter Lombard of the previous century, who was responsible for the famous Sentences, which contributed so much of the study of Theology, during this period of the Middle Ages; King Solomon, Denis the Areopagite, Orosius (the disciple of St. Augustine) and Boethius, author of De Consolatione Philosophiae; the others are Isidore of Seville and the Venerable Bede from the early Middle Ages, then Richard of St. Victor of the twelfth century and, finally, on Thomas' left is Siger himself.

A number of fanciful speculations and suggestions were made down the later centuries regarding the identity of this "Sigieri". For example, Rev. Francis Cary, when producing in the middle of the last century the various editions of his English translation of the Commedia theorized that the poet was probably referring to Sigebert "a monk of the abbey of Gemblours, who was in high repute at the end of the eleventh and beginning of the twelfth century" [1].

On the other hand, none other than Pietro di Dante, the poet's own son, had identified the fact that the "vico degli strami" must have referred to the "Rue du Fouarre" where the Faculty of Arts in Paris was situated. He goes on to suggest that the individual in question was a philosopher from Brabant, who, it seemed, must have gone on subsequently to become a theologian too [2].

In fact, most commentators down the centuries were able to make the link between the "vico degli strami" and the Schools of Liberal Arts situated in the Latin Quarter of Paris and indicated that Siger must have been a teacher there. Some went further, speculating, as a result of the phrase "sillogizzo", that he must have been a specialist in logic. In point of fact, this would have been unjustified as all formal argument and discussion were officially undertaken in syllogistic form. (The present writer well recalls participating in a philosophical disputation of this kind as an undergraduate in Rome in the early 1960s).

2.2.   Fourteenth Century Averroism.

Following the 1277 Condemnations by Stephen Tempier in Paris, it was of course intended that the influence of Ibn Rushd (Averroes) should be cut off in full flow. It was, however, felt by many others that support for Thomas Aquinas was broad enough to ensure that his writings would not only survive but his thought would continue to flourish.

On the other hand, it was clearly the desire of the Condemnations that the influence of Siger, Boethius of Dacia and their comrades, whatever it might have been, should be clearly rooted out and that their memory and writings should disappear from public awareness.

Bruno Nardi (1884-1968), to whom great credit must be given for much of the research outlined in this and the subsequent section, was convinced that, early in the fourteenth century, the Franciscan theologian Pietro Aureoli was familiar with some of Siger's work, at least with his De Anima Intellectiva, as well as with Thomas' De Unitate Intellectus contra Averroistas [3].

John of Jandun (1275-1328), Master of Arts at the College of Navarre, certainly claimed to be the "ape of Aristotle and Averroes" [4]. Despite the Condemnations of 1270 and 1277, Ibn Rushd himself had continued to be the subject of teaching and study in Paris and John was the major figure in fourteenth century France to pursue this line, commenting on several occasions on doctrines such as the eternity of the world and the unity of the intellect [5]. In 1315, he was lecturing in the Faculty of Arts in Paris on the Expositio Problematum Aristotelis of the Averroist physician-philosopher Pietro of Abano (1257-1315), who, as Professor at the University of Padua, had introduced the ideas and scholarship of the Arabs to Italy, especially through the medium of medicine [6]. John came out strongly against Thomas' interpretation of Aristotle and may in this sense therefore be described as an Averroist. In 1326, he was to join Marsilio of Padua, a follower of Ibn Rushd and perceived to be particularly dangerous as a result of his political teachings, in seeking refuge at the court of Louis of Bavaria in Nuremberg. This was prompted by John's own fears of having incurred the wrath of the Roman Curia, while he was himself teaching in Padua.

Ibn Rushd (always named as Averroes by John) is for him the most perfect defender of philosophy [7]. John attempts to resolve the dilemma of the apparent contradictions with Christian teaching by claiming, in a similar way to the later Siger - as we shall see later in this study - that doctrines of faith must be unconditionally accepted by the believer [8]. Indeed, he goes further by declaring, perhaps with some echoes of Saint Augustine, that such a step would be particularly meritorious if it enables faith to be freely given although it might appear to be in conflict with what reason tells the believer [9]. This, of course, is in contrast with Thomas' idea of faith building on reason and gives rise to some scholars accusing him of "double-truth".

However the question remains: did he know of Siger and/or his works or only those of Ibn Rushd? In fact, there seems little doubt that Bruno Nardi's investigations do prove that John was also familiar with De Anima Intellectiva [10]. His teaching is identical and he does refer explicitly to the first words of this tract, attributing it to "Remigius de Brabantia" [11]. Indeed, it is interesting to note that, on occasions John himself is referred to as "Joannis de Gandavo" [12]. It does not appear to have occurred to Nardi nor any other scholars that if this is a reference to Ghent in Belgium, we may have found a link with Siger, that is at least national, if not of greater import.

It is, perhaps, noteworthy that John of Jandun did not seem to know Siger's other writings on this topic. Does this suggest that, as a result of Siger's sudden departure from Paris in 1277, few copies of his teaching would have been available?

This may well be the case, but, since Thomas had explicitly declared that he had written his tract with the "Averroists" in mind, it would have been harder to suppress the actual reply to this. Nevertheless, John does not hesitate himself to promulgate views which have already been condemned. The unusual nomenclature given to Siger may reflect an acceptable alternative or it may even reflect the success of the process of the authorities in trying to suppress memory of his teaching, particularly in view of the accurate quotation of the first few words of the tract.

Perhaps, from the perspective of the end of the twentieth century, we are more surprised than we should be that the influence of important thinkers could disappear so quickly, since we are discussing a time before mass-circulation of writings as a result of the invention of the printing-press.

Indeed, in the Arab world, the reading and memory of Ibn Rushd (Averroes) also seems to vanish quite rapidly on his death, in marked contrast to the way in which he was regarded in his lifetime; he was not to assume scholarly or indeed any other popularity again until the second half of the nineteenth century. As Renan points out, not one of Ibn Rushd's followers achieved any notable fame [13].

It seems fairly certain that Thaddeus of Parma, James of Piacenza and other Italian Averroists of the University of Bologna in the fourteenth century appear also, via John of Jandun, to be aware of Siger's De Anima Intellectiva [14]. However, did they know of Siger himself? Again, it seems more than possible though it cannot be proven at the present stage of research.

The English Carmelite John of Baconthorp (c.1285-1348) explicitly refers to Siger, in so far as he claims that both Ibn Rushd (Averroes) and Siger had disagreed with Aristotle [15]. Before becoming Provincial of the Order in England, he had studied and taught in both Oxford and Paris, the latter around 1323-1325. So it does seem that in Paris, two generations later, the memory of Siger had not disappeared, though there was probably by then a very considerable range of rumours and counter-rumours about the events of fifty years or so before. Baconthorp apparently wants to be an authentic follower of Ibn Rushd and claims that the latter had only postulated monopsychism as a possible theory and that it did not correspond to his own views. He further claims that Siger felt that the

1270 decree did not condemn nor threaten his own sincerely held beliefs, since he was really in no conflict with it.

Although Nardi may well be right in suggesting that Baconthorp has misunderstood Siger (perhaps as a result of his limited access to his writings!), the fact remains that Siger's memory is very much alive in the academic ambience of Paris itself, as compared to its relative disappearance in Italy although Averroism was flourishing there.

2.3.   "Italian Averroism" of the Pre-Reformation Period.

In the fifteenth and early sixteenth centuries, there was a sizable school of thought in Italy, which, because of its very considerable debt to Ibn Rushd, is often described as Italian Averroism.   Certainly, in the fifteenth century, he was the dominant source as "Commentator" par excellence for thinkers in Padua and Bologna such as Paolo Nicoletti of Udine (sometimes known as Paul the Venetian).

Nicoletti seems to have had in Padua in 1408 a copy of De Intellectu, purportedly Siger's reply to Thomas' De Unitate Intellectus.   This is very interesting since, a century earlier, Thaddeus of Parma, as we have seen, appears only to know of Siger's views in De Anima Intellectiva - and those through the medium of John of Jandun (16).   Perhaps Nicoletti had acquired a manuscript copy from either Paris or Oxford and brought it now to Italy?

By the sixteenth century, there seems to be a split developing between writers.   On the one hand, there are those such as Alessandro Achillini (1453-1518) and Agostino Nifo (1473-1538).   Although the latter was to modify his views somewhat from the monopsychism of his master Nicoletto Vernias, in order to harmonize it with Catholicism after the Fifth Lateran Council in 1512, they can be contrasted with those of others such as Pietro Pomponazzi (1462-1525) who followed the Aristotelianism of Alexander of Aphrodisias rather than that of Ibn Rushd himself.   What these writers seem to have in common, however, is some adherence to the "double-truth" theory in one form or another; in fact, Pomponazzi's view of the function of religious truth finds some echoes in the views of some recent thinkers, such as R.B. Braithwaite, who perceive such beliefs as having primarily a normative function for human conduct.

We make another interesting discovery, via a student's written account of the lectures on Aristotle's Physics, given by another Bolognese teacher of this period, Tiberius Bacilieri. Our lack of knowledge of Tiberius is probably explained by the fact that he ended up in the relative backwater of Pavia. However, the preface to the student's account mentions both "Subgerii" and "Joannis de Bacone Carmelite" in its preliminary dedication. Although Siger is not subsequently mentioned by name in the text, Nardi finds that many of the ideas and themes are those defended by him in De Intellectu and also in the opusculum De Felicitate to which Agostino Nifo refers [17]. It is quite possible that these views may have been derived via Alessandro Achillini, who was often called the "Second Stagirite" as a result of his commentaries on Aristotle [18]. Likewise, Antonio Bernardi (sometimes known as Bernard of Mirandola), who was to be appointed Bishop of Caserta in 1552, seems to mirror ideas both of Siger and of Alessandro Achillini, when teaching twenty years or so earlier in Bologna [19].

Nardi also finds these ideas current in Giovanni Pico's attempt, in the spirit of Siger and contrary to Thomas Aquinas, to reconcile the unity of the intellect with the individuality of the intentional act; he does this in a way that Siger had apparently been unable to do. He speaks of a doctrine of "descent", whereby the same universal essence can descend and be particularized in individuals, without its losing any of its immortal and undivided nature [20].

This is one of the rare occasions when we can say that the Italian school attempted to develop further the ideas of Ibn Rushd and, more particularly, of Siger himself. Nardi had good reason to see Achillini, Bacilieri and the others as being predominantly philosophers re-presenting the earlier ideas rather than as being original thinkers [21]. It does however beg the question as to whether Siger himself is a true Aristotelian or rather an Averroist. This question will be considered from several aspects later in this study.

Agostino Nifo had also referred in his book <u>De Immortalitate</u> to what he describes as monopsychist views of "Suggerius et Rogerius uterque Bacconitanus" which had, he claimed, been derived from Averroes. Clearly, Siger and John Baconthorp are intended, despite the relatively vague nomenclatures given. There is probably by now a copyist's error and Nardi seems to be quite close to the mark in suggesting "Suggerius vel Rogerius Ioannesque Baconthorp" to be the correct version [22]. Roger is certainly an alternative name for Siger in this context, as can be seen from the use of it made by a Spanish master, John Montesdoch, who taught in Bologna firstly and then Padua from 1521 onwards. It is especially interesting that the latter claims to have seen manuscripts of Siger's (Roger's!) in the Library of St. Dominic's at Padua and in that of the Canons of the Lateran also. Nardi is convinced that these included at least <u>De Intellectu</u> and <u>De Felicitate</u>, but not, on the other hand, those better known ones of today to which no reference is made, as would certainly have been otherwise expected [23].

Van Steenberghen feels that Nardi has exaggerated the importance and influence of Siger during this period [24], but it may well be that the overall view of the totality of Siger's thought, with the consequent inbuilt balance, has not come down to these Italian thinkers some 250 years after his death. However, it is particularly intriguing that it is possible that it could be precisely those writings and ideas, which have not yet been discovered at the end of the twentieth century, that were familiar at that time.

Does this mean that, following the condemnations of the Fifth Lateran Council in 1512, these writings were destroyed whenever possible, while most of the others had been destroyed or hidden around the end of the thirteenth century, following the 1277 Condemnations and the subsequent academic climate at Oxford and Paris? Certainly both supporters and opponents of Thomas Aquinas would have had strong, though different, reasons for not wanting the ideas of Siger, Boethius of Dacia and their colleagues to add to the intellectual conflict and turmoil at the end of the thirteenth century.

However, as these last two sections have indicated, there does seem to have been a vaguely linked kind of school of Sigerian/Averroist thought off and on down the centuries. We must recall that we are not considering the kind of historical and academic situation, which was to prevail in later times, when the ideas and writings of groups, such as the English Empiricists, were to be so freely and easily available.   Perhaps, likewise, Van Steenberghen is being less than entirely fair in his comments above on Nardi's evaluation of Siger's importance for the thinkers of the Late Middle Ages considered in this and the previous section; certainly, in the context of those times, there is probably no significance in the failure to make the link with the Siger found in Dante's <u>Paradiso</u>.

However, both Nardi and Van Steenberghen are certainly right to be united, despite their many disagreements, in acclaiming the importance of Siger as a profound thinker with a philosophical system of ideas that may put him in the first rank of medieval thinkers, alongside Thomas Aquinas, Scotus and William of Ockham.   The greater then is the tragedy that, because of sustained persecution and opposition, his ideas subsequently remained fairly static and rigid in his followers - pace the example of Giovanni Pico to which reference has been made above - instead of developing dynamically as in the case of the schools of followers of the other three outstanding thinkers.

This may well explain much of his subsequent failure to merit much mention or reference in the theological and philosophical scenes until his rediscovery in the nineteenth century, when all our modern academic skills and techniques have enabled a fresh and positive appraisal to be undertaken.   What his legacy is to subsequent centuries will indeed be discussed in later chapters.

2.4.   Victor Le Clerc.

The first scholar in modern times to rediscover Siger was Victor Le Clerc towards the end of the first half of the nineteenth century.

With five colleagues, who were fellow-members of the Académie des Inscriptions et Belles-Lettres, he had taken over the responsibility for producing the massive series on the Literary History of France from the St. Maur Benedictines. Le Clerc, in fact, reserved for himself the task of undertaking the research on Siger. He provides us with this in some thirty pages or so of Volume XXI [25].

For centuries, Siger had remained only a name for those who were commentators on the Divine Comedy. Hence, for example, De Venturi, writing in Florence in 1774, describes Dante's words as referring to a Professor of Logic in Paris (so much had been surmised from the word "sillogizzo") [26], while a little later Biagioli describes him as a "French theologian and philosopher" [27].

Le Clerc was therefore breaking new ground in his research and this is clearly recognized in his introduction to this volume [28].   Indeed, despite his inevitable mistakes, his contribution at this stage is quite remarkable. He outlines his discovery of more than a dozen different examples of scholars or clerics of the later Middle Ages, bearing the names Sigier, Siger, Syger or other variations. He has little difficulty in establishing that Dante's reference is indeed to Siger of Brabant but then goes on to identify the latter with Siger of Courtrai [29]. He does not really attempt to justify this decision as such, but the following may help to understand it.

He had discovered the involvement of Siger of Brabant with the strife in the Faculty of Arts between 1272 and 1275 over the election of Albéric of Reims as Rector. As a consequence of the objections of the Norman Nation, this had resulted in the election of two Rectors, the double awarding of degrees and so on; indeed this state of affairs was to remain until the intervention of Simon of Brion (later to become Pope Martin IV) [30].

48

It seems that Le Clerc was influenced to make this mistake by the Dominican writer, William Tocco. In his life of Thomas, written around the time of the latter's canonization in 1323, Tocco speaks of his hero as destroying "Averroism" at first and then "later" a new error, with origins not from outside but from within the faith. This, he says, was propagated by "William of Saint-Amour, Siger and their followers" [31].

Now, William of Saint-Amour had been involved in the earlier secular-mendicant controversies of 1252-1257 [32]. So, clearly, Tocco's chronology is seriously at fault. This probably indicates that he is writing with a serious lack of hard evidence, perhaps on a basis of rumours over half a century later. In any event, we shall see that, even if Tocco's order of events were reversed, Siger of Brabant could hardly have been actively involved in William of Saint-Amour's conflicts of the Fifties, except as a very young student. Even if we were to concede the possibility that his later notoriety was to give him an unjustified prominence in events of which, at most, he could only have been on the very fringes, yet another difficulty remains. It seems virtually inconceivable that he could have been directly involved with William, since the latter's quarrel was predominantly an internal one within the Theology Faculty, which resulted in William's banishment in 1259 [33].

Le Clerc had further discovered that a bequest was made to the library at the Sorbonne of some books of Thomas Aquinas, which apparently referred to the names of the donors as Siger of Courtrai and Bernier of Nivelles in a text which then proceeds to refer to the latter in connection with Siger of Brabant and the events of 1277 [34]. This, combined with another later reference in his source to Siger of Brabant and Bernier of Nivelles as "masters in theology" rather than philosophy [35], led him to conclude that Siger of Brabant must have become a theologian, even lecturing on the Summa Theologiae of Thomas Aquinas, as well as being a philosopher. Perhaps, the writings of Siger of Courtrai would, he reasoned, help to make the necessary connection.

It does seem that Le Clerc was further persuaded to make this identification between the two Sigers on account of Dante's eulogy. To Le Clerc, it is almost impossible to imagine a loyal admirer of Thomas giving such a prominent and positive role, as Dante does in his poem, to a man who had otherwise been such a major opponent of his. Thus, it would seem to be the supreme accolade, in Le Clerc's view, for a theologian who had opposed the religious orders, and Thomas in particular, and for a man who had been denounced for heresy by a Dominican Inquisitor, to be not only absolved from his crime but also now to be so acclaimed before the heavenly court by Thomas himself [36].

Later in his article, Le Clerc refers to a writing, entitled De Recuperatione Terrae Sanctae, which has subsequently been accredited to Pierre Dubois by Van Steenberghen [37]. The author is constructing a series of arguments, suitable for young people who might be persuaded to offer themselves for helping in the task of recapturing the Holy Land. He decides that philosophy is the most appropriate and attractive tool to serve as the lynchpin for this. Then, somewhat in the tenor of Dante, he recommends the study of topics taken from the Quaestiones Naturales "tam fratris Thomas quam Segeri (sic) [whether of Thomas or of Siger]". The author goes on to say that he had been a student of Siger of Brabant himself [38].

For Le Clerc, the implication is clear. Siger must have lived to redeem himself from his controversial "Averroist" writings which had been condemned by Thomas. Furthermore, this must have been done under the name of Siger of Courtrai, as if he were starting a new life, now in full communion with the Church.

Le Clerc suggests that both this author and Dante must have been present at lectures of Siger, sometime in the last two decades of the thirteenth century [39]. However, it is equally possible that Pierre Dubois had been impressed with Siger's teaching before 1277 and that he recommends him, simply as one of the most learned and impressive philosophers of the Faculty of Arts and greatest interpreters of Aristotle, despite the censures directed against him. Besides, surely his acquaintance with Ibn Rushd would also make his teaching a suitable source upon which to build up some sort of dialogue with which to enter into argument with Muslims?   Furthermore, Le Clerc, following Echard, suggests that the Sorbonne Library would not have accepted the bequest of books from a Siger, unless he had been properly reconciled with the Church [40].

Finally, he believes his theory regarding Siger's apparent re-conversion or reconciliation is confirmed by dramatic anecdotes, such as that of Andrew of Orvieto, apparently taken from Benvenuto of Imola, which implicitly consider him to have been, in a metaphorical sense, an unbaptized pagan and not merely a heretic [41].   Le Clerc's confusion of the two Sigers is unfortunate but understandable in view of the barely developing stage of research in this area in the middle of the nineteenth century.

However, after we have eliminated those writings which we can now clearly attribute to Siger of Courtrai, we are left with only four, known to Le Clerc at that time, which we can classify today as belonging to Siger of Brabant.   These include two fragments of Quaestiones Naturales, De Anima Intellectiva (which he takes to be part of the former work) and a small fragment of Quaestiones Logicales.   These are all found in a continuous section of manuscript, which is known as Manuscript Nat. Lat. 16133.   The only other work known to him is Impossibilia, which he himself had discovered in Nat. Lat. 16297.

From Le Clerc's perspective, the fragments from Quaestiones Logicales would explain Dante's use of the word "sillogizzo"; he links the Quaestiones Naturales with Pierre Dubois's forementioned coupling of Siger's name with that of Thomas.   De Anima Intellectiva would of course confirm his loyalty to Aristotle rather than the Christian faith.   Impossibilia, according to Le Clerc, does indeed reveal heresy and heterodoxy, since he cannot conceive that a Christian place of study could possibly have permitted what he sees as the exercise of frivolous sophistic arguments, in the manner of the Greeks in the pagan world of nearly two thousand years earlier [42].

While Le Clerc, as we have seen, has included some of the works attributed to Siger of Courtrai, he is nevertheless very ready to acknowledge that his first survey and assessment of Siger of Brabant may well contain a number of mistakes. He accepts that many more works of Siger must, at that time, lie undiscovered. His aim has been to rediscover after five centuries his life and writings, to some extent, and to pave the way for future scholars [43].

2.5. Ernest Renan.

In the third edition [1867] of his seminal work Averroes et l'Averroisme, which had been first published in 1852, Ernest Renan devotes a section to the Condemnations of 1270 (though he does seem a little confused as to whether it was actually 1269) and of 1277 [44]. He identifies Siger as one of those whose views had been singled out for sanction. By analysing some of the 1277 Condemnations, he concludes that Siger and his comrades were Masters within the Arts Faculty, rather than that of Theology [45].

The continuation of the confusion between Siger of Brabant and Siger of Courtrai, moreover, means that Renan is now, as we clearly see, mistaken about some of the details and chronology of Siger's life. This is of course compounded by the fact that he too makes the identification of Siger with the teacher venerated by Dante's Thomas Aquinas. This leads him to conclude that Siger, although originally a "blasphemer", had been converted by a vision of hell and had subsequently taken holy orders, rather in the mode of those contemporary stories which were spread about to edify and encourage the faithful [46].

However, despite all these inaccuracies, we must acknowledge that Renan succeeds not only in making the identification of Dante's Sigieri with his prominent role in the controversies of the 1260s and the 1270s, but also in providing a wider historical context for this "Averroism" as part of a larger movement.

2.6.   Clemens Baeumker.

The next important work to be devoted to Siger is that of Clemens Baeumker, Professor at the University of Breslau and later at Strasbourg, who in partnership with Georg Hertling, produced a series of volumes on the History of Medieval Philosophy.   Baeumker's major contribution to research on Siger was to publish for the first time in 1898 one of his works in its entirety [47], alhough there had been fragments of this same work, Impossibilia, published earlier by Potvin [48] and Hauréau [49].

In this book, Bauemker also offers a biography of Siger, which updates the contributions of Le Clerc and Renan, although he does acknowledge the provisional status of this too, in so far as it still leaves many questions to be answered [50].   With the benefit of Denifle's and Chatelain's recently published edition of the Chartularium Universitatis Parisiensis, he points out how Siger is first prominent in the University in 1266, is a member of the Picard nation and yet apparently led the Norman faction in the opposition to Albéric's election as Rector in 1272 [51].

He also recognizes Delisle's discovery, reported in 1874, that Siger of Courtrai was Procurator of the Sorbonne in 1315 and bequeathed his books of Thomas Aquinas in 1341.   This would mean therefore that this Siger of Courtrai could in no way have been involved with Robert of Sorbon and William of Saint-Amour in the secular/mendicant controversies nearly a century earlier.   Likewise, he could not be the Siger to whom Dante makes reference, since his journey to Paradise was supposed to be dated to the year 1300 [52].

However, he decides to follow Cipolla's hypothesis that there must have been two Sigers of Courtrai, with the earlier one having been a colleague of Robert and William [53].   He also repeats the view that Siger and Bernier of Nivelles were both, at some time, Masters in Theology and that they settled respectably, after being reconciled with the Church, as Canons in Liège [54].

Baeumker's other positive contribution is his acceptance of Castets' conclusions regarding the authorship of Il Fiore, an Italian poem, which was based on an earlier French work of Jehan de Meung, entitled Roman de la Rose. Castets had discovered the Italian poem in the Faculty of Medicine at Montpellier and considers the author, who uses the nom-de-plume "Durante", to be none other than Dante Alighieri himself [55].

There are three very interesting lines, from our point of view, in Sonnet 92. They are put into the mouth of Faux-Semblant, who represents Hypocrisy (somewhat in the manner of Bunyan's Pilgrim's Progress). They are especially fascinating since they do not occur in the original French poem and therefore almost certainly represent the personal work of "Durante":-

> Mastro Sighier non ando guai lieto.
> A ghiado il fe' morire a gran dolore
> Nella corte di Roma, ad Orbivieto [56].

[Master Siger ended up far from happy. I made him die by the sword in great pain in the Papal court at Orvieto.]

Baeumker's cautious opinion, that Mastro Sighier is "probably" to be identified with the Sigieri of the Commedia Divina [57], sheds more light on the possible circumstances of his death, as we shall see in the next chapter.

Other aspects of Baeumker's scholarship are, however, far more dubious. For example, he follows Hauréau in misunderstanding the nature of Impossibilia. We have already seen above how Le Clerc had misinterpreted this work [58], but both Hauréau and Baeumker take this, on the other hand, to be the work of an unknown writer who is showing the errors of Siger in maintaining the six sophisms stated [59]. This is a very fundamental mistake and would imply, for example, that he denied both the existence of God and that of the external world. In fact, a decade later, Baeumker was to acknowledge this particular error, even if somewhat halfheartedly [60].

We might also well query whether Impossibilia, as a work primarily devoted to logic, is the best choice to use as a basis for beginning to discover Siger's distinctive thought.   Surely De Anima Intellectiva would have better fulfilled this purpose, particularly when we bear in mind that Baeumker was well aware of his conflict with Thomas Aquinas over this issue, that had prompted the latter's riposte, which was indeed known in one of its codicils to be entitled "contra magistrum Sigerum" [61].   Presumably, it was his almost blind following of Hauréau's misinterpretation of Impossibilia that led him to exaggerate its importance as being particularly distinctive of Siger's thought and position.

2.7.   Pierre Mandonnet.

Over the preceding fifty years or so, the only other writings which had become available for research since the time of Le Clerc, were De Aeternitate Mundi (discovered by Charles Potvin in 1878) and the sophism Utrum haec sit vera: Homo est Animal Nullo Homine Existente (found by Denifle in Vienna in 1889).   In fact, Coxe had discovered in Oxford the presence of Quaestiones in Tertium de Anima as early as 1852 and Denifle had found in 1891 another sophism Omnis Homo de Necessitate est Animal, which is attributed to Siger amongst several collected together in the Vatican Archives. However, these do not appear to have come to the notice of any relevant scholars and the references remained to be unearthed many years later.   Indeed, the same fate was subsequently to affect Schimek's discovery in 1891 of Compendium magistri Sigeri super Librum de Generatione et Corruptione in Lilienfeld in Austria.

Pierre Mandonnet, the Dominican scholar from Fribourg in Switzerland, writing only one year after Baeumker's publication of Impossibilia, was to initiate great advances in the knowledge and understanding of Siger.   He was to edit these five previously unpublished works already known at this time, and furthermore to lay to rest finally and definitively the confusion caused by the erroneous identification of Siger of Brabant and Siger of Courtrai.   His critical study and the unedited texts were first to be published in the year 1899, and then to be partly revised and republished in 1911.   The first study provides much interest, in so far as it contrasts to some extent with Baeumker's views, and there was to develop over the next decade or so a bitter professional wrangle between the two professors. He attempts an outline of Siger's life and of the main themes of his thought. He also tackles a number of associated issues, to which frequent reference will be made in the course of this study.

Mandonnet was able to track down the origin of the errors concerning the two Sigers to William of Tocco's biography of Thomas Aquinas. This had been very vague and mistaken on a number of points of fact. It had created an anachronism by linking Siger with William of Saint-Amour [62]. Charles Meusnier, in his seventeenth century history of the Sorbonne, had then gone on to make the mistaken identification with Siger of Courtrai, which was to be spread by Échard and many others [63]. Meusnier's conclusion had been that Siger of Courtrai/Brabant, whom he had linked with William of Saint-Amour, had died before 1260. Mandonnet rightly rejects this view as impossible, since Siger of Brabant's name does not appear in the <u>Chartularium Universitatis Parisiensis</u> until 1266, as we shall see in the next chapter.

He also rejects Baeumker's notion, derived from Échard, that Siger and Bernier of Nivelles retired to Liège as canons. He feels this is confirmed by the discovery of a letter of John Peckham, dated 10 November 1284. This letter speaks of the two principal protagonists of the theory of the "unity of forms", which clearly is a reference to Siger and his companion-in-exile, as having "finished their days in misery on the far side of the Alps" [64]. It will in any case be recalled from the previous section how Delisle has shown that Dante's Siger of Brabant could not have lived beyond 1300.

Although he had published a few short articles in the immediately preceding years, the great significance of Mandonnet's volume is that it constitutes the first major work devoted to the study of Siger alone. It represents the fruits of lengthy and very professional research, with evidence of considerable flair, a real feeling for history and an ability to isolate important material from what is merely peripheral. It is a very scholarly work, although naturally, with the discovery of many more texts and academic advances building on his earlier ideas, many corrections must be made today. Nevertheless, it remains substantially accurate in its general assessment of Siger's life and of his role in thirteenth century Parisian thought.

It is of somewhat more than passing interest, however, to see the development, over the first decade of the twentieth century, of the bitter polemical academic and professional conflict between Mandonnet and Baeumker. This was to come to a climax with an article of the former, published in 1911 in the Revue Thomiste [65].

In his second edition of his work on Siger (published in two volumes between 1908 and 1911), Mandonnet had still grudgingly acknowledged some basic attempt at scholarship on the part of Baeumker. However, he continued to criticize the narrowness of the latter's basis for assessing Siger's views, in so far as he only uses one work. This, he maintains, is compounded by Baeummker's erroneous misunderstanding of the nature of Impossibilia and utter failure to see the disputations as a sophistic device [66].

Above all, Mandonnet despises Baeumker for taking eight years to make a public admittance of this error, and then only by means of a very small and obscure footnote [67]. He furthermore resents the lack of acknowledgement by Baeumker of his own work and scholarship, to which the latter only makes three minor references. This is surely a justified complaint, considering the extent and importance of Mandonnet's research.

Mandonnet goes on to express his professional suspicions, regarding the doctoral thesis of a young student called Bruckmuller, which had been supervised by Baron von Hertling in Munich. The latter had indeed been the co-author with Baeumker of the multi-volume Beiträge zur Geschichte der Philosophie des Mittelalters, while the doctoral thesis failed to take any account of Mandonnet's case that Siger was an Averroist [68].

He also feels that Baeumker's assertion that it was Hauréau and Denifle who had established Siger's Averroism is quite inaccurate in the former's case and only partially true in the case of the latter. He wants much of the credit to be given to himself and resents Baeumker's failure to do so [69].

It is sad that these two scholars exhibited their bitterness towards one another so publicly, since it probably deflected both of them to some extent from their investigations into Siger, but it does seem as if the matter assumed much greater importance for Mandonnet than it did for Baeumker. At the same time, it is probably fair to say that Baeumker's overall scholarship covered a much greater range of the history of mediaeval philosophy (but especially of the Platonists) than Mandonnet, while the latter concentrated much more of his attention and research on this particular historical period in question.

Indeed, despite the many limitations and unavoidable errors within Mandonnet's scholarship, which will become more clear as this study develops, it should be fully acknowledged that it was these dedicated investigations of his which really enabled later writers to begin to become aware of the nature of the teaching and thought of Siger.

2.8.　　　　Munich MS.9559.

Martin Grabmann (1875-1949), the successor of Clemens Baeumker as editor of that vast collection of volumes, published in Münster under the name of the Beiträge zur Geschichte der Philosophie des Mittelalters to which reference was made in the previous section, has been highly regarded for both the breadth of his learning and for the clarity of his writings. His major contribution to our knowledge of Siger lies in his discovery of quite a number of previously unknown manuscripts as a result of his extensive scouring around the libraries and archives of Europe. Some of these were second or third copies of writings, with which scholars were already familiar.

However, his most significant announcement came in 1924, following his discovery in Munich the previous year in Clm 9559 of a collection of eight series of "Quaestiones", the last of which "In Metaphysicam" is attributed to "magistro Sogero". After examination of these Commentaries, he declared that he believed them all to be the authentic writings of Siger of Brabant [70].

The great Belgian scholar Fernand Van Steenberghen also accepted Siger's authorship of them for many years. Indeed, he published them in their entirety in edited form in 1931 in the first volume of his earliest major work on Siger, although even then he acknowledged there to be a pressing need to conduct an internal investigation of them [71]. Some doubts about Siger's authorship had already been voiced by Duin, though for the most part he retained the earlier view [72].

However, in 1958, Geza Sajó, librarian at the Hungarian National Library in Budapest, was able to demonstrate conclusively that the first and the seventh of these were in fact the work of Boethius of Dacia [73]. Subsequently, it has been suggested by Van Steenberghen that perhaps some, or even all, of the other Commentaries (that is to say, with the exception of "In Metaphysicam" which is explicitly attributed to Siger) may well be the work of his Danish colleague [74].

It still remains a mystery, however, as to why the collector of this manuscript should only make the one single attribution at the end of the list of these eight similar Commentaries. Could it be simply ignorance or could it even be that, whereas Siger was by this time known to be dead, Boethius, on the other hand, had escaped much censure, was still alive and now held a respectable position? This latter may well be suggested by the Catalogue of Stams, which indicates that Boethius probably went on to become a Dominican [75]. Perhaps such an explanation becomes much more likely, when we note that the collector of MS.9559 does in fact attribute other works in the same manuscript to Thomas Aquinas and other dead, including Arab, authors. Certainly, he appears to be a student of the Faculty of Arts and it would have seemed in his interests to have known the identity of each author. At the very least, we can safely declare that all seven of the other Commentaries are clearly the work of the Sigerian school.

2.9.   Other Major Manuscript Discoveries.

A number of other manuscript discoveries were made during the period between the two World Wars. Although these were frequently additional redactions of works already known, nevertheless they helped greatly in the later production of more reliable recensions, closer to the original versions.

However in 1930 F. Stegmüller quite by chance stumbled across a manuscript, in the Portugese National Library in Lisbon, numbered G. 2299, which explicitly contained the name of Siger.   He announced in an article, in the following year, the contents of his discovery; these included several texts already known, but also, for the first time, five Quaestiones Morales and six completely new Questiones Naturales [76].

Then, in 1931, the renowned historian Mgr. Glorieux announced his discovery that MS. 16297, which had been discovered by Mandonnet and contained a number of Siger's writings, had in fact been compiled by Godfrey of Fontaines, a contemporary who remained in the Faculty of Arts after the 1277 Condemnations [77].   Some of these texts had indeed been included in the second edition of Mandonnet's great work in 1908 [78].

In 1946, Annaliese Maier reported her discovery in the Vatican Archives of some Quaestiones super Secundum Physicorum, that is to say, a commentary on the Second Book of Aristotle's Physics [79].   This was not however to be published till ten years later by A. Zimmermann [80] who, like Dunphy [81], rejects other texts commentating on the Physics which had previously been attributed to Siger.

Meanwhile, new versions of the Quaestiones in Metaphysicam had been discovered in 1939 in Paris by J. Duin and then another in 1950 in Cambridge by A. Maurer.

60

The most recent major discovery was that announced in 1966 by A. Dondaine and L.J. Bataillon [82]. These two Dominicans had found in the National Library in Vienna a manuscript numbered S. 2330, which includes yet a fourth version of Quaestiones in Metaphysicam, and a copy of Quaestiones super Librum de Causis, whose Sigerian authenticity can be shown by some detective work, involving a little decoding, to be beyond dispute. This latter is particularly useful for our understanding of Siger's thought, since we have an example of neo-Platonic influence on him through this work of Proclus, rather than of Aristotle. Furthermore, it almost certainly represents the latest extant teaching that can be definitively accredited to Siger. One of the other writings in this manuscript, Sententia super Quartum Meteorum, can also attributed to Siger, although his name has been touched up so that it could be replaced by that of Peter of Auvergne. Some others here may well belong to him too, but, if so, they will date from the very beginning of his teaching career [83]. However, it is interesting in that they may in fact reveal his Aristotelian roots in so far as they indicate how Adam of Buckfield was a major influence on his teaching at that time [84].

2.10.　　Important Modern Publications on Siger and of his Texts.

Following in the footsteps of Le Clerc and Mandonnet, Van Steenberghen has been the scholar in recent years, who, throughout the whole of his working life, has devoted most critical thought to Siger and his school, although Pinborg, a Danish scholar, has edited those works which can now fairly be attributed to Boethius of Dacia [85].

Reference has already been made to Van Steenberghen's earliest work of 1931, in which he also edited the texts of Grabmann's Munich recension, some of which were erroneously attributed to Siger. This work was then supplemented by his own volume Les Oeuvres et La Doctrine de Siger de Brabant, which was published in 1938 and which fairly represented knowledge and scholarship on our subject up to that time [86].

In his later life, however, the Louvain Professor produced in 1977 a much revised study in the "Philosophes Mediévaux" series [87]. Frequent reference will be made to this excellent work in the course of this study, although evidence will also be provided here to demonstrate the need for us to revise a number of the judgments and conclusions offered by Van Steenberghen.

In this same series, for which Van Steenberghen had taken on overall direction and responsibility, there can be found major publications of texts of almost all of those works which can now be safely attributed to Siger. They were produced over a number of years by Duin (1954), Marlasca (1972), Bazán (1972) and (1974), Zimmermann (1974), Dunphy (1981) and Maurer (1983). The last two of these conclusively replace an earlier edition by Graiff of Siger's Questions sur la Métaphysique (1948). The writer will be referring to all of the above texts at various stages in later chapters of this study.

One other text Quaestiones Metaphysicae Tres has been published separately by Vennebusch (1966), and in fact has clear similarities, as we shall see, with three questions found in the fuller Commentaries on Aristotle's Metaphysics [88].

Finally, Sententia super Quartum Meteorum is as yet unpublished, though some very small parts of this, as well as of other possible Sigerian texts, can be found in the article of Dondaine and Bataillon to which reference has been made in the preceding section. However, these early texts do all appear to be very straightforward commentaries from which it is not possible to derive any distinctive teaching.

2.11.   Most Recent Research on Siger.

Over the last thirty years or so, a number of articles have been published in numerous periodicals around the world on the subject of Siger or of the Faculty of Arts in his time. Reference will be made later in this study to many of these and also to a number of papers delivered at conferences which have been subsequently published. Unfortunately, though not surprisingly, most do not offer insight in great depth, even within a very limited area of research. Additional mention should however be made of three other pieces of research completed within the last few years.

The Italian scholar, Adriana Caparello, published in 1987 a book entitled La "Perspectiva" in Sigieri di Brabante [89], which endeavours to examine his views on that aspect of physics, sometimes described as "optics", which is concerned with the functioning of light as a means to acquiring knowledge. She also tries to link this to his metaphysical views, in the manner developed some fifty years before Siger by Robert Grosseteste and others [90]. Its value, however, in the context of this study is somewhat peripheral, but, while further reference to it will be minimal, it must be acknowledged that it does indeed cover an area of Siger's teaching which has been little researched previously.

In addition, two different scholars have presented doctoral theses on Siger in 1990, both at the University of Navarra in Pamplona. Antonio Carol has written the Naturaleza de la Metafisica segun Siger de Brabant, the heart of which was published in the following year under the title La Distinción entre "Esse" y "Essentia" en Siger de Brabant [91]. Much of this can provide great interest to the specialist student of the metaphysics of this period.

His sometime colleague, Raimondo Sanfilippo, followed up a Master's dissertation presented at the University of Palermo in 1985 on the distinction between essence and existence in the teaching of Siger with a doctoral thesis entitled I Fondamenti Metafisici della Psicologia di Sigieri di Brabante. This complements to some extent Carol's research in so far as it relates to Siger's views on psychology and, as in his case above, part of this has been published recently under the title La Composizione dell'Ente Finito in Sigieri di Brabante [92].

Some mention could also be made of a small book entitled Menschliche Seele und Kosmischer Geist written by two authors, W.-U. Klünker and B. Sandkühler and published in 1988. They examine the relationship between Thomas Aquinas' De Unitate Intellectus contra Averroistas and Siger's De Anima

Intellectiva. Probably, the greatest contribution they make is to provide a translation of the latter in German. It would not be unfair to say that their knowledge of wider issues is somewhat limited and they provide little original insight, other than to suggest that Siger may possibly have believed in reincarnation [93]! They then endeavour to find links between Siger's teaching and the "pneumatosophy" of Rudolf Steiner [94].

Finally, a little booklet entitled Siger van Brabant: De Dubbele Waarheid, published in 1992, should be acknowledged. Unfortunately, it does not go into much depth about the issues considered. However, in so far as it is written in Dutch and also offers Dutch translations of a few extracts of Siger's teaching, it can be commended for opening up a greater awareness of the Brabantine scholar to a new and wider readership.

CHAPTER THREE

THE LIFE AND TIMES OF SIGER UP TO

THE END OF HIS TEACHING CAREER IN PARIS

3.0.   Introduction.

This chapter examines the events of Siger's life up to and including his exile from Paris following the publication of Stephen Tempier's second series of Condemnations on 7 March 1277.   Chapter Nine will later offer a speculative investigation of the period following the enforced end of his teaching career up to and including his death.   His early years will inevitably be somewhat speculative too, though many of the episodes of the years in the Faculty of Arts in Paris are documented by the Chartularium Universitatis Parisiensis and a number of other sources, now available in many archives and records.   Since the previous chapter offered an outline of the gradual unfolding of our knowledge of Siger and of the rediscovery of his writings, the approach here will be from the contemporary state of knowledge.   This does not, of course, preclude reference to the opinions of earlier writers (including indications, where relevant, of how more recent discoveries may have made some previously-held views no longer tenable).

3.1.   The Early Years.

As is not unusual for this period of the Middle Ages, the only detail
which we know for certain about Siger's background is the fact of his origin as
being from the province of Brabant in the Low Countries.   We are also aware
from the decree summoning him and two colleagues to appear before the
Inquisitor that his diocese was that of Liège, where he held the title and, most
importantly for his financial security, the benefice of Canon of St. Paul's [1].
During this period, it was ruled by a duke, subject to the Holy Roman Empire, and
covered quite a large area of modern Belgium (both Walloon and Flemish
speaking) and also part of the southern area of the modern nation of the
Netherlands, which still possesses today a province retaining the name of Brabant.

However, from which part of Brabant did Siger come?   Sassen thinks
that the fact that he became a member of the Picard Nation indicates the French-
speaking area, since otherwise it would have been more usual to have joined the
English Nation [2].   However, Van Steenberghen points out that Siger, as a name,
sounds Teutonic in origin - probably a Latinization of the German Sieger and the
Dutch Zeger (or, come to that, the equivalent of the English Victor) [3].

On   the other hand, because a number of Siger's associates have
French-sounding names, he postulates that he was probably Flemish by birth, may
have gone to Liège for his early studies, linking up with French-speaking Picards
there, with the result that he joined that Nation in Paris instead.   There does,
however, seem reason to question this last hypothesis, when we note that Siger's
first appearance on the recorded scene of history is as a result of his fierce
involvement in the controversy over the reception of John of Ulliaco into the
French rather than the Picard Nation [4].   Besides, several of the later internal
crises within the University, and the Faculty of Arts in particular, do cut across
national boundaries.

It does seem to the writer far more likely, therefore, that he did come
from the geographical area which really did belong to the Picard Nation.   It may
be a far more likely eventuality that Siger was a Flemish-speaker by birth and

family origin, who came from a part of Brabant, where there were some Flemish and some French speakers, perhaps near the language borderline area. In some cases, there must have been, for example, Flemish overlords in predominantly French-speaking areas. Certainly, it would be more than feasible that he came from a relatively well-to-do family of Flemish origin, but grew up in a French-speaking area that would have been covered by the Picard Nation.

It is interesting to note that Siger is known by his region rather than his town or city. This might suggest that he probably came from a small village or a rural area. Another possibility - which does not seem to have been previously discussed - is that he came from an aristocratic background of nobility, even from the extended family of the Dukes of Brabant. If primogeniture, or some other method of attempting to maintain the inheritance of lands and possessions, applied at this time in the culture of Siger's family [5], it could well be that he was a bright younger son sent initially to the Cathedral or Latin School in Liège, as a result of family influence or contacts. With other middle-class and noble boys, he would have studied reading and writing as well as Latin grammar [6]. He may have shown such early promise that he was awarded the benefice of Canon of St. Paul's, again possibly as a result of patronage, which would, in modern terms, provide him with the equivalent of a scholarship to Paris [7]. Such a scenario is at least as likely as Van Steenberghen's reliance on his having been simply identified at an early age as an exceptional scholar meriting a benefice as a bursary for study [8]. In any event, this would provide Siger with unusual security, since even many of the young Regent Masters of Arts did not possess this financial advantage, which was much sought and fought for [9].

When was Siger born? Mandonnet calculates that it would have been around 1235 [10], but of course he comes upon this date partly as a result of the confusion with Siger of Courtrai. Van Steenberghen puts his birth at around 1240 to allow for the fact that he was still a Master of Arts in 1277 [11]. The date of his birth must indeed remain uncertain, while, of course, we must ultimately acknowledge that it remains of little importance. The normal timescale for qualification as a Master of Arts would suggest, however, on calculating back from Siger's first recorded public appearances, that 1240 must be a fairly close estimation, though it could be two or three years later, if we are to date the beginning of his magisterial career as no earlier than 1266.

3.2.   Siger as a Young Master of Arts in Paris.

Cardinal Simon of Brion, later to become Pope Martin IV, was appointed Pontifical Legate to the University of Paris in 1265 [12]. It would not be long, however, before Siger of Brabant was to come to his notice.

A row developed early in 1266, because, as noted in the preceeding section, a young Master of Arts, John of Ulliaco, had joined the French Nation, which at this time amounted in numbers to about the total of the other three Nations added together.   The Picards would normally have laid claim to the geographical area from which he had come [13].   John was then kidnapped and suffered some violent abuse at the hands of the Picards.   As a result, the French indignantly broke off relations with the other three Nations and chose a Rector without consulting them.   Presumably they feared that they would be outvoted in the election of a Rector, according to the special system of voting already described in the first chapter.   Such a Rector may then have very well found the French to be in the wrong.

However violence was to escalate and Simon of Brion now decided to intervene.   Siger of Brabant was suspected of being involved in the illegal arrest of a French Canon, William of Tulle [14].   Furthermore, his name was one of several being cited as members of a group of fellow-countrymen, who, albeit with the apparently full approval of the Picard Nation, had allegedly attempted to seize the ritual Books of Hours, belonging to some of the French Masters, while the latter were actually singing the Office of the Dead in memory of a former Master, William of Auxerre, who had died over thirty years earlier [15].   What is also intriguing about this last episode is that another name cited was Simon of Brabant. When we consider how rarely this geographical epithet seems to have been used, it is worth speculating as to whether he could even have been a relative.   We find no further mention of Simon so it is possible that he joined another faculty to pursue a career in the Church or even in Law back in Flanders, while Siger was able to channel any aggressive instincts in academic disputations and conflicts.

On 27 August 1266, Simon of Brion, as Papal Legate, delivered his judgment that, if there were a future case of dispute over the election of a Rector, then a joint commission of theologians and lawyers would have to report and come up with a decision within a month. In addition, probably to ensure stronger leadership in the Faculty of Arts, he decreed that the election of a Rector should take place quarterly, instead of monthly.

No sanction seems to have been imposed in the actual case in question, nor incidentally at this time is any mention yet made of any heterodox teaching in the Faculty. Van Steenberghen suggests that this may be because Simon of Brion has only arrived so recently [16]. On the other hand, it could equally well be that Simon felt discipline and good order were needed as priorities at first, or even that no real controversy in the doctrinal field had yet come into the open. We really do not know and can only speculate.

Van Steenberghen believes that Siger's part in this episode shows the immaturity and impetuosity of a young and unscrupulous leader [17]. However, Gauthier argues to the contrary that Siger still appears to be only an insignificant figure at this stage of his career [18]. Whatever may be the truth, those involved clearly had widespread support from within the three Nations. It is hard for us, in an age of professional policing, law and order, to appreciate the difficulties and frustrations involved in solving disputes, even in the cultured ambiente of the fledgling University. In previous years, there had been after all a range of other conflicts, strikes and temporary closures.

Recent research has discovered a series of texts of William of Baglione, holder of the Franciscan Chair of Theology in 1266-1267, in which he attacks three of the teachings, which were to be condemned by Stephen Tempier in 1270 [19].

It may well be, following the increased access to the works of Aristotle and of his commentators, that there would have been opportunities for purely academic discussion on these topics. However, the evidence of William of Baglione indicates that some of the theologians were certainly concerned about the teaching within the Faculty of Arts in 1266. Furthermore, it seems far more likely that, with the growth in the study of Aristotle and Ibn Rushd, there would have been for some years now undercurrents of experimental thought. There would surely have already been an exchange of ideas about the implications of a whole range of ideas and teachings. Furthermore, Van Steenberghen's assertion that William of Baglione could only have had Thomas Aquinas in mind as an opponent, since there were no heterodox Aristotelians in Paris at this stage, is actually begging the question at issue [20].

We have already wondered, in the first chapter, whether John Sackville might not have been so involved to some extent ten years earlier [21]. Certainly, it is possible that others, such as Adam of Buckfield, may have been floating some such similar ideas around at this stage in England. Adam had been involved in student disturbances in Oxford, was an avid commentator on Aristotle and does seem to have resigned his canonry at Lincoln about 1276-7, the height of the troubles in Paris [22]. It is probably no more than sheer coincidence, but the question mark remains there.

Another issue that has never really been considered is the relationship between supposed irresponsibility in the field of University discipline and possible irresponsibility in the area of academic teaching and learning. Yet surely many may well have seen a link between the two! Certainly, Van Steenberghen does admit that, in the following year, Bonaventure warns the Franciscan General Chapter in Paris, in his Lenten Conferences of 1267 (known as Collationes de Decem Praeceptis) of the danger of heterodox errors and subversive teaching in the Faculty of Arts [23]. Indeed, Bonaventure must surely have been warned some time in advance of suspicions that this was the case. He condemns, as three errors against the Christian faith, the positions of some Masters on the topics of the eternity of the world, of the oneness of the intellect and of the fixed determinism of fate. The latter would have invalidated man's efforts to achieve salvation. All three of the above teachings were subsequently to figure among the thirteen propositions to be condemned in 1270.

The following Lent, in a similar series of conferences, known as Collationes de Septem Donis Spiritus Sancti, Bonaventure continues his warning on these three teachings, now adding others also, such as the impossibility of creation "ex nihilo" (24). It is interesting, incidentally, to note Bonaventure's views on the relationship between philosophy and theology. In his Fourth Conference of this Lent of 1268, he follows the normal university practice up to this time of perceiving philosophy merely as a preliminary area of study before a student moves on to theology, unless one wants to "fall into darkness" (25). We can fairly contrast this with Thomas Aquinas' use of philosophy as a worthwhile support to help formulate and understand theological ideas and, of course, even more so with the position of Siger and Boethius of Dacia (which we shall consider later in this study), claiming that it is a subject worthy of study in its own right.

Clearly, warnings, such as these now being given by Bonaventure, would have alerted the authorities to the teaching which had been going on in the Faculty of Arts. If the Church authorities felt a dangerous situation was in danger of being created, then they would have to intervene. This would be particularly the case, when we bear in mind the importance of Paris as a centre of study, the potential for other universities to follow its leadership and, above all, the fact that every future academic leader within the Church had to study Arts before going on to Theology. In fact, even in the case of theology, it is worth noting that, as has been pointed out by Sarayana very recently, Bonaventure fails generally to make Thomas' distinction betwen theology as a spiritual means of contemplating God and theology as a speculative discipline of intellectul study (26). The result is that he sees theology almost entirely as serving the spiritual development of the individual believer.

Thomas Aquinas was also about to enter the fray. He had been holder of the Dominican Chair of Theology from 1256 to 1259 and was now teaching in Rome. We can only speculate on the reason for his unusual return to Paris early in 1269 and it may well be unconnected with events in the Faculty of Arts.

Nevertheless, it did mean that he was to find himself right in the thick of it all before long. He tried to steer a narrow, but dangerous, middle course between those in the Faculty of Arts who were apparently prepared, at least under the cloak of open intellectual investigation of Aristotle, to present ideas that conflicted with accepted orthodoxy of belief, and those who felt that study of Aristotle should really be avoided because of the high risks and major threats which it might offer Christianity.

Bazán appears to be right in dating four extant works of Siger to the period prior to 1270, namely the Compendium de Generatione et Corruptione, the sophism Omnis Homo de Necessitate est Animal, the quaestio Utrum Haec sit Vera: Homo est Animal, Nullo Homine Existente and the Quaestiones in Tertium de Anima [27]. The first of these appears to be an abridged version of a work of the English scholar Geoffrey of Haspall and Bazán thus produces cogent arguments to suggest it dates from the very beginning of Siger's teaching career, certainly before 1268. It probably reflects his use of lecture notes, whether his own or Geoffrey's, at a stage before he had the time or opportunity to develop his own distinctive ones.

A fifth work, Sententia super Quartum Meteorum, also seems to belong to Siger but, like the first work above, also appears to owe considerable, though not quite so much, dependence to an English scholar, in this case to Adam of Buckfield [28]. Thus, for similar reasons, this should probably be dated to one of the first years of Siger's teaching.

Stephen Tempier, who had been appointed Chancellor three years earlier, about the same time as Simon of Brion had become Pontifical Legate, became Bishop of Paris in 1268. He was to issue a decree on 10 December 1270, condemning under penalty of excommunication, thirteen alleged errors in teaching in the Faculty of Arts. These, corresponding to a large extent with the earlier warnings of Bonaventure, concentrated on the four areas of monopsychism, the eternity of the world, determinism and the denial of divine providence [29].

A small work of the Augustinian Giles of Rome, entitled <u>Errores Philosophorum</u>, is also an interesting witness to what was happening at this time. Although he may have been a few years junior to Siger, he is writing after moving on to study theology, while clearly retaining considerable interest in his old faculty [30].

Of the five works of Siger listed above, three appear to have little direct relevance to the Condemnations. However, the quaestio <u>Utrum Haec sit Vera "Homo est Animal, Nullo Homine Existente"</u> does speak of the eternity of the world and some of the <u>Quaestiones in Tertium de Anima</u> refer to the unicity of the human intellect. As we shall see later, there can be little doubt that much of these goings-on reflected a direct response to the rapidly growing concern about the influence of the teaching of Siger and some of his colleagues [31]. However, he is again about to take centre-stage in the internal politics of the university.

3.3.   Siger's Teaching Career in Paris from 1270 to 1276.

At Christmas 1271, Albéric of Reims was elected Rector (since 1266, as has been noted, such an appointment was for three months). A minority group felt him to be incompetent and unworthy. They appealed to the recently constituted Commission of Appeal of senior theologians and lawyers, which subsequently found in favour of Albéric. The minority now further appealed to the Papal Legate, Simon of Brion [32].

Mandonnet plays down the rebellion and calculates that it only included about one-sixth of the total members of the Faculty [33], while Van Steenberghen thinks there would have been about a quarter of the total [34]. Clearly, it is difficult to be more accurate, when we are so uncertain about the numbers within each Nation and the exact relationship between the Nations. However, on Van Steenberghen's estimate, we are still talking about virtually half the Faculty, when we exclude the large committed French Nation. It is quite extraordinary that so many would have been prepared to take the risk of standing up for their principles and to go into open opposition and schism within the

Faculty. When this large group of members was excluded from voting in the next election, they promptly set up as a separate body. They elected a series of their own Rectors, awarded their own degrees and so on. Of course, their exclusion could well indicate, not only a gesture of punishment, but also a fear that their influence might be growing.

The larger, mostly French, "loyalist" group all took oaths on 1 April 1272 to avoid any disputation on so-called "theological" questions, such as the Incarnation and the Trinity. They vowed never to comment on or to discuss texts which might seem opposed to the Christian faith [35].

How great was Siger's involvement in all these comings and goings? We can only speculate. Nevertheless, since the minority group is described by the "Chartularium" as "Pars Sigeri" - in opposition to the "Pars Alberici" - it would seem that he was certainly the leader and the focus of the opposition [36]. Van Steenberghen even claims he was probably the first rival Rector to be elected [37], though more recently Gauthier has tried to present a case, suggesting that his role was really very minor [38].

We cannot say to what extent the dispute was really over teaching, disciplinary or personal matters. Perhaps it was a combination of all three. Certainly, as we shall see later in this study, it was far from Siger's mind to want to pronounce on such theological matters. It was his aim to establish the independence of the Faculty of Arts from that of Theology. While he was to acknowledge that some philosophical questions were of concern to theologians in so far as revelation might have a bearing upon the issues considered, he did not claim authority in such matters of revelation for the philosophers. However, in a fledgling situation of democracy, such as that pertaining in this case, feelings and resentment would have run very deep. This would be especially the case with decrees of excommunication flying around, with the right to teach, personal livelihood and so much else at stake.

It is even possible that there was a hidden agenda regarding moral behaviour. Brewer believes that Roger Bacon's testimony that a number of Paris theologians were expelled from Paris for several years following a public condemnation of homosexual activities referred to the same year of 1271 [39].

Bonaventure was to have one more onslaught in his Eastertide Conferences of 1273 - known as <u>Collationes in Hexaemeron</u> - before he was summoned back to be invested as Cardinal, never to see Paris again. Here he condemns in very strong language the use of philosophy, rather than Scripture, to determine the truth of questions and, in doing so, gathers together a list of mistakes which have recently arisen as a result of doing so:

> In tantum aliqui nostri temporis in iis profecerunt ut, erecta cervice contra veritatem Scripturae, in iacturam matris Ecclesiae dicerent et scriberent mundum aeternum, animam omnium unam, non esse tutum votum paupertatis et castitatis, non esse peccatum fornicari, et plurima deteriora, quae non sunt digna dici [40].

[What is more, some people in our days, by raising their heads against the truth of Scripture, have gone so far in them ('adulterous areas of learning') as to speak to the detriment of the Church. Furthermore, they have written that the world is eternal, that there is only one soul for everyone, that the vow of poverty and chastity is not desirable, that fornication is no sin, along with very many worse things that are quite unmentionable.]

As we have already seen, many theologians in Paris perceived only too clearly what they saw as the threat to Christian discipline and order, posed by the discovery of the so-called "pagan" authors. Even Albert the Great, now away from Paris, in response to a plea from a young theologian Giles of Lessines, had produced a small work, entitled <u>De Quindecem Problematibus</u>, in an attempt to defeat what he thought were the positions of the so-called "Averroists" [41].

On the other hand, there clearly existed a deep split, quite apart from the conflict described above, within the Arts Faculty itself. About four or five years after his <u>Errores Philosophorum</u>, Giles of Rome published a new work called De Plurificatione Intellectus Possibilis, to counter some of the arguments of Siger's "De Anima Intellectiva", while others within the Faculty of Arts remained very anxious to retain their philosophical and academic independence. They were anxious to avoid any interference or censorship from such theologians, after the hard-won gains of a few decades earlier, including permission to teach the Aristotelian corpus in its integrity.

Simon of Brion was to issue a decree on 7 May 1275 on his return to Paris from the Council and Curia in Lyon, in which he makes no personal reference to Siger nor indeed to any doctrinal question [42]. He does, however, determine that the division must end and takes it upon himself to appoint Peter of Auvergne as the new Rector for the entire Faculty. The schism is healed, but he makes noises, threatening sanctions if splits recur. The fact that it had taken well over three years to resolve indicates well the strength of feelings and the depth of the split involved. The Chartularium Universitatis Parisiensis also states that he declares the legitimacy of Albéric's election. It should also be noted that Simon of Brion was renowned for his excessive nationalism, even when he was later to be elected Pope Martin IV, and it is almost inconceivable that he would have found against the French Nation [43].

Some eighteen months later, however, on 23 November 1276, Simon du Val, the Dominican Inquisitor General of France, issued a summons calling upon Siger of Brabant, Gosvin of La Chapelle and Bernier of Nivelles, all Canons of Liège, to appear before him at Saint-Quentin on 18 January 1277 to answer a charge of heresy [44]. It seems however that they had already fled from Paris.

Preliminary moves had already been made. On 2 September 1276 a university-wide decree had been published which prohibited all teaching in private places of any material except within the basic subjects of logic and grammar [45]. About a fortnight after the summons by the Inquisitor, Simon of Brion issued a decree about the outbreaks of what he saw as scandalous behaviour in the University. He threatened excommunication for those found guilty of alcoholic excess at parties, hooliganism and getting involved in fights! [46]

Certainly, the Solemn Condemnation of 7 March 1277 was to include, quite apart from the doctrinal questions which we are considering in this study, condemnations of sexual intercourse before marriage and other sexual practices, considered by the Church authorities to be immoral but which were presumably fairly widespread at this time.

Finally, on 18 January 1277, the newly elected Pope John XXI (Peter of Spain) had written to Stephen Tempier, asking him to investigate alleged events in the University [47]. The upshot on 7 March was this famous Solemn Condemnation of 219 propositions "contra errores Boetii et Sigeri" [against the errors of Boethius and of Siger], although, of course, as we have seen, its scope was very much wider than their own teachings and indeed included many aspects of Thomas Aquinas' teaching. This move was to be followed, eleven days later, by a similar condemnation on the part of Robert Kilwardby, Archbishop of Canterbury. This involved thirty, mostly Thomist, propositions which were, he claimed, being taught at Oxford.

Yet another interesting development was the issuing by John XXI on 28 April 1277 of a letter, headed "Flumen Aquae Vivae", which instructed Tempier to make a fresh investigation into the teaching in Paris "tam in artibus quam in theologia" [in Arts and Theology alike] [48].

Undoubtedly, the witchhunt was much wider in scope than merely to silence Siger and his colleagues; many were aiming at Thomas, no doubt, while many others would have been affected somewhat by association with the scandals over alleged immoral behaviour. However, it did mean that Siger's teaching career in Paris had come to a premature end.

There is very little hard evidence about his subsequent life in Italy before he was eventually murdered but some considerable speculation about this period will be offered later in Chapter Nine.

3.4.   Events Surrounding Siger's Flight into Exile.

As has been noted above, this syllabus of 1277 contains 219 statements condemned as errors, of which 179 are concerned with philosophical questions and forty deal with strictly theological issues [49].

Since a number of these latter, which are contained in a block as the final forty theses, refer anyway to teaching contained in the <u>De Amore</u> of Andreas Cappelanus, a kind of lover's manual, it is clear that the main focus of attack was on issues arising from some of the Aristotelian teaching in the Faculty of Arts. Stephen Tempier, as Archbishop of Paris and Simon of Brion, as Papal Legate - even possibly along with Simon du Val, the Inquisitor - may well have been making a concerted attempt to stifle challenges to their authority from any of the independent-minded philosophers, along with reinforcing the traditional Augustinian approach now being challenged by those theologians such as Thomas Aquinas, who had been developing new ways of understanding, using Aristotelian methodology.   At the same time, it is worth noting the strong French element among these Church leaders.

It is clear that, in any case, there is quite some considerable lack of organization and muddle about the order in which the statements are formulated [50].   This may well represent some measure of haste about its compilation and possibly also some element of delegating different aspects of the investigation to different members of the Theological Commission that had been set up [51].

In the prologue, the double-truth accusation is brought up by the Archbishop:

> Dicunt enim ea esse vera secundum philosophiam, sed non secundum fidem catholicam, quasi sint duae contrariae veritates, et quasi contra veritatem sacrae Scripturae sit veritas in dictis gentilium damnatorum ... [52].

[Thus they state things to be true according to philosophy, but not according to the Catholic faith, as if there are two contrary truths and as if there is a truth in the sayings of pagans in hell that is opposed to the truth of sacred scripture.]

The next five chapters will examine the works of Siger to see if this accusation is justified, whether in those early works of Siger to which reference has been made above in Section 3.2 or in any of his other works that reflect his teaching between 1270 and 1276. A reconstruction of the probable chronology for all of his works can be examined in Appendix A.

Following a general examination of Siger's views regarding the nature of truth in the next chapter, the four main areas of scrutiny covered in the 1270 Condemnations are considered separately. All come under suspicion again in the 1277 Condemnations and can be examined in detail in Hissette's excellent study Enquête sur les 219 Articles Condamnés à Paris le 7 mars 1277 which investigates possible sources of the articles censured.

CHAPTER FOUR

SIGER'S GENERAL VIEWS ON

THE NATURE OF TRUTH

4.0.   Introduction.

Before examining individually some of the major issues considered by Siger, it is desirable to examine his general views on the nature of truth in general. Much of this will be ascertained by looking at his writings on logic and, to some extent, on metaphysics, though it will be necessary to refer to other texts too.

It will be recalled from the introduction to this study that it is intended to place Siger's views in their historical context.   This will also include an awareness of their origins, though by no means always their resolution, in his research into Aristotelian positions.   Likewise, he will often be influenced by the commentaries of Ibn Rushd, though he will not hesitate to deviate from these when he considers it right to do so.   At the same time, this chapter will show how many of the processes and procedures of considering problems of the thirteenth century were not too dissimilar to some of those examined in the twentieth century.

Furthermore, we can have some sympathy with Kenny's case that it is important to understand philosophers close to us in time and culture, if today we are really to succeed in getting to grips with the theological implications of the thought of the Middle Ages [1]. Hence, in the next section, it will be useful to examine some of the arguments of the logical positivists. Their views on the nature of truth and its verifiability are very relevant and well-worth examining at this stage, particularly as they also had further implications for viewing the nature and role of theology and so-called religious truths. While, of course, this philosophical school did for several decades hold considerable sway in this country, some of the insights offered by linguistic analysis were also to provide a very valuable contribution to that self examination undertaken by a number of theologians in the face of the perceived threat to their traditional ways of thinking and expression.

Then, following a brief description of the way in which Siger's contemporaries employed the device of universals to help to make sense of the nature of intellectual knowledge, it seems desirable in this chapter, the first of the theoretical ones, to offer some relevant ideas on the practical teaching context in which most of Siger's extant writings would have been produced.

It will then be possible to examine in some detail Siger's views on the relationship between the external world, ideas and language. Issues such as the nature of certainty, error and doubt will also be considered before looking at the use of different kinds of language, such as metaphor and myth. This will then enable firm conclusions to be formed regarding the justice or otherwise of those accusations of "double-truth" made against Siger and preliminary judgements can be made about his understanding of the relationship between philosophy and theology.

4.1.   Some Twentieth Century Approaches to Truth, Knowledge and
          Language.

          The key philosophical question in examining the nature of truth
involves the triangular relationship between mental concept in the brain, language
as verbalized in any form - vocal, written or whatever - and external reality.

          There have of course been thinkers who have questioned whether it is
really possible to prove the latter's actual objective existence; and, to some extent,
such relativistic tendencies can be seen in the British Empiricist traditions of
Berkeley, Locke and Hume.   Logical Positivism certainly finds its roots in this,
rather than in Continental Idealism, though it is also influenced by the
mathematical-type strictures of Russell, Whitehead and other contemporaries.   At
this point, in view of the later claims by Logical Positivists to have eliminated
metaphysics, it is worth noting that Russell's system of analysis of logical atomism,
which, though starting from the analysis of observable facts, goes on to consider
what he calls "problems of complexity".   This process could in effect be
considered to involve searching for metaphysical solutions in its final "residue in
analysis" [2]; it is indeed an attempt to discover the ultimate basic character of
language and of the world.

          The young Ayer, the best known of British Logical Positivists, was
captivated as a young postgraduate by the discussions and arguments of
Wittgenstein and his colleagues in the so-called Vienna Circle.   Wittgenstein, in
his early Tractatus Logico-Philosophicus, originally published in 1922, describes
the relationship between language and reality by means of Russell's relationship of
atomic propositions to atomic facts.   He compares this to the correspondence
between a picture of a scene and the elements of the actual external scene in reality
itself.   Hence, "an atomic fact is a combination of objects" [3], while "the
configuration of objects forms the atomic fact" [4].   Hence, meaning and
signification in the use of language becomes paramount and philosophy becomes
almost entirely centred on the logical use of language.   It is as a result not
concerned, as it had traditionally been, with theories regarding the underlying
nature of reality, but rather with the meaningfulness of language and its actual

ability to describe external reality, as it can in fact be known and experienced rather than merely theorized about.

   In <u>Language, Truth and Logic</u>, first published in 1936, Ayer introduces the principle of verification, which he claims is essential for any sentence, or proposition that it expresses, to be meaningful.   In this respect, he feels therefore that the traditional concentration of philosophy down the centuries, with its arguments and counter-arguments about truth and falsity (as we shall see, for example, in this study) is ignoring the far more fundamental question as to which propositions can even be considered to be potentially meaningful.   If it is not possible for them to be verified to his satisfaction, as is the case both with all theological statements and with what he terms "metaphysical" statements, then not only is there no point in considering them, but they are also of no value or concern to us.   In this way, philosophy is reduced to logic and the analysis of language.   No further speculation is justifiable, for a putative proposition of that kind is "neither true nor false, but literally senseless", as he declares in his preface to the first edition of this book [5].

   Ayer argues that there are two kinds of valid statements.   Firstly, there are "analytic" propositions, which are concerned with the truths of logic itself; into this category fall, for example, definitions and mathematical principles, which are really self-verifiable, since they are in effect tautologies from which it is not possible to learn anything new [6].   He does concede of course that we may not always be fully aware of their deeper implications, as, for example, in a difficult mathematical problem, which our mind may not be able to grasp immediately [7]. His empirical pedigree is fully revealed in the second kind of valid statement, which he describes as "synthetic" (a phrase, however, borrowed likewise from Kant).   He declares that to ask for the nature of truth is really tantamount to asking for a "translation of the sentence (stating that the proposition) p is true" [8]. Consequently, he argues that it is the verifiability of the language contained in the sentence that is crucial.   The actual truth or falsity is for Ayer, at this early stage of his career, less relevant from a purely philosophical perspective.

The vital ingredient in this part of his theory is, then, to examine if a proposition, whether general or particular, is capable of being verified empirically through the senses. He accepts that these propositions, unlike the tautologies of analytical statements, cannot be absolutely certain, since effectively they are really hypotheses, which are subject to the test of observation by further sense-experience [9]. In this way, the laws of empirical science are able to develop.

For Ayer, therefore, ethical or theological statements are totally incapable of fulfilling these requirements of his verification principle since they are neither analytic nor synthetic according to his definition. Ethical statements cannot be fully normative in an objective sense but tend rather to be expressions of feeling on the part of the individual [10], while theological statements are, according to Ayer, metaphysical. He even describes a statement of disbelief by an atheist as being "nonsensical", since even the word "god" must according to this criterion be considered as devoid of any meaningfulness [11].

In fact, Ayer later acknowledges that only analytic statements are not open to doubt or question, although he does also maintain that it is at least theoretically possible to verify synthetic statements from sense-experience. Hence, inductive reasoning is for him an acceptable process for developing general judgments, despite the lack of cast-iron certainty [12].

These indications of the basic thrust of early Logical Positivist thought are offered to the reader at this point, so as to make it easier to spot some of the similarities and some of the differences regarding the problems that Siger also faced over language and truth.

As criticisms came to be made, with respect to the exclusive claim of the verification principle as presenting apparently all the answers, Wittgenstein, Ayer, Quine and the others soon began to re-assess the rigidity of their positions [13]. There is no need to go into details here, but this process did have the side effect that the awareness and practice of linguistic analysis did become more widespread. At the same time, it came to include a demand that any area of knowledge could be required to produce and present its own equivalent principle and criterion for its particular "language-games".

Indeed, some Christian philosophers, such as Braithwaite, took up this point with their own interpretation and understanding of what he saw as the real nature of religious language [14]. Likewise, some theologians, such as van Büren, felt impelled to describe themselves as "Death of God" theologians, in the light of the criticism of the actual use of the word "god", developing a theology in which Christianity was to be virtually reduced to concern with the present world alone [15].

Another problem, highlighted by Mary Warnock, is that the term "metaphysics" is often now employed in different ways. Indeed, most often, it is used to express opposition to apparently unsubstantiated religious or theological claims that prompt disdain and condemnation, rather than strictly philosophical principles as such [16]. In fact, it has been argued that the verification principle itself is really a metaphysical proposition [17]. Wittgenstein acknowledges this in his <u>Tractatus Logico-Philosophicus</u> [18] and Ayer comes very close to an admission of it in his later writings [19].

Furthermore, Wittgenstein himself, in his posthumously published <u>Philosophical Investigations</u>, declares that it is in fact illogical to claim, in the manner of Humean empiricism, that sense-content can be conceived as an essentially private and incommunicable entity [20].

It is also worth noting that, while quite often today the idea has remained that the truth or accuracy of theological statements is very dubious, even if not quite meaningless in the sense of Ayer and his colleagues, scientific statements have frequently been accorded the status of indubitable fact. However, Einstein has already shown us that we cannot ultimately talk in terms of absolutes in the universe, but that distance, time and so on are relative to the position of the observer, as the latter employs the use of his senses. More recently, Popper has shown us the provisional nature of scientific theories - even, of course, that of Einstein - and that the scientist makes conjectures as to the regular nature of occurrences in the world, in order to establish so-called laws. The inductive process is of course used at first, but then subsequently the laws have to be tested by attempting to refute whatever be the initial conclusion. If they survive this challenge relatively unscathed, then the scientist tends to accept them. However, they can of course only remain probable, not certain, and may need to be reviewed or re-formulated at some time in the future [21].

This must be kept in mind when we come to look soon at how in the thirteenth century Siger perceives the nature of truth, at a time when philosophy, which of course included the study of physics, can really be considered as the "science" of its period. It can therefore be argued that Aristotelianism, and, in particular, the radical form of Siger, is very relevant in its attempt to make sense of the nature of knowledge, ideas and language and well worth another look for modern thinkers, both philosophical and theological. At the same time, it is fair to recall that this breadth of knowledge, contained in the notion of philosophy from the middle of that century, was of course an extension from the far narrower confines of logic and epistemology of those years before the official acceptance of Aristotle's corpus of works for university teaching. Later, of course, physics and the other sciences were to branch off from the "Faculty of Arts" and the umbrella of philosophy was to change again. Perhaps, it is a little ironic that, as we have just seen, much of Anglo-American philosophy in the twentieth century involved an attempt to restrict its boundaries so narrowly to theories of logic, knowledge and meaningfulness, as we have just seen.

Of course, the ideas of Wittgenstein, Ayer and their colleagues would, in their own view, be far more fundamental than the concerns of Abelard and the earlier medieval logicians. Certainly, their conclusions, and possibly also their presumptions regarding the lack of verifiability of theological and, what they call, metaphysical statements, introduce a fresh dimension. Nevertheless, their basic area of interest is indeed broadly similar and, in this respect, the wheel has turned full-circle as the efforts of Wittgenstein to liberate philosophy from Cartesian prejudices has enabled us to take a renewed look at Scholasticism [22].

Furthermore, we should note that many thinkers now see logical positivism as having involved a sterile journey down a blind alley. Indeed, Wittgenstein, like Ayer, was to acknowledge, in his later years, that the issues were far more complex than he had formerly thought [23]. Nevertheless, the process of linguistic analysis did offer a blunt challenge to religion and to theologians that they should not make unjustified assumptions about the language which they used to describe their beliefs.

Hence, theologians, such as Ian Ramsay with his theory of "models" and "qualifiers" [24] and John Macquarrie in his acceptance of the multiplicity of distinctive "language-games" [25], demand that the theologian should define his terms and parameters of meaning before going any further. John Hick also, with his theory of "eschatological verification", claims to be answering the logical positivist challenge, while avoiding the more extreme limitations of their self-adopted premises [26]. Certainly, this represents an important step in recognizing that both theological and traditional metaphysical language need to be understood as having their own codes of language and understanding, when they require acceptance of particular claims or assertions.

This point is again very relevant in a different way when we come to a more detailed examination of the 1270 and 1277 controversies, for we need to inquire as to which particular teaching each condemnation was referring, as well as asking if in fact the latter had fully grasped its actual intended meaning. It can be recalled with interest that Pope John XXIII, in his opening address to the Second Vatican Council on 11 October 1962, reflected an awareness of the same difficulty, when he declared that, while there is a timeless absolute quality about dogmas of belief, nevertheless this does not apply to the temporal use of the words to express these same dogmas [27]. That is to say, the actual use and meaning of language can vary, develop or change, as may the way in which ideas and beliefs are presented. Wittgenstein and Ayer would have been as interested in that statement as would have Siger and Thomas Aquinas, albeit not for quite the same reasons.

4.2.   The Role of Universals in the Middle Ages.

Our attention now turns directly to the thirteenth century and to the lively debates during the Middle Ages regarding the nature of knowledge and the relationship between ideas, language and reality.   Much of this was centred upon the discussions regarding the nature of universals.   Put simply, this concerned the relationships of groups of beings (genera and species).   Are they simply mental concepts or do they really exist independently of the mind?

Following Plato and later Neoplatonic thought, those such as John Scotus Erigena in the ninth century and William of Champeaux in the twelfth century were extreme realists in this sense.   They considered that individual objects which we see and touch are really only copies of an eternal archetype, on which they depend for their existence.   On the other hand, Roscelin in the eleventh century described universals as "flatus vocis", that is to say, sounds signifying words and no more.   Such nominalism ultimately reached its inevitable dead-end with William of Ockham in the fourteenth century.   The latter, for whom the individual object represented true reality and experience - foreshadowing, in this respect, the British Empiricism of later centuries - declared that a universal is not anything real existing in a subject, either inside or outside the soul [28].   For Ockham, universals represented a purely mental and psychological process whereby individuals could be grouped together, but without any real basis in reality [29].

A middle position between these two extremes had been adopted by Peter Abelard in the twelfth century.   He saw universals as not having real existence in themselves, although they did actually reflect something of reality. Despite representing something real, they could only be understood as concepts, when abstracted from the world. This more moderate position was to be further developed by Thomas Aquinas, who actually allowed universals an independent existence in reality, albeit only as subsisting in individuals.   In this way, he develops Abelard's purely logical category into a metaphysical one [30].

This very brief overview of the mediaeval discussions on universals cannot possibly begin to do justice to the topic. However, it is hoped that it will enable the reader to relate to some extent the views of Siger himself to the historical and intellectual context in which he found himself.

It is incidentally interesting at this point to reflect on the claims of Ballard, a deaf-mute with no awareness of actual language, as reported by William James. He asserted that he had experienced wordless thought, had possessed the ability to do mental arithmetic successfully and was able to reflect on, what we would call today, fundamental ultimate questions [31].

4.3.   The Practical Context of Siger's Written Corpus.

It has already been noted, at the beginning of Section 4.1, that, in any examination of the notion of truth, the key question is to examine the relationship between mental concept, language and external reality. It is now possible to undertake this task with regard to the views of Siger by beginning an analysis of those parts of his extant writings which refer to this question and to his general views on the nature of truth.

In fact, it should be stressed that many of these will not be his own original personal writings, but rather a collection of notes ("reportationes") taken by others. Sometimes, these latter may be very brief summaries, leaving scholars to attempt to fill in the gaps, using our historical, textual and other intellectual skills. On other occasions, they may involve a more detailed analysis of a course of lectures, which usually has taken place on the content of one of Aristotle's books. In the latter case, we cannot of course be completely sure that the thought of Siger (or of any other lecturer, come to that) has been fully and faithfully recorded.

One very good example of this is his Quaestiones in Metaphysicam, for which today we have general consent that the four extant versions have different qualities, positive and negative. It is indeed likely that they may well reflect notes taken from different series of lectures delivered in different years.

Another practical factor, invariably underestimated and sometimes even ignored, is that it is highly probable that a master lecturing to a group of young students publicly, will be more restrained in expressing his views than in a published treatise of any kind, intended for fellow-scholars, despite the obvious dangers of putting anything potentially dangerous down in writing. Reference will be made to this factor later in this book. This judgment is further confirmed by Thomas Aquinas' oblique reference to some of the Paris Masters of Arts (including, quite possibly, Siger) as being reprehensible in discussing certain ideas "in angulis coram pueris" [in corners in front of mere boys] and his challenge to them to come out into the open to make such statements publicly, where they could then be openly considered and attacked [32].

In this chapter, as has been noted, we shall consider Siger's views on the basic issues concerning the nature of truth, before going on to analyse more specific teachings of his in subsequent ones. It is the nature of this current investigation to show that he did not hold particularly unusual opinions, in so far as these general questions are concerned, particularly if we reflect on the historical and intellectual context of his time. For this reason, the reader will appreciate why, in the rest of this chapter, this analysis does not follow a chronological development, since Siger does not apparently need in this case to react to external circumstances, whether of events or of other writers. It makes much more sense to develop a logical order in our examination of relevant points and arguments, wherever they may happen to be found in the Sigerian corpus.

4.4.   Our Knowledge of the External World.

It will be recalled that it was explained earlier (Section 2.6) how Baeumker had misinterpreted the nature of Siger's Impossibilia. He had taken them at face value and imagined that Siger held extremist views which an orthodox writer was refuting. In point of fact, Mandonnet showed quite conclusively that these six topics were partly exercises in sophistry, which nevertheless in their refutation made Siger's own position quite clear [33].

Siger is quite determined elsewhere in his Quaestiones in Metaphysicam, to stress the difference between a straight sophist and a philosopher like himself. For the former, the whole process is just a game. For the philosopher, it is the pursuit of knowledge:-

Sophistae non quaerunt in vita nisi apparere scire, philosophus autem non appetit in vita nisi scire [34].

[While sophists only seek to give the appearance of knowledge, the philosopher seeks nothing else in life except knowledge.]

It is at this point interesting to note that the Second of the Impossibilia does in fact deal with the issue of the existence of the external world. In the Greco-Roman cultural period, there had indeed been thinkers, such as Zeno, who had claimed that the above was an unwarranted assumption. Naturally, if we were to accept this premise, we would be unable to make any claims regarding truth nor would we have the ability to achieve verification of the evidence of our senses at all. Siger affirms that what is apparent to our senses cannot be simply figments of our imagination, akin to what we may think we are experiencing in our dreams. He acknowledges that there is a difficulty regarding verification, in so far as our senses are sometimes deceived and we seem to have no other way of correcting or confirming our sense-impressions, except through the medium of another sense. How can we then ever be certain that we are right or decide which sense is to be trusted? This of course is a problem that the logical positivists of the twentieth century had to tackle and which Ayer clearly recognizes [35].

Siger's solution is the pragmatic one, developed from our own human experience that we can confirm our interpretation of more fallible sense-experiences by reference to more reliable ones:

Magis enim credendum est ei quod apparet de prope quam de longe, et vigilando quam dormiendo, et sano quam infirmo (36).

[We can rely more on what is near rather than distant, when watchful rather than asleep and when healthy rather than ill.]

Thus, Siger argues that we can rely on the accuracy of our eyesight much more, if we are fairly close to an object than if we are some distance away. Likewise, if someone is ill - here Siger is presumably referring to situations such as delusions or hallucinations that might arise from suffering from a fever - his claims will be less reliable than those of a perfectly healthy person. Furthermore, sometimes our intellect is able to recognize that it cannot trust one or more senses in a particular situation; this then acts as a correcting filter in a balancing process, when we may at first be deceived:

Et huius ratio est quia sensus cui apparet aliquid quod est apparentia tantum, non habet secundum suam naturam iudicare quod hoc sit apparentia tantum. Et ideo ei non creditur, sed alii cuius est iudicare, ut intellectui (37).

[And the reason for this is that the sense to which something seems to appear, does not have the natural capability to judge what is a mere appearance. And hence belief comes not from this but from that whose role it is to judge, that is to say, the intellect.]

Similarly, Siger affirms the irrationality of those who believe themselves unable to accept even the most basic objects of our knowledge (per se nota). (These, it must be stressed, are not what Ayer would be calling 750 years later analytic judgments, but rather those fundamental synthetic judgments that the mind makes). On the other hand, it is reasonable to seek confirmation for what we believe to be true:

...ratio deficit eo quod in per se notis rationem quaerit, omnium quaerens rationem; ... et in omni credito (ratio) quaerit aliud per quod sciatur esse verum illud quod creditur (38).

[... it is unreasonable, if seeking an overall reason for everything, to seek one for things which are self-evident; ... whenever it does believe something, it (reason) seeks an alternative through which the object of belief is known to be true.]

Certainly, we can sometimes mistake at first the evidence of our senses. Siger's example of the river-bank appearing to move in the opposite direction as we sail down a river in a boat could be paralleled by the modern experience of the traveller in an Underground train, looking out of the window at the walls of the tunnel (39). It would however be quite irrational and unreasonable to assume that we can never trust our senses, just because of such occurrences. Indeed, we are even more aware that such an experience is merely illusory and Siger becomes quite cynical about anyone who fails to accept this:-

... credere oppositum illius supernaturale videtur et miraculosum magis quam naturale (40).

[...to believe the contrary seems to involve the supernatural and to be more of a miracle than natural.]

He accepts there is a real problem with the person who perversely refuses to accept these arguments, since such a step does lead ultimately to total scepticism and an inability to be ever certain about anything:

Qui autem aliquem sensum esse digniorem quam alium et alicui sensationi per se credendum non accipit, sed huius rationem quaerit quae ostendat quod sit ita sicut apparet, huic nihil probari potest, iste de nullo certus esse potest (41).

[Let us consider the case of someone who does not accept that one sense can be more worthy than another and that any sensation is itself worthy of belief, but also seeks the reason why something should be as it appears to be. Nothing can be proved to such a person and he can never be certain about anything.]

Siger thus does not indulge in Descartes's provisional doubt to try to overcome this, but leaves his students in absolutely no doubt that we can trust our senses in general and that they give us reliable knowledge. The intellect helps achieve this by acting as a final instrument of judgment in unearthing realities in the external world. In all this argument, Siger assumes that our powers of knowledge are themselves in the first place naturally infallible, unless there is some reason for them to be defective. Furthermore, as Van Steenberghen has rightly observed, it does not seem to have occurred to Siger, any more than to any other of his contemporaries, to question whether the senses and intellect actually acquire penetration of external objects in themselves, rather than merely sense-perceptions that may ultimately have no ultimate basis in objective reality [42].

Indeed, we would say that Siger views our apparent knowledge of external reality in a similar way to that of those twentieth century scientists, who would simply declare that their task is to report and analyse what our senses tell us experimentally, although the transcendental method of Lonergan would acknowledge and understand this process [43]. In this respect, Siger could indeed be more accurately compared with a modern scientist of this kind than to many contemporary philosophers. Perhaps, such a question would have seemed quite irrelevant anyway for a person sincerely inquiring into the nature of truth, but who was living in a world that made pragmatic and basic demands on everyone, even those on the staff of universities, in the struggle to survive physically and intellectually.

4.5.   Our Potentiality for Knowledge of Truth.

In his <u>Quaestiones in Metaphysicam,</u> Siger follows Aristotle in affirming the link between language and knowledge, that is to say, between human ideas as expressed in language and those ideas as truly representing external reality.   He argues that our senses can confirm the truth of a judgment:-

Experimentum sermonum verorum est ut conveniant rebus sensatis [44].

[The test of true words is that they agree with the objects of the senses.]

When we link this with the gist of the argument, covered in the previous section, concerning the circumstances whereby we can safely rely on our senses, we can see that not only can we be sure in our own minds, but that we can also communicate truth to another person.   It is even possible, Siger immediately indicates, to persuade that person to change his or her judgment.

In the following Quaestio, Siger follows Aristotle in declaring that we have a natural desire to learn and to discover the truth [45].   This statement presumes that this is at least potentially feasible and that there is indeed such a reality knowable outside of our own interior selves.   There is, incidentally, absolutely no indication at this stage that there could be more than one truth as such, for which we should be searching or examining in our discovery of the external world.

4.6.   The Essential Nature of Truth.

Siger follows Aristotle in seeking where the nature of truth lies. Is it in the mind (in intellectu) or in the objective world (in rebus)?

In the Munich version of his Quaestiones in Metaphysicam, he speaks of truth as being located in both of the above but declares that it is fundamentally in the mind and only in the objective world through the latter's relationship with the former:

> Dico quod veritas est in rebus et veritas est in intellectu. Et
> est intelligendum quod duplex ratio veritatis invenitur in
> rebus, cum veritas sit in intellectu, nam veritas non potest esse
> in rebus nisi per comparationem ad intellectum, et hoc vel
> practicum vel speculativum [46].

[I state that truth lies both in the objective world and in the intellect. Furthermore, it should be realized that there are two ways in which truth is found in reality. While truth is in the intellect and it can only be in the objective world through a relationship to the intellect, this latter can be either practical or speculative.]

By the "practical" intellect with regard to the discovery of truth, he is referring to the situation when, for example, a work of art faithfully represents the image which has been in the mind of the artist.   Likewise, the content of the "speculative" intellect, with which we are more directly concerned here, is reflected in the external world, unless we happen to be confused as a consequence of having dreams or some similar illusions, which do not have a genuine basis in reality.

Thomas Aquinas speaks of truth as the "adaequatio rei et intellectus" [identity between object and intellect] [47].   Siger too accepts this Aristotelian identification of truth with being itself, the two elements only being distinguished by and in the mind alone.   Hence, as he elaborates further in the Cambridge version, which Dunphy believes to have been taken from a later series of lectures [48], (probably a year or two afterwards and therefore representing a marginally later stage in the development and clarification of his thought), he states that truth seems to lie in the identity of the mind with the object in the external world [49]. Certainly, there is again no suggestion or hint that truth is anything other than single and individual in nature. Indeed, if there is only one external reality, it is hard to see how, from Siger's point of view, it could possibly be otherwise.

He accepts later in this Commentary that mistakes do sometimes occur but here explains that, in his view, this must not be blamed on the sense-perception itself but rather on the human rational interpretation of the former:

> Homo errat circa sensibile, non tamen sensus, quia sensus non
> sentit rem nisi secundum quod est [50].

[It is the human being, rather than the sense (sense-faculty), which is mistaken about the object of sensation, because the sense senses the object only as it is.]

This is an interesting comment in view of, to give an example, our similar modern understanding of colour-blindness, which indicates that the brains of some people are unable to distinguish between the messages given by the rods and cones in our eyes, regarding the rate of billions of vibrations per second of different colours. Perhaps errors in taste, such as when we are sick, are more difficult to explain away like this, for it does seem to be the deadening of the taste-buds, with the result that they cannot send the correct messages to the brain, that seems to make food appear bland to the eater. In fact, Siger himself, in the fourth book of his <u>Quaestiones in Metaphysicam,</u> explains such an error as arising from the effect of the illness on the infected tongue, so that consequently the actual taste-experience becomes bitter, although the food may be naturally sweet. Hence, even in this situation we cannot say that it is the actual sense of taste itself that is wrong. It is merely reflecting and reporting how one sensation overwhelms the awareness of the other:-

Cum gustus iudicat dulce esse amarum, non solum est dulcis,
sed etiam amari humoris in lingua existentis...   Magis est
credendum uni sensui quam alii... [51].

[When taste judges sweet to be bitter, the taste is not only of the sweet
thing, but also of the bitter humour present on the tongue.   One sense should be
believed (in such a case) rather than another.]

Of course, for Siger and his contemporaries, the problem is
predominantly a metaphysical one (perhaps rooted in the idea of a Creator
designing an appropriate final cause for each faculty), so that our senses are
naturally inclined to be faithful in their representation of reality. This contrasts
with the psychological and epistemological issues, on which Freud, Russell or
Ayer concentrated.   However, from our perspective, the really important point is
that ultimately modern empiricists should be able to relate to the general
implications of Siger's explanation of the apparent problem, arising from the fact
that we can make mistakes when we take on board the fruits of our sense-
perception.   This has important lessons for our understanding and discovery of
the nature of truth, in so far as it implies that truth is essentially one and there is
not the slightest hint in these texts that there could be any kind of "double-truth".

4.7.   Roots of Error.

We have already seen in the previous section that the mind can fail to
interpret the evidence of the senses correctly, but that Siger's underlying
assumption is that the latter are as such infallible in themselves.   Otherwise, as
was explained earlier (Sections 4.4 and 4.5), it would be virtually impossible to be
able to make any statements which could imply knowledge and certainty.

He accepts that sickness may influence us to make mistakes, although
he points out that, if, for example, we may be unable to rely on our taste-buds, we
can still check and confirm our opinion by referring to someone else affirming
something which may be generally accepted too:

Si tunc unus dicat verum, alius similiter, magis credendum est
dicenti verum famosius [52].

[If then one person claims to be telling the truth and another person likewise, the one with the greater reputation for telling the truth should be believed.]

However, he does make it clear that the evidence of others must not be considered a direct source of knowledge, but rather merely as a means of indirect confirmation.   He has harsh words for anybody permitting emotional attachment or love to be a reason for believing the word of another person.   Reason must be the only criterion:-

Qui enim credit opinioni alicuius propter amorem eius ..., non
quia rationem habet, vituperandus est [53].

[Anyone who believes somebody's opinion for reasons of love ..., not because (s)he is right, should be despised.]

One is tempted to wonder if this perspective comes solely from the stark rationality of a philosopher or if it indicates any coldness of personality, whether because of the practice of celibacy or not, or indeed if it is the fruit of a bitter experience of a love betrayed.   Certainly, it is interesting to refer to one of the only five Quaestiones Morales of Siger which we possess and which are generally considered also to reflect fairly late teaching in his career [54].   Here, he argues that celibacy is much the best lifestyle for a philosopher or an intellectual, if he is to avoid being too distracted in his pursuit of truth:

Status enim coniugalis multas habet mundanas occupationes,
ut circa filios et uxorem, quas non habet existens in statu
virginali [55].

[For the married state brings worldly tasks, like those concerning wife and children, which someone living in the state of virginity does not have.]

It is interesting how this view echoes that expressed by Héloise in one of her letters to Abelard, after their enforced separation:

> What harmony can there be between pupils and nursemaids, desks and cradles, books and distaffs, pens and spindles? Who can concentrate on thoughts of scripture and philosophy and be able to endure babies crying, nurses soothing them with lullabies, and all the noisy coming and going of men and women about the house? Will he put up with the constant muddle and squalor which small children bring into the home? (56).

Nevertheless, for whatever reason, this nuance has disappeared a year or two later in the Cambridge version when Siger concentrates more on the danger of excessive attachment to one's own opinion:

> Et est hoc intelligendum de eis qui amore suae opinionis contra multitudinem eam sustinent; qui tamen opinioni propriae contra multos innituntur ut rationem multorum iudicent, non sunt reprehendendi (57).

[And this should be understood with regard to those who uphold their own opinion against a large number (of opponents). On the other hand, those who persist with their own opinion against many others, in order to make a rational judgement of their position, should not be reproved.]

In the Munich version, Siger had in fact already warned that, we must in any case be particularly wary of accepting a majority opinion, simply because it is that of the majority. He suggests, with an apparent touch of the cynicism of the academic, that most people do not attempt to go beyond the superficial when making a judgment:-

Valde pauci et subtiliter perscrutantes, quia multitudo in cognitione non se extendit ultra sensibilia [58].

[Very few people make a detailed examination, because most do not go beyond what they learn through their sense-knowledge.]

He offers a particularly poignant warning in this respect, especially regarding more abstract notions which transcend the senses, and declares that we must not accept the judgment of the majority in deciding who has wisdom and right views on their side.   We must not be influenced by anything except genuine objective evidence:-

...sicut non iudicatur verum de rebus, praecipue in transcendentibus sensum, ex testimonio multitudinis, ita nec quis sit sapiens, quis insipiens, debet iudicari ex testimonio multorum.   Et ideo non sufficit dicere quod credendum est magis iudicio sapientis, quia quis sit sapiens non est per se notum;   sed ex re debet iudicari opinio cui est magis credendum .... [59].

[... in the same way as we should not make judgments about things, particularly when they transcend the senses, just because the mass of people says so, likewise we should judge anyone to be wise or foolish just because many people say so.   Hence, it is not enough just to say that we should believe the judgment of a wise man more, for we do not automatically know who is wise. However reality must be the guide in judging whose opinion is to be believed the most.]

Another danger to look out for arises from the experience of having been habitually exposed for a long time to a view that conflicts with the true one. This may be especially acute where the source of the mistake is a person who is normally esteemed to be an expert in the matters under consideration.   Siger goes on to give the particular example of Ibn Rushd, who had highlighted Ibn Sina's error, which many people had simply accepted, of believing it to be possible for man to procreate without semen [60]. It is again quite clear that Siger is certainly convinced that there can be only one truth.

On the other hand, it is perfectly possible for someone mistaken, even over basic principles, to be guided to the truth by good, learned teachers. This would not be done however in the case of someone who was incredibly stupid and so was naturally incapable of achieving accurate knowledge. Indeed, Siger indicates that levels of intelligence and attitudes towards learning need to be taken into consideration when pupils are to be admitted for learning:-

> Unde simile est quaerere huic: an asinus posset philosophari
> .... oportet respicere ad complexiones puerorum si quis debet
> poni ad scholas [61].

[It is therefore like asking if an ass can be a philosopher. It is necessary to look at the levels of boys' ability in the case of decisions over school entrance.]

Is this remark deliberately omitted by Siger in the Cambridge version a year or two later or is it a comment added by the editor in the Munich version, perhaps as a result of a question from the floor put to Siger after his lecture and exposition or could it even just be a note added by the editor himself on his own initiative? In any event, Van Steenberghen seems to be clearly wrong in attributing this to a reference to a medical examination [62]. Although this may at first seem the meaning to the reader, the whole context of the word "complexiones", on deeper examination, seems to refer to "shades" of greater or lesser intelligence.

Likewise, he is surely wrong in affirming that the invincible ignorance, referred to above, simply stems from failures in temperament. In this Quaestio, Siger is discussing what we would today call a low intelligence quotient. Perhaps, Van Steenberghen was misled by a cursory examination of the word "doctores" in line 37, which must refer to teachers rather than medical doctors.

Later, in the Fourth Book of Quaestiones in Metaphysicam, Siger again avers that another factor that may influence the accuracy of an interpretation of our sense-experiences is the degree of its difficulty, as, for example, in the case of sight, the distance which we may be from the object. Likewise, in the same section, he ruminates on the possible effects of the imagination in misleading us:-

> Nec etiam aequaliter creditur tantas esse magnitudines, quales eas iudicat sensus in remoto et in propinquo. Nec etiam aequaliter creditur sic esse sicut quis imaginatur et sicut quis sentit [63].

[We do not believe equally that the sizes of things are as the sense (of sight) judges them to be, regardless of whether they are far away or at close quarters. Nor do we have equal belief that reality is how someone imagines it and how someone senses it.]

Again, the question that Siger does not tackle is the psychological and epistemological one as to how we can be sure that we are genuinely receiving reliable sense-impressions and how we can distinguish this experience from fantasy and imagination. The borderline is narrow and, like the modern scientist today, Siger, the medieval philosopher, argues that, in cases of real doubt, we should turn to further evidence from other senses as a balance and counter-check:-

> ...cum iudicat per gustum esse amarum, deponit opinionem quam habuit per visum quod esset dulce [64].

[...when (someone) judges through taste that it is bitter, he discards the view which he had through sight that it was sweet.]

It seems that, in this respect, Siger would be well able to relate to the perspective of Popper and other philosophers of science that conjectures have to be made and tested, so that they can then be either confirmed or rejected [65]. Moreover, as was implied in his arguments for the reality of the external world and earlier in this section, we can turn for confirmation to others, whose judgment of their senses we would normally be able to trust. This, he again reminds us, is always provided that our judgment here remains rooted in reality and is not dependent on the vagaries of mass-opinion. Surely, this is an approach with which a modern scientist would find little to quarrel.

In the ultimate analysis, we have to rely of course on basic "primo et per se nota" principles to get us started, without which we could never be certain of anything:-

> Alius est si aliquis semper in iudicio de sensibili vellet quaerere aliquid certificans: esset enim sic procedere in infinitum; et si non esset aliquid quod sit primo et per se notum, non erit aliquid notum [66].

[Another (error) is if, in making a judgment about a sense-impression, someone always wants to seek confirmation for it since that would mean an infinite regression; and, if there were nothing which was immediately self-evident, there would be nothing known at all.]

These are the medieval philosopher's equivalent of generally accepted premises which the modern scientist assumes when he analyses the external world and draws conclusions about it. Otherwise, we could not avoid an infinite regress and would naturally and unavoidably be led into total scepticism.

4.8.   The Use of Philosophical Doubt as a Methodolology.

Modern readers are of course familiar with Descartes' methodological doubt, starting from his own existence, which he employed ostensibly to buttress his whole epistemological system by proving this first.

Almost equally well known is Anselm's temporary dismissal of his belief in the existence of God, in employing the Ontological Argument, so as to try to understand this very act of faith [67].   Both are examples of the use of doubt as a method of understanding or developing our knowledge of reality in the widest sense.

Siger likewise, in the Preface to his <u>Quaestiones super Librum de Causis</u> (probably the last and certainly one of the most reflective examples of his thought), may well be defending the use of methodological doubt as an essential tool in acquiring knowledge.   If we were not to have doubts, he says, we would be like someone on a journey, unaware of his destination.   In such a case, even if we happened to stumble on the truth, we would probably be unable even to recognize it:-

> Sic non praeconcipiens dubitationes ad cognitionem veritatis
> non dirigetur nisi casu, quia, si veritatem attigerit, nesciet
> utrum ibi quiescendum vel ulterius procedendum [68].

[In such a case, if he does not have preliminary doubts in the first place, he will not be directed towards knowledge of the truth, except by chance. This is because, if he did get to the truth, he would not know whether to stop there or to keep looking further.]

He goes on to argue that therefore doubt is essential and inevitable, but of course must be resolved.   He uses the analogy of a person's feet being tied up.   The bonds must be loosened if he is to make further progress.   So, indeed, doubts must be resolved, but this is best accomplished by listening to both sides of the argument.   It is by this method that we are able to discover the truth:-

> Cognitio   enim   veritatis   in   aliqua   rerum   solutio   est
> dubitatorum [69].

[For to know the truth in something is to get rid of doubts.]

Of course, what Siger is thus advocating is to some extent based on Peter Abelard's "Sic et Non" methodology and not essentially different from his and indeed the regular university practice at this time and for many more centuries afterwards. We see it in the style of academic delivery in the presentation of a topic in both the Arts and Theology faculties at Paris and elsewhere [70].

However, what we are discussing here, as a philosophical tool for the discovery and understanding of the truths of reality, is very different from those factors described in the previous section, which Siger rightly perceives as obstacles to the development of learning about the external world.

4.9.   The Principle of Non-Contradiction.

Towards the end of Section 4.7, reference was made to principles which are "primo et per se nota". For Siger, Thomas Aquinas and their contemporaries, these include the four "causes" of Aristotle, i.e. final, efficient, material and formal causes. However, for our purposes here, the most important, and indeed the most basic, of all principles is that of non-contradiction.

The Sixth of the Impossibilia was devoted to proving this principle; and later a much deeper analysis was made by Siger in the Fourth Book of his Quaestiones in Metaphysicam. Indeed, this is the point at which we properly enter in a logical way into the realm of language. It enables the closing of that triangular process, involving external reality, mental concept and language, to which reference has already been made in Section 4.1.

The problem is to some extent similar to that of Ayer and his colleagues. How can we construct a knowledge-system if we are not sure of its accuracy? Ayer, as we have seen, demands verifiability for a statement to have any meaning and to avoid rejection. For him, there are only two kinds of statements which meet this criterion, namely those which are either synthetic or analytic ones.

For both types, he accepts the impossibility of a process "in infinitum". He asserts that "there must be some statements of empirical fact which are directly verified....and a similar argument applies to a priori statements" [71].   The latter he describes as "tautologies" [72], but states that they are essential for the use of language.   Indeed, he goes on to declare that these basic laws of formal logic (and indeed of mathematics too), such as the law of contradiction [sic] and that of the excluded middle are necessarily true [73].

Siger, likewise, accepts the need for certain fundamental principles. He sees philosophical ones as being the most basic of all and therefore the most certain too:-

Illa scientia est certissima ex cuius suppositione procedunt omnes aliae [74].

[That knowledge is the most certain, which acts as the assumed foundation from which all others develop.]

Siger asks the question as to what is the most basic principle of all. He declares that it must indeed be whatever is the most certain, so that it is impossible for us to be genuinely mistaken about it, and that it must be universally and naturally known (rather like Ayer's certainty with "an appeal to intuition") [75]. He proceeds to demonstrate that the principle of non-contradiction (essentially what Ayer and other modern philosophers formulate in their mathematical style of terminology as the law of contradiction) fits this bill.   Quite simply, something cannot both be and not be at the same time in the same respect:-

... dicendum quod non contingit aliquid simul esse et non esse, neque contradictoria simul esse vera [76].

[... it must be stated that something cannot be and not be at the same time, nor can contradictories be true at the same time.]

Such a discovery is carried out through the process of composition undertaken by the intellect:-

Intelligendum est quod duplex est operatio intellectus. Quaedam est quae est indivisibilium intelligentia, apprehensio ipsius quod quid est; alia, compositio vel divisio intelligibilium apprehensorum (77).

[It should be understood that there are two ways in which the intellect operates. One involves the understanding of indivisibles, i.e. the grasp of an essence, while the other involves the combination or the separation of the essences thus grasped.]

It is as fundamental to the former as is knowledge of being itself to the intellect in its apprehending role:

Sicut enim ratio entis est id quod primo notum est intellectu apprehendente, ... ita supradictum principium ... est id quod primo notum est intellectu componente et a cuius cognitione dependet cognitio cuiuslibet noti intellectu illo (78).

[In the same way as the underlying principle of being is what is first known by the apprehending intellect,... so the forementioned principle ... is what is first known by the composing intellect and that on whose knowledge there depends the knowledge of anything known by the latter intellect.]

The apparent difficulty posed by the existence of future contingents is not in fact relevant, for here and now the future event is neither true nor false (79).

An example of Siger's employing this principle in the course of one of his arguments can be seen in his Quaestio utrum haec sit vera: Homo Est Animal, Nullo Homine Existente (80).

It is indeed impossible, he declares, to be mistaken about this principle, although it is possible for us to verbally assert the opposite of what we are thinking:

Circa ipsum enim impossibile est errare mente, licet voce contingat dicere oppositum: non enim necesse est quae aliquis dicit voce, haec estimare [81].

[It is indeed impossible to err in the mind, although it can happen that the opposite is expressed verbally, since it is not necessary for someone to say verbally what he is thinking.]

Hence, he goes on to acknowledge that some thinkers have condemned Heraclitus for his writings on the non-stability of reality, as implying that things can in fact be and not be simultaneously [82]. (It is somewhat ironic that some of the ethos of that interpretation of Heraclitus' position on this matter has now been subsumed by modern scientists and thinkers, theorizing about the changing and dynamic nature of the universe.) In any case, by the time of the Cambridge version of the Quaestiones in Metaphysicam, Siger seems to suggest by implication that he certainly does not subscribe to this interpretation of Heraclitus' views for the phrase "sicut dicitur de Heraclito" [as is said about Heraclitus] in the previous reference is now replaced by the milder expression "etsi aliqui crediderint Heraclitum dixisse..." [although some thought that Heraclitus had said] [83].

This is more than a nuance or change of emphasis; it is rather a clarification of Siger's more positive understanding of Heraclitus. It is typical of a scholar who puts so much store by honesty and integrity - here, in disparaging the sort of excesses of some scholastics in extracting the teaching of others from its context so as apparently to demolish more easily a position that the original proponent never actually held. Indeed, it is the type of practice, still common in many of the Church universities of Europe, at least until the Second Vatican Council.

4.10.   The Use of Words as a Means to Communicate Ideas.

The Law of Contradiction (or, as Siger preferred to call it, the principle of non-contradiction) is of course fundamental to logic, modern and medieval.   Opponents of logical positivism have rightly asked whether this Law is itself analytic or synthetic.   However, we can see that it is certainly a basis for the former kind of statement and also, of course, for the development of subsequent logical reasoning.   This latter is today more often formulated, as we have already seen, in mathematical forms rather than the scholastic syllogistic form, though both involve progressive argumentation and judgments.   It is at this point, however, that there arises with its full force that process of abstraction, which was considered in medieval times under the title of universals.

Siger, of course, was well-schooled in the principles of logic, both theoretical in his academic circles and also pragmatic in its practical application, where he was able to develop arguments and themes in all areas and levels of learning within the Faculty of Arts.

In the only one of the Quaestiones Logicales of Siger which we still possess, he considers the meaning of common terms, especially of nouns.   As Bazan has rightly pointed out, Aristotle had well established the fundamental role of the meaning of words for human language and communication, in order to make the study of the sciences possible [84].

In the Fourth Book of his Quaestiones in Metaphysicam, Siger argues that the use of "nomina" [nouns] is "ex institutione nostra" [of our human origin] [85].   Although this suggests a practice that is of human origin and not a reflection of some pre-existing Platonic-type entities, it is clear that some universal understanding of this use is necessary for anyone who wishes to embark on learning and discovery of truth by the use of language.   Indeed, if a person has already grasped this basic use of words correctly, then they can even be inducted into the use and practice of a different language [86].   (It is very interesting, incidentally, how in the Cambridge version of this reference one of the examples given is the more practical everyday language of French, replacing the classical Greek mentioned in the Munich version).

It is this underlying understanding that words have been given a specific meaning, which is, in all cases, vital.   Much of this acceptance of the nature of what we might well call language-codes would be comprehensible to writers such as Wittgenstein.

How then does language, according to Siger, function?   Words quite clearly not only refer to objects outside of the self in external reality, but also reflect the actual understanding of these by the individual:-

Dico quod voces significant res, non secundum quod existunt,
sed secundum quod intelliguntur [87].

[I state that words signify objects, not in the way they exist, but according to the way they are understood by the intellect.]

This is the reason why, for truth to be present, there must be internally an accurate representation in the mind of what is in fact present in external reality. Nevertheless, the will has also played a part in this, in so far as it has freely determined and accepted a particular meaning:

Dico ... quod quid significet nomen non est de per se notis,
sed fit notum argumentatione aliquali.   Nomen enim
significare hoc vel illud est per voluntatem [88].

[I maintain ... that the meaning of a noun is not self-evident, but becomes known by some kind of argument, for a noun comes to mean this or that by choice.]

4.11.   Siger's View of Universals.

There are, for Siger, two dimensions to the term "universal": that is to say, the essence of actual concrete objects found in reality and the abstract idea of this which is found in the mind:-

> Considerandum est quod, cum in universali sint duo, id quod est universale et universalitas ipsa: id quod universale est, natura quaedam est, non conceptus mentis;   sed universale, secundum quod universale, est conceptus mentis tantum [89].

[One should take into consideration that, in the case of universals, there are two aspects, namely, the object which is universal and universality as such: the object which is universal is of a certain nature in reality and not a concept of the mind, while a universal, as such, is a mere concept of mind.]

It is this which makes human language possible and this moderate realism brings Siger's position quite close to that of Thomas Aquinas [90].   Siger is quite insistent that universals as such are merely mental concepts, since all objects in external reality are individual and singular:-

> Quod si universale, secundum quod universale, non est substantia, tunc apparet quod in universali sunt duo, scilicet res quae denominatur universalis, ut homo vel lapis, quae non est in anima, et ipsa intentio universalitatis quae est in anima; et sic universale, secundum quod tale, non est nisi in anima [91].

[If a universal, with regard to that dimension by which it is universal, is not a substance, then it is clear that there are two aspects to universal; namely the object in reality which is described as universal, such as a man or a stone, which is not in the (intellective) soul, and, on the other hand, the universality which, by the very act of intentionality, is in the soul.   Thus, a universal, in so far as it is a universal, is only in the soul.]

This is then how for Siger it is possible legitimately to apply meaning within the universal concept in the mind to the intended object to which reference is being made. This view is of course taken from Aristotle, for whom, unlike Plato, every substance in the universe is individual, while the universal is always something, which, though perfectly real and objective, has no separate existence at all.

It will now be possible to compare Siger's position with those of Roscelin on the one hand and William of Ockham on the other, as outlined in Section 4.2 above.

However, while Ayer and his colleagues in the twentieth century reduced philosophy largely to the analysis of language alone, Siger and Thomas Aquinas of course root their use of universals, which are employed to identify and describe the truth of propositions, firmly in the reality of the external world. Nevertheless, the two positions would be mutually comprehensible, if not acceptable, to one another across the span of seven centuries, despite Ayer's earliest protestations about meaninglessness, in situations where he cannot find true verifiability.

In the sophism Omnis Homo de Necessitate est Animal, Siger makes it clear that, in so far as universals involve an abstraction in the mind of the nature of a being in reality, they also involve an abstraction from any temporal context:-

> Dicitur autem universale esse ubique et semper, non quia sit actualiter et substantialiter ubique...sed dicitur esse ubique et semper quia non determinatur aliqua differentia temporis vel loci [92].

[A universal is described as being in every place and in every time, not because it is actually everywhere in substance ... but is described in such a way because it is not determined by any difference in time or place.]

It is the actual stability of the idea or concept within the intellect that makes possible and preserves the uniformity of the term, although the object, which it represents, may even have ceased to exist:-

Quia igitur, quando cessat entitas rei, non cessat intellectus eius, sed manet unus et idem, ideo vocis rem illam significantis manet eadem significatio [93].

[This is because, when the entity of an object ceases in reality, the understanding of it does not cease. On the contrary, it remains one and the same so that the meaning of a word indicating the same object remains the same.]

It is indeed in the sophism referred to above, that we can see how Siger develops his theory of logic, which underpins his justification for the use of language to express judgments of truth, as reflected in reality. The details of this theory need not concern us here, but it is worth commenting on how Siger felt it vital to justify in a schematic way his methods of describing reality.

There is no question that the discovery, maintenance and description of any truth identified by the intellect, as a result of sense-experience, is paramount to him as a thinker. In this respect, indeed, his perspective, though different, is again not opposed to Ayer's view of synthetic judgments while his underlying approach shows the same earnestness for the discovery of truth, as is demonstrated by any modern scientist.

4.12.   Siger's General Attitude to the Views of Other Writers.

Siger, of course, develops his ideas, in the first place from his reading of Aristotle, often with reference made to other writers, especially Ibn Rushd, and sometimes, as we have seen, he comes to conclusions, similar or even identical to those of Thomas Aquinas. He is no slave to Aristotle, however, as has sometimes been implied [94]. There are a number of examples of his departing from what appears to be Aristotle's original position. For him, Aristotle's philosophy can and does provide a framework on which to build, but even this must be carefully examined to root out any mistakes and errors:-

Philosophus quantumcumque magnus in multis possit errare (95).

[A philosopher, however great he may be, can be wrong about many things.]

Hence, in his methodology, in so far as he is a Professor in the Faculty of Arts, he sometimes presents it as his duty to explain and interpret Aristotle, even though the latter may be wrong over a number of matters:

Haec autem dicimus opinionem Philosophi recitando, non ea asserendo tamquam vera (96).

[This is stated in exposition of Aristotle's view, not as an assertion of its veracity.]

Later in this study, especially in the next chapter which will examine the possibility of the eternity of the world, we shall see how the maturing Siger became very ready to depart from Ibn Rushd's interpretation of Aristotle. Likewise, we shall see how at times he agrees with Thomas Aquinas, even being influenced to some extent to change his opinions, especially over the question of the unity of the intellect.

Certainly, he has some considerable respect for both Thomas and Albert the Great, who, of all his contemporaries, he describes as being "praecipui viri in philosophia" [leading men in philosophy] (97). However, being so close in time and place, he rarely seems to quote them directly. Nevertheless, it must be virtually certain that he must have heard Thomas speaking publicly, even if he may possibly have never entered into personal and private discussion with him (though it does seem far more probable that they would have done so, even if only privately, in such a relatively small academic ambience in Paris).

In fact, in the case of Albert, it appears from the first of the three Quaestiones commenting on the Metaphysics in the text enumerated Nat. Lat. 16133, (though covering, in this case, the same material as is found in the seventh Quaestio of the Introduction in the Munich version), that Siger may have heard Albert teach publicly at some time too. Certainly, he states that "hoc enim dicentem viva voce audivi" [I have heard him say this live.] [98].

Vennebusch suggests that these "quaestiones" may have been issued separately for some special reason [99]. Be that as it may, it will be recalled that Albert had only taught in Paris from 1242-1248, when Siger would only have been a young lad. Van Steenberghen follows Vennebusch in suggesting that he may have gone to Strasbourg or to Cologne to hear Albert, while he was teaching in one of those cities [100]. It seems just as possible, however, that Albert may well have visited Paris, especially to confer with Thomas, his fellow-Dominican. In such a scenario, Albert may possibly have delivered a public lecture as a prominent guest-speaker or Siger may have been introduced to him privately where he would have heard him expound his views. In either event, we note how Siger was ready to take into account the views of others, whom he could respect professionally in what he saw as his search for true knowledge and understanding.

Whatever may have been the case, it is clear that Siger was more than ready to turn to a whole range of sources, ancient and contemporary, in maintaining his professional integrity. In his Quaestiones in Metaphysicam, he does indeed declare implicitly that he does not believe there is one truth for philosophy and another one for religion:-

> Sic autem velare philosophiam non est bonum: unde   non
> est hic intentio Aristotelis celanda, licet sit contraria veritati
> (101).

[To cover up philosophy in this kind of way is not good.   Therefore, what Aristotle intended must not be hidden here, although it may be contrary to the truth.]

118

In fact, in the Cambridge version, he makes it clear that he disagrees with those who attempt to alter the real position of Aristotle to make it appear as if his views were compatible with the Christian faith:-

> Propter etiam ea quae fidei sunt non est velanda intentio Philosophi, sicut quidam voluerunt, dicentes Philosophum non intendere mundum simpliciter esse aeternum [102].

[We should not cover up Aristotle's meaning even for reasons of faith. This is what some people have wanted when they state that Aristotle did not mean that the world is in all respects eternal.]

Thus, we can see how Siger, like Thomas Aquinas and others of his contemporaries, viewed the notion of "auctoritas" [authority] which, after all, does derive from the word "auctor" [author].   By the middle of the thirteenth century, different authors were graded according to their respective considered authority [103].   Just as in the Faculty of Theology, Peter Lombard's Commentary was used to explain the revealed authority of scripture, but remained of course itself merely the fruit of human reflection, so in the Faculty of Arts, Siger was claiming the right to follow the esteemed non-revealed authority of Aristotle to guide him, where appropriate.

4.13.   The Implications of Siger's General Views on Truth.

We have already seen (Section 4.4) that Siger is definite that there is an external world which we experience firstly via our individual senses.   These senses are sometimes misinterpreted, for one reason or another, by the mind (Section 4.7), and this is how error can arise in our understanding of actual external reality.   Furthermore, we must beware of the danger of following majority opinion irrationally in forming our judgments for it is our own individual rationality that leads us to truth:

Qui enim iudicat aliquid secundum dictum multitudinis hominum, indicat se non habere rationem [104].

[The person who makes a judgment, as a result of what a mass of people say, indicates his lack of rationality.]

However, he is in no doubt that it is possible for us to experience reality as one and not simply as relative or multiple. There is here clearly no question of there being more than one truth (Section 4.5).

Although it is perfectly legitimate in our search for knowledge to put to one side beliefs of which we feel personally certain, as a temporary practice of methodical doubt (Section 4.8), he goes on to show that there are some basic "per se nota" principles and truths, of which the most fundamental of all is the principle of non-contradiction. Up to this stage, his medieval starting-point for the reality-concept-language triangle (Section 4.6) is different from that of Ayer and modern proponents of logical positivism, although it does seem likely that they would be able to grasp Siger's own language and methodology in arriving at a similar conclusion regarding their own "law of contradiction" and other basic analytical statements.

We have also seen that what can be described as the moderate realism of Siger, and indeed of Thomas Aquinas too, depends on the notion of universals, implying that the mind is able to abstract general elements from independent individual objects known by sense-experience. In this way, a judgment can be determined in the mind and be meaningfully expressed in language which reflects what is actually present in reality (Sections 4.10 and 4.11). It is on this bedrock of the expression of reliable knowledge that, of course, the whole system of logic during this medieval period was able to develop according to carefully determined rules. The role of these was to provide the underpinning which would ensure that nothing illogical or inaccurate should mislead either student or master in the quest for still greater knowledge, whatever be the field in which they happened to be working. This, of course, was important for the whole procedure of disputations, where attempts were often made to show the illogicality of consequential conclusions and to point out the source of apparent mistakes.

It is very likely that Siger would have been influenced as a young student by the logic of Peter of Spain (later to become Pope John XXI). It is also probable that this scholar, who was to become the only Portuguese Pope in history, was studying medicine in Paris around the time that Siger was completing his studies in philosophy [105]. Peter of Spain concentrated on the analysis of the structural elements of propositions unlike the Aristotelian approach of analysis from illustrative examples [106]. We have already seen a similar approach in Siger's writings on logic.

Less well known a logician is the Englishman William of Sherwood, who seems to have influenced not only Peter of Spain but also Albert the Great and Thomas Aquinas [107]. William also deals in his treatise on logic with this question of consequences [108], which governs the laws of valid inference.

These questions and conclusions were being widely and openly debated during Siger's time as student and teacher in the Faculty of Arts. It was in the midst of this environment within which we know Siger to have become a leading figure, that (Section 1.5) every aspiring theologian, lawyer or physician had to pass through, unless exempted by reason of his membership of a religious order. It has in recent years been shown that such laws and rules can in fact be expressed properly in the mathematical formulations of modern propositional logic [109]. Up to this point, then, as has already been said, Siger and Ayer could at least be on speaking terms and able to understand one another's approach. Furthermore, there is absolutely no doubt that the theoretical basis of his views on logic imply that Siger sees truth as being only single in reality.

Of course, much similarity can be detected in Siger's views and in the Aristotelian influence on him, to what is found in the writings of Thomas Aquinas, especially in the first eleven Quaestiones of the first book of his De Veritate. However, the latter does, as a theologian, develop his theory of truth very much with religion and revelation in mind, while Siger is much more empirical in his approach. He approaches philosophy as a means to learn more about the nature of the world, much as a modern philosopher of science like Popper would do. Thus he employs methodical doubt where appropriate and tests his theories by making conjectures, followed by attempts to confirm or disprove them through a fair and balanced study of the evidence. It is already possible to begin to see how he has often been underestimated as a leading thinker of the thirteenth century, whose academic career was to be sadly and prematurely truncated. Nevertheless, it is still possible for him to offer a very real contribution, through his overall perspective, vision and approach, to our modern processes of searching for greater and greater knowledge and understanding in the universe today.

4.14.   The Role of Myths and Fables in a Theory of Knowledge.

It may seem very strange at first to come upon this section, immediately after the writer has endeavoured to indicate Siger's singlehearted sincerity in the pursuit of knowledge and of truth.   To many people today, brought up in an age that may in some respects seem more hardheaded and cynical, the very perception of myths and fables tends to suggest images of error and untruth, which contemporary man has ostensibly outgrown in a so-called scientific age. Perhaps even some of the comments of Siger noted above, which contain warnings against being too ready to accept majority public opinion rather than searching for evidence on truly rational and impartial grounds, may conjure up ideas of what have often in the past been described as old wives' tales.

In the Second Book of his Quaestiones in Metaphysicam, Siger indeed discusses the role of what he calls "fabulosa et falsa" [fables and falsehoods] in influencing citizens to keep human laws and he criticizes the ancient so-called law of Pythagoras which threatened the wicked with their souls being reborn into a brute animal:-

In lege Pythagorae tradebatur sub comminatione quod anima hominis boni post mortem intraret aliud corpus bonum, mali autem corpus alicuius bestiae; quod non fuit verum, sed propter terrorem positum [110].

[In the Law of Pythagoras, it was handed down as a threat that after death the soul of a good man would enter another good body while that of an evil man would enter the body of some farm-animal. This was untrue but intended to frighten.]

Such a tale may evoke memories of the bogeyman for children - and no doubt there were many such tales prevalent in the thirteenth century - while the latter Pythagorean example may even perhaps, interestingly enough, suggest ideas of "karma" [actions and their consequences in this and the next life] and "samsara" [cycle of repeated birth and death] in Indian religions, which are nevertheless generally alien to Western European thought.

Siger again takes up some of the same area for discussion in his Commentary on the Third Book. Maurer points out how Aristotle had shown great impatience with mythologists who spoke of the ancient Greek gods in metaphorical terms as, for example, tasting nectar and ambrosia for their pleasure and delectation [111]. We see here, however, that Siger is quite prepared to take an independent and more positive line than Aristotle did on this topic. It is also interesting to note that while the relevant section in the earlier Munich version is merely contained in the general commentary [112], it is expanded in the later Cambridge version into an independent "Quaestio" of Siger himself entitled "Utrum philosophantibus competat loqui de divinis fabulose" [113]. This positive decision to insert it in this way may specifically suggest that Siger had developed his own independent views on this topic, not in full agreement with Aristotle. At the same time, he may have found that this section of his course constituted a suitable stage at which he could proclaim them to his listeners.

Hence, he goes on here to concede that there may be some justication for people describing beliefs about God in mythical and metaphorical language, if the speakers or the listeners find it impossible to grasp them intellectually in an accurate way, but may find it helpful to use their imaginations to depict truths in a more physical way:-

> Verum est quod de divinis loqui fabulose contingit aliquibus vel propter impotentiam intellectus: cum enim non possint intellectum elevare ad ea quae sunt intellectualis naturae, depressi ad phantasmata, intellectualia speculantur tamquam sensibilia (114).

[It is true that it is appropriate to speak about divine matters in fables to some people, if the ability to understand is lacking. This is because they are unable to raise the intellect to those things which are of an intellectual nature. When reduced to mental images, intellectual matters are viewed as if they are of the senses.]

He goes on to show that, on the other hand, he is far less happy and cannot justify the conduct of those - suggesting that perhaps Plato was guilty of this - who deliberately employ the same approach in order to try to hide the truth in such a way. He believes that a philosopher, precisely because he is a philosopher, should not indulge in the use of metaphors and fables, which are more appropriate for "poets". (He does not comment on Peter Abelard's double role here!). Can one fancifully hear Siger demanding through the centuries hard evidence for ghosts, flying saucers, magic rings or little green men? Secondly, since metaphors and fables do hide the truth to some extent, this conflicts in principle with the proclaimed role of philosophers to discover and expose the truth. Does not such a comment seem familiar when one considers the proclaimed dedication of modern scientists to do the same? Thirdly, there is, he says, the danger of students misunderstanding their nature by taking them to be literally true and so holding an inappropriate belief in them.

Despite this latter warning, which most modern liberal theologians would repeat regarding many fundamentalist Christian approaches to doctrines and to scripture, Siger finds two good reasons which would justify teaching "sub

124

fabulis et metaphoris" [with the help of fables and metaphors] under certain circumstances [115].

In the first place, our mind may be unable to grasp fully some realities without their use, as is the case with the First Cause, which, he says, human language is quite incapable of describing adequately:-

> Quando enim intellectus noster non potest ad plenum capere aliqua intelligibilia propter eorum excellentiam et improportionem intellectus nostri ad ea ... tunc licet in simili ea declarare [116].

[So, when our intellect is unable to grasp some intelligible things to the full, as a result of their excellence and the lack of proportion of our intellect to them ... it is then acceptable to explain them by means of a comparison.]

Then, secondly, he elaborates on his earlier comments to justify such use by someone, who may himself fully understand the underlying truth, but whose audience may be unable to do so without the help of metaphorical language. In this latter case, did he have in mind the use of parables by Jesus or of stories by preachers in the pulpit? Or was he merely trying to justify his own pedagogical practices with young students in his lecture-room? We can but surmise on the range of possibilities.

Certainly, Moses Maimonides, and indeed other Jewish writers, had considered elements of the Bible, even of the unchangeable Torah given by God, to be metaphorical, symbolic and not literal in an historical sense. We see an example of this in the declaration of the third principle of his Fundamentals of the Jewish Faith, when he declares that "we must realize that whatever the Torah or the Prophets speak about God, they do so in a metaphorical and allegorical manner" [117].

Ibn Rushd too states that "whenever a statement conflicts in its apparent meaning with a conclusion of demonstration ... there will invariably be found among the expressions of scripture something which in its apparent meaning bears witness to that allegorical interpretation or comes close to bearing witness" [118], while, as Bello points out, he accepts that for the mass of the faithful the literal interpretation still remains appropriate [119].

Such ideas, of which we can even see traces in St. Augustine's three levels of "visio" - corporeal, spiritual and intellectual, of which the interpretative ability of the latter was necessary for biblical prophecy [120] - were also no doubt developing in Christian circles. Maurer gives the example of William of Conches, who spoke of Eve's body having its origin in Adam' rib as being a typical fable in scripture which was nevertheless intended to express the truth, by means of what was not literally true but should be interpreted in order to discover a hidden truth [121].

It has thus been clearly demonstrated how Siger of Brabant became very much an independent thinker. He did not justify myths, fables and metaphors as such in the first order search for truth by a philosopher, any more than an empiricist or a scientist of the modern age would. Nevertheless he was able to see that it was a possible and even legitimate use of language to do so on those occasions when it would enhance the transmission of knowledge and truths to others. Siger is speaking, indeed, in a way that can be very comprehensible and acceptable to modern thinkers and intellectuals. What we must not do, of course, in interpreting such teachings, is to imply that there can be two literal truths at the same time.

4.15.   Siger and the Double-Truth Accusation.

We have already noted how many earlier scholars had simply accepted as true the accusations of Tempier and others that Siger was a proponent of the position that a teaching could be true for philosophy, while being false for theology, or vice versa. It is not our concern in this study to determine whether this view, often known as the "double-truth" theory, may well have been held in later centuries just before the Reformation for political or other reasons by some of the so-called Italian Averroists.

However, as will become clearer in subsequent chapters, it is probable that Siger can be seen as a man searching for the truth, not always certain of his own position and indeed willing to amend it at times, when faced with convincing counter-arguments. This provisional approach also implicitly acknowledges the existence of truth on more than one dimension - not in the traditional interpretation of the "double-truth" position as such, but somewhat akin to the different perspectives posed by the question of the origin of mankind at the time of the Evolution controversies in the nineteenth century. Here, it would be widely accepted by most non-fundamentalist Christian believers, that it is perfectly possible to maintain without any contradiction that the origin of the human race comes from God and at the same time that it derives from apelike ancestors.

A good illustration of this which reflects the scientific-type theories of the period can be seen in one of the Quaestiones in Metaphysicam (Cambridge Version) where Siger, who like his contemporaries simply takes the reality of acts of magic for granted, discusses whether the power to carry them out derives from the heavenly bodies or from separated substances such as demons or devils. A superficial reading of his resolution of the problem - "Sed unum scio, aliud autem credo" [I have knowledge of one thing while I believe something else] (122) - might, if taken out of context, suggest "double-truth". However, his explanation sums up carefully and succinctly what this chapter has been suggesting in terms of the two dimensions or domains of truth. He agrees with Aristotle that there must be a rational mechanistic-type explanation that could only imply that the causality must lie in heavenly bodies. However, he explains that faith may reveal truth on a different level, that which would otherwise be unknowable through the natural knowledge of the philosopher, namely that the heavenly bodies may come into play as immediate causes precisely through the more remote causality of demons:

> Non enim intendo negare tales substantias intellectuales quas daemones dicimus, nec quod a substantia aliqua intellectuali separata possit procedere immediate aliquid novum. Credo

tamen quod opera talia, facta per artes magicas, non sunt facta immediate a virtute talis substantiae intellectualis, sed a virtute corporum caelestium [123].

[Indeed I do not intend to deny that there are such intellectual substances as what we call demons, nor that something new can proceed immediately from some separated intellectual substance. I believe however that such works, accomplished through magical arts, are not carried out immediately through the power of such an intellectual substance, but through the power of the heavenly bodies.]

Hence both apparent alternatives are not in reality genuine alternatives at all, but are both true according to different levels of knowledge and in no way contradictory to one another. The fact that in the twentieth century the whole question would be viewed in a totally different light makes no difference to our understanding of the process by which it is resolved by Siger according to the philosophical/scientific knowledge and religious faith of his day.

We have a further insight into how Siger viewed the relationship between philosophy and theology, by examining a Commentum that lies between the first and the second Quaestio in the Sixth Book of the Quaestiones in Metaphysicam. Here he contrasts natural theology and revealed theology in six different ways. It appears almost to constitute a personal statement, laying down a marker regarding the independent status of the two faculties - indeed in the earlier Cambridge version he used the phrase "nostra theologia" [our theology] to describe the former. While he is perfectly happy to acknowledge that actual revelation is more certain than philosophical enquiry, he also emphasises that this does not apply to any human reflection which proceeds to develop or elaborate on the actual revealed truths:

... modus considerandi in ista theologia, quae est pars philosophiae, est procedere ex principiis quae sunt nota nobis via sensus, memoriae et experimenti, ex lumine et ratione naturali. Modus autem considerandi in theologia quae est

> sacra scriptura non est procedere ex principiis quae sint nota
> via sensus, memoriae et experimenti et lumine naturali, sed
> proceditur in ea ex principiis notis per divinam revelationem
> .... Deinde autem ex illis principiis, sic notis per revelationem
> divinam, proceditur per investigationem humanam ... [124].

[... the method of reflection in that theology which is a branch of philosophy is to proceed from principles which are known to us through the senses, memory and experience, by means of natural vision and reason. The method of reflection in that theology, which is sacred scripture, is not to proceed from principles known through the senses, memory and experience by natural reason but from principles known by divine revelation... Then, however from those principles, known by divine revelation, the method proceeds by human investigation ... .]

Nowhere in this Quaestio is found the slightest suggestion that truth itself is anything but one and single, while the indications from the previous text that Siger is predominantly concerned about asserting the independence of academic investigation into non-revealed philosophy seem to be confirmed by some of his concluding remarks:

> Sic ergo quantum mihi videtur nunc, ipsae differunt in his sex
> iam dictis. Ex quibus ... apparet quod pessime volunt
> procedere illi qui in illa scientia volunt procedere in omnibus
> modo demonstrativo. Principia enim demonstrationis debent
> esse nota via sensus, memoriae et experimenti [125].

[It therefore seems to me at this point in time that the two sciences differ in the six forementioned ways. It thus seems that it is a very bad procedure for those who want to continue in the former science (revealed theology) by demonstrative method in all matters. This is because the principles of demonstration are known by means of the senses, memory and trial-and-error.]

This may well be prompted by some of his fears or even resentment that genuine thought in the Faculty of Arts over topics which are not in themselves revealed was at risk of condemnation by theologians. Furthermore, the very phrase "scientia", used by Siger like his contemporaries, indicates that he did not think of philosophy or theology as being merely concerned with certain bodies of knowledge but rather with an ongoing process of knowing and discovering truths within reality. In a similar way, a twentieth century Christian of the academic stature of Teilhard de Chardin was able both to recognize that he is almost certainly bound to be wrong over a number of matters and also to see science and theology as complementing one another, in so far as they look at the same reality in different ways [126].

In the next four chapters, it will be argued that Siger was indeed likewise searching for truth over a number of controversial matters. Moreover, while he was accused of holding the double-truth theory, nevertheless there is not the slightest justification for maintaining that he believed there can be two different truths in content, but merely that he asserted there can be two different processes in investigating and discovering the truth.

CHAPTER FIVE

SIGER'S VIEWS ON THE ETERNITY OF THE WORLD

5.0.   Introduction.

        This chapter is the first to analyse one of the more specific aspects of
Siger's teaching to see if any evidence can be discovered of his upholding,
explicitly or implicitly, the "double-truth" theory.   It will look thus at his views on
the creation of the world and, in particular, whether this act should be considered
to be an event of a temporal or an eternal nature.   Such an investigation will also
be able to cast some light on Siger's approach to the relationship between religious
belief and philosophy.   Again, it will be the process of his methodology, rather
than the mere content alone, that will ultimately be of the greatest importance for
evaluating Siger's significance today.   However, much of this chapter will
inevitably be concerned with the content of his teaching, but, as was outlined in the
beginning of the last chapter, this will be undertaken not in isolation but in its
historical and intellectual context.

        As in the next three chapters, when the other topics raised by Tempier
in the 1270 Condemnations are considered, Siger's teaching will be carefully
scrutinized.   However, it will be worthwhile to begin with a brief look at the
context and adversarial nature of those articles of Stephen Tempier in both 1270

and 1277 which are relevant to this area. There will follow an outline of Christian teaching on creation, as expressed in the Bible and the early Christian Fathers. A survey of the relevant teaching of the Christian magisterium from the Middle Ages onwards will be complemented by a brief look at medieval Jewish and Islamic writers. A brief overview of the historical origins of the range of the diverse views on creation will then be carried out so that the immediate context of the controversies can be understood, along with the divisions of the various camps around 1270. It will be useful at that point to provide an examination of the relevant philosophical, theological and religious questions surrounding this topic, in a non-critical way, so that the range of distinctive issues can be clarified before attempting any actual assessment of them.

After a brief consideration of the more immediate academic context with regard to creation, the next stage will be to investigate the interpretations of earlier writers and scholars regarding Siger's views on this topic. Only after this will there be attempted an in-depth analysis of those relevant texts, which we can assign with some confidence to the Sigerian corpus. In following the probable chronological order of teaching, this will show clearly the evolution in his thought and any development in his responses to that historical and intellectual environment in which he found himself. Following this analysis, which will be undertaken with some reference of course to the views of some of his most important contemporaries, an assessment will be made regarding the validity or otherwise of the accusations of "double-truth" in this matter and of Siger's approach to the relationship between religion and his teaching in the Faculty of Arts. Finally, a brief overview of some of the more recent views of present-day scientists, astronomers and theologians will be offered, so that some evaluation can be attempted of the possible contemporary relevance of Siger's views on this topic, whether in terms of content or of process.

5.1.   Tempier's Condemnations of 1270 and 1277 with Regard to Creation.

In the preamble to the 1277 Condemnations (as we saw in Section 3.4), Tempier makes it clear that many of the opinions held within the Faculty of Arts, which were now being censured, were in his view and that of the Theological Commission charged with the investigation, guilty of implying "double-truth":

> Dicunt enim ea esse vera secundum philosophiam, sed non secundum fidem catholicam, quasi sint duae contrariae veritates, et quasi contra veritatem sacrae scripturae sit veritas in dictis gentilium damnatorum [1].

[Thus they state things to be true according to philosophy, but not according to the Catholic faith, as if there are two contrary truths and as if there is a truth in the sayings of pagans in hell that is opposed to the truth of sacred scripture.]

We shall examine in this chapter whether such an accusation can be levelled fairly at Siger's views on creation.   In fact, specific condemnations of certain opinions concerning the eternity of the world were made.   Thus, Article 83 clearly refutes the suggestion that the world was not made "de novo".   Likewise, Articles 80, 84, 85, 87, 88, 89 and 90 develop condemnations of various particular arguments or reasons adduced to support the eternity of the world.

As we come to a more profound consideration of the issues and arguments involved, it should also be noted that there are a number of other relevant articles, concerned with opinions regarding the existence of non-material creatures from eternity, e.g. Article 39, and of the creation of the human race itself from eternity, e.g.Article 138, which have clear implications for and relevance to this topic [2].

Of course, these condemnations did not suddenly arise and come upon the scene without any warning.   There had been the major explicit condemnation by Stephen Tempier himself on 10 December 1270, much earlier in Siger's professional career, of thirteen opinions judged to be heretical. Of these, the fifth and sixth are particularly relevant in this case [3]. As we shall see later in this chapter, there is a whole context of controversy in Paris surrounding this, involving Bonaventure, Thomas Aquinas and many others, which will need careful examination.

5.2.   The Biblical Background to the Topic.

How did Christians come to think that revelation demanded a belief in a temporal creation? Where did they find a scriptural justification for this?

Perhaps at first sight the most obvious reference is the first verse of the first chapter of Genesis, cf. "In the beginning God created the heavens and the earth". Does "in the beginning" demand a temporal creation or could it be a metaphorical way of describing by myth the dependence of the universe for its existence on its one sole creator? While the first is the most obvious meaning of Jerome's Vulgate "in principio", which was of course the version familiarly used in the thirteenth century in Western Europe, we have to acknowledge today, as does for example the Revised Standard Version, that the original Hebrew is also capable of being understood as "when God began to create" - an expression which might emphasize more the mythical nature of the Priestly story of the Six Days of Creation.

Another text commonly used in support of this teaching is Proverbs 8:22, where Wisdom is personified as being a creation of God "before the beginning of the earth". While some Christians today may reinterpret this in their own way to refer to the Second Person of the Trinity, this would not of course have been the original Jewish meaning. The Hebrew word "qanani" strangely enough was rendered as "acquired me" or "possessed me" by Aquila and subsequently by Jerome in the Vulgate, presumably to avoid the kind of misinterpretation that was implied by the Arians, who maintained that, since Wisdom was supposed to personify the Word, the latter was therefore merely a Created Being [4].

Another interesting text can be found if we turn to the Book of Wisdom, which was included in the Greek Septuagint, where can be seen a reference to the "hand that from formless matter created the world" (Wisdom 11:17 - Jerusalem Version). This would certainly seem to suggest an ordering of the cosmos out of pre-existing chaos or prime matter.

What is more pertinent however is Peter Lombard's own interpretation of Genesis 1:1 in his Sentences. Since this had become the seminal commentary in the latter part of the thirteenth century in the Faculty of Theology, - much to Roger Bacon's disapproval, it had largely replaced direct commenting in lectures on biblical texts - it was to overshadow any other possible interpretations of the text at that time:

> In principio creavit Deus coelum et terram. His etenim verbis Moyses spiritu Dei efflatus, in uno principio a Deo creatore mundum factum refert, elidens errorem quorumdam plura sine principio fuisse principia opinantium [5].

[In the beginning God created heaven and earth. Thus with these words Moses bestowed with the Spirit of God declares the world to be made by the Creator God in one initial beginning and destroys the error of those particular people who think there were many beginnings without one initial beginning.]

In any event, we might indeed wonder if the above references, and others such as Psalm 90:2, John 17:5 and Ephesians 1:4, cannot be fairly construed as referring to what might well be called the metaphysical precedence of God over dependent creation rather than requiring a temporal precedence. Besides, as will soon become clear, there are a number of different philosophical and theological implications involved and this topic is very much more complicated than does at first appear. However, it really does seem that the weight of traditional teaching, when allied to Peter Lombard's Sentences, certainly had created the climate in the Faculty of Theology that the inspired word of Scripture demanded a temporal creation.

5.3.   Ancient and Patristic Thought on Creation.

It would not have occurred to Aristotle seriously to doubt the eternity of the world.   For him, an effect needs a cause that itself must possess both simultaneous and preceding existence. Hence, if the world had been made in time, it would have been necessary to refer back to an earlier time and movement [6]. This kind of argument, albeit in somewhat inferior form, indeed probably predated Socrates, Plato and Aristotle, as Thomas Aquinas acknowledges [7].   This contrasts, of course, with the view of a modern empiricist, such as David Hume, who denies that cause and effect can demonstrate with certainty anything other than observed sequences of temporal succession, and then goes on to declare that we should simply accept the fact of the existence of the universe and not try to question philosophically or theologically either its duration or even hypothesize the need for a designer at all [8].

Some of the early Church Fathers, such as Origen, seem to accept the eternity of creation, though, truth to tell, they come to it from a different direction from that of Aristotle.   God did not at some point start to become a Creator and his providence was always there [9].   Hence, while this particular material created world has not always existed and actually came into existence as a result of moral fault [10], nevertheless there has always been a finite world as such.   Likewise, Justin had taught that God had created the "cosmos" out of informed matter which involved a process of being carefully shaped and organized [11].   While there were other dissenting voices, we should remember the context of those early centuries when orthodox Christians were fighting against the dualism of the Gnostics and the Manicheans.   That meant that they had to explain whether or not matter was evil or if it could, in origin, have come completely from God.   The whole issue seemed very complicated to writers of that time.   It is now possible therefore to focus upon the first critical distinction in understanding whether creation should be seen as either "ex nihilo" [out of nothing] or as a result of the re-organization of some pre-existing matter or indeed as a two-stage creation, incorporating both of the above.   This is the position that some writers interpreted Philo as holding, apparently as a means of explaining what appeared to him to be two different consecutive creations of the human race in Genesis 1:27 and Genesis 2:7 [12].   It seems that, around this time, most writers felt that a temporal creation would imply a change in the divine will and therefore could not be a viable position. They do not seem to have considered the issue as to whether an eternal universe could possibly have compromised the status of God.

It certainly can be argued that it is from the second half of the second century that Tatian and then Theophilus of Antioch - ironically, probably following the Gnostic Basilides a generation or so earlier who had arrived at the same view for different reasons - may have been the first orthodox writers to affirm the idea of "creation ex nihilo" as such [13]. This, of course, is by no means the same as affirming a temporal creation. It seems that that particular debate continued for a while longer, though gradually more and more writers, including St. Augustine, presented the case that it was at least a philosophically viable position until eventually Philoponus went on the offensive, arguing in 529 that the universe must have had a beginning [14].

St. Augustine had indeed been preoccupied with the nature of time and seems to teach that both time and the world were created together [15]. His influence was of course to be vast on the medieval theologians, especially the earlier ones. This teaching also highlights the second of the distinctions that will need to be made to avoid possible confusion, namely that between eternity and perpetuity, meaning respectively either a co-eternity with God or simply as having always existed ever since a temporal creation of the cosmos. Indeed, it can certainly be well argued that it has been such confusions that has led to much misunderstanding of earlier writers. Following the pre-eminent authority attributed to St. Augustine, it came about that Christian thinkers thought it was essential to believe in a temporal creation, although, as we shall see in the next section, it does not seem to have been considered necessary to state this as a doctrine that must be believed. However, as the thirteenth century developed, this teaching was to fall into sharp contrast with the eternalism of the Islamic philosophers, referred to in the previous section, as much as with the newly rediscovered ancient writers.

This sharp difference of teaching was, not surprisingly, to be highlighted by all the other tensions occurring between philosophy and theology in the University of Paris and also those regarding the nature and use of authority within the much wider ecclesial context. To what extent would the teaching of these views, even when merely presented as opinions of so-called pagans and non-believers, whether ancient Greek or Islamic, constitute a danger to young impressionable minds? Would the study of them provide a specific threat to the unity and teaching magisterium of the Church?

5.4.   Creation and the Magisterium.

It might be useful and interesting at this point to ask why this should be considered so vital an issue for orthodox teaching and why some of these views should seem to require so severe a sanction as that of a proclamation of heresy. Naturally, there were arguments and counter-arguments on the level of purely intellectual discussion, but why should teaching over this be considered necessary as a measure of Christian (or, come to that, of Jewish or Islamic) orthodoxy?

Our first historical port of call should be the decree in 1215 of the Fourth Lateran Council in its definition against the perceived dualism of the Albigensians and the Cathars. Within this decree is included a requirement for a profession of faith which includes:

> Firmiter et simpliciter confitemur, quod unus solus est verus
> Deus ... creator omnium visibilium et invisibilium, spiritualium
> et corporalium: qui sua omnipotenti virtute simul ab initio
> temporis utramque de nihilo condidit creaturam, spiritualem
> et corporalem, angelicam videlicet et mundanam [16].

[We confess strongly and in all respects that there is only one true God ... who is creator of all things, visible and invisible, spiritual and corporeal: who, by his almighty power, established simultaneously from the beginning of time both kinds of creature, spiritual and corporeal, that is to say angelic and earthly.]

While no doubt the prime aim of the decree was to oppose some of the views of the forementioned heretics regarding the dual nature of creation and the origins of evil, the phrase "ab initio temporis" indicates clearly the further intention to exclude the view that creatures, whether of the spiritual world or of this, could be temporally co-eternal with God.   Certainly, a century after this Council at the time of the notorious Montaillou Inquisition, this latter view does appear to be linked with those Albigensians, at least at the level of popular peasant belief [17]. While a similar condemnation was to be made by Pope John XXII of Meister Eckhardt in 1329 condemning the statement that the world has been "ab aeterno" [from eternity] [18], the very selfsame words of the 1215 decree were to be quoted again in 1870 over six and a half centuries later by the First Vatican Council, choosing further to emphasize that God has also created "bonitate sua ..... liberrimo consilio" [out of his goodness and freewill] [19].

At this stage it could well be asked whether, from a Roman Catholic perspective, this specific point has been defined as a matter of faith.   Pius XII clearly believed so, if we scrutinize the evidence within "Humanae Generis", his famous encyclical letter of 1950, in which he claims that he is reasserting the teaching of the First Vatican Council by condemning recent theological tendencies to assert both the eternity of the world and the necessity of creation [20]. However, we could also query whether the Pope's interpretation of the actual intentions of the First Vatican Council is in fact correct.   The Council Fathers probably did assume that belief in a temporal creation is necessary, but, as we shall see later, they just as probably did not distinguish between the relative importance of the concepts "ex nihilo" and "post nihilum".   Their main aim was to reinforce the earlier condemnations by Pius IX, in the Syllabus of Errors and elsewhere, of the ontologist views of writers such as Malebranche and Rosmini for what was seen as inclining implicitly towards a virtual pantheism:

> Deus idem est ac rerum natura et idcirco immutationibus obnoxius, Deusque reapse fit in homine et mundo, atque omnia Deus sunt et ipsissimam Dei habent substantiam; ac una eademque res est Deus cum mundo ... [21].

[God is to be identified with the nature of things and hence subject to changes. God indeed is found in Man and in the world. All things are God and have the very substance of God while God is one and the same thing with the world ...]

Pius XII for that matter was probably also failing to make the same distinction, in so far as he was trying to uphold the need to believe in God's foreknowledge of all human actions, as indeed, later in the same letter, he enters the arena of the relationship betwen science and theology, in so far as he declares that he is unable to see how polygenism can be reconciled with belief in original sin (22). Hence, it seems certain that the Bishops at both the Fourth Lateran Council and the First Vatican Council, as mentioned above, were not immediately concerned with trying to uphold the teaching of a temporal creation as such. Their concerns were elsewhere with attempting to control movements perceived as heretical for other reasons. Consequently, it can be fairly questioned whether such a view is a definitive Christian dogma within the Roman Catholic Church and not merely representing implicit assumptions in accordance with contemporary teaching. For example, the Council of Florence where the main concern is clearly to uphold the freewill of God as Creator rather than anything else in this respect, does nothing to discourage this interpretation of events (23).

On the other hand, of course, neither John XXII's nor Pius XII's statements demand, from a theological point of view, any definitive and obligatory assent. Vollert's view that "the doctrine that the universe has a temporal duration is defined as a dogma of faith" (24) is therefore very debatable, although of course this is not the immediate issue of concern in this study of Siger's views in their historical context. However, this is a point that perhaps should not be forgotten, as we come to see the vitriolic condemnation of this particular position in the thirteenth century.

At the same time, it might well also be worth retaining at the back of one's mind the question as to how important it is to a modern Christian to believe in creation, as if it were a single temporal event in the past. It has been suggested that even neo-Thomists today (ironically, almost certainly more in tune with contemporary hierarchical leadership than was their mentor and guide in his own day) understand the phrase "in the beginning" in an almost entirely non-temporal sense, linking the metaphysical concepts of creation and conservation of the world together theologically [25]. Perhaps a particularly good example of such theology is to be found in the scientist-theologian Teilhard de Chardin, though he cannot of course be properly described as a neo-Thomist, despite the fact that his writings are imbued with the use of Thomist and scholastic language, e.g.

> There is not one moment when God creates, and one moment when the secondary causes develop.   There is always only one creative action (identical with conservation) which continually raises creatures towards fuller-being by means of their secondary activity and their earlier advances [26].

In another section of the same book Christianity and Evolution, he writes:

> Creation, Fall, Incarnation, Redemption, these vast universal events no longer appear as fleeting accidents occurring sporadically in time - a grossly immature view which is a perpetual offence to our reason and a contradiction of our experience.   All four of these events become co-extensive with the duration and totality of the world;   they are, in some way, aspects (distinct in reality but physically linked) of one and the same divine operation [27].

Jolivet, a much more mainstream Thomist writes that:

> ... to assert that the world is created does not mean that the world began in time, that is to say, to be more precise, that from the moment of creation a finite time (however long) has passed. Nor does it mean the opposite.   I say simply that the world does not exist of itself, nor in virtue of itself, but that it

proceeds absolutely and wholly from God and from an act of
his sovereign freedom [28].

It will appear then that there is substantial theological evidence that the
subject today seems to be nothing like as clearcut as Tempier might have wanted
to maintain, particularly when we take into consideration some of the ambiguities
within the relevant biblical texts that we have already seen.

5.5.   Jewish and Islamic Thought regarding Creation in the Middle Ages.

Having looked at Christian teaching, it is worth taking at least a
passing glance at Jewish and Islamic thinkers on this topic.

Although Maimonides teaches temporal creation, yet we should note
that he does emphasise the continuous dependence of all of creation on the Creator
and it is this aspect of contingency that he sees as being central [29]. Nevertheless,
even he, in speaking of the Torah, certainly declares its permanence and perhaps
even implies its timelessness in some sense or other [30]. In fact, some ancient
rabbinic traditions do speak of the Torah as being co-extensive with God himself,
while the Zohar, whether literally or metaphorically, speaks of it as existing before
Creation, using language very reminiscent for the Christian of that used about the
Word, the Second Person of the Trinity [31]. Perhaps the Neoplatonic influence
of emanations with regard to the Sefirot is to be associated with this kind of
thought.   In any event, such texts serve to show that, even for the Jewish
community, the issue is not as clearcut as perhaps tradition might at first appear to
suggest.   Certainly, Maimonides does on a number of occasions, like Thomas
Aquinas later, make clear that he believes that there is no clear philosophical proof
either for or against a temporal creation and that the question can only be solved
by revelation [32].   In this, of course, their position differs from the later Jewish
philosopher Hasdai Crescas, who believed an eternal creation "ex nihilo" was
necessary to explain God's existence as a Necessary Being.

Likewise, there are parallels in Islamic teaching. The Qur'an implies a temporal creation of the universe [33] and of course Islam does not even countenance the possibility of the theory of evolution of living species. Nevertheless, the controversies surrounding groups such as the Mu'tazilites who supported the created nature of the Qur'an and the Mutakallimum who supported its uncreated nature will be recalled. The Islamic philosophers, however, were very happy to follow Greek thought in affirming the eternity of the world, albeit from different directions. So, for example, Ibn Sina is dependent on Neoplatonic thought and is led there from the nature of necessary emanations, while Ibn Rushd looks more towards Aristotle and develops his perspective from the nature of causality [34].

5.6.   The Immediate Historical and Academic Context.

It was around 1230 that William of Durham and others began to compose theological "quaestiones" on the eternity of the world. They were involved in investigating the relationship of time to eternity as well as what is to become the more important question as to whether the world was, or could have been, eternal. While this, as we have seen, does seem to have arisen because of the need of theologians to comment on it from Peter Lombard's Sentences, nevertheless it was to lead to an examination of the more precise nature of Aristotle's teaching on creation, now that his works were gaining a much wider and officially permitted readership. Hence, on one side, some such as Philip the Chancellor and Alexander of Hales argued that Aristotle had never in fact himself claimed that the world was actually eternal. Others, such as Robert Grosseteste and William of Auvergne, rightly insisted that this was his teaching and consequently was heretical and in conflict with Christianity [35].

How could there have been such confusion about Aristotle's actual views? We should make allowances for the difficulties in getting copies of authentic texts of Aristotle. William of Moerbeke was not to complete his Latin translations of the Corpus Aristotelicum until well into the second half of the century. We must also remember that there was a predisposition among many loyal Christian philosopher-theologians to avoid imputing any views to the newly discovered and rehabilitated Greek writer that might derogate from the teaching of the Church, lest he should become compromised in the eyes of the Church authorities. Indeed, some writers tended almost to identify him with reason and believed it virtually impossible for his writing therefore to be truly in conflict with the faith of the Church over this or any other issue. By the time of Albert the Great, however, these fears and apprehensions were decreasing and he was able to rationalize the authority and status of Aristotle into what he considered to be the appropriate context. Thus, he should be offered due intellectual respect and authority, while recalling at the same time that this involved merely secular rather than divine insight [36].

It should, of course, be noted at this point that, while the theologians took as their starting-point the Commentaries on Genesis, the Sentences and the doctrinal teaching of the Church, the philosophers were coming in the opposite direction (not necessarily, of course, with contrary conclusions), starting from their readings of Aristotle's Physics and other writings. In the latter case, there was now to develop an investigation of the precise nature of Aristotle's teaching, particularly as a result of the greater access both to more of his writings and to the Commentaries of Ibn Rushd and Maimonides. This was especially to focus on the central question as to whether there was a temporal or eternal creation of the world and also as to whether a temporal creation could be demonstrated by reason alone.

So, during the 1260s and 1270s, we are now to see a whole series of intellectual discussions and conflicts on this hotly argued topic in Paris through the three main protagonists Bonaventure, Thomas Aquinas and Siger of Brabant, as well as among a whole range of lesser known writers. These were to climax in the Condemnations of 1270 and 1277.

5.7.　　　A Brief Review of Earlier Writers on Siger and Creation.

The traditional view has been to see Bonaventure as totally committed to the position that we can prove the non-eternal existence of the world and that Siger followed Ibn Rushd (and Ibn Sina, come to that) in the heresy of maintaining its eternity.　In this scenario, Thomas Aquinas, while acknowledging Christian orthodoxy, is seen as steering a middle position in so far as he felt nothing could be proved one way or the other by reason alone.

We shall look at Bonaventure's and Thomas Aquinas' respective teachings later on, but in this section we shall begin our analysis of Siger's views with a brief overview of opinions over the last hundred years or so regarding his teaching on this matter.

Mandonnet had simply assumed from his reading of Sigerian texts that the philosopher had slavishly followed Ibn Rushd and was an unquestioning "Averroist", particularly regarding the eternity of the human species, of prime matter, of movement, of time and of the separated substances [37].

Van Steenberghen in his research began to differentiate between different stages in Siger's career.　In his earliest writings, such as the two-volume work of 1931 and 1942, Van Steenberghen states categorically that the doctrine of the eternity of the world is found throughout Siger [38].　However, his subsequent research was to lead him to moderate this position considerably.

For example, in his Introduction à l'Étude de la Philosophie Médiévale, published in 1974, he declares that before 1270 Siger proclaimed in the style of the great Islamic philosophers that metaphysical causality demands the eternity of the world (recalling the phrase "Averroist"), and that even afterwards this was still to be found in his writings, albeit now on occasions with some hesitation [39]. However, by the time of his great work of 1977, Van Steenberghen differentiates between the period before 1270 and the writings of Siger after 1270.　He claims that in the first period Siger teaches quite openly the eternity of species and, as a more probable opinion, the eternity of the single intellect of the human species,.

However, Van Steenberghen then argues that Siger acknowledges subseqently that the eternity of the world is opposed to Christian teaching while the eternity of the Intelligences and of the heavenly spheres is merely hinted at. Towards the end of his teaching career, according to Van Steenberghen, Siger tends to hide behind the position of wishing merely to expound the "teaching of the philosophers", while by his final extant work he argues that, with the benefit of the Christian faith, we are better able than ever to see the weaknesses of Aristotle's arguments regarding the eternity of the Intelligences [40].

In 1969, Bukowski had written a very brief article on Siger in this context in which he purported to revise some earlier views of Müller [41]. Bukowski now claimed that, as a result of greater knowledge of authenticity and non-authenticity of texts, we are forced to conclude that Müller's position "must be modified to allow that, in Siger's doctrine of the eternity of the world, although metaphysics' arguments are no better than probable, natural philosophy's are demonstrative" [42].

Argerami has denied, on the other hand, that Siger ever maintained eternalist theses [43]. However, the actual process by which he came to his conclusions must also be rejected, since he too uses texts, now identified as belonging to Boethius of Dacia [44] and other writers of unknown and doubtful identity [45]. The more recent writer Bianchi provides an outline of the same case with greater conviction than Argerami [46], while Dales in his recent major work on this general topic entitled Medieval Discussions of the Eternity of the World does not enter into the question as to whether we can detect development in Siger's thought, in so far as he concentrates almost entirely on the one work De Aeternitate Mundi alone [47].

Following this brief summary of previous writers regarding Siger's views on the eternity of the world, we should now be able to begin an in-depth examination of his relevant texts, which will be considered in what can be considered a likely chronological order.

5.8. Quaestio utrum haec sit vera: Homo est Animal, Nullo Homine Existente.

In this quaestio which appears probably to constitute the earliest evidence that we have of Siger's teaching on this issue, he does seem to teach the eternity of the human race, as indeed of any other species, without any hesitation. He follows Aristotle, in so far as he declares:

> De ratione humanae naturae est quod ipsa est ens simpliciter,
> non pro determinato tempore, sicut Socrates vel Plato [48].

[It is fundamental to human nature that it is itself a being without qualification, not just for a fixed period of time like Socrates or Plato.]

He uses the principle of contradiction in such a way as to suggest that, if we were to claim that there could ever be a time when no man existed, then we would also be forced to conclude that there was no fundamental essence to human nature. This would have the inevitable consequence that no individual (such as Socrates) could ever be accurately described as being essentially human [49]. He then goes on to conclude his case with an "ad hominem" argument:

> Hypothesis autem quae dicit nullum hominem existere seu
> esse ens, implicat contra naturam humanam idem oppositum
> eius rationis [50].

[However the hypothesis, stating that no man exists or is a being, implies the very opposite meaning to human nature.]

But is Siger himself uncritically proclaiming the eternity of the human race and of all species? On the surface, one could of course be forgiven for thinking so. Indeed, even Van Steenberghen seems to believe this to be the case [51] and in this he follows Bazán who has edited this text and affirms quite fairly that Siger shows no indication of either reserve or prudence, unlike in other works [52].

148

On reflection, however, we should firstly recall that this is indeed one of the earliest of his writings and all seem agreed that it is certainly to be dated prior to 1270. Further, there is no reason to suppose that he was doing anything other than offer, as a young Master, an academic commentary in defence of Aristotle's thesis. In this regard, the last paragraph of the Quaestio is very interesting:

> Huic ergo sententiae firmiter adhaerendum est, nam cum fuerit considerata, acquiescat intellectus et sileat; recedat vanitas verborum in hac materia ne cognitionem impediant. Qui enim in omnibus manifestis et immanifestis aequaliter disputare voluerint, contingit eis saepius dicere ab ipsis rebus extranea, ut dicit Commentator supra 'secundum Caeli et mundi' (53).

[This opinion should be firmly upheld, for, when it has been considered, the intellect should pause and rest. Let empty words recede in this matter lest they hinder understanding. Indeed, those who want to argue equally about everything, whether obvious or unclear, usually say irrelevant things, as the Commentator states with regard to the Second Book of the 'Heaven and Earth'.]

Again, this could at first appear as if Siger is closing the door, saying that the conclusion of the Quaestio is so proven that he wants to warn against empty verbiage by people who want to get off the point and to bring up other matters. However, closer observation here shows that he is quoting a saying of Ibn Rushd that he has come across from a different context. In this sense, both here and in the Quaestio as a whole, we can understand how as a fairly new Master of Arts lecturing, as was his duty, on the writings of Aristotle, he may not have seen it as his primary task as to dissect and criticize him. Certainly, we can see that Siger is warning against vain verbosity on this issue. Aristotle's actual teaching is for him as plain as can be and his explanation should therefore be accepted as accurate. Whether Aristotle is completely right or not does not come into real consideration here. It would surely not be too cynical even to suggest that Siger could be trying to preempt any awkward objections.

Furthermore, we should not ignore the fact that, as Bianchi points out [54], the basic context of these remarks is to find logical arguments which would support Aristotle's views on the nature of universals, an issue of great philosophical importance during the whole period of the Middle Ages, as has been indicated in the previous chapter. So this Quaestio could well be understood as a state-of-the-art demonstration of this, without any direct introspective investigation or judgment of its own credibility or value. Some internal evidence for this can also be indicated by the fact that, unlike his more usual practice, Siger never uses the first person singular (e.g. "dico") to preserve his own position, but nearly always uses the third person singular in the passive mode, with the sole exception of three instances of the use of the more formal first person plural.

This general interpretation of the status of Siger's lecturing at this early stage of his career would seem to be confirmed by the way in which he does not yet develop his own distinctive positions and views but - according to common practice of the time - was quite prepared to use the arguments and material even of relatively recent writers and masters. So, for example, Duin has found a substantial indebtedness of Siger in his Compendium super De Generatione et Corruptione to Geoffrey of Haspall [55]. Likewise, the Sententia super Librum Quartum Meteorum which is itself a literal commentary, without any questioning, on this pseudo-Aristotelian work, acknowledges a clear debt to Alfred of Sarashel and frequently demonstrates a very close, almost word-for-word, dependence on Adam of Buckfield [56]. Although this is not acknowledged, the latter would almost certainly have been a lecturer during Siger's student days [57].

It is not hard, if we pursue our historical method of investigation into the ideas of Siger, to visualize the young Master as beginning his teaching career, heavily dependent on earlier commentators and being uncritical in any overt way of Aristotelian thought. He would not, in this scenario, have seen it as his duty in the Faculty of Arts to have taught in any other way, at least while his own ideas were still in a relatively early stage of development. We must recall that this was all happening at a time when the different faculties in Paris were jostling one another in a very competitive way to maintain and increase their respective status and authority. Of course, Tempier's Condemnations in 1270 had not yet been issued to create a much sharper and more tense atmosphere, with everyone looking over their shoulders even more.

5.9.   Quaestiones in Tertium de Anima.

It is the Quaestiones 2, 3 and 5 of In Tertium de Anima which are going to be the most relevant to our current investigation. This commentary is (as we shall see in much greater depth in the next chapter) primarily concerned with the nature of the intellective soul but, in these early questions, Siger also examines whether it is eternal and the nature of its relationship to earthly time. Van Steenberghen seems to want to emphasize the heterodoxy of Siger at this stage so as to fit in with his theory of the subsequent development of Siger's thought to a greater compatibility with the Church's teaching, as he matured in response to the 1270 Condemnations. Thus he describes him as teaching the eternity of the unique intellect of humankind "comme l'opinion la plus probable" (as the most probable opinion) [58]. Is this the case? Let us examine the text most carefully.

First of all, however, as Bianchi has noted [59], the thrust of the debate, as presented by Siger immediately before his solution, is the contrast and conflict between the position of Aristotle and that of Augustine. The former claims that since the soul is not generated into existence then it must be eternal, while the latter teaches that the soul was created at the moment of infusion [60]. Siger goes on to explain that from Aristotle's perspective, were the First Cause to create "de novo", this would involve change in the will of the First Cause. This is for Siger what he technically calls a "probable" rather than a "necessary" position:

> Estne hoc necessarium?   Dicendum quod, licet hoc sit
> probabile, non tamen hoc est necessarium [61].

[Is this necessary? It should be stated that, although this is probable, it is not however necessary.]

It is, according to him, in God's power either to create an eternal intellect or not, "secundum formam voluntatis suae" [according to whether or not his will so desires] (62). The only way in which anyone would ever know for certain would be if we were able to investigate fully God's inscrutable will, which he declares, in the form of a rhetorical question, to be quite impossible for anybody:

> Qui ergo voluerit scire utrum intellectus factus sit de novo vel
> factus sit aeternus, oportet eum investigare formam voluntatis
> Primi. Sed quis erit qui eam investigabit? (63).

[It follows that anyone who has wanted to know whether the intellect has been made anew or has been made eternal, should investigate the form of the will of the First Being. But who will there be to investigate it?.]

In fact, this passage is echoed in the treatise De Aeternitate Mundi of his colleague Boethius of Dacia, who suggests the contrary view is bordering on madness:

> Metaphysica non potuit demonstrare quod mundus non sit
> coaeternus voluntati divinae. ... Metaphysicus non potest
> demonstrare talem fuisse formam voluntatis divinae ab
> aeterno: dicere enim quod metaphysicus possit hoc
> demonstrare, non solum figmento, sed etiam, credo, cuidam
> dementiae simile est: unde enim homini ratio, per quam
> voluntatem divinam perfecte investiget? (64).

[Metaphysics cannot demonstrate that the world is not coeternal with the divine will. ... The metaphysician cannot demonstrate that such was the form of the divine will from eternity. To say that the metaphysician can demonstrate this is not only a figment (of the imagination) but also, I believe, akin to madness.

152

Indeed, whence does the reasoning come to man, through which he might perfectly investigate the divine will?.]

Siger then twice states that, since the above is the case, if we should be forced to choose between the two positions, we must come down on the side of Aristotle, which, although not definitive, is "more probable" than that of Augustine (65). What then does he mean when he says that if we follow Aristotle, then we will reject Augustine, but if it is the other way round and we accept Augustine's view, then we shall still accept the argument of Aristotle?

> Si ergo credatur Aristoteli, planum est quod non est credendum Augustino. Si vero credatur Augustino, erit aequaliter (66).

[Therefore, if Aristotle is believed, it is clear that Augustine is not to be believed. However, if Augustine is believed, it will be an equal belief.]

Perhaps Da Palma offers a clue when he states that Siger has an acute awareness of the independence of human knowledge and investigation in its own field of philosophy and is jealously defending it from external influence and infiltration (67).

Surely we can again see the process going on in Siger's mind, where he says that one position is more likely - indeed the Latin word "probabilior" implying the comparative is twice used rather than Van Steenbeghen's rendering "le plus probable" (superlative) of all possibilities. This is of course a long way from "double-truth" and this interpretation of Siger's actual way of thinking seems to be confirmed by deeper analysis of the actual words "probabilis" and "probabilior" on the technical level of medieval usage in such contexts, where, as Van Steenberghen himself acknowledges elsewhere, "probabilis" means "with evidence in its favour" and "probabilior" means "with greater evidence in its favour" (68). It is comparatively easy these days, even for a scholar, to miss sometimes such an important point because of our exposure to the slant of our contemporary use of the word "probability" - and surely no one would want to accuse Albert the Great and Thomas Aquinas, who were no different from Siger in this respect, of "double-truth"! Siger himself employs this usage in the fourth of the Impossibilia, where he avers that, although a solution is "probable", it cannot be upheld - even on purely natural philosophical (scientific) grounds:

> Quamquam vero haec sententia probabilis sit, tamen stare non potest [69].

> [Although there is evidence for this opinion, it cannot however be upheld.]

We can fairly conclude therefore that Van Steenberghen must be wrong to suggest that Siger has merely been saying that one must make a decision and choose between Aristotle or Augustine [70]. His interest and aim has been to assess the relative strengths of the evidence for the arguments rather than comparing with any actual reality or truth that might itself only be known by faith.

There is yet another twist in our investigation of this text, particularly relevant to this comparison between Aristotle and Augustine. No scholar has as yet been able to discover the text attributed to the latter in any of his extant writings. Clearly, this may not be very significant in itself, were it not for the fact that we do find a very close correspondence between the relevant language quoted by Siger and a text of Bonaventure, which the latter does not attribute to Augustine [71]. This could well indicate that the Sigerian text is here intending, perhaps for good and deliberate reasons, to contrast Bonaventure, rather than Augustine, with Aristotle. If this is so, then the comparison is really an assessment of the relationship between Aristotelian philosophy and one particular theological school. So, for example, we can contrast Siger's comments above about the inscrutability of God's will with those of Peter of Tarantaise, Regent Master of Theology in Paris at about this time and later to become Pope Innocent V:

> Si mundus ab aeterno fuit, nunquam potest non fuisse; ergo non esset productus a Deo voluntarie [72].

[If the world existed from eternity, it can never have not been in existence. If this were the case, it would not be produced by the freewill of God.]

In the context of this particular Quaestio, therefore, Siger appears to be declaring that to speak of the infusion of bodies by souls after the creation of the former is an unproven theological theory. The rational Siger would further argue that, even if true, it would not invalidate philosophical investigation.

The third Quaestio is of less relevance here and will be looked at in the next chapter (73). However, the fifth is worth a brief examination at this point in so far as Siger goes on to maintain that theoretically the intellect is corruptible on the grounds that it did come from nothing. Nevertheless, because it is dependent for its existence on the First Cause, we can say that it is kept in existence by the will of God:

Dico quod Primum perpetuat intellectum voluntate sua [74].

[I state that the First Being perpetuates the intellect by his own freewill.]

He has openly acknowledged here again his willingness to depart from Aristotle's position, using the first person singular "dico" in pronouncing his resolution of the Quaestio. It is interesting to see how he is now beginning to develop and pronounce his own views at this stage of his career, in contrast to Van Steenberghen's assertion that he is blindly following heretical positions over the matter of eternity of creation up to 1270, since evidence strongly suggests that this particular commentary must be placed prior to that year and is certainly no later [75].

5.10.   Quaestiones in Physicam.

We have already noted that much of the work, previously attributed to Siger under the general heading of Quaestiones in Physicam (see Sections 2.9 and 2.10), can no longer be done so safely and indeed that some has been subsequently accredited to Boethius of Dacia. However, Zimmermann has edited what does appear to be authentic Sigerian material, consisting almost entirely of a commentary on Aristotle's Second Book of the Physics. Here we find another text, probably contemporaneous or slightly subsequent to the dating that has been offered for the Quaestiones in Tertium de Anima [76].

In some of the later questions found here, Siger identifies the problem of the nature of time with respect to the relationship between cause and effect. Thus, in Quaestio 19, he makes the basic distinction between the source of origin of an object and its actual beginning in time:

> Duplex est principium rei: 'ex quo' et 'principium in tempore' [77].

[There are two ways in which we can speak of the origin of something: the source from which it comes and its beginning in time.]

This is of course very relevant to the attacks being made by Bonaventure at this time [78].

In his conclusion, Siger makes it clear that he is only reflecting on the level of natural causes and that it may be different for anything that is made eternally:

> De factionibus aeternis non disputatur hic, et forte sunt secundum istum ordinem, si sunt [79].

[This disputation has not been concerned here with those things which have been made eternal and, perhaps if they are eternal, they may be so according to that dimension.]

He is clearly implying, as Van Steenberghen has noted [80], that, in the hypothesis of eternal causality, then the effect could be equally eternal.

Indeed, in the following Quaestio, he also distinguishes between something which is made by the process of change and what derives from creation out of nothing. He clearly sees the latter, whether temporal or eternal, as affirming a different process from that normally seen in the changes of the natural world:

> Et cum arguunt philosophi quod non fit aliquid nisi possibile
> sit ipsum esse per suam naturam, dicendum quod illud quod
> fit est dupliciter: aut secundum transmutationem, et sic bene
> arguunt: illud enim quod fit per transmutationem, habet ex
> quo fit; aut fit aliquid ex nihilo non per transmutationem, et
> sic non valet eorum ratio [81].

[And when philosophers argue that nothing comes to be unless it is by nature the kind of thing that is able to exist, it must be noted that 'comes to be' has two senses: either 'by being altered' - in this sense the argument is sound, for, when something comes to be by being altered, there is something from which it comes to be; or 'from nothing' (as distinct from 'being altered') - and in this sense their argument is invalid.]

In the final Quaestio, Siger attempts to demonstrate that nothing is capable of being produced out of non-being:

> Dicendum quod ex non ente nihil generatur per naturam, sicut
> et dicunt philosophi [82].

It should be stated, just as philosophers say, that nothing is generated naturally from non-being.]

Yet again we have a golden opportunity, providing potential for his opponents to attack him for apparent heresy, if such a statement is extracted totally out of context!   However, following the earlier references, it is not surprising to note that Siger is obviously speaking about empirical experience of the natural world and is not discussing here the deeper theological and religious issues associated with the creation of the universe as a whole.

5.11.   Impossibilia.

We have already noted above (Section 5.1) how Tempier's thirteen Condemnations of 10 December 1270 include two Articles (5 and 6) which are relevant to this issue.   While it does appear to be highly likely that, even before this date, Siger was innocent of the "double-truth" kind of accusation regarding the nature of the creative act, it is clear nevertheless that he was trying to defend the philosophical process from what he saw as non-intellectual and anti-intellectual encroachment by some theologians.   He was strongly committed, in this respect, to upholding the independence and integrity of the Faculty of Arts.

However, from 1271 onwards, he does appear to introduce a greater element of prudence into his writings, in so far as he does offer sometimes the disclaimer that he is speaking or writing as an interpreter of earlier philosophers. So, for example, in the first of the Impossibilia on the question of the existence of God, he practises the usual sophistic type of disputation-argument, even offering in his solution to suggest that the Intelligences (according to medieval scientific opinion, both spiritual beings, such as the angels, and heavenly bodies, such as the stars and the planets) may well be eternal:

... intelligentia caret potentia ad non esse [83].

[An Intelligence lacks the potentiality to not-exist.]

Nevertheless, he goes on to conclude this Quaestio by declaring that:

Hoc autem dicimus secundum sententiam philosophorum [84].

[We however say this according to the opinion of the philosophers.]

This would again seem to indicate a similar approach and process of reasoning, albeit not based on empirical evidence, to that of a modern scientist who happens to be a religious believer, trying to work independently from any religious beliefs of which he might otherwise take account. This is confirmed by his analysis of the nature of the relationship and difference between a particular moment in time and time itself in his third of the Impossibilia on the question discussing "quod Bellum Troianum esset in hoc instanti" [that the Trojan War would be occurring at this moment] [85]. Van Steenberghen may well therefore be reading more into what he believes to be Siger's development in teaching and thought than is truly warranted. Indeed, he does acknowledge that, while the eternity of the Intelligences is "insinuée mais non affirmée expressement", [implied but not explicitly stated], Siger "s'abrite pourtant derrière les philosophes" [is however sheltering behind the philosophers] [86].

5.12. De Aeternitate Mundi.

Although De Aeternitate Mundi is considered by Bazán to be approximately contemporary with the Impossibilia [87], it is nevertheless a different kind of work from those already considered in this chapter. These have been either commentaries on works of Aristotle or lectures based on the style of sophistic-type disputations of an adversarial nature within the Faculty of Arts. These latter were conducted according to strict procedural rules much as the British legal system functions according to an adversarial framework, where it is the task of each Counsel to try to produce the strongest ("probabile") evidence in support of his case and against that of his opponent. This basic characteristic within the nature of many of the works of medieval philosophy is often forgotten, neglected or ignored, leading to misunderstandings regarding the actual perspective of the philosopher himself. Attention has already been implicitly drawn in this chapter to this element within some of the texts examined, so as to indicate how Siger, just like any other great scholar, is able to develop his ideas and to mature as a thinker within his own historical and academic milieu. We have also seen how he nevertheless adhered to that perspective, which is central to this study, by which he understood philosophical study to involve a self-contained body of investigation. This is independent from, though not inherently contradictory to, that of religion and the Christian faith, although it might run counter to certain particular erroneous religious and theological themes.

Tracts, written as freestanding statements of a position, such as the De Aeternitate Mundi, are however more likely to offer the writer scope to elucidate more precisely his own actual position, both as regarding the topics under discussion or dispute and also as regarding the views of other writers, both earlier and contemporary. There are, it should be noted, many other treatises, such as this, written around the same time by other authors such as Peter of Tarantaise, Bonaventure, Thomas Aquinas and Boethius of Dacia. Some are predominantly theological, others predominantly philosophical (even most recently de Grijs has argued for the former and Aertsen for the latter in respect of Thomas' work (88)), though each kind will be aware of the other, even if only to criticize or to condemn.

Nevertheless, it is intriguing that, in this Tractatus, Siger explicitly uses the divine name [Deus] where in earlier writings he has spoken of the First Being (Primum) - with the notable exception of the first of the Impossibilia, of the same period, which did explicitly concern itself with the existence of God as such. Here, Siger tackles the question from a slightly unexpected angle with overt links to the problem of the nature of universals, which he explicitly lays out in his third chapter; and, to a lesser extent, when he examines the relationship between act and potency in the fourth and final chapter.

He makes it clear in the Introduction that his purpose in writing is to refute philosophically those who claim that they can demonstrate creation-in-time:

> Propter quamdam rationem quae ab aliquibus demonstratio
> esse creditur eius quod species humana esse incepit cum
> penitus non praefuisset, et universaliter species omnium
> individuorum generabilium et corruptibilium, quaeritur ...
> secundum viam Philosophi procedendo [89].

[This tract is produced because there are some who believe they can demonstrate that the human race, and, in general, the species of all individual beings which are subject to generation and corruption, had a beginning after not having previously existed. Its investigation ... proceeds according to the Philosopher's (Aristotle's) approach.]

He introduces the question by declaring that every individual human being - or, come to that, any particular member of any other species - has a finite beginning in time:

> Species autem humana talis est, et universaliter species
> omnium individuorum generabilium et corruptibilium, quod
> quodlibet individuum huiusmodi specierum esse incepit cum
> non praefuisset [90].

[The human species, however, is such - and in general the species of all individual beings subject to generation and corruption - that any individual whatsoever of this kind of species had a beginning, when previously it had not been in existence.]

At the same time, he acknowledges that "...omne ens est a Deo Causatum" [every being has its cause in God] [91].

In the first chapter, Siger argues that the only way in which a human being, as an individual, can come into existence is through generation from another human being. Moreover, we can only speak of the human species as possessing human existence, in so far as it exists in particular human beings. Hence it must have always existed from eternity [92]. Indeed, this argument, depending on the premise that universals only exist in particular individuals, will be examined explicitly in the third chapter [93]. It is important, however, to note that, on no less than three distinct occasions in this first chapter, Siger stresses that he is speaking from a philosophical perspective [94]. In the same way, a religious believer and scientist today would distinguish the process of his own empirical research from that of his religious belief and would accept that his faith or his religion might introduce a new dimension or a new perspective of which he would not otherwise be aware.

In the next chapter, Siger sets about trying to defeat the opposing case of those such as Bonaventure who attack Aristotle's argument for the eternity of past time:

> ...solutio apud Aristotelem est quod, licet quodlibet tunc sit finitum, quia tamen in tempore est accipere tunc ante tunc in infinitum, ideo non totum tempus praeteritum est finitum [95].

[Aristotle's answer is that, although any particular past moment in time is finite, nevertheless any moment can precede another in the past to infinity. Hence past time in its entirety is not finite.]

While he again stresses that he is merely arguing at a philosophical level - "secundum philosophos" [96] - he does conclude by admitting the negative nature of his own submission here. That is to say, he has argued that the opposing premise, that the human species cannot possibly be made from eternity unless there is at least one determined eternal individual human being who has always lived, rests on superficial reasoning:

> Et cum in individuis hominis nullum aeternum inveniant, totam speciem incepisse cum penitus non praefuisset demonstrasse putant, frivola ratione decepti [97].

[And they have been deceived by flimsy reasoning into thinking that, since they find no individual man to be eternal, they have demonstrated that the species as a whole began to exist after it had previously not done so.]

It is then that Siger offers the disclaimer that he is not undertaking at this stage to show the truth of his position but merely the weak reasoning in the case of those who maintain a temporal creation:

> Non conamur autem hic oppositum conclusionis ad   quam
> arguunt ostendere, sed solum suae rationis defectum... (98).

[We are not trying however to demonstrate the opposite of the conclusion for which they are arguing, but only the defect in the reasoning. as is clear from what has been already said.]

In the fourth chapter, ostensibly to investigate whether act or potentiality comes first, the difficulty of being able to prove anything one way or the other from the level of philosophy or science is demonstrated.   Sperm is needed for a man to come into being, while of course sperm cannot be produced unless there is already a man.   This process of reasoning, on the level of observation, would appear to go on for ever without a solution:

> ...sperma est ex homine et homo ex spermate in infinitum,
> secundum philosophos (99).

[The view of philosophers is that sperm comes from man and man from sperm to infinity.]

He even goes on later to make a comparison with the classic chicken-and-egg situation:

> ...sicut etiam qua ratione gallina ovum tempore praecedit et
> ovum gallinam, sicut vulgus arguit (100).

[... like the reason why a chicken precedes an egg in time and the egg precedes the chicken, just as the common argument goes.]

Indeed, in this critical section, we are able quite clearly to see how in this treatise it has been Siger's purpose, in the footsteps of Aristotle, to demolish on philosophical grounds those philosophy-based arguments in favour of a creation-in-time, which were, he says, attempted by some poets, theologians and natural philosophers [101]. It might well be imagined that he has in mind among his contemporaries those such as John Peckham, who declares unequivocally that there is no way in which the world could be created eternally:

Dico, igitur, quod mundus nullo modo capax fuit aeternae vel interminabilis durationis. Qui autem posuerunt mundum Deo esse coaeternum ex falso fundamento ad hoc moti sunt, vel quia sine mundo Deum credebant esse otiosum; vel quia non credebant Deum aliquid facere novum nisi voluntate affectum, et per consequens mutatum [102].

[I say, therefore, that it is in no way possible for the world to be of eternal or neverending duration. Those who have claimed that the world is coeternal with God have arrived at this conclusion from a false premise: either because they believed that without a world God would be idle, or because they believed that God only makes something new if he is so influenced in his will and consequently changed.]

In the context of potentiality and act, as delineated by Aristotle and Ibn Rushd, Siger considers it appropriate to touch briefly on the cyclical theory of the universe [103]; here too he steers an agnostic line, making it clear that even so he is not committing himself to such a view:

Haec autem dicimus opinionem Philosophi recitando, non ea asserendo tamquam vera [104].

[In repeating these, we are however stating the opinion of the Philosopher, not asserting them to be true.]

He does subsequently explain his position as being akin to that of Aristotle, who sees man in potentiality as always having existed in prime matter just as God has always existed in actuality:

> Sicut enim Deus semper est, sic et, apud Aristotelem, potentia homo, cum accipitur ut in prima materia [105].

[For just as God always exists man also, according to Aristotle, does so in potentiality, in so far as inherent in prime matter.]

It is however only in this potential sense that we can speak of man or any finite being as being eternal:

> ...dicendum est quod ens in potentia non est sempiternum nisi cum accipitur in prima materia [106].

[... it must be stated that a potential being is everlasting only in the sense that it is inherent (as a possibility) in prime matter.]

Finally, at the very end of the tract, the "Explicit" (as seen in one of the "reportationes") reasserts the purpose of the treatise as being the refutation of the claim that it is possible to show creation-in-time philosophically. He declares his position on this matter to be agnostic - unlike Aristotle! - and that the former can only be upheld by an act of faith:

> Explicit tractatus Magistri Sigeri de Brabantia super quadam ratione ab aliquibus reputata generationem hominum tangente, ex cuius generationis natura putant se demonstrasse mundum incepisse, licet neque hoc, neque eius oppositum sit demonstrabile, sed fide tenendum quod inceperit [107].

[Here ends the treatise of Master Siger of Brabant concerning a certain argument of some people regarding the generation of human beings. From the nature of this generation, they think they have demonstrated that the world came into existence, although neither this nor its contrary can be so demonstrated but it is by faith that it must be maintained that it had a beginning.]

It is worth noting that Van Steenberghen casts doubt on Bazán's upholding of the authenticity of this "Explicit", which is indeed omitted from one of the families of texts (108). This in itself would not of course be a pressing reason and it is true that it presents a position more akin to that of Thomas than the actual content itself of this little tract might fully lead one to expect. Nevertheless, we must assert that Van Steenberghen does tend to neglect the fact that Siger adopts a negatively neutral pose, especially in so far as, particularly in the second and fourth chapters, he attacks those who claim to be able to produce philosophical proof of the temporary nature of the world. Furthermore, we have seen that he consistently - no less than sixteen times - refers to the philosophical perspective of the work.

Finally, this is surely confirmed by the fact that his colleague Boethius of Dacia also, albeit with a slightly different emphasis, declares his agnostic position too as a philosopher. Creation as such does not even strictly fall into the ambit of the natural philosopher:

> Natura enim omnem suum effectum facit ex subiecto et materia, factio autem ex subiecto et materia generatio est et non creatio. Ideo naturalis creationem considerare non potest ... (109).

[For nature produces all its effects out of a subject and matter. However, production out of a subject and matter is generation and not creation. Therefore the natural philosopher is unable to study creation ...]

Nevertheless, Boethius continues, neither the mathematican nor the metaphysician can do so either (110).

However, is Dales fair to dismiss Siger's treatise as a "not particularly impressive performance"? [111]. What Dales describes as a "limited purpose" is in fact a statement of the agnostic neutral position of the philosopher and very close to that adopted by Thomas Aquinas. Indeed, it is not too dissimilar to that of a modern astronomer, faced with the variety of Big Bang, Steady State and other possible theories on the purely scientific level, who might wish to indicate that none can be simply ruled out of court on purely rational grounds at this point in time. In fact, Dales' evaluation of this work does not appear strengthened by the fact that he goes on to discuss a Commentary on the Physics which, although for quite some time in the past it had been attributed to Siger, has not been so claimed for many years now [112].

Furthermore, it is fair to say that Siger's De Aeternitate Mundi, considered in isolation, does not have the breadth nor the depth of examination of the issues as has the treatise of Boethius of Dacia with the same title. We can only speculate as to whether this is because Boethius has had considerable access to the ideas of Maimonides [113] or because Siger's aims were more specifically directed against a small group of his own contemporaries, whether within the Faculty of Arts or that of Theology. There may even be the more prosaic explanation that it was hastily produced in a relative hurry. At the same time, we should recall that one of Boethius' major arguments, indeed derived from Maimonides, to show from the inscrutability of the divine will that it is impossible to prove anything one way or the other on the philosophical level, had already been employed by Siger in his Quaestiones in Tertium de Anima [114].

Finally, it is worthy of note, in the light of what has already been said in this section about Siger's aim of trying to affirm the independence of philosophy from faith, that Dales asserts that Boethius, far from predominantly offering a survey of the arguments regarding the creation of the world, had as his main purpose "...to vindicate the freedom and independence of philosophy by showing that there was no conflict between the Christian faith and philosophy" [115].

5.13.   De Necessitate et Contingentia Causarum.

Another work of the same period, <u>De Necessitate et Contingentia Causarum</u>, can also be dated to some time approaching 1272 [116]. Siger explains that his purpose is to investigate the taxing question as to whether things happen by necessity and are predetermined or not:

> Incipit quaestio difficilis determinata a magistro SIGERO DE BRABANTIA.   Quaestio tua non immerito dubitabilis est, utrum omnia futura necessarium sit fore antequam sint, et de praesentibus et praeteritis etiam: utrum fuerit necessarium ea fore antequam fierent [117].

[The beginning of a difficult question determined by Master Siger of Brabant. Your question is quite rightly controversial as to whether, in the case of all future things, it is necessary that they will be before they are; and similarly with present and past things, whether it was necessary that they would be before they came to be.]

Siger does make the development and determination of this question very much his own.   For example, he uses the first person singular "dico" five times in less than twenty lines at the beginning [118] in the context of his explanation of what he sees as the true position of philosophy - "secundum intentionem philosophorum" [according to the intention of philosophers] [119]. Again, the process appears to be very much like that of a modern scientist who is trying to demonstrate that his theory represents the truth more closely than do those of his adversaries.

So he goes on later to declare that some of his colleagues in fact argue against what he understands to be the clear teaching of Aristotle by saying that, even those effects which occur as a result of particular intermediate causes must be necessary and predetermined, in so far as all depends on the First Cause [120]. They are, however, wrong, he goes on, because the First Cause, although nothing can stand in the way of its own effects, can nevertheless itself cause effects through the means of intermediate causes which can themselves be prevented. These are therefore contingent and not absolutely necessary:

> ...errant...quod, licet Causa Prima non sit causa impedibilis seu cui concurrat accidens impedimentum, ipsa tamen producit effectus inferiores per causas medias et non immediate; ... licet ergo Causa Prima non sit impedibilis, producit tamen effectum per causam impedibilem [121].

[... they are wrong ... because, although the first Cause is not an impedible cause, or one to which an accidental impediment can happen, it does however produce, through intermediary causes, subordinate effects which are not immediate. Therefore, although the First Cause is not impedible, it does however produce an effect through an impedible cause.]

It is therefore in the context of arguing his case against that of other thinkers that Siger indicates what he believes to be the true interpretation of Aristotelian philosophy. It will also be noted that this should be considered in conjunction with Siger's understanding of the impenetrability of the divine will and of God's underlying omnipotence and freewill, which we have already examined in his Quaestiones in Tertium de Anima [122]. Thus, this implication that God is capable of determining that things should not be predetermined fits in well with the Christian idea of human freewill.

Having examined thus the heart of Siger's thesis in this treatise and seen that he is predominantly concerned with the way in which effects depend on their causes and whether they are necessary or contingent, we are now better able to understand the context of his earlier remarks in the first section, which Van Steenberghen took to imply quite simply the eternity of the world. He does speak of the First Cause as having an automatic, immediate and necessary effect, which is also simultaneous:

> ...causa primae intelligentiae per se, immediata, necessaria, et qua posita simul et ponitur causatum eius primum [123].

[... the cause of the First Intelligence is self-explanatory, immediate, necessary; and as posited it is simultaneous with its first caused effect.]

However, granted that he is speaking of what he calls "First Intelligence", nevertheless, in so far as this is part of a survey into the nature of causality amd the actual relationship between causes and effects, he is surely saying no more here than that the first and immediate effects of the First Cause are actually at the time dependent on it as their cause. This kind of approach will not be alien to the view of the theologian who might argue that the world is actually dependent on God for its very existence. Likewise, the phrase declaring Cause and Effect to be of the same duration - "simul erunt secundum durationem" [they will be of simultaneous duration] [124] - could also be very close to the Christian idea of God's continued conservation of the universe, rather than concentrating an emphasis merely on an initial creation; duration is not, in this context, significant in terms of a timescale as such, but in the context of declaring that, wherever there is an effect, then the Cause must also be simultaneously acting upon it. This interpretation is surely confirmed by Siger's earlier comparison of how effects can occur later than causes, if there have intervened intermediate effects and causes:

Nihil enim prohibet quasdam causas praesentes esse necessarias super effectus futuros, eo quod sunt causa illorum effectuum mediante motu et per ordinem ad motum, qui posterioritatem in duratione causat [125].

[For there is nothing to prevent certain present causes from necessitating future effects. In so far as they cause those effects, they may have moved an intermediary object, so that through a relationship to this, it causes posteriority in duration.]

After all, the philosophical point which he is making and which a Christian could then adopt in the context of the dependence of the created universe on God - much as a modern theologian might build on an apparent empirical scientific discovery - is that an effect must exist at the same time as its immediate cause.

In fact, it is now beginning to be possible to discover that Siger was by now able to determine that the important question was not whether the universe has always existed but whether it depends totally upon God for its capacity to exist in actuality.   As we have seen, it was the failure of some philosophers to accept that we cannot fully understand the nature of God's will and that it is possible for him to choose to determine either that the universe should exist eternally or that it should begin to exist, which, in Siger's view, leads to error.   Siger, Boethius of Dacia and Thomas Aquinas might well agree in declaring that, as Christians, revelation and faith appear to demand the latter alternative.   Yet, Thomas argues vehemently in his own De Aeternitate Mundi against John Peckham, Bonaventure and other theologians that the former is possible for God, had he so willed.   It is the finite contingency of the world that is central, vital and must be upheld.

5.14.   De Anima Intellectiva.

The tract De Anima Intellectiva, which is generally dated to 1273-1274 [126], will of course be considered in greater depth in the next chapter.   It is, however, also relevant here in so far as it considers whether the intellective soul is eternal or temporal.

In the fifth chapter, which is central to this theme and in which the basic question is asked whether the intellective soul has always existed, Siger again makes a great point of declaring on numerous occasions that it is the teaching of Aristotle which he is expounding [127].   To some extent, of course, this reflects his stated aim in the prologue of keeping his friends happy by providing a tract according to texts of approved philosophy, rather than presenting his own personal position:

Et ideo, exposcentibus amicis, eorum desiderio pro modulo
nostrae possibilitatis satisfacere cupientes, quid circa

praedicta sentiendum sit secundum documenta philosophorum probatorum, non aliquid ex nobis asserentes, praesenti tractatu proponimus declarare [128].

[And, therefore, at the demand of friends and wishing to satisfy their desire as best as we can, we propose to declare in the present treatise what should be felt about the foresaid matters, according to the texts of proven philosophers rather than statements made on our own initiative.]

Later, Siger's natural philosophical/scientific method of approach is again expressed, as he declares how Aristotle followed natural reasoning:

Hoc etiam apparet rationibus naturalibus quas Aristoteles secutus est [129].

[This is also clear through the natural reasoning followed by Aristotle.]

In this fifth chapter, the first of the three arguments for the eternal prior existence of the soul stems from the reasoning that something will be incorruptible if there is no reason for it to cease to exist in the future. This is a point that Siger certainly had endeavoured to demonstrate in the previous chapter on the grounds that the soul is not composed of matter and form and is free of matter:

Omne corruptibile seu mortale est compositum ex materia et forma, vel est forma materialis. Anima intellectiva nec est composita ex materia et forma, nec est forma materialis, sed liberata a materia, per se subsistens. Ergo non est corruptibilis seu mortalis [130].

[Everything which is corruptible or mortal is composed of matter and form or is a material form. The intellective soul is neither composed of matter and form nor is a material form. but is freed from matter and subsists of its own accord. Therefore it is neither corruptible nor mortal.]

Here, he now goes on to argue that future incorruptibility relies philosophically on the same principles which would apply if we looked into the past and so this would inevitably demand eternal past existence:

> Quod si ex eadem causa aliquid non semper erit in futuro et non semper fuit in praeterito, quod igitur caret causa quod non semper sit in futuro, caret et causa quod non semper fuit in praeterito.   Quare, si anima intellectiva est aeterna et semper ens in futuro, fuit igitur aeterna et semper ens in praeterito (131).

[If something deriving from the same cause will not always exist in the future and has not always been in the past, this is because what lacks a cause to exist for ever in the future also lacks a cause to have been for ever in the past. Therefore it follows that, if the intellective soul is eternal and will be for ever in the future, then it has been eternal and has been for ever in the past.]

It may be significant that, in the argument in the whole of the previous chapter, no reference whatsoever is made to Aristotle or to any other writer. Could this indicate in a subtle way that Siger, whether consciously or not, is fairly convinced in his own mind of the thesis here presented, while of course being aware of the theological and religious implications of the content of this chapter? If so, this would explain his decision to stress again in this fifth chapter, just as he did in the Prologue, his more limited field as a Master of Arts.   This may be the case, though of course it may simply be that he does not believe that it is necessary to quote other sources of support for what is so obviously true.

In any case, Siger now goes on to present the second argument quite explicitly as an explanation of Aristotelian thought, in so far as it maintains that there is no more rational justification for arguing against the eternal existence of the intellective soul than against eternal change in the eternal world as a whole:

Praeterea dicit Philosophus ... quod mundum semper non fuisse et incipere nullam habet rationem. Quare enim nunc magis esse inceperit quam prius et in toto praeterito infinito? Et sicut arguit de motu et mundo, similiter argui potest de anima intellectiva ...[132].

[Besides the Philosopher says ... that there is no rational basis for the world not to have existed for ever and to have had no beginning. Why should it have begun now rather than before and through the entire infinite past? And just as he argues about movement and the world, a similar argument can be offered about the intellective soul.]

Likewise there is a third 'ad hominem' argument that Siger employs, asserting that there is no way in which we can speak of a non-material being as only existing in potentiality, rather than in actuality:

Quod si accepit illam virtutem cum esset in potentia ad eam, cum omnis virtus essendi quam praecedit potentia ad illam virtutem sit virtus existens in materia, virtus essendi animae intellectivae esset virtus essendi materialis, et sic corruptibilis [133].

[This is because if it (the intellective soul) received that property (incoruptibility) when it was in potentiality for it, then, since every property of being preceded in potentiality is a property existing in matter; consequently the property of being of the intellective soul would be a material property of being and so the latter would be corruptible.]

Nevertheless, it is very significant that Siger does go on to stress that the above does not, in Aristotle's view, imply that the intellective soul does not itself have a cause for its very necessity and eternity:

... quamquam secundum Aristotelem anima intellectiva sit aeterna in praeterito et in futuro, tamen causata est. Nihil

enim prohibet quaedam necessaria et aeterna habere causam
suae necessitatis et aeternitatis ... (134).

[... although Aristotle says that the intellective soul is eternal in the
past and in the future, it has however been caused.   This is because there is
nothing to prevent certain necessary and eternal things from having a cause of their
own necessity and eternity ...]

To this extent, it does not have independent self-explained existence
but needs the First Mover.   Siger here, like Thomas, is arguing that, on
philosophical grounds, there is no reason to pre-determine that it is impossible for
an effect to be caused from eternity.   It is like the classic example of the eternal
footprint in the dust.   Siger then goes on to offer an explanation of why we should
reject the notion that something can arise out of nothing, either in the order of time
or in the order of nature (135). Again, on this level of natural philosophy, we can
see the scientific-type process and reasoning quite clearly.

Finally, it is interesting to note that, at the very conclusion of this
chapter, he does use the first person singular apparently to declare his belief in the
eternal, but contingent, existence of the soul:

Et intelligo animam intellectivam de se semper esse ens sic:
quia in eius ratione seu definitione est semper esse, cum
careat materia.   Istud tamen semper esse, quod est de sui
ratione, non habet ex se effective, sed ab alio (136).

[And I understand the intellective soul automatically to be always a
being in this way.   It follows from its underlying principle or definition that it
always exists, since it lacks matter.   This basic property to exist always is not self-
caused but caused by another.]

Is it possible to read into this a departure from his stated procedure of
dispassionate exposition of Aristotelian thought?   As suggested earlier, it may be
that there is some subtle psychological basis for this interpretation.   Certainly,

Thomas rarely uses the first person singular [137], but he was a different personality, much more aware of his religious position in the Church. Moreover, much as he was to argue against those with whom he disagreed philosophically or theologically, he perceived the implications of his role as a priest and a churchman, differently from Siger, who was keen to assert his independence as a philosopher.

However, it may be no more significant than stamping his own personal authority as a Master of Arts on this determination of the question at the conclusion of the chapter. To some extent, this seems very likely, if we take cognizance of the fact that the above quotation again stresses the need to emphasize that the soul must have an external efficient cause. After all, as Thomas and others also stress, this is the important factor in demonstrating the relationship of created beings to the Creator. This contrasts with the viewpoint embraced by so many of their contemporary philosophers and theologians, who were sidetracked into wanting to stress the temporal nature of creation, since they were unable to see how, without affirming this, it was possible to maintain the former.

It is Siger's independence as a philosopher, whatever his religious beliefs may or may not have been, that enables him, like many later thinkers of the Enlightenment several centuries later over other issues, to affirm the importance of the causality aspect so clearly. Van Steenberghen may therefore be going a little bit too far with his somewhat snide remark that Siger seems to be expressing his personal convictions over all this [138]. Does he expect Siger to continue here to provide even more references to Aristotle than he has done already? Siger's procedure of offering a philosophical exposition has been very lucidly presented. No doubt, he is making one or two personal points as a philosopher against the perceived logical errors of others, as one would expect of someone brought up in the adversarial system of the disputations of the Faculty of Arts. We would expect no less today from a scholar, whether an atheist or a religious believer.

After all, in an earlier chapter, where he has referred to other philosophers and to theologians, such as Albert and Thomas, he has asserted quite bluntly that his perspective was that of natural reason and of philosophy and that he is prescinding from issues of revelation and of divine miracles:

> Quaerimus enim hic solum intentionem philosophorum et praecipue Aristotelis, etsi forte Philosophus senserit aliter quam veritas se habeat et sapientia, quae per revelationem de anima sint tradita, quae per rationes naturales concludi non possunt. Sed nihil ad nos nunc de Dei miraculis, cum de naturalibus naturaliter disseramus [139].

[For here we seek only what the philosophers, and especially Aristotle, mean. However, the Philosopher may have felt differently from what constitutes the truth and wisdom, which have been handed down about the soul through revelation but could not have been concluded through natural reasoning. Nevertheless, divine miracles are not our present concern, since we are discussing natural matters on a natural level.]

There is no reason to take Siger at less than his word here or anywhere else in the tract, than he asks us to do in the Prologue above [140] and we have little evidence to go on to enable us to speculate about Siger's own personal beliefs. On the other hand, he has also shown that he has little brief for woolly and unsubstantiated claims to be able to prove philosophically what he believes cannot be so proved.

5.15.   Quaestiones in Metaphysicam.

Another of our later sources for Sigerian thinking is found in the various versions of the Quaestiones in Metaphysicam. Although this work is not of course in any sense directly concerned with the topic under consideration in this chapter, there are certain underlying assumptions about the nature of his views at this time, which can be gleaned from it, as Dales, for example, briefly implies [141]. In the latter's case, however, it is very unfortunate that he is still using the texts produced by Graiff, although these have been superseded by those of Dunphy (1981) and Maurer (1983) for a number of years now.

There are, in particular, a significant "Commentum" and "Quaestio" in Book III (Munich Version), the former of which is then found presented as a separate question in the Cambridge version [142], already identified as being of particular potential importance by Duin [143]. Here, in the midst of his explanation of how Aristotle, on his own level of philosophical investigation, was able to deny that being could come from non-being and yet might well be wrong, Siger is found denying that this would give us any justification for concealing or denying the former teaching:

> ...sic autem velare philosophiam non est bonum: unde non est
> hic intentio Aristotelis celanda, licet sit contraria veritati [144].

[To cover up philosophy in this kind of way is not good. Therefore, what Aristotle meant must not be hidden here, although it may be contrary to the truth.]

Indeed, Siger warns, while we must be careful to rely on reason rather than mere opinion, nevertheless there are some beliefs for which reason is not enough and which need the prophets to enlighten us:

> ...aliis credimus quod magis fuerint ex prophetis, et non
> secundum viam rationis. Item, quidam credunt magis suis
> opinionibus quam rationibus, ista autem non debent ducere in
> errorem [145].

[... we believe in other things which have come from prophecy rather than by reasoning. Likewise, some believe more in their own opinions rather than solid reasons. However, they must not be sources of error.]

In the subsequent question, which is concerned with differences between corruptible and incorruptible beings, Siger explains how, according to

178

Aristotelian metaphysics, species must be perpetual and everlasting. What is very interesting again is, however, his final sentence in which he appears to reflect wistfully on the dilemmas of conflict between faith and reason and how true knowledge and intellectual satisfaction can only be achieved, once there is no doubt left:

> Unde, licet oppositum huius per fidem teneatur, quamquam non possit per demonstrationes probari, et quamquam rationes Aristotelis possint impediri, non tamen videtur quod possit ad plenum satisfieri intellectui humano; unde dicit Aristoteles quod cognitio veritatis est solutio dubitatorum: unde, quod aliquis cognoscat veritatem et nesciat solvere rationes in oppositum, non videtur [146].

[Hence, despite the fact that the opposite of this may be held through faith although it cannot be demonstrated conclusively, and although the reasoning of Aristotle can be challenged, it does not however seem able to satisfy fully the human intellect. That is why Aristotle speaks of knowledge of the truth as dissolution of doubts. Therefore,it does not seem that someone could know the truth and not know how to defeat opposing reasons.]

We can only speculate as to what Siger himself really thought and believed, but a greater defence of the value of the pursuit of knowledge for its own sake would be hard to find. The fact that these words are not found in the Cambridge version may indicate that they reflect spontaneous comments made at the end of his lecture or in response to a question in the particular year that his teaching gave rise to the Munich version.

In the Cambridge version, the last two quotations seem to have been coalesced at the end of the previous question, in the context of the eternity of non-material beings, along with a much clearer expression by Siger that it is his personal belief that there may well be circumstances in which it may be impossible to argue convincingly and rationally against some positions, although faith may indicate the opposite:

Et credo quod, sicut ea quae fidei sunt per rationem humanam probari non possunt, ita sunt aliquae rationes humanae ad opposita eorum, quae per humanam rationem dissolvi non possunt. Propter hoc tamen in his quae fidei sunt non est errandum; sed est alia via credendi ea quam per rationem humanam, ut dictum est. Propter etiam ea quae fidei sunt non est velanda intentio Philosophi, sicut quidam voluerunt, dicentes Philosophum non intendere mundum simpliciter esse aeternum et alia huiusmodi. Via enim credendi intentionem Philosophi est ratio humana, et alia est via ad credendum quae sunt fidei, ut dictum est [147].

[And I believe that, just as matters of faith cannot be proved through human reasoning, so there are some human reasons for opposing the above, which cannot be dispelled through human reasoning. That is not a reason for being wrong about matters of faith. There is a different way of believing those things known through human reason, as has been stated. Even for matters of faith, the meaning of the Philosopher should not be concealed, as some have wanted when they have said that the Philosopher did not mean that the world is in all respects eternal and such like. The way of believing what the Philosopher meant is human reasoning which is different from the way of believing matters of faith, as has be stated.]

While Siger insists that it is wrong to misinterpret Aristotle's teaching, nevertheless it is very clear that he is declaring that the validity of the distinction between reason and faith involves not the single content of truth, but the way or process of arriving at the truth. This is critical for understanding why he is not guilty of holding the "double-truth" theory as presented by his adversaries. Moreover, we may well understand how important it must have seemed to Siger and Boethius to defend this procedure and practice in the interests of free speech, when faced with opposition from within both the Faculty of Arts and the Faculty of Theology, where of course they also found an ally in Thomas Aquinas.

There is one other interesting question for us (included in the Munich version but omitted from the Cambridge version) that investigates whether something incorruptible can be the immediate principle of anything corruptible. This is a particularly relevant topic to our present investigation because Siger refers back to the earlier Quaestio 16, where, he reminds us, it was stated that to say that the First Being could eternally will an effect to begin without any intermediary involved a contradiction in terms:

> Dicebatur prius ... quod, si dicatur quod Primum voluit ab aeterno quod effectus suus inciperet et quod immediate ab eo recipiat esse, ista non stant simul, sed contradictoria implicantur: unde velle hoc, est velle impossibile et ideo hoc esse est esse impossibile [148].

[It was stated above ... that, if it be said that the First Being willed from eternity that its effect should have a beginning and that it should immediately receive existence from it, these two factors are not compatible but a contradiction is implied. Thus, to will this is to will the impossible and therefore this is impossible to exist.]

On the level of human reason alone, continues Siger, there is strong, but not overwhelmingly conclusive evidence to support this:

> ... dico quod propositio probabilis est tantum, non necessaria [149].

[... I say that the proposition is only probable, not necessary.]

The difficulty lies in our inducting a universal principle from only a limited number of examples from within our empirical sense-experience, and then re-applying it incorrectly:

> Quando accipitur universale aliquod attendo ad plura particularia et non ad omnia, illud universale est verum pro

pluribus et non pro omnibus: unde si etiam accipiatur pro aliquibus quae non sunt eiusdem rationis cum particularibus ad quae attendit, propositio probabilis est [150].

[When some universal is accepted by relating to a large number of particulars but not to all, that universal is true for the large number but not for all. Therefore, if it were accepted also for some which are not of the same category as the particulars to which it relates, the proposition is probable.]

Likewise, it is easy, he warns those who disagree, to ignore the fact that the First Cause acts on a different and higher level than we usually operate:

Cum ergo tu dicis: si causa est ab aeterno unde debet esse effectus, tunc effectus erit ab aeterno, tu consideras ad ista inferiora et non respicis ad Primum, quod est alterius rationis. Sic ergo potest aliquis errare, et sic propositio assumpta probabilis est et non necessaria [151].

[When therefore you state: a cause which is from eternity must produce an effect which is from eternity, you are considering those lower things and you are not looking at the First Being, which is of a different level. It is thus possible for someone to err, so that the assumed proposition is probable and not necessary.]

5.16.   Quaestiones super Librum de Causis.

We need now to turn to Siger's final extant work to discover any late indications of his views on the topic under consideration in this chapter. Early in the Quaestiones super Librum de Causis, we have a reminder that Aristotle not only considered it possible for each individual human being to have an infinite number of ancestors but that it was indeed essential:

... sic accidit ut Socrates generetur ex infinitis hominibus praecedentibus; et non secundum Aristotelem est hoc possibile, sed necessarium (152).

[... so it comes about that Socrates is generated from an infinite number of previous human beings. Indeed, it is Aristotle's view that this is not merely possible but that it is necessary.]

He then goes on to begin an examination of the nature of eternity. Using Aristotle's definition of time as 'the measurement of change according to before and after' - "numerus motus secundum prius et posterius" (153) - he declares the essence of eternity to lie in the apprehension of that uniformity which is utterly and totally incapable of change:

Et consistit ratio aeternitatis in apprehensione uniformitatis se habendi eius quod est extra motum et omnino immutabile (154).

[And the principle of eternity lies in the apprehension of a uniformity within itself which is external to change and completely immutable.]

This itself, he explains in the next Quaestio, is caused by the unchangeability and eternity of the First Being:

Aeternitas consequitur immutabilitatem, et sicut immutabilitas quaedam est causata et participata a primo immutabili, ita est aeternitas quaedam causata a primo aeterno (155).

[Eternity follows from immutability and, just as a certain immutability is caused and participated in by the first immutable being, so is a certain eternity caused by the first eternal being.]

Subsequently, Siger is now able, he feels, to demonstrate that, when we speak about eternity in this sense regarding the First Being, then this has a completely different meaning from that eternity which those supporters of the eternity of time have in mind:

> ... aeternitas differt a tempore in hoc quod tota simul est aeternitas, tempus autem non, ita quod etiam secundum ponentes tempus esse aeternum, sine principio, sine fine, nihilominus tamen praedicta differentia differt tempus ab aeternitate [156].

[... eternity differs from time in the respect that eternity is at the same time complete whereas time is not. It follows that, even for those who posit that time is eternal and has no beginning nor end, nevertheless there is the forementioned difference between time and eternity.]

The difference is that eternity is present with no potentiality, whereas time would imply continuity or perpetuity with both actuality and potentiality:

> Aeternitas enim, cum sit tota simul, nec finem habet nec principium in potentia; tempus autem continuum cum priori et posteriori semper existens, finem et principium habet in potentia ... [157].

[This is because eternity, since it is at the same time complete, has neither an end nor a beginning in potentiality. Continuous time, on the other hand, while always existing with a before and an after, has an end and a beginning in potentiality.]

Time and eternity, indeed, are not on the same dimension and therefore there is no problem about their simultaneous co-existence:

> Diversae tamen mensurae durationis quae non sunt eiusdem rationis et generis et naturae, sicut sint tempus et aeternitas, nihil prohibet simul esse [158].

[There is nothing to prevent different measures of duration, which are not of the same level, genus and nature, as is the case with time and eternity, from existing at the same time.]

However, because any simultaneous link between the two is not on the same level, we can only understand the relationship by looking at the differences:

Nec est intelligenda ista simultas quasi sint una mensura mensurata tempore vel aeternitate, sed est intelligenda ista simultas secundum negationem, quia unum eorum non habet esse prius et posterius, reliquum autem habet [159].

[That simultaneity should not be understood as a single measure for measuring time or eternity but rather as implying a positive difference, because one of them does not possess existence before and afterwards while the alternative does.]

We can see the agreement here with the same basic assumptions of a writer such as Robert Grosseteste, when he first drew attention to the possible problems for Christian belief of Aristotle's clear teaching. This was in spite of attempts by some to argue for the contrary lest Aristotle's prestige take a battering. However, we also see very clearly how he proceeds to conclusions, diametrically opposed to those of Siger:

Cum igitur Deus sit eternus, mundus quoque et motus et tempus sint temporales, tempus vero et eternitas non sint eiusdem generis mensure... Deus autem eternus causa est mundi temporalis et temporis, nec praecedit ista tempore sed simplici eternitate [160].

[Since therefore God is eternal but the world, change and time are temporal, time and eternity are indeed not of the same genus of measurement... Everlasting God is however the cause of the temporal world and of time and does not precede the above in time but by simple eternity.]

Siger goes on to draw an analogy between the unity and diversity of time and that of the three dimensions of space, in so far as both involve change and changeability:

> Haec autem unitas secundum esse mobilis non manet sed variatur continue sicut mobile unum esse non tenet in spatio sed continue variatur [161].

[This mobile unity regarding existence does not last but is subject to continuous variation in the same way as one mobile object does not maintain existence in its space but is subject to continuous variation.]

On turning to look at what were known as Intelligences, Siger explains how Aristotle felt that they were directly created by God, albeit from eternity:

> Et supposita aeternitate intelligentiae, debet intelligi sic ipsam esse causatam et factam, non quod a prima causa procederet aliqua factio quae esset transmutatio ad esse eius, sed quod esse intelligentiae ab aeterno invenitur a causa prima ... [162].

[And if we were to suppose the eternity of an Intelligence, it must be understood that the latter is caused and made like that. This is not because some manufacture has proceeded from the First Cause which would involve a transmutation to its existence, but because the existence of an Intelligence is found eternally from the First Cause.]

Aristotle, Siger continues, could do no other than maintain this view, upholding the eternity of movement in the heavens:

> Haec opinio fuit apud Aristotelem valde necessaria, ita quod pro constante habuit motum caelestem esse sempiternum, continuum et unum [163].

[This opinion was, according to Aristotle, highly necessary so that he considered it to be a constant that the movement of the heavens is everlasting, continuous and single.]

He had apparently considered the possibility of an eternal will producing a non-eternal Intelligence, but had rejected it as lacking full logical coherence:

> ... cum voluerit primum ab aeterno quod intelligentia esse inciperet, oportet ab hac voluntate aeterna non aeternam produci intelligentiam. Et hanc solutionem vidit Aristoteles ..., nec sibi fuit ad plenum satisfactum [164].

[... when the First Being willed from eternity that an Intelligence should begin to be, it follows that a non-eternal Intelligence would not be produced by an eternal will. Besides, Aristotle saw this response ... and it did not fully satisfy him.]

Despite all this, Siger nevertheless declares that philosophy must take second place to the authority of the Christian faith on this question, although there is no proof for the latter:

> ... (quia) auctoritas fidei christianae maior (est) omni ratione humana et etiam philosophorum auctoritate, dicamus intelligentiam non esse in aeternitate, licet ad hoc demonstrationem non habeamus [165].

[... because the authority of the Christian faith is greater than all human reason and even than the authority of philosophers, let us state that an Intelligence does not exist in eternity, although we do not possess a demonstration for this.]

Yet again we see the parallel with the problems that may be faced by a Christian scientist of today as Siger concludes here, close to what turns out to be the end of his teaching career, that there is a need for an unquestioning and loyal Christian faith:

> Rationi autem illi quae innititur auctoritate fidei christanae firmiter et pie sine ampliore inquisitione credendum est [(166)].

[Faith without any further investigation should uphold that reasoning which relies firmly and loyally on the authority of the Christian faith.]

5.17.   A Summary of Siger's Thought on the Eternity of the World.

Now that we have examined Siger's extant works in some detail regarding the eternity or otherwise of creation, we may quite reasonably ask if there is any evidence in this respect of the "double-truth" accusation. Furthermore, it would now be appropriate to recall the relevant condemnations of 1270 once more to see if they refer to his early works, before turning to the much more all-embracing ones of 1277.

We have already seen (Section 5.8) that Van Steenberghen is probably wrong in stating that, at the very early stage of writings such as Quaestio utrum haec sit vera: Homo est Animal, Nullo Homine Existente, Siger is himself accepting Aristotle uncritically.   As a young Master, not yet fully established in reputation, he would in his first years have seen it as his task to expound Aristotle's teaching as authentically and as well as he could, just as a young scientist at a university today might do the same for theories of quantum physics, the Big Bang or whatever, regardless of his own religious beliefs. There is a world of difference between an approach such as this and a blind following of Aristotle.   Moreover, it was at that time, far more than would be contemplated today, the academic reputation of individual writers or commentators that provided the major motivation for acceptance of particular viewpoints.   Even in the Faculty of Theology, the Sentences of Peter Lombard had become in a similar way the paramount text for interpreting the Scriptures.

We must again recall that, in the actual historical context of the time, the Faculty of Arts had not long been authorized to teach all of Aristotle's works and that both the ecclesiastical authorities and the Faculty of Theology had for some time harboured more than a few reservations about this. So it would be more likely to be in the context of a maturing professional self-confidence and probably also of greater wisdom and tact in the increasingly dangerous intellectual climate that we can speak of an apparent evolution in Siger's thought on this matter. This seems a far more likely scenario than Van Steenberghen's more stark assumptions of an actual evolution in his thought and teaching from heresy to a new and eventual acceptance of Christian orthodoxy.

Then, we can note that Augustine really did seem to have doubted whether a creation from eternity was even possible and he claimed that the idea of a created, but eternal, universe is scarcely intelligible [167]. However, the contemporary Augustinian theologians, following the Sentences of Peter Lombard and the Declarations of the Fourth Lateran Council (Sections 5.2 and 5.4) against the Albigensians and the Cathars, were seeking to oppose not only eternal creation but also to claim that there could be no possible logical support for it at all.

That this was the actual situation seems to be confirmed by Siger's affirmation in his Quaestiones in Tertium de Anima (Section 5.9) that he considers that, intellectually, the Aristotelian arguments seem to hold water better than the Augustinian ones. When we recall that most of the theology taught at this time was in the Augustinian tradition, we can again see that Siger is unwilling to allow Bonaventure, Peckham or other theologians to claim without challenge that the temporal nature of creation could be proved logically. Siger certainly is not suggesting any kind of "double-truth" doctrine here, for he asserts quite positively that the key issue here is the impenetrability of God's will, which cannot be known on the level of natural philosophy, but only by faith. That is why, according to Aristotle, only a trigger of some sort can cause a change to occur [168], which of course would not be possible, he says, in a changeless God. Thomas Aquinas had already indicated that any mover who possesses a will, as distinct from any other agent that does not, is quite capable not only of deciding to do something, but also of postponing its actual implementation to some other determined time:

... nisi praecedat aliqua immutatio vel in natura moventis vel in mobili, non incipiet a movente naturali esse motus, qui non fuit prius.   Voluntas autem absque sui immutatione retardat facere quod proponit: sed hoc non est nisi per aliquam immutationem quam immaginatur, ad minus ex parte temporis (169).

[... unless it is preceded by some absence of change either in the nature of the mover or in the movable object, motion will not begin to be from a natural mover, which did not exist previously.   The will however needs internal change if it is to implement what it proposes, but this is only by means of appearing to be unchanging, at least from the perspective of time.]

In the authentic Quaestiones in Physicam, Siger does not attempt to deny that Aristotle asserted that eternal causes would have eternal effects because of the necessary link between the two.   However, he now declares that there is an essential difference between transmutation, as it would normally occur in the natural world, and actual creation.   This leads to the fundamental distinction between seeking the source of origin of an object and asking whether it has an actual beginning in time.   This illustrates Siger's perception that the critical issue - which was not comprehended by Peckham and some other opponents (170) - is in fact not of when creation did or did not take place [post nihilum] but the actual nature of creaturehood and the contingency implied in this, regardless of time or change [ex nihilo].

While there is then no evidence to support Van Steenberghen's assertion that Siger baldly taught the eternity of the world as a fact prior to 1270, we do see him, however, being much more cautious following Tempier's decree. For example, he offers more frequent disclaimers, as in Impossibilia, about his exposition of Aristotle arising from his stance as a philosopher, at the same time of course implicitly declaring his support for the independence of the teaching in the Faculty of Arts.

In <u>De Aeternitate Mundi</u>, he attempts on the other hand to refute those philosophers who choose to support creation-in-time on rational grounds, while in <u>De Necessitate et Contingentia Causarum</u> he returns to the theme of contingency as being the main issue. In <u>De Anima Intellectiva</u>, he looks at the issue of creation of immaterial beings, which, briefly touched upon in <u>Impossibilia</u>, he declares to be no different from material beings in needing an external efficient cause. This, he argues, is not affected by Aristotle's demand, on the grounds of the principle of like-cause and like-effect, that the universe must be eternal. Here, then, we see the development of the notion of co-eternity, where contingency is maintained between effect and First Cause.

This kind of approach is further developed in the <u>Quaestiones in Metaphysicam</u> where, although this difference between corruptible and non-corruptible beings is accepted, he defends as a philosopher the Aristotelian approach regarding the impossibility of being coming out of previous non-being. However, he offers the very clear statement that this is at the lower level of understanding and that faith does and must transcend reason. In his final work, the <u>Quaestiones super Librum de Causis</u>, we saw how he further analysed the implications of Aristotelian philosophy regarding the difference between the nature of the eternity of the Pure Act of the First Being and that of the created world with its actuality and potentiality as a result of change. Yet again, however, we came across here the strong reminder that the teachings of the Christian faith should take precedence.

How genuine were these caveats of Siger? Ultimately, of course, we have no way of being sure. It is of course a misconception to imagine that everyone in the medieval world was a committed believer and so we could interpret some of his references regarding the priority of the Christian faith to an act of intellectual, and perhaps physical, self-preservation! However, in any event, we have seen a continuous thread running through his writings on this topic, whereby he stresses the independence of the process of philosophical investigation, regardless of the apparent dictates of faith. This is, of course, poles apart from an assertion of the so-called "double-truth", as presented by Tempier and others.

Just as Thomas Aquinas [171] was perhaps arguing primarily against those traditionalist churchmen who felt that it would be a contradiction for God to have been able, even hypothetically, to create an eternal finite universe, so Siger and Boethius were arguing against colleagues within the Faculty of Arts who claimed the opposite could be proved and encouraging others to support the fight against a takeover of the autonomous research and teaching undertaken in that faculty by the Faculty of Theology and the ecclesiastical authorities.   So, for example, Siger's philosophical argument about the impenetrability of God's will in the Quaestiones in Tertium de Anima, can be seen around the same time in theological form based on scripture in Thomas' Quaestiones Quodlibetales of 1270 [172].   Likewise, Thomas' De Aeternitate Mundi, unlike those of Siger and Boethius from the Faculty of Arts although they bear the same title, is a predominantly theological work [173].   It is not in the usual "quaestio" form but is clearly written with the intention of settling the dispute authoritatively.

It therefore appears inaccurate to hold, as earlier writers such as Van Steenberghen have done [174], that there were three groups of thinkers - those conservative theologians and their philosopher-colleagues who held that the temporal creation was both demonstrable as well as true;   those "Radical Aristotelians", like Siger and Boethius, who denied both of the above;   and those, like Thomas, who believed it on the witness of faith but denied that it could be shown rationally.   It has been shown that it is unlikely that Siger really adhered to the position of Aristotle as such but his aim, as we have seen, was to defend the independence of philosophy.   His position, and perhaps that of Boethius, may really be much closer to that of Thomas himself and, whatever might or might not have been discussed informally and off-the-record in the academic equivalent of the Senior Common Room in Paris, there was not a separate group of Radical Aristotelians as such who stood in open opposition to the faith of the Church as such over this particular issue [175].

Indeed, if Wippel is correct in believing that it was not until his De Aeternitate Mundi contra Murmurantes (to give it its full title) [176] that Thomas was willing to assert explicitly the possibility of an eternally created world [177], we might also be inclined to feel that he and Siger, though coming from opposite backgrounds and directions towards one another, could well have been mutual influences on each other and that their aims in this crusade against the Augustinian theologians and their supporters in Philosophy may well have been a common one with some interchange of suitable points of view.   Furthermore, it would have been the bad feeling following the events of 1270 that would have prompted this reaction from them both.   Despite Siger's relative youth and inexperience when compared to Thomas' seniority and stature, this hypothesis would fit in well with Dante's remarks in Paradiso X 133-138 (see Section 2.1) where he has fulsome praise for Siger from the lips of Thomas.   Hence, Thomas and Siger alike would have agreed in their respective settings that this particular dogma offers no genuine embarrassment to philosophical reflection.   The theoretical possibility of creation from eternity and the possibility of solving the problem by reason alone remain legitimate objects of philosophical enquiry.   Likewise, we might argue today for the same independence of scientific enquiry.

Siger does employ a wide range of arguments - many of which find echoes in Davidson's careful schematization of his Jewish and particularly Islamic predecessors dividing this question into arguments either from the nature of the world or from the nature of God [178].   Truth to tell, however, it is probably fairer in the actual historical context of the thirteenth century to divide them into three categories.   These would contain, firstly, the arguments from the natural world; secondly, those from the eternal cosmological world of the Intelligences and so on with its "aevum" rather than time;   and, finally, those from the metaphysical perspective of the nature of the First Mover, of causality and of the unchangeability of God.

However, when we actually examine the strength of Siger's arguments as such, we need to acknowledge that, not only are they not original and can also be found in earlier writers, but also that they are not necessarily presented in the most powerful way that they might have been.   Siger, of course, was clearly recognized as an outstanding Master of Arts among his contemporaries but it is his stance in defence of the philosophical independence and of the intellectual and professional integrity of the Faculty that is of such great significance for us.   Since the Fourth Lateran Council and Peter Lombard's teaching on this topic declare it to be a matter of faith, the temptation must have been very great for many theologians to try to take over and insist on philosophical support as well.

His position has thus become very close to that of his colleague Boethius of Dacia, who arguably clarifies the position of the independent-minded philosophers even more succinctly than Siger:

> Dicimus autem quod mundus non est aeternus, sed de novo creatus, quamvis hoc per rationes demonstrari non possit... Si enim demonstrari possent, non esset fides sed scientia [179].

[We state however that the world is not eternal, but created anew, although this cannot be rationally demonstrated ... For if it could be demonstrated, it would not be faith but science.]

Likewise, it may well be that it is a combination of Van Steenberghen's strong personal religious commitment to the need to affirm the temporal creation of the universe, allied to his general neo-Thomist sympathies - though of course he is critical of Thomas over this question [180] - that explains his failure to appreciate the closeness of the positions here of Thomas, Siger and Boethius.

5.18.   Siger and the 1277 Decree.

Having examined in some detail Siger's teaching on the question of eternity, it is appropriate to look briefly at the relevant articles in the 1277 decree [181] to see how justly they can be levelled against him in particular. They are of course much more far-reaching than those two of 1270 referring to the eternity of the world as such and that of the human race [182]. This brief investigation, since this topic was one of those at the heart of the controversy, will also act as a good exemplar for examining the nature and validity of the whole process of such condemnations at this time.

Article 80 - "Quod ratio philosophi demonstrans motum caeli esse aeternum non est sophistica; et mirum quod homines profundi hoc non vident" [That philosophical reasoning demonstrating the movement of the heavens to be eternal is not a sophism; and it is astonishing that thinking people do not see this] - does not seem to be upheld anywhere by Siger. Certainly, he discusses this aspect of Aristotelian teaching on a number of occasions, but, even in his relatively early Quaestiones in Tertium De Anima, he stresses that he does so in order to compare the relative strengths of the respective Augustinian and Aristotelian arguments [183]. He discusses it as being part of Aristotle's teaching in the Quaestiones super Librum de Causis but nowhere does he express wonder at those who do not uphold it, though of course this could have been the impression that some opponents may have gained with Thomas Aquinas and Boethius of Dacia offering similar comments. Certainly, we have already noted the latter's comments that those who held that the temporal creation of the world by God could be proved were close to needing their brains examining [184]. Could this article be a riposte to that?

Article 83 does find an echo in the Quaestiones in Physicam and in De Necessitate et Contingentia Causarum, where Siger, as we have seen above, does declare contingency to be the vital issue. However, it is clear, as he indicates in his Quaestiones super Librum de Causis where he emphasizes the difference between Pure Act and Potentiality in creatures, that the Christian faith should take precedence [185]. It is quite possible that some young students may have been causing problems by omitting this reservation in their informal conversations, whether in the University, in their lodgings or in taverns.

Articles 84 and 87, which both refer to the claim that eternity in the future must also demand the existence of eternity in the past, find an Aristotelian echo in Siger's second quaestio in his Quaestiones in Tertium De Anima - "Omne enim habens virtutem per quam potest esse in toto futuro, habuit virtutem per quam potuit esse in toto praeterito" [Every being which has the power to exist through the entire future, has the power through which it has been able to exist for the entire past] [186] -, in De Anima Intellectiva - "(Aristoteles) vult ... quod omne aeternum in futuro, est aeternum in praeterito, et e converso" [Aristotle requires that everything which is eternal in the future is also eternal in the past and vice versa] [187] - and in the Quaestiones in Metaphysicam - "Aristoteles ... ostendit quod, si aeternus est in futuro, quod in praeterito" [Aristotle shows that, if it is eternal in the future, then it is eternal in the past] [188]. However, as Hissette (189) points out, in the first instance as we have already seen, the context is a comparison with the evidence for the Augustinian case; in the second instance he immediately makes it clear that Aristotle is only following natural reasoning [190] and in the third case we were warned that he was explaining the teaching of Aristotle even if it were opposed to the truth [191].

Article 85, with its general all-embracing statement on the eternity of the world, has already been very carefully dealt with and we have seen there is no evidence that Siger even openly claimed to believe in it himself and indeed could appear to believe quite the opposite.

Article 88 seems somewhat obscure and may reflect some misunderstanding of what philosophers may have actually been saying. Its references are more applicable to texts of Aristotle and Ibn Rushd than Siger and Boethius, though Hissette has discovered echoes in an anonymous text [192]. However, texts such as De Aeternitate Mundi when discussing the notion of time may have been the catalysts for the theologians to issue this condemnation, though again Siger is stressing that the teaching is that of Aristotle rather than of himself (193).

Article 89 may well refer to Siger's comment in his Quaestiones in Metaphysicam that Aristotle would believe it to be a contradiction in terms to declare that God as First Cause could desire something to begin, without the use of an intermediate cause, rather than cause an eternal effect:

> Dico quod Aristoteles diceret quo implicarentur contradictoria, quia velle quod incipiat et etiam quod immediate a Causa Prima, hoc est velle opposita: unde enim aliquid ponitur incipere, requirit causam novam; unde autem a Causa Prima immediate, aeternum ponitur [194].

[I state that Aristotle would declare that it would imply contradictions, because to will it to have a beginning and also that it derive immediately from the First Cause is to will opposites. Therefore, for something to be posited to have a beginning requires a new cause, while for it to derive immediately from the First Cause, is for it to be posited eternal.]

Nevertheless, we recall that at the conclusion of the Quaestio he refers to faith as requiring the opposite of this, even though it cannot be proved and Aristotle's arguments may be hard to counter [195]. There is no suggestion that he in any way agrees personally with Aristotle. The problem was that even to discuss such matters seemed in some circles to represent a possible threat in the theological climate of the day.

Article 90 declares the eternity of matter in the universe. We will recall that in the Quaestiones in Physicam Siger stressed the difference between transmutation, which is referred to here, and creation [196].

Article 39 refers to the co-eternalism of non-material beings, such as the Intelligences and the intellective soul, with God. This is a thesis familiar to Siger which we have already come across in several of his works, such as De Anima Intellectiva - "Ipse (Aristoteles) enim dicit animam intellectivam separari ab aliis virtutibus animae corporeis sicut perpetuum a corruptibili" [For Aristotle states the intellective soul to be separated from other corporeal powers just as something perpetual from something corruptible] [197] - and in Quaestiones super Librum de Causis, where we have seen him refer to its Aristotelian pedigree and to its conflict with Christian faith [198].

Article 138 has the clear intention of referring to the alleged eternal generation of the human species. There were clear references to this in Quaestio utrum haec sit vera: Homo est Animal, Nullo Homine Existente [199]. In this very early work, Siger does not see a need for any cautionary statement about the context of his Aristotelian teaching in the Faculty of Arts, whereas in those works that are subsequent to 1270, such as <u>De Aeternitate Mundi</u> [200] he does so clarify his teaching position.

In summary, therefore, there does seem evidence to confirm the preamble to this syllabus of 219 theses, declaring them to be directed against Siger and Boethius, that the Theological Commission appointed by Stephen Tempier did indeed have Siger in mind over this particular issue.   However, there is no real evidence that they were seriously taught as something to be accepted and believed, rather than representing the professional presentation of the teaching of Aristotle, Ibn Rushd and others.   Indeed, once they were warned by the 1270 decree of the danger, Siger and Boethius were much more cautious in the way they circumscribed their teaching, showing open respect for Christian doctrines and authority.   Whether young and immature students neglected this or not, we do not know.   However, even a cursory examination of this Condemnation provides clear evidence from the sometimes very inaccurate and clumsy wording within the individual Articles, along with its lack of organization of order, that the whole Syllabus was very hastily and carelessly drawn up.

There is likewise no evidence to suggest that, in this matter, Siger was either explicitly or implicitly guilty of "double-truth", despite the accusations levelled against the Masters of Arts by Tempier, referred to at the very beginning of this chapter and worth repeating here:

> Dicunt enim ea esse vera secundum philosophiam, sed non secundum fidem catholicam, quasi sint duae contrariae veritates, et quasi contra veritatem sacrae scripturae sit veritas in dictis gentilium damnatorum [201].

[Thus they state things to be true according to philosophy, but not according to the Catholic faith, as if there are two contrary truths and as if there is a truth in the sayings of pagans in hell that is opposed to the truth of sacred scripture.]

Furthermore, on this particular issue, the teaching of Siger and Boethius was not far from that of Thomas Aquinas, whose teaching on other topics is condemned in a number of the other Articles. Hence, in the historical context, we must also take into consideration not only a struggle for and against the academic independence in the Faculty of Arts, but also the struggle to impose a particular neo-Augustinian theological movement on everyone.

5.19.   Medieval and Modern Concepts and Theories of the Beginning of the Universe

The medieval concept, based on the Ptolemaic system of three-dimensional space, with a flat earth at the centre surrounded by a number of spheres, is very familiar and was, taken for granted by Siger and his contemporaries. Likewise, until the fourteenth century, the only reliable way to tell the time was by means of a sundial (though, of course, observation of the phases of the moon also had important significance for many cultures, especially outside Europe), for the only mechanical means was the relatively unreliable use of water-clocks. Although time was defined by philosophers as the measurement of change, it does seem that they were not aware of the full significance and implications of this.

The uniformity of the movement of the heavenly bodies (stars, planets, etc.) was seen as not being total, following observation in subsequent centuries and, despite attempts to explain anomalies by the theory of epicycles, it was gradually found that this could not be an adequate explanation. The mechanism of the measurement of time in a linear way - unlike the cyclical theories of some Ancient and Eastern concepts of time - was in sharp contrast with all this.

Under the Copernican system, the movement of the heavenly bodies was, on the other hand, seen to be totally uniform. This, of course, led to the period of mechanistic scientific world-views of the Renaissance, which, for so many reasons, was for centuries often perceived to be a threat to religion and to theology. Hence, this scientific approach came to be held up as a contrast to what was often described as a mythical approach.

More recently, in this century, we have learned of the relativity of time, how one event can be seen by one observer to precede another but that the two events can appear to be chronologically reversed by another observer elsewhere in the universe. So, we even see the light from stars reaching us here on earth, which mathematical and astronomical calculations tell us come from those stars which a closer observer would know no longer to exist. Our new scientific cosmology has therefore left the realm of absolute certainties, though, for all practical and most scientific purposes, we still assume that time is simply and in all respects uniform and linear, that light travels in straight lines, that the laws of observation of the natural world are absolute and even, more often than not, that the world is flat!

It can therefore be seen that we have passed from the radical realism, with regard to the absolute, independent nature of time, of Copernicus and Newton, through the radical idealism of Kant, for whom time is merely a subjective category and not an empirical notion, to the moderate realism of today, which is in many ways closer to that of Aristotle, Thomas Aquinas and Siger [202].

At the same time, this discovery that knowledge of the universe is dependent on the observer's position and time in the development of the expanding universe also throws up a number of other interesting observations. As Bergmann points out, it is possible for two particles, a finite distance apart from each other, to travel on perfectly reasonable trajectories, yet be incapable of interacting with or being known to each other in any way [203].

Most scientists seem to find that the Big Bang theory, by which the universe is developing with more distant galaxies moving away from each other at proportionately greater speeds than less distant ones, represents a more useful, and perhaps more accurate, model than the Steady State one. It is intriguing that not only has the balance of sub-atomic particles had to be within a very narrow ratio to enable intelligent life of humankind to arise at any time, but that it is theoretically possible that there are many (infinite?) other universes of which not only could we ourselves as a species never possibly have knowledge, but from which no conscious life could possibly arise either [204]. We must note however that physicists are more aware than ever of the limitations of all our modern theories. In some ways, we can see them as models useful for interpreting the universe and our environment just like any of the models, or even myths, of the past. Misner suggests indeed that once a theory has been falsified and its limits are known, it becomes a better and more useful theory [205]. Hence, we may soon find that both the Big Bang and the Steady State theories will need to be partly adapted to explain new observations about how the universe functions and develops. It is quite clear that our awareness of our ignorance is growing in parallel to, if not actually faster than, our growth in knowledge [206].

This newfound awareness of the limitations of our natural knowledge, combined with the desire of academics to roll back the frontiers of knowledge more and more over the issue of the origin and development of the universe strikes a close analogy with what we have seen in this chapter of the search by Siger and his colleagues to find ways of describing and of making sense of the underlying rationale and source of the universe. The Big Bang theory, suggesting that the entire universe started from a minutely compressed basic source of exploding energy some 15,000 million years ago, may indeed seem a useful model for a scientist, but of course it leaves open on another level the question whether the universe is self-explanatory or was created "ex nihilo" or indeed whether it simply reflects an instant in an eternally oscillating universe of expansion and contraction. The latter possibility must and can only remain on the level of speculation since it would be intrinsically unknowable empirically. All this recalls the process of the controversy enunciated at different levels within the Faculty of Arts in Paris in the thirteenth century and also the contribution of religious faith at that time. In particular, it will recall the very dispute over the eternity or otherwise of creation.

Furthermore, the awareness that the cosmos is in a dynamic state forces us to face the issue that it makes more sense to ask why an eternal First Cause should only be considered to influence the existence of the universe at the one point of creation, particularly if we understand God himself to be timeless and transcending time [207].   Siger, as we have already seen, emphasizes that the important question is in fact that of the contingent relationship of the created universe to God rather than the "date" of its initial creation. As Moltmann puts it, "the expression 'creatio ex nihilo' is meant to convey both the freedom of the Creator and the contingent character of everything that exists; ... (this) refers not just to the origin but to the ongoing fundamental nature of everything that is" [208]. Indeed, the question as to whether or not it is theoretically possible for the universe to have existed in an infinite past time is still just as much disputed by scientists, as is the question whether the actually, rather than the merely potentially, infinite makes valid sense by mathematicians, as ever they were in the Faculty of Arts seven centuries ago [209].   Those debates of the thirteenth century enable us to see today some confirmation of the claim that it is the idea of God's changelessness that is of much greater importance than that of his so-called "timelessness" [210].

This again opens up the whole question of the actual relationship between cause and effect with regard to God and Creation, which in recent years has been particularly examined by Whitehead, Hartshorne and the other Process Theologians.   Peacocke draws an analogy of this relationship with that of the developing foetus within the pregnant mother and then developing, after she has given birth, into an interdependent relationship which can involve and influence change in both [211].   This model would perhaps not have seemed all that illogical to Siger as he puzzled over these matters.   Siger was, as we have seen, faced with the external limitations imposed on the content of his teaching, and, whatever he felt about no single position adequately providing all the answers, he did not want to give up the search.   Similar sentiments are expressed today by thinkers such as Barbour who declares that "all models are limited and partial, and none gives a complete or adequate picture of reality" [212].   They are fortunate that they are not faced by powerful men such as Tempier who could so effectively and abruptly stop them in full flow.

A further irony that would not be lost on Siger is that a number of modern exegetes, who try to eschew any preconceived beliefs - as opposed to those theologians and scripture scholars who tend to interpret scripture subsequently in the light of what they already believe - are now telling us that it is extremely unlikely that the Priestly writer of Genesis 1 did conceive creation as being "ex nihilo" at all but pre-supposed pre-existent material [213].

Finally, while science has subsequently shown that the human race has not always been on earth, there is little doubt from what has already been seen regarding Siger's approach and of the methodology and process of his reasoning and investigation, that his free spirit would have no problem about accepting the discoveries of subsequent centuries. Nevertheless, one can perhaps imagine his rueful smile at learning of the conception of human beings through "in vitro" fertilization, and even of the possibility of the fertilization of virgins, when noting the Church's even recent insistence, at the time of "Humani Generis", echoing in 1950 the teaching of earlier Councils, that original sin must be transmitted through finite time by means of natural generation [214]. This would become even more poignant when we consider Rahner's very cogent case that "the Fathers of the Council of Carthage thought of 'generatio' in an Augustinian way, as involving 'libido'; in other words, they thought of generation as communicating original sin because and in so far as it is bound up with sexual desire; and we must say that this idea was one of the reasons which made them formulate the statement in just the way they did" [215]. He and Thomas, perhaps for different reasons, would not have wanted the Church to commit itself to particular positions of just one school of thought that would restrict the opportunity for manoeuvre for later generations of scholars, which could even lead to apparently ridiculous situations.

CHAPTER SIX

SIGER'S VIEWS ON THE INTELLECT

AND THE INTELLECTIVE SOUL

6.0.   Introduction.

This chapter will examine the nature and significance of "monopsychism", that is to say, the teaching that there is only one single unique intellect for all of humankind. This will begin with a look at the relevant articles of the 1270 and 1277 Condemnations to establish its importance in the view of the religious authorities in Paris, as well as the danger for orthodoxy which they perceived from it. There will follow a short examination of the roots and origin of the teaching, especially in Aristotle and Ibn Rushd, comparing this briefly with the early religious teaching of the Jewish Tenakh (Old Testament), the New Testament and Qur'an, as well as with some of the early Christian Fathers and Islamic scholars.

Having established this basis of the problem, its issues and religious implications, there will be undertaken an in-depth analysis of the relevant texts of Siger, especially the Quaestiones in Tertium de Anima, the De Anima Intellectiva and the Quaestiones super Librum de Causis. Other Sigerian texts will be briefly considered and also both the most important <u>De Unitate Intellectus contra Averroistas</u> of Thomas Aquinas, written at the height of the controversy, and, to a lesser extent, parts of that <u>Commentarium in I et II Libros De Anima</u> which is edited by Maurice Giele but whose authorship has not yet been established.

It will then be possible to discuss the nature, meaning and significance of Siger's writings on this topic and whether there are any developments in his views over a period of time, before making evaluations and assessments of them, both in their immediate historical and intellectual context, as well as that of the succeeding centuries. Finally, we shall relate the evidence of this chapter to modern views of the nature of the mind and of the soul and discuss whether all scientists of today see the issue in quite so clearcut and straightforward a way as many would have claimed on empirical evidence, even until comparatively recently.

6.1.   Official Condemnations of Monopsychism.

With regard to Tempier's first decree of 10 December 1270 [1], no less than five of the thirteen Articles are relevant to this chapter, namely:

1.   Quod intellectus omnium hominum est unus et idem numero. [That the intellect of all human beings is one and the same in number.]

2.   Quod ista est falsa vel impropria: homo intelligit. [That the following is false or inappropriate: the human being has intellection.]

7.   Quod anima quae est forma hominis secundum quod homo corrumpitur corrupto corpore. [That the soul which is the form of the human being in so far as it is human is corrupted when the body is corrupted.]

8.   Quod anima post mortem separata non patitur ab igne corporeo. [That the soul when it is separated after death does not suffer from corporeal fire.]

13.   Quod Deus non potest dare immortalitatem vel incorruptionem rei corruptibili vel mortali.   [That God is unable to bestow immortality or non-corruption on a corruptible or mortal thing.]

The major role of monopsychism in this ecclesiastical decree of censure, particularly when we also recall the strong condemnation of other contemporary writers such as Albert the Great, Bonaventure and Thomas Aquinas, demonstrates clearly that it is as a result of this issue rather than of any other that the term "Averroist" came to be coined.

In the first Article, the essential assertion of monopsychism is condemned, while in the second what appeared to many to be its corollary is tackled.   The other three Articles delineated above consider apparent implications of that teaching, namely the lack of individual immortality, the denial of both the corporeal fires of hell and of the resurrection of the body - all doctrines strongly asserted by the Church of this period.

Of the 219 theses to be condemned by Tempier and his committee of theologians on 7 March 1277, about thirty or so are concerned directly or indirectly with this.   They are listed in the notes to this chapter [2], though it should be noted that the actual source of the stated opinion is often difficult and sometimes impossible to find.   On occasions, indeed, it is also very difficult to unravel what the actual condemnation in the Articles could even possibly have had in mind since the actual statement seems too farfetched for anybody realistically to have been claiming.

6.2.   The Origins and Roots of Monopsychism.

At the heart of the problem is the dualism inherent in Greek philosophy involving the opposition between the material, physical world and the spiritual world.   This was to find one resolution in both Jewish and Christian Gnosticism, but, more importantly from our point of view, the neo-Platonic version of this was to lead to Augustine's bipolarization of body and spirit, which was for many centuries to pervade Christian religious thought.   Then, in the thirteenth century, the rediscovery of Aristotle meant that the philosophers were often struck by the potential changeability and destructibility of all physical beings, consisting of matter and form, in this lower world;   this was in contrast to the eternal permanence and immutability of spiritual beings in the celestial world. Consequently, it is possible to see the implicit tension between, on the one hand, Aristotle's metaphysics which demands that, since matter is the principle of individuation, there can only be one unique intellect if it is truly spiritual and, on the other hand, his psychology which recognizes that each human being, as a rational animal, is a distinct thinking individual.

We need to be aware of the particular Aristotelian significance of "anima", which refers to the form of living beings animating their matter as the principle of their lives, so that, in this sense, writers speak of the "soul" of intellective, sensitive (animal) and vegetative (plant) beings.   It is important to beware of making an identification, therefore, between the Christian notion of soul and the Aristotelian notion of "intellective soul".   Furthermore, it is vital to distinguish between this "intellective soul" and that faculty of reasoning which includes the ability to abstract by making use of universals, which is called the "intellect".

Ibn Rushd was, we have seen, honoured with the title "Commentator" by Aristotelians from the thirteenth century onwards, both for what was seen as the lasting value of his interpretation and also because of the corrections and amendments which he made to those of earlier writers.   However, truth to tell, he was very much more than this nomenclature implies, especially in his shorter

Commentaries, where he frequently departs from the actual Aristotelian text to express his own views on the topic under consideration [3].

As we shall see, a number of late thirteenth century writers had access to his <u>Commentarium Magnum in Librum De Anima</u>, but it is in the <u>Tahafut al-Tahafut</u> that he speaks not as a Commentator on Aristotle. Hence, this represents more authentically his explicit and personal defence, as an Islamic philosopher, of many of his own views in the face of attacks against philosophy by Al-Ghazali and other Islamic theologians. This, however, was not available in Latin till 1328 and even then four critical disputations on the Physics were omitted and were in fact unknown even to Nifo and Pomponazzi and the "Italian Averroists" till they were included in 1527 [4]. For this reason, consideration of the <u>Tahafut al-Tahafut</u> will be excluded here and most reference will be made to Ibn Rushd's Commentary on the Liber de Anima. It can even be argued that, had the availability of the breadth of his writings not been so limited, much of the hostility between the Artists and the Theologians might have been avoided [5].

However, it can certainly be safely said that he sees Aristotle as the greatest of the ancient philosophers, while Ibn Sina, for example, had owed most to the Neoplatonists. In Book III of the De Anima, Aristotle had established the attributes of the intellect to be impassible and unmixed:

> This (thinking) part of the soul, then, must be impassive but receptive of the form and potentially like this form, though not identical with it: and, as the faculty of sense is to sensible objects, so must the intellect be related to intelligible objects [6].

Ibn Rushd in his Commentary declares that the proposition that each man has his own distinct intellect is indefensible:

> Quoniam, si res intellecta apud me et apud te fuerit una omnibus modis, continget quod, cum ego scirem aliquod intellectum, ut tu scires etiam ipsum, et alia multa impossibilia.

Et si posuerimus eum esse multa, continget ut res intellecta apud me et apud te sit una in specie et duae in individuo; et sic res intellecta habebit rem intellectam, et sic procedit in infinitum (7).

[Since, if the object of my understanding and of yours should have been single in every way. it would mean that whenever I knew something so would you also know the very same and many other impossible things. Also, if we posited that it was multiple, it would mean that the object of my understanding and of yours should be single in species and double in the individual. Thus, the object of understanding will have an object of understanding and it would proceed like this to infinity.]

However, if there is only one unique intellect for all of humanity, does this mean that Ibn Rushd does not believe in the multiplicity of the soul in each individual? He attempts to solve this apparent difficulty by suggesting that while the intellect, as an "unmixed" power, can judge an infinity of objects, not known through the senses, the judging powers of the soul are "mixed individual powers" capable only of judging individual finite objects of its intentionality:

Et possumus scire quod intellectus materialis debet esse non mixtus ex iudicio, et eius comprehensione. Quia enim iudicamus per ipsum res infinitas in numero in propositione universali, et est manifestum quod virtutes animae iudicantes, scilicet individuales mixtae, non iudicant nisi intentiones finitas necesse est ut non sit virtus animae mixta. Et cum huic coniunxerimus quod intellectus materialis iudicat res infinitas et non acquisitas a sensu, et quod non iudicat intentiones finitas, continget ut sit virtus non mixta (8).

[And we can know that the material intellect must be non-mixed with regard to judgment and comprehension. This is because we judge through it an infinite number of objects in a universal proposition. Also, it is clear that, because the judging powers of the soul, needless to say individual and mixed ones, only judge finite objects of its intentionality, it cannot possibly be a mixed power of the soul. Further, when we add to this that the material intellect does judge infinite objects which are not sense-acquired and because the latter does not judge finite objects of intentionality, it would mean that it is a non-mixed power.]

The soul is indeed in one sense rational but, unlike the intellect (according to the interpretation of Ibn Rushd), it can only know objects - since it is a power dependent on the senses - in their individual forms rather than in their universality as such:

> (Aristoteles) non intendebat quod sensus comprehendit essentias rerum, sicut quidam existimaverunt: hoc enim est alterius potentiae, quae dicitur intellectus; sed intendebat quod sensus, cum hoc quod comprehendunt sua sensibilia propria, comprehendunt intentiones individuales diversas in generibus et in speciebus; comprehendunt igitur intentionem huius hominis individualis, et intentionem huius equi individualis, et universaliter intentionem uniuscuiusque decem praedicamentorum individualium [9].

[Aristotle did not mean that the sense comprehends the essences of objects, as some people have thought, for this is from a second power called the intellect. He meant on the other hand that the senses, in so far as they comprehend objects in their own sense-characteristics, comprehend different individual intentions in genera and in species. They therefore comprehend the intention of this individual man and the intention of this individual horse and universally the intention of each of the ten individual basic predications.]

This naturally prompts a number of questions whose answers, although they are not found clearly in the Commentary on the Liber de Anima, are however further elucidated in the Tahafut al-Tahafut. Hence, Ibn Rushd, while maintaining that the soul is in some way rational, does not abandon Aristotle's position that it is basically physical and material. He upholds a fundamentally monistic stance, whereby the soul, as a form of the body, at death ceases to retain its activity. This is because it is linked irreversibly to the body, although it does continue to survive in some inactive form. Nevertheless, it does not possess the ability to operate independently, as can be discerned from the analogy with sleep for the bodily senses in the ordinary way:

> Et similitudo mortis somno in hoc est ratio evidens permanentiae animae. Quoniam destruitur operatio animae in somno ex destructione instrumentorum eius, et tamen ipsa non destruitur. Igitur necesse est ut sit dispositio eius in morte, sicut est dispositio eius in somno [10].

[The similarity of death to sleep lies in the obvious permanence of the soul. This is because, while the operation of the soul is destroyed in sleep as a result of the destruction of its instruments, yet it is not itself destroyed. Hence it follows that its disposition in death will be similar to its disposition in sleep.]

However, this does not mean that each soul preserves some kind of individual existence on its own:

> Ponere autem animas absque materia multas numero est quid non notum ex opinionibus Philosophorum. Nam causa multitudinis numeralis est materia apud eos; causa vero distinctionis in multitudine numerali est forma. Reperiri autem multa numero, eadem tamen forma absque materia, est quid dubium [11].

[However to posit that souls without matter are many in number is something not known from the opinions of the Philosophers. For they maintain that matter is the cause of multiplicity of number while form is the cause of distinctiveness in multiplicity of number. Moreover, the discovery of things many in number, but with the same immaterial form, is something open to doubt.]

The whole human being, body and soul, will of course, according to Quranic teaching, be resurrected on the Day of Judgement. We can perhaps therefore see Ibn Rushd as attempting to reconcile Aristotelian ambiguity regarding soul and intellect with a monistic, rather than a dualistic, understanding of man and with a religious destiny in an afterlife [12]. Hence, the human soul, for Ibn Rushd, is not naturally immortal but the human being is a united psycho-physical or soul-body organism, dependent on God for its resurrection to its complete entity beyond the grave.

We do of course recall that Siger and his contemporaries, whether supporters or opponents, did not appear to have the direct benefit of this clarification of Ibn Rushd's views which we can find in the Tahafut al-Tahafut. This lack will naturally have affected their understanding of his interpretation of Aristotle and of his own philosophical views, most especially on this particular question of his monopsychism. Certainly, we should not forget that he believed that his teaching here was in complete agreement with the teaching of the Qur'an and he clearly submits to the authority of revealed prophecy:

> Et ideo verissima omnium propositionum est, quod omnis Propheta est sapiens et non omnis sapiens est Propheta; sed sunt sapientes, de quibus dicitur quod sunt haeredes Prophetarum [13].

[And therefore it is the most true of all propositions that every prophet is a wise person and that not every wise person is a prophet. There are however wise people about whom it is said that they are the heirs of the prophets.]

Hence, in the tradition of the Mu'tazilite and post-Mu'tazilite theologians too, he saw apparent difficulties with some of the literal descriptions of the Qur'an, such as the descriptions of the banquets and of the virgins in Paradise [14]. These were considered to be symbolic metaphors with a religious teaching role for the ordinary simple believer. In his Fasl al-Maqal (On the Harmony of Philosophy and Religion), he speaks of all theologians as agreeing that an allegorical interpretation of the Qur'an is a tenable alternative position to that involving a literal understanding. He asserts that the disagreements arise when one starts deciding in specific instances which interpretation should or should not be employed [15]. The critical point here to appreciate is that he was certainly committed totally to the unity of truth [16], albeit the fact that he considered it possible to express it by means of different kinds of language [17]. Indeed, the Qur'an acknowledges the value of the use of reason as a means of religious exhortation:

> Call men to the path of your Lord with wisdom and kindly
> exhortation. Reason with them in the most courteous manner
> [18].

6.3. The Nature of the Theological Problems arising from Monopsychism.

It will be noticed that from the perspective of a Christian theologian - and to a lesser extent that of Muslims and Jews too - a number of possible problems would appear to arise if a monopsychist position is to be maintained.

Some are directly concerned with the nature of humankind: for example, does a human being have an individual soul of some kind and, if so, what is the nature of its relationship to the body? What kind of relationship does the human race have to other species? Should we or should we not identify mind with soul? What is the nature of spirit? Can we manage to preserve individual responsibility without maintaining a plurality of intellective souls?

Other issues have general theological implications such as the meaning of original sin and the questions as to whether this is passed on genetically via our parents. Yet others have eschatological implications, such as the question as to what part of the individual, if any, exists after death? What is the nature of life beyond the grave? Is there a hell or a heaven? Are they necessarily eternal? Are these states physical, spiritual or merely metaphysical?

When we recall the established pre-eminence of the theologians - and, in particular, of those of the Augustinian School, itself dependent on Neoplatonism rather than Aristotelianism - we can begin to understand how they felt in 1270 and

1277 the need to reassert their suspicions about Aristotelian philosophical approaches and especially those involving any suggestion of dependence on Ibn Rushd or other Muslim writers. This climate, when allied to the perceived need to preserve the unity of the Western Church under the centralized authority of the Pope and his nominated Bishops, helps us to understand their negative reactions to those independent-minded scholars in the Faculty of Arts in Paris.

6.4.   Scriptural Perspectives on Personal Identity after Death.

It certainly is a fact well-known to Biblical scholars that the idea of a life-after-death developed relatively late in the pre-Christian period. Indeed, even in the first century of the Common Era, the Sadducee priestly group continued in its total denial of such a separate spiritual existence.

In the New Testament, the concept of the ultimate finality of death is also largely accepted on a merely natural level. The Kingdom of God is present among those who accept the Messianic message of Jesus and it is only faith in him that will bring men and women victory over death. Death is, we see again here, a stage akin to sleeping. Christ is "the first to rise from the dead" (Acts 26:33) and it is the resurrection of the dead which is central to the Christian message of liberation, for "it is sown a physical body, it is raised a spiritual body" (I Corinthians 15:44). When we recall how the very first Christians had assumed the Second Coming of Jesus was imminent (Mark 13:26 and 13:30), we can better grasp how the notion of the existence of the disembodied spirit only really developed under the later influence of Greek thought. This would also have been reflected in the Christian acceptance of that Genesis account of Creation where God breathes his spirit into Adam (Genesis 2:7) who is seen as an animated body rather than that "spirit-in-a-body" notion. This was particularly to develop in patristic and medieval Christian thought, as did the idea of a Particular Judgment of the individual soul, alongside that of the General Judgment on the Last Day.

Although the Qur'an throughout implies the immortality of the soul, Montgomery Watt/Bell claims that nevertheless it "does not assert a natural immortality of the soul, since man's existence is dependent on the will of God" [19]. It is the resurrection of the whole human body, rather than a separate existence of the soul after death, which is most strongly upheld in the Qur'an:

> From the earth We have created you, and to the earth We will restore you; and from it We will bring you back to life [20].

6.5.   Quaestiones in Tertium de Anima.

After placing the topic of this chapter in its broader theological and philosophical contexts, it is now appropriate to begin an examination of Siger's views by looking at those texts which can be attributed authentically to him. This commentary can provide an insight into his early teaching. Bazán concludes in fact that this work is a "reportatio" dating from towards the end of the first stage of Siger's teaching career (1265-1270), quite probably from the academic year 1269-1270 [21]. He joins earlier writers in concluding that, particularly since the content seems to take no heed nor notice of Tempier's Condemnation of 10 December 1270, it must certainly predate that event [22].

The work itself is divided into four sections, although, inevitably, there is some overlap of thought and general content:

> [a]   The difference between the intellect and other parts of the soul (qu. 1).

> [b]   The intellect in itself (qu. 2-6).

> [c]   The relationship of the intellect to the multiplicity of human bodies (qu. 7-9).

> [d]   The powers of the intellect - the "receptive" and "agent" intellects (qu. 10-18).

[a]   In the first quaestio, Siger considers whether the intellective principle is rooted in the same substance and the same subject as the vegetative and sensitive principles, concluding that the union within the human soul must be "composite" (rather than a "simple" union with the latter two principles, which we find of course in non-rational animals):

> Dicendum enim quod intellectivum non radicatur in eadem anima simplici cum vegetativo et sensitivo, sicut vegetativum et sensitivum radicantur in eadem simplici, sed radicatur cum ipsis in eadem anima composita.   Unde cum intellectus simplex sit, cum advenit, tum in suo adventu unitur vegetativo et sensitivo, et sic ipsa unita non faciunt unam simplicem, sed compositam [23].

[It must be stated that the intellective (power) is not rooted in the same simple soul along with the vegetative and sensitive ones, in the way that the vegetative and the sensitive are in the same simple soul, but it is rooted with these very ones in the same composite soul.   Therefore, since the intellect is simple when it comes, then in its coming it is united to the vegetative and sensitive souls. Thus, when these powers are themselves united like this, they do not make one simple soul but a composite one.]

Nardi has rightly pointed out that this is not a novel position but can also be found in several earlier writers, such as Adam of Buckfield and Alexander of Hales who, it will be recalled, were quite probably Masters of Arts in Paris during Siger's own student days [24].

In any event, as we have seen, Neoplatonic influence had already very much stressed the dualism of body and spirit. However, theologians had tended to understand this in terms of distinct substance with regard to the body and the soul within the individual human being, while attempting at the same time to stress their distance from the more extreme views of the Manicheans and the Cathars.   Thus. there was real potential for conflict between theologians and philosophers. Albert the Great had come up with a novel compromise solution, whereby the intellective soul is directly created by God and is united to the vegetative-sensitive soul(s), which is rooted in matter, to form one single composite substance, hence partly of internal and partly of external origin [25]. Of course, as we shall see, Thomas develops his own unique solution to the question of the unity of the human soul, but we must note that Siger, as a Master of Arts, takes no account of the possibility of any special divine intervention in so far as he follows a scrupulously philosophical line.

Siger himself had already discussed the position of those (probably the theologians) who, with the intention of trying to preserve the "simple" unity of the soul, maintain that the sensitive and vegetative parts are also external in origin. He goes on to conclude in accordance, he believes, with Ibn Rushd's understanding of Aristotle, that one "composite" soul is formed in the subject:

> Per hoc patet ad illud quod dicit Averroes quod Aristoteles opinatur vegetativum, sensitivum et intellectivum esse unam animam in subiecto. Verum est: unam compositam, non autem unam simplicem [26].

[It thus becomes clear, as Ibn Rushd says, that Aristotle considers the vegetative, sensitive and intellective souls to be single in the subject. It is true that there is one composite, rather than one simple, soul.]

Perhaps it would be fair to recall at this point that, whereas theologians were using the term "soul" in what we have to come to see as a distinctively religious sense affirming its potentiality to subsist independently in its own right, Siger as a philosopher views it on the other hand more in terms of what we would describe as a life-force.

[b]   In the previous chapter of this study we have already examined in some detail the second quaestio of this commentary which examines the eternity of the intellect;   we have seen how Siger dispassionately leans to Aristotle's view

rather than that of Augustine and how he affirms in philosophical language the impossibility of understanding the Will of the First Being [27].

In the third quaestio, he demonstrates the other-worldly non-temporal nature of this creation:

> ... intellectus est de novo factus ... licet eius substantia nec sit
> in tempore nec sit in nunc temporis sed sit in nunc aevi [28].

[...the intellect is made from new ... although its substance is neither in time nor in the 'now' of time but is in the 'now' of the 'aevum'.]

Then, reaffirming his fidelity to Aristotle in his declaration that the intellect is of external origin [29], he sets out in the fourth quaestio to show that the latter, since it abstracts universal principles (such as those that might apply, for example, to all triangles, even though we do not have actual personal experience of every individual triangle that exists in the world [30]), must have an immaterial nature and therefore be ungenerated:

> Quare intellectus est immaterialis.   Sed si immaterialis est,
> ingenerabilis est etc. [31].

[Therefore the intellect is immaterial.   However, if it is immaterial, it cannot be generated and so on.]

Hence, it is in the unique operation of the intellect in human beings that there lies the difference from the material senses which need organs to create phantasms:

> Sed actio sive operatio intellectus, qui modo est in nobis,
> separata est nec utitur organo [32].

[But the action or operation of the intellect, which is only in us, is separate and does not employ an organ.]

218

This therefore marks an important difference between humans and other animals. For example, when a sheep perceives a threat to be posed by the particular sighting of a wolf, this is only on a non-rational level:

> Unde, etsi ovis in lupo accipiat inimicitiam, hoc non est nisi quia simul apprehendit colorem talem, magnitudinem et sic de aliis. Intellectus autem, etsi quidditates accipiat cum phantasmatibus sensibilibus, nunquam tamen illas actu intelligit cum phantasmatibus sensibilibus simul [33].

[Therefore, although a sheep may perceive hostility in a wolf, this is only because it grasps a particular colour, size and so forth for the other qualities. The intellect however, although it may perceive essences along with the sense-phantasms, nevertheless does not ever understand these in act at the same time as the sense-phantasms.]

The fifth quaestio, in which he argues from the incorruptibility of the intellect, particularly demonstrates the nature of Siger's philosophy of reasoning. Here he is probably emphasizing that this solution is his own personal contribution by using the first personal singular form of the word "dico" five times in less than twenty lines [34]. The intellect, as a contingent created being, is made perpetual through the First Cause, rather than being eternal of itself and in its own right:

> Dico ergo quod intellectus de se est corruptibilis. Unde, sicut eductus est de nihilo, sic per naturam propriam reductibilis est in nihilum. Sed dico quod intellectus habet hoc ex influentia Primae Causae, unde hoc solum a Prima Causa habet, scilicet quod sit perpetuus [35].

[I therefore state that the intellect is intrinsically open to corruption. Therefore, just as it has come out of nothing, so through its particular nature it can be reduced to nothing. However, I state that the intellect is like this as a result of the influence of the First Cause.   It therefore possesses this characteristic only from the First Cause, namely that it is perpetual.]

This does not occur by means of what the theologians might call conservation in existence but is determined at the very moment of its creation through the Will of the First Being:

> ... dico quod intellectus non perpetuatur per hoc quod continue recipiat aliquid de novo a Primo, sed quia ... recipit ab origine sua a Primo per quod postea in aevum perpetuatur. ...dico quod Primum perpetuat intellectum voluntate sua [36].

[I state that the intellect is not made perpetual through the fact that it continually receives something from the First Being, but because ... it receives from its origin from the First Being through which it is subsequently made perpetual through the 'aevum'.   ... I state that the First Being perpetuates the intellect by means of his own Will.]

Whatever might seem the validity of such an argument, we do very clearly see the independent philosopher arguing on his own terms, albeit with, of course, the guidance of Aristotle and other writers to influence him in the development of his ideas.   The theological import of revelation does not come into his consideration at all.

In the sixth and final quaestio of this section, after a long discussion with supporters of so-called "spiritual matter", he excludes all matter from the intellect:

> Credo esse dicendum (quod) in intellectu non sit materia aliqua sicut nec in substantiis separatis [37].

[I believe that it should be stated that, just as in separated substances, there is no matter in the intellect.]

[c]   It is here in the third part of this commentary, where it examines the relationship of the intellect to the plurality of physical human bodies, that we really come to the heart of its controversial material.

The ninth quaestio is the key one where Siger asserts that the immateriality of the intellect demands its unicity:

> ...concluditur quod intellectus, (cum) sit immaterialis, in eius
> natura non est quod multiplicetur secundum numerum [38].

[... the conclusion is that it is not in its nature that the intellect, being immaterial, is multipliable in number.]

To the counter-argument, attributed to Ibn Sina, that the intellect is multiplied on the other hand because of its ability to perfect matter - "multiplicatio secundum numerum ... tamen creatur sub habilitate perficiendi materiam" [numeral multiplicity ... is created with the capacity to perfect matter] [39] - he claims the support of Ibn Rushd that this would only happen if the intellect is seen as a power within the body:

> Ideo arguit Averroes quod, si intellectus multiplicaretur
> secundum multiplicationem hominum individuorum, esset
> virtus in corpore [40].

[Therefore Ibn Rushd argues that the intellect would be a bodily faculty if it were multiplied according to the multiplicity of human individuals.]

The contrary position is rejected because it is matter that is the principle of differentiation and it is not contained in immaterial forms such as universals:

Si ergo formarum immaterialium, quae sunt sub una specie, si sit ita quod una non est melior quam alia, ergo non magis habet appropriari huic materiae quam alii [41].

[If therefore this referred to immaterial forms, which belong to a single species, if it were in such a way that one is no better than another, then there is no reason for it to be appropriated to this individual matter rather than another.]

Presumably, Siger here is speaking in metaphysical terms rather than allowing for the psychological and epistemological possibility of error, which we noted in Chapter 4 when looking at his theory of truth and reliability of knowledge [42]. He goes on to explain that the senses achieve union with the material part of the individual human being, while the intellect does the same with the formal part:

Nota ergo quod intellectus et sensus copulantur nobiscum in actu, sed diversimode. Sensus enim copulatur nobis per partem eius quae est materia. Sed intellectus copulatur nobis per partem eius quae est forma [43].

[Note therefore that the intellect and the senses are linked with us in act, but in different ways. The senses are linked to us through the part which is matter but the intellect is linked through the part which is form.]

By "form", it would seem that Siger is referring to the vegetative-sensitive soul or life-force, as seen in the first quaestio, whereby he has tried to show that the intellect itself can only be rooted to it to set up a "composite" soul.

This union, it was argued however in Quaestio 7, is not one of substance, but achieved through the operative power of the intellect:

Intellectus perficit corpus, non per suam substantiam, sed per suam potentiam, quia, si per suam substantiam perficeret, non esset separabilis [44].

[The intellect perfects the body not through its substance but through its potentiality, because if it were to perfect through its substance it would not be separable.]

He follows Aristotle in drawing the analogy of a sailor causing a ship to move:

> Et hoc scripsit Aristoteles ... : si intellectus est actus corporis
> sicut nauta navis, sic est separabilis [45].

[And Aristotle wrote the following: if the intellect is the act of the body like a sailor of a ship, then it is separable.]

The union is twofold. Siger can safely declare that the intellect, as the principle of intellection, does not use a bodily organ (presumably, here he means what we might call the brain) but communicates with the imagination which operates through it. On the other hand, as mover of the body, while it acts "per se" on the body as a whole, it only does so "per accidens" on any particular part of it [46].

It should be noted that the phrase "operante" [operating] which is also found elsewhere in this section of the commentary [47], contrasts with Albert the Great's phrase that "intellectus communicat non corpori, sed potestati quae communicat corpori, scilicet phantasiae et imaginationi et sensui" [the intellect does not communicate with the body but with the faculty which is in communication with the body, namely the concept, the imagination and the sense] [48]. When we recall Albert's idea that the intellect is directly and individually created by God, whether at conception or in the womb [49], the additional significance of this word-phrase "operans" stands out. It really does seem that earlier scholars have not fully grasped the dynamic nature of this claim for Siger. They have generally interpreted this section of text by considering Siger's theory of the union of the intellect with the vegetative-sensitive soul in too static a way. Because Thomas Aquinas seems to take this theory in such a manner [50], subsequent writers, themselves imbued with Thomism and Neothomism, have tended to follow suit, even though they do acknowledge to some extent his references to operative powers of the intellect. Even Van Steenberghen appears to fall into this trap [51].

The ancient world took for granted the influence of the stars on our lives and actions. For Siger, the union of the intellect with each individual is, however, more intimate than this:

> Nam plus communicat intellectus noster nobiscum quam motores caelestium orbium [52].

[For our intellect communicates more with us than the movers of the heavenly orbs.]

It is not just through but actually in the very act of knowledge that the union between the intellect and the vegetative-sensitive soul, which was outlined in the first quaestio, takes place. The imagination is "operans" and the intellect is perfecting the body of which that soul is the form:

> Intelligo autem intellectum esse perfectionem quantum ad suam potestatem, quia perficit corpus quoad suam cooperationem" [53].

[I understand however that the intellect is perfection with respect to its power, because it perfects the body as regards its cooperation.]

If Bazán's transliteration "cooperationem" is re-read as "co-operationem", this can be seen even more clearly. This would then even more strongly support Caparello's view that Siger's position has often been misrepresented as advocating that the active operation is almost tacked on to that one static substance, which is the composite of the two static souls [54]. Perhaps this error is not as surprising as it might otherwise be, when we recall again the very powerful dualism of body and spirit, found in the medieval religious world under the influence of Neoplatonism.

224

Siger overcomes the obvious objection that a single intellect would rule
out different items of knowledge for different people, by pointing to the priority of
the phantasm-images in the imagination over the action of the intellect:

> ... dico quod hoc est verum, si intellectus secundum
> substantiam prius sit in omnibus quam intentiones imaginatae.
> Hoc autem falsum est.   Immo prius intentiones imaginatae
> quam intellectus sit in hominibus [55].

[... I state that this would be true, if the intellect with regard to
substance preceded phantasm-images in all respects.   However, this is false.   On
the contrary, phantasm-images precede the intellect in human beings.]

Perhaps, with hindsight, one can say that Aristotle's analogy, employed
by Siger, of the sailor making the ship move, has been a little misleading and a
better comparison would be with the single source of the sun.   This is able to
provide warmth for each person to live and, to take a more modern example, even
to provide entire heating systems for buildings by means of solar panels and so on.
So again in this section Siger has used his professional expertise in a strictly
philosophical, almost scientific, style, without any reference or regard being made
to any religious teachings or views.

[d]   Ibn Rushd had spoken of six powers of the intellect - viz. agent
intellect, possible intellect, speculative intellect, intellect in habit, "intellectus
adeptus" and material intellect [56].   He does, however, declare that these are in
fact different aspects of what he calls the "two intellects", that they have a single
mode of action in one sense [57] but a different mode in another [58].

Siger, in speaking of the agent and possible intellects, makes it clear in
the fourth and final section of this commentary that they must not be seen as two
different substances but as two powers of the same substance:

Adhuc de intellectu agente et possibili intelligendum quod non sunt duae substantiae, sed sunt duae virtutes eiusdem substantiae [59].

[At this point it should be understood that, as regards the agent intellect and the possible intellect, there are not two substances but that they are two powers of the same substance.]

He has already used the phrase "passibilis", especially in Quaestio 10, to describe the latter (mainly, it seems, because he wishes to consider the implications of the suffering of the separated soul in the next quaestio). Perhaps indeed we would do well to think of them as active and passive elements when we use those phrases better known to students of scholasticism. It is probably best rendered in modern English by the phrase "receptive" if we are to convey most fully the nuances of its meaning. In this quaestio, in ruling out any material element to this, he has hinted at this aspect:

Alia vero est passio, quae consistit in sola receptione, et sic passio, quae consistit in sola receptione, non est per naturam materiae, et talis passio est in intellectu [60].

[Sufferance is indeed different and consists in receptivity alone. Hence sufferance, in consisting of receptivity alone, does not exist through the nature of matter and such sufferance is in the intellect.]

In Quaestio 12, this is further developed by the use of the word "oblatio" for, when speaking of fundamental first principles, he says that:

... ita sunt quaedam quae intellectui oblata maximam faciunt cognitionem [61].

[... thus there are certain things offered to the intellect which create the greatest knowledge.]

He has already ruled out the innatism theory of, for example, Albert the Great to account for these:

> Dico et credo quod intellectui nostro non est innata aliqua cognitio intelligibilium, sed est in pura potentia ad omnia intelligibilia, nullius intus habens innatam cognitionem, sed ex phantasmatibus intelligit quidquid intelligit [62].

[I state and I believe that there is not any innate knowledge of intelligible things in our intellect, but that it is in pure potentiality with regard to all intelligible things.   It has no innate knowledge within but whatever it does understand it understands as a result of coming from phantasms.]

In doing so, Siger asserts that the only innate aspect is that potentiality - somewhat similar to that exemplified by a blank blackboard or slate on which we are able to draw - which is possessed by the receptive intellect:

> ... dicendum intellectus praeparatus est ad intelligibilia sicut tabula ad picturas.   Sed hoc non est per cognitionem aliquorum intelligibilium sibi innatam, sed per potentiam sibi innatam naturalem praeparatus est ad intelligibilia [63].

[...it should be stated that the intellect is prepared for intelligible things just as a blackboard is for pictures.   However, this is not by means of an innate knowledge of intelligible things but through a natural potentiality innate to itself it is prepared for intelligible things.]

In Quaestio 13, he acknowledges, very much in the manner of a modern scientist making conjectures from his observations of the world, that, while not all is yet fully comprehensible, nevertheless there must be a link in understanding between the receptive and the active powers of the intellect:

Rationes ... bene concludunt quod nos non experimur in nobis
qualiter intellectus possibilis agentem intelligat vel quod etiam
non intelligat, non tamen concludunt quin ipsum intelligat [64].

[There are good reasons for concluding that we do not experience
within ourselves in what way the receptive intellect understands the agent or even
how it does not do so.   There are no good reasons for concluding that there is no
self-understanding.]

He then proceeds to assert that this is accomplished through the
process of abstraction from the phantasms possessed by the imagination:

Dico ergo quod ad intelligere nostrum requiritur receptio
intelligibilium abstractorum universalium cum factione eorum
et etiam abstractio eorumdem, cum prius fuerunt intentiones
imaginatae [65].

[I therefore state that for our understanding there is required a
reception of intelligible abstract universals along with their manufacture and there
is also required an abstraction of the same, when there have previously been
phantasms.]

Having established that there is nothing innate about the knowledge of
the intellect, he also rules out at some length some form of illumination or radiation
as the explanation [66].   He avoids dualism, however, and preserves the
"composite unity" of knowledge in the individual subject, which had been asserted
in the first quaestio, by explaining the whole process in more detail:

Dico quod intellectus agens nihil penitus recipit, et dico quod
intellectus agens intelligibilia universalia abstracta actu facit in
intellectu possibili.   Unde dico quod, praesentibus imaginatis
intentionibus in organo phantasiae, facit intellectus agens
intentiones universales intentionibus imaginatis, et ab illis

intentionibus similibus abstrahit rationes rerum intelligendi universales [67].

[I state that the agent intellect receives nothing within. I further state that the agent intellect actually manufactures intelligible abstract universals in the receptive intellect. I therefore state that, when phantasms are present in the organ of the imagination, the agent intellect manufactures universal concepts with the phantasms. From those similar images it abstracts the universal aspects of things for understanding.]

The idea of illumination or enlightenment is contrasted with that union between the vegetative-sensitive soul and the intellective soul, achieved through operative activity. This is again twice emphasized by the use of the verb "facere". Indeed, in the beginning of this quaestio, he had declared that it is only through the act of intellection that we can speak of "species" as having any form of existence:

Sed non est locus specierum nisi per actum intelligendi" [68].

[There is however no place for species except through the act of understanding.]

Siger acknowledges that Ibn Rushd taught that the union of the unique and eternal intellect with the human race as a whole is more fundamental than any union with a particular individual human being. To the extent that Ibn Rushd sees the human race as eternal, this is, for Siger, a reasonable interpretation of the situation:

Et intellectus copulatio humanae speciei essentialior est quam copulatio quae est huic individuo, propter hoc quod humana species aeterna est (et) quia intellectus (qui) ei copulatur aeternus est [69].

[And the linking of the intellect with the human species is more essential than the linking to any particular individual. This is because the human species is eternal and because the intellect linked to it is eternal.]

However, he does remind us that this can of course only take place through operative activity working on the phantasms of an individual:

> ... tunc dico quod intellectus huic (individuo) copulatur quia intentiones imaginatae: aliter enim nunquam fuissent actu intellecta (70).

[I state then that the intellect is linked to a particular individual as a result of phantasms since otherwise they would never be actually understood.]

These points are once again emphasized in Quaestio 15, where he also shows how it serves to explain how different people understand in different ways:

> Et cum dicitur: intentiones intellectae sunt unius intellectus, dico quod, licet intentiones intellectae sint unius intellectus simpliciter in se, tamen (sunt) intellectae huius intellectus secundum quod copulatur isti et non absolute. ... Sed quia intelligit ex intentionibus imaginatis copulatis diversis hominibus, et diversis secundum diversitatem hominum, ideo intelligere diversificatur in diversis. ... Sed dico quod anima rationalis potentialiter est copulata humanae speciei eo quod natura suae virtutis activae est agere talia, quae nobis sunt copulata (71).

[And when it is said that the objects of the intentionality of intellection belong to a single intellect, I state that, although the objects of intentionality of intellection do belong to a single intellect in every respect in itself, they belong however to the intellection of this intellect in that it is linked in this way and not in an absolute sense... However, because it has intellection from the objects of the imagination as linked to different human beings and differently according to the diversity of human beings, it follows that intellection will be different in different people... Moreover, I state that the rational soul is potentially linked to the human species in that it is the nature of its active power to effect those things which are linked to us.]

In Quaestiones 16 and 17, Siger attempts to demonstrate that, while spiritual (separated) substances can actually have self-knowledge, they cannot however have knowledge of one another, because they are incapable of having a material physical species or phantasm of each other. The only exception is the First Cause, precisely because they are its immediate effects. Hence, this is how our intellect does immediately recognize God rather than by means of those Neoplatonic theories of emanation:

> Similiter noster intellectus immediate respicit Primam Causam tamquam suam causam et non per intelligentias medias [72].

[In a similar way our intellect immediately sees the First Cause as its own cause and not through intermediary intelligences.]

Finally, in the last quaestio of this commentary, so as to avoid any misunderstanding on the part of the student, Siger repeats his earlier descriptions of the operative and active way in which the intellect enables us to have understanding:

> Ideo credo et dico quod intellectus, etiam secundum quod noster est, particulare particulariter non intelligit, nec primo nec ex consequenti. Intellectus enim noster non est (talis) ut intelligat per organum, sed separatus est secundum utramque partem suae virtutis, et secundum possibilem et secundum agentem; communicat tamen operanti per organum [73].

[I therefore believe and state that the intellect, even in the respect in which it belongs to us, does not understand a particular thing as a particular, whether in the first instance or as a consequence. This is because our intellect is not such that it understands through an organ, but is separate according to both parts of its power, receptive and agent. However, it communicates with the subject of operation through an organ.]

However, as we have seen earlier in this chapter - and indeed in Chapter 4 too - a certain knowledge of the particular is possible because the content of a universal includes the particular which is represented by it, although of course it is not known in that very individuality by which the particular is formally constituted:

> Immo dico quod universale (cum) idem sit cum suo particulari, per cognitionem universalis cognoscitur particulare, sed non (ut) est in forma propria, sed solum in universali, quia haec forma universalis vere est particularis secundum suum esse. Particulare enim aliam formam ab universali non habet (74).

[Moreover, I state that, since the universal is one with its particular, the particular is known through knowledge of the universal. This is not however in a form peculiar to it, but only in the universal form, since this very form belongs to the particular according to its (i.e. the particular's) existence. This is because the particular does not have a form distinct from the universal.]

6.6. Nature and Methodology of Siger's Approach in Quaestiones in Tertium De Anima.

It will be clear how on initial and cursory glance Siger might well be thought to be in opposition to several of Tempier's 1270 Articles, which were detailed in Section 6.1 above.

An interesting insight into Siger's level of reasoning can be seen by looking at the Eighth Article, which condemns any denial that the soul may suffer from bodily fire after death. In fact, such a thesis is upheld by Siger in Quaestio

11 of this Commentary. It comes immediately after the one which discusses what is meant by the possibility of the intellect being able to suffer, when he asserts that he believes that he is being faithful to the Aristotelian tradition in declaring that what he understands by the intellect is unable so to suffer in a material sense:

> Alia vero est passio, quae consistit in sola receptione, ... non est per naturam materiae, et talis passio est in intellectu [75].

[Different indeed is suffering which consists merely in receptivity ... and is not through the nature of matter. Such suffering is in the intellect.]

In Quaestio 11, he acknowledges that this is a "quaestio non multum philosophica" [a not particularly philosophical question], but does offer what he sees as a basic rational and philosophical perspective on it. This is very interesting for the light it shines on Siger's methodology and general approach of investigation over the general topic of the intellective soul. He argues that the soul can only suffer if it is united to the body, since in itself it does not contain matter:

> Omne quod patitur, per naturam materiae patitur... Anima non patitur a corpore nisi ab eo cui unitur [76].

[Everything which suffers does so through the nature of matter... The soul only suffers from the body to which it is united.]

This would almost certainly, says Siger, not have posed a problem for either Aristotle or Ibn Rushd, since for them the intellective soul is always united to some body or other at any given time:

> Forte, si quaeretur ab Aristotele utrum anima intellectiva esset passibilis, ipse responderet quod ipsa intellectiva separata impassibilis est, et forte ipse cum Commentatore eius diceret quod ipsa inseparabilis est, et si separetur ab hoc corpore, non tamen ab omni corpore simpliciter separatur [77].

[Perhaps if Aristotle were asked whether the intellective soul were able to suffer, he would reply that in so far as separate and intellective it could not suffer. Furthermore, perhaps he would say with Ibn Rushd that it cannot be separated and that, if separated from a particular body, it would not however in every respect be separated from every body.]

In fact, in this quaestio, Siger does seem to stray a little out of his depth and gets involved in exegesis regarding Aristotle which suggests to him that the latter was speaking about brute animals when he declared that the soul does not enter every body [78]; and, earlier, in opposing the thesis of some theologians, he attempts to identify their philosophical weakness over this matter [79]. However, as regards the central thesis in question, despite the lengthy consideration, he sits on the fence - perhaps because he feels that Aristotle's vagueness must leave him neutral as a philosopher:

> Solutio. Non videmus quod Aristoteles aliquid dixerit de ista quaestione, quia non invenimus quod ipse alicubi determinaverit de statu separationis [80].

[The answer is that we do not see that Aristotle said anything about this question because we do not find that he had anywhere made any determination about the state of separation.]

This all sounds very much like a modern scientist who might choose to abstain from religious speculation but does want to affirm what he sees to be possible pitfalls for the unwary theologian. He does thus seem to see it as more important to take notice of Aristotle's original views rather than Ibn Rushd's interpretations of his thought, despite the latter's stature and importance as Commentator for him.

The Thirteenth Article, which should be understood as referring to the Resurrection of the Body, would not be a philosophical issue for Siger either. If the condemnation is interpreted as demanding the mortality of the human soul, as commonly understood by Christians, Siger would begin by denying the full validity of this definition. He would then turn back to what he has said about the operative and dynamic nature of the union between intellective soul and vegetative-sensitive soul. We can well understand however the concern of Tempier. Perhaps, indeed, some of the implications of this dynamic union can in some sense be better appreciated, than even Siger could possibly have imagined, now in this era when we speak of electrically-charged particles. This contrasts even with the relatively recent past, when the Copernican and Newtonian views still saw the universe as in one sense regular and static, albeit differently from the way in which it was generally perceived in the medieval period.

Van Steenberghen seems surprised that the unorthodox character of his philosophy in this Commentary does not seem to trouble Siger and suggests that he would have expected him to have avoided a conflict with religious belief [81]. However, that is the whole point. His view of philosophy does not involve him here in looking over his shoulder at the moral and religious implications but is an assertion of its value and integrity on an independent level. On this dimension, it is a very powerful plea that philosophy really is worth studying for its own sake. For the same reason, Van Steenberghen's hint elsewhere [82], that a reading of the early quaestiones could be interpreted in an orthodox sense before Siger shows his true colours in the Third Part of the Commentary, is interesting. However, the whole episode almost certainly reflects some display of his views, although its strict and logical development remains neutral and independent from religious belief and its implications. Even in the second quaestio, he has suggested, in a very different way from his attempts to avoid what he sees as possible basic philosophical errors on the topic of corporeal fires in Quaestio 11, that he would almost certainly not want to delve into the deeper theological issues involved in the nature of the divine will:

> Qui ergo voluerit scire utrum intellectus factus sit de novo vel factus sit aeternus, oportet eum investigare formam voluntatis Primi. Sed quis erit qui eam investigabit? [83].

[Anyone therefore who would want to know whether the inellect is made anew or is made eternal needs to investigate the form of the will of the First Being. But who will there be who will investigate that?]

It may very well be that, despite the surprise of so many earlier writers that he does not directly and explicitly address the psychological question of Tempier's Second Article - "utrum hic homo singularis intelligit" [whether this individual man has intellection] -, he could be quite deliberately avoiding it. This may be not simply out of some fear of being condemned, but because he considers it to be irrelevant to the metaphysical issues being discussed. Besides, he probably believes that his own dynamic approach to the nature of the union of the intellect with the individual actually explains the problem in a much more effective and more profound way than could possibly be done by the more superficial everyday expression of individual awareness of knowledge. He was certainly not naive enough to oppose such a statement on the more obvious level any more than, as has already been suggested in earlier chapters, a modern scientist would attack someone in everyday conversation for speaking of the sun rising or setting.

After all, we have already seen in Quaestio 15 how he was quite prepared to go back over old ground to some extent, in order to answer some objections, in re-explaining his position. He does this in a professional manner, affirming once more his overall dedication to the stature and independence of philosophy. This professionalism is again demonstrated in the way in which he is very ready and prepared to take a personal and different line from earlier writers, even in his public commentaries. In the previous chapter, we noted how his very earliest works do not reveal this willingness.

Salman has suggested that, whereas Ibn Rushd had seen the agent intellect and the possible intellect as being perfectly distinct and separate substances, Siger understands them as being two powers of the same substance (84). Caparello takes this even further by saying that in Siger the perfective activity of the agent intellect is exercised on the vegetative-sensitive faculty, while in Ibn Rushd it was on the possible intellect (85). Certainly, Siger does, as we have seen, through his special theory of active union in the dynamic activity of intellection, set himself in deep opposition to any suggestion of Neoplatonism, of which there were vestiges in the dualism of the contemporary Christian theologians when they spoke of the realms of body and spirit.

In any event, he really does seem to assert his own individual professional independence, much as a scientist would so insist today in discussing the theories, or even in using the terminology, of his predecessors. For example, he himself prefers not to use the term "speculative intellect", although he acknowledges its use by Ibn Rushd [86]. This of course does not prevent him from developing some of the latter's ideas. Likewise, he avoids the use of the phrase "material intellect".

Be that as it may, we can perhaps take Tempier's Seventh Article as having Siger in his sights, if by "soul" is simply understood his vegetative-sensitive soul. Such confusion and misunderstanding may have led some to see Siger as a heretic in this matter as a result. It is even more likely that Tempier could have had Siger, as well as Ibn Rushd in mind, in the First Article, whether or not he was able to grasp the more subtle and deeper nuances of Siger's intellectual theories.

6.7.   The Reaction of Thomas Aquinas.

The best-known and most important source for understanding Thomas' views at this time (though, of course, not the only one) is his treatise with the full title of Tractatus de Unitate Intellectus contra Averroistas, although some versions do give variations on this title. Indeed, Codex 225 of Corpus Christi College Oxford adds explicitly that "haec scripsit Thomas contra Sigerum de Brabantia et alios plurimos Parisius in philosophia regentes anno Domini 1270", while the Introduction to the Munich version (Latin 8001) likewise mentions Siger by name [87]. At the very least, we can safely say that Thomas was subsequently perceived to have had Siger, and perhaps some of the latter's colleagues, in mind and that this treatise was written within the atmosphere developing after Tempier's first set of Condemnations.

In fact, we know that Bonaventure had already come out very strongly against monopsychism - as evidenced in his two series of Lenten sermons "Collationes de Decem Praeceptis" of 1267 and "Collationes de Septem Donis Spiritus Sancti" of 1268. He was very concerned about what he saw as its unavoidable heretical implications:

> Tertius (error) est de unitate intellectus humani in omnibus ...
> Secundum tertium, non est differentia in merito et praemio, si
> una est anima Christi et Judae proditoris.   Totum   est
> haereticum [88].

[The third error concerns the unicity of the human intellect in everyone ... According to this third, there is no difference in merit and reward, if there is one soul for Christ and for the traitor Judas. This is complete heresy.]

We must recall, however, as we have seen in the previous chapter, that such comments should be viewed in the context of similar attacks on the eternity of creation and so on. The Faculty of Arts was, it seemed to Bonaventure, a dangerous hotbed of potential dissent, in so far as some of the Masters like Siger claimed an independence for philosophy as a separate discipline in its own right. This, he felt, led to a rationalism which, while it was not dependent on faith, was however unacceptable in his view for a Christian:

> ... philosophica scientia via est ad alias scientias, sed qui vult
> stare, cadit in tenebras [89].

[... the science of philosophy leads to the other sciences, but the person who chooses to remain there falls into darkness.]

Both Wéber [90] and Van Steenberghen [91] feel that D'Albi [92], in his study on Bonaventure's influence on the events in Paris from 1267 to 1277, exaggerates in turn both Thomas' apparent wavering in condemning these dangerous teachings and also the importance of Bonaventure's role in forcing the struggle against them. They find it impossible to believe that Thomas would not be fighting fervently against such perceived dangers to Christianity and can only assume that he is biding his time. However, while Brady and Gauthier may both be right in thinking that Thomas reached Paris in the first few months of 1269 [93], is it not more than feasible that the Neothomist views of Wéber and Van Steenberghen have clouded their judgment? This may then have led them into an exaggerated defence of Thomas' so-called orthodoxy and D'Albi may be right to some extent in that, even if Thomas was not totally supportive of Siger, nevertheless he did have some sympathy for his position and for his methodology. He would not then be expected to have issued attacks on Siger's position earlier. As an Aristotelian, he may perhaps have understood some of what Siger had been trying to say about the dynamic relationship between the operations of the intellective soul and the vegetative-sensitive soul. In any case he himself did not agree with the more extreme dualistic tendencies in Augustinian thought, which ultimately owed their origins to Neoplatonism. This might well account for his initial reluctance to enter the fray, until he felt that he had no alternative but to throw his own hat into the ring.

In this treatise, however, Thomas does begin by declaring that he is aware that the view that the intellect is a separated substance is against the Christian faith and that it creates problems regarding reward and punishment. He will argue however on mainly philosophical, rather than theological, grounds:

> Et sic tollitur retributio praemiorum et paenarum et diversitas eorundem. Intendimus autem ostendere positionem praedictam non minus contra philosophiae principia esse quam contra fidei documenta [94].

[And so there is removed the retribution of rewards and punishments and the diversity among them. We intend however to show that the foresaid position is not less opposed to the principles of philosophy than it is contrary to the documents of the faith.]

The first half of the book is devoted to demonstrating that the answer, for Thomas, lies in the fact that the human soul, in its entirety, is the form of the living, but material, body rather than in the analogy of the sailor and his ship. At the same time, talk of a soul-in-common is merely metaphorical:

> Hoc ergo habito, quod anima determinatur vegetativo, sensitivo, intellectivo et motu, vult ostendere consequenter quod quantum ad omnes istas partes, anima utitur corpori non sicut nauta navi, sed sicut forma. Et sic certificatum erit quid sit anima in communi, quod supra figuraliter tantum dictum est [95].

[I therefore uphold this that the fact that the soul is defined by its vegetative, sensitive and intellective impulse means in consequence that, with regard to its relationship to all those elements, the soul uses the body. not as a sailor uses a ship but as a form. Hence, it will be clear what is the nature of the soul-in-common and that it was only spoken of above in a figurative sense.]

The first chapter is very much involved in trying to demonstrate that Ibn Rushd is not a reliable interpreter of Aristotle's original thought, accusing him twice of perverse statements [96]. It claims that the human soul is unique among forms united to matter, precisely because it has a power of operation within the intellect, which does not require a bodily organ; it is in this sense that Aristotle could speak, says Thomas, of the soul being "separate":

> Manifeste apparet ... quod intellectus (possibilis) sit aliquid animae quae est actus corporis; ita tamen quod intellectus animae non habeat aliquod organum corporale, sicut habent ceterae potentiae animae [97].

[It is absolutely clear ... that the (receptive) intellect is the part of the soul which is the act of the body. This, however, is in such a way that the intellect of the soul does not have any bodily organ in the way that the other powers of the soul do.]

In the second chapter, Thomas yet again accuses Ibn Rushd of being "perverse" [98] and, more particularly, in its conclusion where he condemns the latter's so-called Aristotelianism in most scathing terms:

> ... qui non tam fuit Peripateticus, quam philosophiae peripateticae depravator [99].

[... who was not so much an Aristotelian as a source of distortion of Aristotelian philosophy.]

Could these attacks on Ibn Rushd in this first part of the treatise, when considered in conjunction with what Thomas has claimed to be his defence of the real Aristotle, not amount just as much to an attack on those Augustinian opponents of Aristotelianism, like Bonaventure, as on what Siger himself was actually teaching? We have seen in the previous chapter that such a scenario was recognized by Van Steenberghen and other more recent writers with regard to the question of the possibility of demonstrating by reason alone the temporal creation of the world although it is not so considered by them for this issue. It might make much more sense not to draw such a sharp distinction between Thomas' approach on these two issues. Certainly, Thomas' disagreement with Ibn Rushd - or with Ibn Sina, come to that - is not so surprising when we consider how he had ostensibly devoted the entire <u>Summa Contra Gentiles</u> to arguing against Muslims.

Thomas' actual exposition of his case that the intellectual soul is the substantial form of man is based on the almost Cartesian premise that:

> Manifestum est enim quod hic homo singularis intelligit: nunquam enim de intellectu quaereremus, nisi intelligeremus [100].

[It is clear indeed that this particular man has intellection: for we would never be inquiring about the intellect unless we were in the process of intellection.]

This case, then, is clearly based on each person's apparent psychological awareness of the experience of individual thought. Whether this is altogether a totally valid attack on Ibn Rushd is perhaps open to dispute. A modern scholar, concentrating on the latter's metaphysics, declares that "Ibn Rushd ... draws an original distinction between the pure, incorruptible substance of this (active) intellect and its act, united with the material intellect and subject to generation and corruption; acts of intellection follow upon one another; wherever a new act of intellection is generated, the previous one is destroyed" (101). However, this is not our main point of concern here, although we are able to note how our explanation of Siger's own teaching in his Quaestiones in Tertium de Anima also reflects his own interpretation of this problem from a metaphysical perspective.

Thomas argues that, unless each human being has a distinct intellect, it would be impossible to maintain unity and continuity of understanding within the individual.   This, for him, is the basic fallacy of Ibn Rushd's position (102). Almost certainly with an eye on some of the views of Siger and others, he does not see that the idea of the intellect being a mover can possibly provide a satisfactory solution:

> Tunc intellectus non se habet ad Socratem, nisi sicut movens
> ad motum.   Sed secundum hoc actio intellectus quae est
> intelligere, nullo modo poterit attribui Socrati (103).

[If this were the case, the intellect is only related to Socrates as a mover to the moved object.   This, however, would mean that the action of the intellect, which is understanding, will not be able to be attributed to Socrates.]

He goes on to deny that his own position implies that the intellect is a material form [forma materialis] (104); it is rather, says Thomas, a form of matter [forma materiae] (105).   That is to imply that it is not precontained within the potentialities of matter, developing naturally through the conception of a new human being.   On the other hand, it is created directly by God so as to enable an actual individual organism to come into existence.   It is noticeable that, in the

242

whole of this section of the corpus which is concerned with the relationship of the intellect, soul and body, although he names Ibn Rushd (under his Latin appellation) on quite a number of occasions, he does not however mention by name Siger or any of the contemporary Artists. This is despite the fact that he does apparently allude to arguments, objections and counter-arguments that could be attributed to Siger.

In the second part of the treatise, Thomas proceeds in his fourth chapter to take up the second aspect of the controversy, that is to say, the notion of a single intellect for the entire human race. He begins by trying to argue that such a view is more in tune with Plato than with Aristotle [106]. If this were maintained, we could not preserve, he says, the differences that pertain between people:

> Si igitur sit unus intellectus omnium, ex necessitate sequitur
> quod sit unus intelligens, et per consequens unus volens, et
> unus utens pro suae voluntatis arbitrio omnibus illis secundum
> quae homines diversificantur ad invicem [107].

[If therefore there is a single intellect for all, it would necessarily follow that there is one person as the subject of understanding. In consequence of this there would only be one subject of willing and one subject of his own freewill, using all those things according to which human beings are differentiated from one another.]

He goes on to argue that such a thesis is also incompatible with a true understanding of Aristotle. Hence, by implication, he again separates himself from Ibn Rushd and anyone else reliant on the latter's apparent interpretation of Aristotle over this question. Matter may indeed be the principle of individuation, but we can also, Thomas argues, have multiplication even of separated substances, let alone the human individual:

> Individuae ergo sunt substantiae separatae et singulares; non
> autem individuantur ex materia, sed ex hoc ipso quod non

sunt natae in alio esse, et per consequens nec participari a multis. Ex quo sequitur quod si aliqua forma nata est participari ab aliquo, ita quod sit actus alicuius materiae, illa potest individuari et multiplicari per comparationem ad materiam (108).

[Therefore separated substances are individual and singular. However, they are not individuated by matter, but rather by the very fact they do not exist by nature in something else, and hence are not participated in by many. It follows from this that any form which is by nature participable by something else, in such a way that is the act of some matter, can be individuated and multiplied by its relationship to matter.]

It is, however, very interesting to discover that Thomas is ready to turn to the possibility of God acting as an external cause in the creation of the multiplicity of human intellects for each person. Furthermore, although he does state his case at first in philosophical terms, as had been intimated at the beginning of the treatise, he now turns to God's omnipotence and ability to perform miracles as a possible solution, since otherwise:

... sic enim possent concludere quod Deus non potest facere quod mortui resurgant, et quod caeci ad visum reparentur (109).

[... for they could so conclude that God cannot accomplish that the dead should rise again and that the blind should be restored to sight.]

For Thomas, of course, the big theological difficulty is the continued existence of the individual after death. He is forced to concede that his arguments would emphasize the imperfection, in the sense of human incompleteness, of life-after-death:

Concedimus autem quod anima humana a corpore separata non habet ultimam perfectionem suae naturae, cum sit pars naturae humanae. Nulla enim pars habet omnimodam perfectionem si a toto separetur (110).

[We concede however that the human soul, when separated from the body, does not possess the ultimate perfection of its nature. This is because no part possesses perfection in every way if it is separated from the entire being.]

In his final argument, he asserts that, far from later writers breaking away from the authentic Aristotle, it is Ibn Rushd who stands out among all philosophers as the one who has deviated from the commonly-held opinion which he has already outlined:

Unde merito supradiximus eum philosophiae peripateticae perversorem. Unde mirum est quomodo aliqui, solum commentum Averrois videntes, pronuntiare praesumunt, quod ipse dicit, hoc sensisse omnes philosophos Graecos et Arabes, praeter Latinos (111).

[We have therefore stated above with justification that he has been a source of distortion of Aristotelian philosophy. It is therefore remarkable how some people, only seeing Ibn Rushd's comment, take the liberty of declaring his statement to be the opinion of every Greek and Arab philosopher as opposed to the Latins.]

It is probably the last three paragraphs of the treatise, which make up Thomas' conclusion, summary and indeed challenge to others, that prove the most fascinating of all. It will be recalled that Ibn Rushd - and, come to that, many other Greek and Arab philosophers too - has been mentioned on many occasions in this work, often pejoratively. There have also been references to those who have, in Thomas' opinion, relied too heavily on him to the detriment of a genuine understanding of Aristotle. At the same time, no contemporary philosopher has been singled out for such treatment. Here, however, Thomas really does indignantly attack one particular person - albeit still unnamed, he is assumed to be Siger - for presuming to suggest that the opposition to the single unicity of intellect is merely a stance held by Latin Christians to remain in accordance with that Church's magisterium:

> Est etiam maiori admiratione vel etiam indignatione dignum, quod aliquis Christianum se profitens tam irreverenter de christiana fide loqui praesumpserit; sicut cum dicit quod Latini pro principio hoc non recipiunt, scil. quod sit unus intellectus tantum, quia forte lex eorum est in contrarium. Ubi duo sunt mala: primo, quia dubitat an hoc sit contra fidem: secundo, quia se alienum innuit esse ab hac lege. Et quod postmodum dicit: haec est ratio per quam Catholici videntur habere suam positionem, ubi sententiam fidei positionem nominat [112].

[It is also worthy of great wonder or even indignation that somebody claiming to be a Christian should presume to speak with such irreverence about the Christian faith. This arises from his saying that the Latins have not accepted this on principle - namely that there is only one intellect - because perhaps their law opposes it. There are two things wrong with this: firstly, because he doubts whether this is against the faith and, secondly, he suggests that he himself is outside of this law. It is even more so because he goes on to state that this is the reason for which Catholics apparently hold their position, when they claim it to be a matter of faith.]

Thomas goes on to impute to this individual the claim that multiplicity of intellects involves a contradiction in terms, but that nevertheless the latter believes it as a matter of faith, while being obliged to reject it on philosophical and rational grounds:

> Nec minoris praesumptionis est quod postmodum asserere audet: Deum non posse facere quod sint multi intellectus, quia implicat contradictionem. Adhuc autem gravius est quod postmodum dicit: per rationem concludo de necessitate,

246

quod intellectus est unus numero; firmiter tamen teneo
oppositum per fidem [113].

[It is no less presumptuous that he dares to proceed to assert that God
cannot effect there to be a multiplicity of intellects, on the grounds that it implies a
contradiction. However even more seriously he states further: I necessarily
conclude by reason that the intellect is one in number although I firmly maintain the
opposite by faith.]

In the penultimate paragraph, Thomas attacks this philosopher's
audacity in discussing issues such as hell-fire and for opposing the views of learned
scholars, for he adds cynically that he might just as well start getting involved in
topics such as the Trinity and the Incarnation:

> Non caret etiam magna temeritate, quod de his quae ad
> philosophiam non pertinent, sed sunt purae fidei, disputare
> praesumit, sicut quod anima patiatur ab igne inferni, et dicere
> sententias doctorum de hoc esse reprobandas. Pari enim
> ratione posset disputare de Trinitate, de Incarnatione, et de
> aliis huiusmodi, de quibus nonnisi caecutiens loqueretur [114].

[He even has the great audacity to presume to challenge those matters
which do not pertain to philosophy but belong to pure faith, such as that the soul
might suffer from hellfire, and to say that the opinions of the learned on this should
be reproved. He would have as much reason to challenge the Trinity, the
Incarnation and other teachings of this kind, about which only someone going blind
would speak.]

Finally, Thomas repeats his claim that he has argued on the
philosophical level without turning to documents of faith [115], before laying down
the gauntlet in challenging the unnamed scholar to come right out into the open if
he wants to maintain his opposition:

... non loquatur in angulis nec coram pueris qui nesciunt de tam arduis iudicare; sed contra hoc scriptum rescribat, si audet ... [116].

[...let him not speak in corners nor in the presence of juveniles who do not know how to make judgments about such difficult matters. On the other hand, let him write back against this writing, if he should dare...]

Van Steenberghen shows no hesitation in following earlier scholars in declaring that the apparently fierce reaction of Thomas is explained by the grave threat posed by his opponent to the Christian faith [117]. While it would clearly be ridiculous to suggest that Thomas was in sympathy and merely acting out a charade, the truth nevertheless may be somewhere in between. We have already noted how, despite Bonaventure's earlier tirade against what he understood by monopsychism, Thomas appears to have taken a year or so before reacting in public. Might not this betray some hesitation or caution, or perhaps even that he was eventually, precisely because of his academic pre-eminence, challenged or pushed into making an open statement himself, on behalf of apparent Christian orthodoxy, but from a mainly philosophical perspective?

While Thomas had presented his analysis of Aristotle's position from a psychological perspective within philosophy, he must have been aware, as Van Steenberghen acknowledges, of the problems arising from the latter's metaphysics, regarding the need for a perpetual immaterial being to be a separate substance [118]. However ingenious Thomas' solution of the intellect as being a "form of matter" able to subsist alone, is it necessarily any more philosophically acceptable - or, indeed, more faithful to Aristotle's thought as a whole, despite his attacks on Ibn Rushd as perverting it - than Siger's idea of the dynamic and composite union in the human being between the single operative intellect and the vegetative-sensitive soul animating the body? Another point is that there are examples in the second part of the treatise where Thomas does tend to interchange the phrases "intellect" and "intellective soul" somewhat gratuitously [119].

Van Steenberghen does make a very constructive point in suggesting that Thomas would have been better advised to have spoken of the essential need for the human soul to be created in, but not necessarily to remain in, a body [120]. This would have been a better approach than to speak of its having to be united to matter, that is to say, the body, since Thomas would have been able to have avoided having to use the argument, more shaky on a metaphysical level than might at first appear, that it is the fact of the destruction of the body that itself prevents the natural union of body and soul after death:

> Essentiale enim est animae quod corpori uniatur; sed hoc impeditur per accidens, non ex parte sua sed ex parte corporis quod corrumpitur [121].

[For it is of the essence of the soul that it should be united to the body. This is however accidentally prevented, not of its own accord but as a result of the body which is corrupted.]

It does seem that he avoids tackling the very real metaphysical points at issue. It is hard to believe that he did not appreciate this. It is of course possible, as Van Steenberghen suggests, that he chooses to do this, so as to avoid presenting his anti-Aristotelian opponents with more ammunition [122]. However, it is also possible that he was in some ways sympathetic to Siger's attempts to resolve this issue.

Even though Siger had no specific published writing on it, Thomas would not have wanted him to have initiated an unwanted, and perhaps unnecessary, conflict with the Church authorities. This desire may very well have been at the heart of Thomas' warning to keep out of theological issues - which, after all, is almost always the case with Siger. After all, Thomas himself has, despite the protestations that he has restricted himself to philosophical considerations, taken his usual approach of using philosophy as a tool to fit in with what he believes to be orthodox Christian teaching. On the other hand, Siger has acknowledged, as we have already seen in Quaestio 11 of his Commentary, that he has very real reservations about even offering some philosophical insights into the topic of the physical fires of hell.

Likewise, that challenge of Thomas, referred to above, where in his summary he calls on his apparent adversary to avoid discussions "in angulis et coram pueris" [in corners and in the presence of juveniles] would make sense in such a scenario if it was intended to act as a public warning. After all, this does not have to be interpreted, as it always seems to have been, as a strong personal attack. It will be recalled that all the students in the Faculty of Arts were young and relatively immature. Hence, they could quite justifiably be described as juveniles, boys or young men. Siger's lectures on the <u>Liber De Anima</u> would have been internal to this Faculty and could well be metaphorically described as "in angulis". Thomas would almost certainly have heard some of the young students or novices at Saint-Jacques, where he lived, discussing these lectures. No doubt, he would have been concerned about their inability to understand fully what Siger might, as an eminent scholar, have been getting at. It is more than likely that, in answering questions and asserting the independence of his Faculty, he may well have over-emphasized on occasions some points which would be bound to upset the authorities and could be interpreted as attacks on the Church.

Certainly, it has been shown - and Thomas himself would probably have had no reason to think otherwise - that Siger nowhere supports the "double-truth" theory that something can be true by reason and false by revealed truth or vice versa. On the other hand, we have seen - and Thomas argued this with some vehemence with regard to the temporal creation of the world - that philosophy and revelation can present truths on two different dimensions, much as the scientist and the theologian might do today. This would explain Thomas' apparent attack above regarding "double-truth" and why he preferred to argue in this treatise on a psychological level. Of course, Siger and Thomas might have even agreed - if they ever had a chance to talk together socially as seems almost certain to be the case in an ambience such as the University of Paris in 1270 - that, on a level of speaking in everyday common parlance, each individual person is aware of himself or herself thinking. It was the deeper philosophical and theological issues that needed to be thrashed out.

Thomas could well be not only protecting his own position regarding his use of Aristotelian ideas, but also encouraging Siger to avoid misinterpretation by his young students. Hence, a reasoned written response would be more appropriate. All this of course is mostly speculation but, on consideration of all the evidence, does not seem less likely than the more usual interpretation, which we have already seen, of taking Thomas' conclusion merely in a most immediately obvious and perhaps superficial way.

An interpretation of events somewhat along these lines would offer a much more probable reflection of attitudes, stances and responses among the main participants within the undoubtedly highly charged academic atmosphere in Paris around the year 1270. It would also provide yet another perspective to the fact that many of the later 1277 Condemnations were apparently directed against Thomas himself.

Bazán [123], Lefèvre [124] and Van Steenberghen [125], despite their almost predictable reactions in denying the possibility that Thomas could have been influenced to amend his views by Siger - as suggested by Wéber in his book La Controverse de 1270 à l'Université de Paris et Son Retentissement sur la Pensée de S. Thomas d'Aquin and further developed in a later article [126] - may well be right to assert that Wéber does not overall provide enough evidence to prove his thesis conclusively. However, it is far more likely, as can well be imagined, that Thomas cleverly accepted Siger as a scholar of stature and even of kindred spirit in his appreciation of Aristotle as providing a framework for developing intellectual thought. Hence, he would have felt it necessary to take account of some of Siger's opinions and suggestions in searching for a valid and constructive way ahead.

It is hard to avoid the feeling that even as great a scholar as Van Steenberghen may sometimes allow his feelings of commitment to Neothomism to cloud his judgment and assessment of the actual historical situation. Certainly, it is possible, as when the former rushes to Thomas' defence in declaring the latter's acceptance of the principle of "agere sequitur esse" [action follows existence], that

Siger may not have fully understood Thomas' position [127]. However, it is equally plausible here that Thomas may not have fully understood the position of Siger, as we have seen it. This would also help to explain the pleas by Thomas for more open dialogue, as would the fact that he is so willing to attack Ibn Rushd, without undermining respect for Aristotle too much. Wéber is probably right in thinking that even Thomas subconsciously does not find it easy to cast aside centuries of Neoplatonic influence [128]. After all, Siger too is susceptible to this, as we shall soon see when we examine his <u>Quaestiones super Librum De Causis</u>.

Furthermore, when Van Steenberghen comments on Thomas' maintenance of the real distinction between the soul and its powers of operation, he does in fact, perhaps understandably, touch upon the very reason why Siger upheld his position so vigorously regarding the immaterial nature of intellection [129]. What must by now be certain is that the true historical and intellectual ambience cannot be fully captured simply by looking at texts in isolation or solely through the eyes of a modern Neothomist.

6.8.   Siger's Initial Response to Thomas Aquinas.

We only know of what seems to be Siger's first and initial written response to Thomas' challenge through secondhand sources. For these indirect discoveries, one is totally indebted to the Italian scholar, Bruno Nardi who discovered that, in the early sixteenth century, Agostino Nifo - and a little later Francesco di Silvestri, a Dominican from Ferrara, probably relying on the former's work then being produced via the printing-press [130] - relates how he is aware of an apparently conciliatory reply from Siger to Thomas:

> Sunt et alii viri in philosophia praeclari, qui voluerunt quasi mediare inter latinos et Averroycos, ut Subgerius contemporaneus Thomae, in quodam tractatu misso Thomae in responsione ad illum Thomae [131].

[There are also other men, distinguished in philosophy, who appeared to want to steer a middle course between the Latins and the Averroists, as did Siger, a contemporary of Thomas, in a certain treatise sent to Thomas in response to that of Thomas.]

It would appear from quotations offered that this was indeed the case. On the one hand, he is said to speak of the receptive intellect (though here Nifo uses the Averroist term "material") as an eternal separated form, unique to all mankind, while, on the other hand, he speaks of man as being differentiated as an individual by the substantial union of his body with this intellect:

> ... opinatur cum averroycis intellectum materialem esse formam perpetuam ex utroquo latere, et quod non est forma materialis, hoc est educta de facultate materiae generalis aut corruptibilis, et quod sit una numero omnibus hominibus ... Amplius, voluit hominem esse per se unum compositum ex corpore et intellectu materiali praedicto, directe reponibile in praedicamento substantiae ... (132).

[...he supposes like the Averroists that the material intellect is a perpetual form from two perspectives, both because it is not a material form, derived from the potentiality of ordinary or corruptible matter, and also because it is single in number for all human beings... Furthermore, he wanted to say that the human being, who is by nature (per se) a single being composed of a body and the foresaid material intellect, could be directly placed directly in the category of substance.]

Siger then goes on to show his continuing philosophical disagreement with Thomas, in that the intellect cannot be the form of matter, as Nifo directly quotes Siger:

> Et addit: nec potest intellectus informare materiam, non informante cogitativa, quia non stat materia sine forma constituta in esse per eam; et non potest intellectus informare

sine sua proxima dispositione et ultima, quae est cogitativa (133).

[He also adds: "the intellect cannot inform matter, unless the imagination is so informing, because there is no matter existing without a form set up into existence through it. Also, the intellect cannot inform without its closest and ultimate disposition, which is the imagination".]

On the other hand, the "imagination", since it is of material origin, is itself able to effect the union between the unique intellect and the vegetative-sensitive soul, thereby enabling the Intellect to be primarily and directly the form and the act of humanity as such, while at the same time it can secondarily and indirectly be the act and perfection of each individual human being:

> Sed est primo et per se forma et actus naturae humanae, et per accidens actus et perfectio secundum postremam perfectionem Sortis et Platonis et aliorum; ... et quia postremae perfectiones sunt numeratae, ideo non sequitur   quod ego intelligam per tuum et tu per meum intelligere (134).

[But it is firstly and intrinsically the form and act of human nature and accidentally the act and perfection according to the final perfection of Socrates, Plato and others... and because the final perfections are individuated, it does not therefore follow that I have understanding through your understanding and you through mine.]

Elsewhere, Nifo tells us that Siger claims the human mind is able to know separated substances, and particularly God, directly without intermediaries. It is this latter knowledge which can be the greatest source of happiness for us (135). This point is further explained, he says, in Siger's "Liber De Felicitate", which may or may not be a different book from that other one "De Intellectu" to which Nifo is referring:

... sed Deus est quo omnes felicitantur, quoniam omnes intellectus felicitantur intelligendo Deum [136].

[... but it is through God that all achieve happiness since all intellects achieve happiness by understanding of God.]

What can be made of these extracts from Nifo? Although it is generally recognized by almost all scholars that they do represent, in some way, Siger's first response to Thomas' challenge, nevertheless they are of course only fragments of this response and, with a few exceptions, only paraphrases of the original at that! Thus, for example, it is highly unusual for Siger, at this stage of his career, to speak directly in this kind of way about God - a point that even Van Steenberghen fails to note. In fact, the latter also seems to misunderstand just what Nifo was declaring Siger to have in common with the so-called Latins by referring to the human being as a "per se" union of the animated body with the intellect of the species. Indeed, Van Steenberghen repeats this mistake from his 1966 book word-for-word in his great work of 1977 [137].

Although he is right in saying that Siger again bases his case on this actual union with the help of the imagination [cogitative], the highest faculty of the vegetative-sensitive soul, Van Steenberghen nevertheless gets carried away regarding what he calls flagrant, but previously hidden, incoherences about this. His accusations of Neoplatonic tendencies in Siger, whether true or not, are found in many other writers, including Thomas himself. Besides, we must recall that the Liber De Causis, for example, although attributed to Aristotle in fact belongs to Proclus.

Van Steenberghen then goes on to get involved in theological speculation regarding the knowledge of God in Himself, such as Thomas does in his theological works regarding the Beatific Vision. Again, the Belgian scholar finds Siger wanting as far he is concerned, although on such scanty evidence this hardly seems justified. Even if - as seems unlikely - Siger had himself dipped further into the realms of theology, there seems every likelihood that this would all have confirmed him in his thesis advocating the independence of philosophy from theology.   As for Van Steenberghen himself, he now concludes this somewhat unreliable analysis by showing his true feelings about Nardi by accusing him of letting his so-called rebellious feelings get the better of him in a way unbefitting someone whom he describes as a son of St. Dominic [138]!   When we note that Nardi had given up the priesthood and indeed left the Church for a while as a young man, it is hard to escape the feeling that Van Steenberghen may be departing somewhat here from his own very high standards of objectivity, particularly as Nardi's research had already forced him to change his views over more than one matter [139].

On the other hand, how much has Siger really changed his own views since the Quaestiones in Tertium De Anima?   Surely caution is needed until and unless we possess the original texts, since Nifo is writing two hundred and fifty years after the events.   However, a preliminary judgment would suggest that there is no fundamental change of position in response to Thomas' De Unitate Intellectus Contra Averroistas.   There is rather, at most, an elucidation of his positions regarding the complete union of Intellect and vegetative-sensitive soul in the individual and regarding the way in which the former can be primarily the form and act of humanity as a whole and secondarily that of each individual person.

Indeed, Pattin has recently claimed that serious doubts should be raised as to whether there really is a separate work De Intellectu and he suggests, mostly as a result of making an ingenious change to Nifo's introductory text, that it should perhaps be identifed with Siger's Quaestiones in Tertium de Anima [140].   The case is certainly not proven, although the evidence presented earlier in this study does make it more than merely possible.   However, in the absence of further indications, the position that they are two separate works will continue to be assumed here. Siger may well have been clarifying his own research and reflection regarding his own stance, as Thomas had demanded following his assertion, which we saw in the previous section, that "hic homo intelligit".   However, he does still emphasize the operative element of the union.   If this is the case, Siger's approach is much like that of a modern scientist, when challenged to explain and back up his theorizing, so as to match apparent empirical experience.

6.9.   De Anima Intellectiva.

Whilw we have seen that Siger's <u>Quaestiones in Tertium De Anima</u> - and perhaps the <u>De Intellectu</u> cited by Nifo - was delivered prior to the Condemnations of Tempier of 10 December 1270, Bazán dates the <u>De Anima Intellectiva</u> to 1273-1274 by means of some carefully documented evidence, both external and internal [141]. This dating has been more or less accepted without controversy by all scholars, with the exception of Caparello, who argues that it predates the <u>Quaestiones in Tertium De Anima</u> on somewhat flimsy evidence developed from her very personal interpretation of the respective texts [142]. She claims the support of some evidence from Nardi that the position, quoted by Nifo as being in Siger's first response to Thomas, is found in the latter work and hence they could be one and the same. However, as we shall see, similarity of teaching is present in all these writings, but development is only understood by interpretation and clarification of the concepts and arguments by scholars. Furthermore, we have already noted the views of Pattin towards the end of the previous section and it is indeed far more likely that Siger, in response to a challenge such as Thomas', would offer reasoned replies in the form of a treatise or treatises rather than merely in a taught commentary.

Siger introduces this most important treatise <u>De Anima Intellectiva</u>, by indicating that it does so constitute a reasoned summary of his research into what reputable philosophers maintain on this topic and in response to requests from his friends:

> Et ideo, exposcentibus amicis, eorum desiderio pro modulo nostrae possibilitatis satisfacere cupientes, quid circa praedicta sentiendum sit secundum documenta philosophorum probatorum, non aliquid ex nobis asserentes, praesenti tractatu proponimus declarare [143].

[And hence, at the pleading of friends and wishing to satisfy their desire as best we can, we propose to declare in this present treatise not our own personal assertions but what is felt about the foresaid matters according to the writings of approved philosophers.]

He has obviously been affected by Thomas' powerful accusations that Ibn Rushd had perverted, rather than faithfully transmitted and interpreted, Aristotle. As stated above, therefore, he looks at a wide range of philosophers, even describing Albert and Thomas as preeminent practitioners - "praecipui viri in philosophia Albertus et Thomas" [Albert and Thomas, men distinguished in philosophy] [144]. On the other hand, apart from the very brief neutral quotation of Ibn Rushd's view of the importance of the issue at the very beginning of the Prologue [145], there is only one other reference to him throughout the entire treatise [146].

After two brief non-controversial chapters on the definition and meaning of the word "soul" as such, it is in the third that Siger really gets to grips with the nub of the issue about the intellective soul, by presenting in his customary scholastic style the two respective sets of arguments. It will in any case be recalled that Siger had amended Ibn Rushd's term "material intellect" to "potential (or receptive) intellect" and emphasized that the latter and the "agent intellect" were really two aspects or powers of the same separated substance, rather than two distinct separated substances [147]. His solution now is to declare that intellection is in one sense united to, but in another sense separated from, matter. This is to preserve, as Thomas had demanded in his treatise, the need to be able to assert that each person understands as an individual, but also to acknowledge that there is no bodily organ of intellection:

> Solutio.   Anima intellectiva non cognoscitur nisi ex eius
> opere, scilicet intelligere. Intelligere autem est quodammodo
> unitum materiae et quodammodo separatum.   Nisi enim
> intelligere esset unitum aliquo modo ad materiam, non esset
> verum dicere quod homo ipse intelligit. Intelligere etiam
> aliquo modo est separatum a materia, cum non sit in organo
> corporeo, ut videre in oculo, ut dicit Philosophus [148].

[The answer is that the intellective soul is only known as a result of its operation, namely its intellection. Intellection is however in one way united to matter and in another separated from it. This is because unless intellection were in some way united to matter, it would not be true to say that a human being itself has understanding. Intellection is also in some way separated from matter, since, as Aristotle says, it is not in a bodily organ, like sight in the eye.]

Siger will of course need to explain this if he is to maintain the Principle of Non-Contradiction which he had upheld in his fourth chapter [(149)]. In point of fact, he begins by looking at the solution of Albert and Thomas, who, he alleges, claim that the intellective soul is united to the body in substance, albeit its potentiality is not:

> ... dicunt ... quod substantia animae intellectivae unita est corpori dans esse eidem, sed potentia animae intellectivae separata est a corpore, cum per organum corporeum non operetur [(150)].

[... they say ... that the substance of the intellective soul is united to the body, giving existence to the same, but that the potentiality of the intellective soul is separated from the body since it does not operate through a bodily organ.]

In fact, Siger does not directly and independently tackle Albert's claim that the power of intellection must be rooted in the same subject as the vegetative and sensitive powers, since, as we shall see, philosophy cannot possibly prove this as such. He reminds us that, since he is a philosophy lecturer, he is not attempting to argue on theological grounds:

> Quaerimus enim hic solum intentionem philosophorum et praecipue Aristotelis, etsi forte Philosophus senserit aliter quam veritas se habeat et sapientia, quae per revelationem de anima sint tradita, quae per rationes naturales concludi non possunt. Sed nihil ad nos nunc de Dei miraculis, cum de naturalibus naturaliter disseramus [(151)].

[Here, however, we seek only the meaning intended by the philosophers and especially Aristotle, although the latter may perhaps have felt differently from what actually constitutes truth and wisdom, which may have been handed down about the soul through revelation and which cannot be concluded through natural reasoning. Nevertheless, we are not concerned at present with divine miracles, since we are arguing on natural grounds about things of nature.]

Siger denies that a power of operation can be more immaterial than that substance from which it flows, as is implied by making the distinction between substance and power, and recalls the axiom that "action is in proportion to substantial form":

> ... cum dicitur 'aliquid agit per suam formam' extensive debet accipi forma, ut et intrinsecum operans ad materiam forma dicatur [152].

[... when it is said "something acts through its form", the form must be accepted in its entirety so that what is intrinsic operating on matter should be called form.]

In fact, Thomas had himself accepted this problem but had attempted to overcome it by means of his own distinction, whereby he described the intellect as the "forma materiae" rather than the "forma materialis" [153]. Needless to say, Siger prefers his own solution which, he feels, does overcome rather better the problem of there being a need for a physical organ in the body for intellection to take place if this union in man has to be of a substantial nature:

> Si substantia animae intellectivae haberet esse unitum ad materiam ita quod dans esse materiae, tunc, cum intelligere sit in substantia animae intellectivae, intelligere haberet esse in aliqua parte corporis, ut visio in oculo, aut in toto corpore, quod negat Philosophus [154].

[If the substance of the intellective soul had existence united to matter in such a way that it was giving existence to matter, then, since intellection is in the substance of the intellective soul, intellection would have existence in some part of the body, like vision in the eye, or in the whole body. This is denied by Aristotle.]

This is why Siger sees the union as an operative union:

Anima tamen intellectiva corpori est unita in operando [155].

[However the intellective soul is united to the body in the process of operation.]

He wants of course also to avoid suggesting that intellection can be attributed to the physical body as its subject:

Si homo intelligeret quia substantia animae intellectivae daret esse materiae aut corpori, non solum homini posset attribui operatio intelligendi, sed et corpori, quod falsum est et negat Philosophus [156].

[If the human being had understanding because the substance of the intellective soul gave existence to matter or to the body, the operation of understanding could not only be attributed to man but also to the body. This is false and denied by Aristotle.]

Siger's solution, therefore, rests on the fact that the intellect does not depend on the phantasm, and hence indirectly the body, as subject but as object:

Et cum intellectus dependeat ex corpore quia dependet ex phantasmate in intelligendo, non dependet ex eo sicut ex subiecto in quo sit intelligere, sed sicut ex obiecto, cum phantasmata sint intellectui sicut sensibilia sensui [157].

[In addition, since the intellect depends on the body because it depends on the phantasm in the process of intellection, it does not depend on it as if on a subject in which there is intellection, but as on an object, since phantasms are like sense objects.]

This theory about operative union is confirmed, Siger believes, by our empirical experience that, if the imagination suffers physical damage, then the human being loses the use of the intellect:

> ... laesa quadam parte corporis, ut organo imaginationis, homo prius sciens scientiam amittit, quod non contingeret nisi intellectus dependeret a corpore in intelligendo [158].

[... if a particular part of the body is injured, like the organ of the imagination, the human being with prior knowledge loses it. Thus would only happen if the intellect was dependent on the body in the act of intellection.]

Hence, Siger sees the solution summed up in the phrase:

> ... intellectus in intelligendo est operans intrinsecum ad corpus per suam naturam [159].

[... the intellect in the act of intellection operates intrinsically and naturally on the body.]

As in his Quaestiones in Tertium De Anima, he again uses the idea of the sailor and the ship to illustrate this, a model which he much prefers to that of the wax and the cast [160].

We may recall that in that earlier Commentary Siger had spoken of the intellect as operating in the body as mover, rather than as using an organ within it, for intellection:

Tunc dico quod intellectus non est in qualibet parte corporis quantum ad istum actum qui est intelligere. ... Secundum autem aliam operationem intellectus est in corpore, id est intellectus est movens corpus vel motor in corpore [161].

[I state then that the intellect is not in any part whatsoever of the body as regards that act of intellection. ... However, according to another operation the intellect is in the body, that is to say that the intellect is moving the body or the mover in the body.]

How different, indeed, are the meaning and the implications of the two above texts? From Chossat [162] to Van Steenberghen [163], scholars have believed that they see a change of teaching and that the chronologically later text implies a natural and intrinsic union of the intellect with the individual human being rather than through the action of the intellect on individual phantasms. To put it another way is the imagination, which provides the phantasms, to be considered an object within knowledge or a subject, as Thomas argued? It is true that we do not here get the expressions of active and receptive (or material or passive, come to that!) intellects, but there does not really seem to be any significant change in the fundamental position expressed by Siger, as Caparello indeed recognizes [164].

Indeed, if we look at the very context of the phrase here in the De Anima Intellectiva, we note that it was used a few lines earlier in the actual context of phantasms:

... intellectus per naturam suam unitus est et applicatus corpori, natus intelligere ex eius phantasmatibus [165].

[... the intellect is naturally united and attached to the body; its status is to have intellection from the latter's phantasms.]

Is there therefore any justifiable reason to suppose that there has been a sea-change within the intended meaning, as compared with the earlier Commentary? There, Siger had spoken of the understanding of the intellect as occurring not through its own substance but through the nature of the composite being with which it communicates:

> Dicendum quod, si intelligere esset proprium intellectus et ei inesset per naturam intellectus, sic intelligere et scire essent substantia intellectus. Unde quod ei accidit intelligere, hoc non est per naturam ipsius, quasi ei accidat per substantiam suam, sed per naturam totius coniuncti cui communicat, cui accidat intelligere (166).

[It should be stated that, if intellection were proper to the intellect and of the nature of the intellect, it would follow that intellection and knowledge would be the substance of the intellect. Therefore the intellection which belongs to it does not come through its very nature, as though it happens to it through its substance, but through the nature of the entire union to which it communicates and to which understanding belongs.]

At the most, then, it may be possible to suggest with some justification that there is a clarification of his position, in response to the comments of Thomas, and probably those of Tempier too. This involves an increased emphasis on the presence of the intellect in the individual at the time of intellection rather than on the actual phantasms of the body needed by the intellect. Hence, Siger believes he can maintain his basic case and at the same time cope with Thomas' main objection that we must be able to speak of the individual as being able to have intellection, just as we can speak of his being able to have sight:

> Sic et homo intelligit, cum tamen intelligere sit in solo intellectu et non in corpore; unde nec corpus intelligit quamquam corpus sentiat; homo autem ipse intelligit secundum partem, sicut videt secundum partem (167).

[And thus the human being has intellection, since however intellection is in the intellect alone and not in the body; therefore the body does not have intellection although the body has sense-knowledge; the human being however does not itself have intellection from the perspective of a part in the way that it sees from the perspective of a part.]

It is clear that here, as when he spoke earlier in this treatise of the process of intellection as being human [168], he is not in any way watering down his concept of the union as a dynamic one brought about by the joint operation within the individual [169]. The context indicates that he is not using the word "pars" [part] [170] in the sense of substantial union, which seems to be how Thomas employs it in his treatise [171].

As a union of interaction, this is therefore different from that within bodily, physical faculties:

> Modus tamen unionis partis videntis ad alias partes in toto
> vidente alius est quam modus unionis partis intelligentis ad
> alias partes in toto intelligente [172].

[The way in which the seeing part is united to the other parts in the seer as a whole is different from the way in which the knowing part is united to the others in the knower as a whole.]

He believes, in particular, that this theory matches the facts better than that of Thomas, because he considers that Thomas cannot, if there really is to be a full substantial union with the body, avoid having to impute intellection to the body:

> Et secundum modum quem dicit Thomas, homo intelligeret
> non tantum secundum intellectum, sed etiam secundum
> corpus, sicut et est ipsum videre anima visiva et corpore oculi,
> propter hoc quod modus unionis animae visivae ad corpus
> oculi est sicut figurae ad ceram, et formae esse tribuentis ad
> materiam [173].

[Also, according to Thomas' argument, the human being would understand, not only according to the intellect but also according to the body, just as it is that he sees with the visual soul and the bodily eye. This is because the mode of union of the visual soul with the bodily eye is like a mould with wax and is of a form being bestowed on matter.]

Hence, it is clear that Siger, without referring to Ibn Rushd, who had been so vehemently criticized by Thomas, believes that his theory, regarding the relationship of the intellective soul to the body, matches the intentions of Aristotle much more closely than does that of Thomas. Indeed, far from changing his position in response to the arguments of Thomas and the Condemnations of Tempier, as so many earlier scholars have sought to maintain, he seems in fact to have re-emphasized his own case. He explains this more carefully, so as to lessen possible ambiguity, while perhaps, as we have seen, putting a greater emphasis on the act of intellection within the individual rather than on the common need for phantasms within the imagination for both body and intellect. It does appear likely that the judgment of those earlier scholars may have been somewhat clouded by the subsequent definition of the Council of Vienne in 1312 that the intellective soul is primarily and essentially the form of the human body:

> ... quisquis deinceps asserere, defendere seu tenere pertinaciter praesumpserit, quod anima rationalis seu intellectiva non sit forma corporis humani per se et essentialiter, tamquam haereticus sit censendus [174].

[... whoever henceforth should presume scornfully to assert, defend or hold that the rational or intellective soul is not intrinsically and essentially the form of the human body should be reckoned as in heresy.]

The significance of Siger's final words in this chapter will be better understood, therefore, if we now keep in mind their actual historical and intellectual context:

Hoc dicimus sensisse Philosophum de unione animae intellectivae ad corpus; sententiam tamen sanctae fidei catholicae, si contraria huic sit sententiae Philosophi, praeferre volentes, sicut in aliis quibuscumque [175].

[We have stated that Aristotle felt this about the union of the intellective soul with the body. However, just as in any other matters whatsoever, we wish to prefer the opinion of the holy catholic faith if this should be opposed to the opinion of Aristotle.]

We have already seen his tentative disclaimer above [176], suggesting with words like "forte" and the subjunctive "senserit" and "se habent" that he prefers to see the possibility of Aristotle being wrong as a mere hypothesis, while, on the other hand, if supernatural reasons should suggest otherwise, it is not his task to investigate. So, likewise, while he re-emphasizes here his feeling that he has fairly presented Aristotle's teaching, he is reminding us that, if the Catholic faith were to teach otherwise, then of course, as over any other issue, this might well persuade him or anyone else to alter his opinion. An example of this was, indeed, noted in the previous chapter of this study with regard to the creation of the universe [177]. Caparello too emphasizes the hypothetical nature of Siger's comment in this text [178]. She may well be reading more into the text than is justified in suggesting that the purity of the Christian faith is somewhat ambiguous for Siger. After all, the actual text of the Seventh Article of Tempier is far from clear in condemning Siger's interpretation of Aristotle, as explained above. The explicit condemnation of the Council of Vienne is still nearly forty years away, although of course Article 123 of the 1277 Condemnations was almost certainly aimed at Siger's views in this respect:

Quod intellectus non est forma corporis nisi sicut nauta navis,
nec est perfectio essentialis hominis [179].

[That the intellect is only the form of the body like a sailor of a ship and it is not the essential perfection of man.]

Siger's partial reluctance to give way for theological reasons still has some justification and, at the same time, of course, he is re-emphasizing as ever his own independence as a philosopher and that of the Faculty of Arts. Certainly, there is absolutely no evidence here to support any suggestion that he held the classic "double-truth" doctrine in any form at all.

The fourth and fifth chapters of this treatise, which we considered in some detail in the previous chapter of this particular study [180], are relatively straightforward, in so far as they state that, since the intellective soul is spiritual and does not contain matter, it follows therefore that it must be eternal both in the future and in the past, as the following two examples indicate:

Anima intellectiva nec est composita ex materia et forma, nec est forma materialis, sed liberata a materia per se subsistens. Ergo non est corruptibilis seu mortalis [181].

[The intellective soul is not composed of matter and form and is not a material form, but is self-subsisting and free from matter. Therefore it is neither corruptible nor mortal.]

Quare, si anima intellectiva est aeterna et semper ens in futuro, fuit igitur aeterna et semper ens in praeterito [182].

[Hence, if the intellective soul is eternal and always existing in the future, it follows that it has been eternal and always existing in the past.]

Nevertheless, it is worth recalling that Siger leans very heavily on Aristotle for his evidence in the fifth chapter, which contains at least eight direct references to him. Moreover, despite Van Steenberghen's claim that in De Intellectu Siger had identified the agent intellect with God [183], he certainly does assert here the contingency of the intellective soul:

Est tamen attendendum quod, quamquam secundum Aristotelem anima intellectiva est aeterna in praeterito et in futuro, tamen causata est [184].

[It is indeed to be expected that, although according to Aristotle the intellective soul is eternal in the past and in the future, it is however caused.]

Thus, Siger has no hesitation in declaring his determination of the issue on these lines:

Et intelligo animam intellectivam de se semper esse ens sic; quia in eius ratione seu definitione est semper esse, cum careat materia.   Istud tamen semper esse quod est de sui ratione, non habet ex se effective, sed ab alio [185].

[I also understand the intellective soul thus always to be a being in its own right. This is because in its underlying nature or definition it is always to exist since it lacks matter.   It does not however have that perpetual existence, which is of its nature, as an effect intrinsic to itself but as deriving from another being.]

So again there has been no concession to Thomas' apparently dubious ambiguity regarding the intellect, by linking it so intimately in substance to matter and leaving only its power or faculty alone as spiritual.   Here, just as he argued from other perspectives in the Quaestiones in Tertium De Anima, Siger has produced the metaphysical justification for his interpretation of monopsychism and a coherent scheme of philosophy to accompany it.   Again, then, it is within a context similar to that of a scientist today, if challenged by a fellow-scholar, perhaps a Christian one, to justify or withdraw the contents of an earlier article or publication.

Having established the temporal implications of the intellective soul as a non-material and non-corruptible, albeit created, being, Siger looks in the sixth chapter at the question as to whether it is able to exist completely separately from the body.   Among a series of seven arguments (some based on the conclusions of the two previous ones) to prove the impossibility of this, he points out, in the manner of an empirical scientist, that it is only possible to discover evidence regarding effects of the soul, when it is joined to the body and using the phantasms of the imagination. There is no such evidence for any effects, if existing in a state of total separation from the body:

> Nec etiam potest videri totaliter separata a corpore per effectus apparentes de ea a corpore separata, cum hominibus communiter, immo etiam ad hoc studere volentibus, non appareant opera animae talem statum habentis [186].

[Nor can it (the soul) be seen, when totally separated from the body, through manifest effe cts coming from it in this state; in the ordinary way, effects of the soul in such a state are not apparent even to people anxious to study the question.]

This is a long way from confirming the accusations of Thomas and of others that Siger had been indulging in an extreme form of dualism, with the soul not united to the body. As we have seen, it is for him an operative, rather than a substantive, union. As such, however, it is a composite union in which the intellective soul cannot function without a body. Of course, we should recall that the problem for Thomas, and for other theologians too, lay in the implications of this for individual, personal existence after death. Siger, on the other hand, makes it clear that he can find no evidence for this on purely philosophical grounds. Thereby, the only sense, in which the soul can be spoken of as continuing to exist after the death and corruption of the body, arises because, in Aristotle's eyes, the human race itself is eternal and the intellective soul can therefore continue for ever to operate through different human bodies:

> ... etsi non sit huius corporis corrupti actus, tamen est alterius corporis actus, cum secundum intentionem Philosophi species humana sit aeterna sicut et eius perfectio quae est anima intellectiva [187].

[... although it (the separated soul) is not the act of this particular corrupted body, it is however the act of a second body, since Aristotle meant that the human species is eternal just like its perfection which is the intellective soul.]

It is worth noting in passing that it really is stretching the creative imagination in an anachronistic way to suggest that either Aristotle or Siger is here arguing for the religious notion of reincarnation or rebirth of souls - as Klünker and Sandkühler suggest in their recent book [188].

However, in considering the theological objection that his teaching would involve injustice in so far it eliminates reward and punishment for those deeds committed in our bodily lives, Siger reminds us that his main aim is to explain Aristotle's opinion:

> Quod si quis dicat hoc esse erroneum animas a corporibus totaliter non separari et eas poenas et praemia recipere secundum ea quae gesserunt in corpore, quod enim non ita fiat, hoc est praeter rationem iustitiae, dicendum ... quod nostra intentio principalis non est inquirere qualiter se habeat veritas de anima, sed quae fuerit opinio Philosophi de ea [189].

[It is fundamentally unjust if anyone were to say it is wrong that souls are not totally separated from bodies and that they receive punishments and rewards according to their deeds when they had been in the body. It must be stated ... that our principal intention is not to enquire just what is the truth concerning the soul, but what had been the opinion of Aristotle about it.]

Indeed, he continues by describing briefly a quasi-humanist view of the ethics of good and evil, based on Aristotle, whereby he implicitly denies the view that morality can only be justified in the context of a life-to-come. As for the latter, yet again he disclaims any expertise in the realms of theology but he does acknowledge that supernatural knowledge ("prophecy") may come to some people on a completely different level to that of his own research:

Et est etiam attendendum quod multa sunt quae expertus circa
aliquam materiam cognoscit, quorum inexperti cognitionem
non habent. Et ideo, licet philosophi non experti operum
apparentium de animabus totaliter separatis eas sic separatas
non ponant, qui tamen experti sunt praedictam animae
separationem noverunt et aliis revelaverunt. ... sic nihil
prohibet naturaliter homines quosdam propheticos
quorumdam cognitionem habere, ad quae communis ratio
hominum non ascendit, nisi credendo testimonio prophetae
(190).

[It is also to be expected that there are many things which an expert
knows about some topic of which a non-expert knows nothing. Hence, although
philosophers not being expert about works that apparently concern totally
separated souls do not posit them to be thus separated, those who are expert have
known however the foresaid separation of the soul and have revealed it to others.
... Thus there is nothing in nature to prevent some prophetic human beings having
knowledge of certain things which ordinary human reason does not reach except by
believing the witness of a prophet.]

It must be declared once again, however, that such a position does not
give any hint of adherence to the "double-truth" theory. Indeed, Siger makes it
clear that the whole question within Christianity, regarding the state of the
separated soul, is outside the ambit of philosophy and that the possibility never
seems to have been considered by Aristotle:

et Philosophus ... mentionem, inter huiusmodi substantias
penitus a materia liberatas, non facit de anima intellectiva
totaliter a corpore separata. Quare nec animam sic separari
verum esse opinari videtur (191).

[Among substances fundamentally separated from matter, Aristotle
makes no mention about the intellective soul as totally separated from the body.
Therefore he does not seem to think that such a separation is true.]

His seventh chapter, in so far as it is linked to the previous one, examines the question as to whether each human body has a separate intellective soul. Siger indeed begins with a familiar disclaimer that he is speaking on a purely philosophical level rather than whatever may be the actual truth as such. Interestingly, he declares, however, that his methodology will not only be that of human reason but also of what he calls experience, perhaps with a nod to Thomas' appeal to that universal experience that each person seems to have as an individual:

> ... diligenter considerandum, quantum pertinet ad philosophum, et ut ratione humana et experientia comprehendi potest, quaerendo intentionem philosophorum in hoc magis quam veritatem, cum philosophice procedamus. Certum est enim secundum veritatem quae mentiri non potest, quod animae intellectivae multiplicantur multiplicatione corporum humanorum. Tamen aliqui philosophi contrarium senserunt, et per viam philosophiae contrarium videtur (192).

[... it must be carefully considered, in so far as it is the concern of the philosopher and can be grasped by human reason and experience, by seeking more the meaning of the philosophers in this matter than the truth, when we proceed in a philosophical fashion. Indeed it is certain, according to the truth that cannot lie, that intellective souls are multiplied with the multiplication of human bodies. However, some philosophers have felt the opposite and the opposite does seem true according to the path of philosophy.]

As can be seen, therefore, Siger appears not only to be acknowledging a single, as opposed to a "double", truth according to the principle of non-contradiction. He is also implicitly accepting here the priority of revelation (supernatural knowledge) over philosophy (natural knowledge). In the case of the latter, just like again any modern scientist who might maintain that his theory and conjecture appear to fit in better with empirical observable experience, Siger is asserting that he considers his case to be the stronger. This comes now, not simply from a study of what other philosophers have thought and taught as Van

Steenberghen states [193], but indeed as a result of an examination of conflicting evidence on a rational level, albeit of course prescinding from revelation. His arguments in this chapter are on very similar lines to what has already been analysed. Once again, Siger sets about clarifying his own position, in the face of Thomas' comments, as is indicated by a reference to the latter's appeal to his personal experience of possessing an individual intellect:

> Quod si quis dicat: cum sit anima intellectiva in me ... [194].

> [Because, if anyone says to me "since there is an intellective soul in me...."]

Caparello may be right in suggesting that, in some parts of this chapter and indeed elsewhere in this treatise too, Siger's allegedly heretical position seems more stark than in the Quaestiones in Tertium De Anima. However, the elucidation of his thought for a written treatise and in response to Thomas' challenge, with of course the many caveats already noted regarding the philosophical limits of his writing, seems to be the reason. Certainly, this seems a far more likely explanation than that of Caparello, noted earlier in this section. Scholars down the years, she claims, must have been making serious mistakes regarding the respective chronology of the two books, since otherwise we could not account for such an apparent development in his views, particularly in response to the strictures of 1270 and of Thomas [195]. There is no solid evidence for her view, and indeed everything else points to the long-accepted respective dating of these two works.

The crux of Siger's case is that, just as it is matter which differentiates in individuals within the same species, so it is abstracted form, not material form, which is common within a species:

> Sola igitur forma materialis abstracte considerata ...
> multiplicabilia sunt in plura suae speciei et de pluribus dicibilia
> [196].

[Therefore only a material form considered in the abstract can be multiplied into many items of the same species and be spoken of in respect of many items.]

Siger is in fact quite happy to acknowledge that even so there is indeed evidence to build up a strong philosophical case, which is not easy to counter, for the opposite position, that each human being does have an intellective soul:

> Sed et sunt rationes multum difficiles quibus necesse sit animam intellectivam multiplicatione corporum humanorum multiplicari, et etiam ad hoc sunt auctoritates [197].

[But there are indeed arguments very difficult to counter that the intellective soul is necessarily multiplied with the multiplication of human bodies and there are also authorities for this position.]

Indeed, he states unequivocally once again, towards the end of this chapter, that he is presenting arguments for and against the proposition within the context of philosophical disputation:

> Nisi forte positionem defendendo et causa disputationis... [198].

[Lest perhaps by defending the position and for the sake of disputation...]

His own case has by now already been fully presented, though he sums it up in the following words:

> Unde prius dicebatur qualiter homo intelligit, seu attribuitur intelligere ipsi homini, utpote quia operatio operantis uniti materiae attribuitur toti composito. Intellectus autem in opere intelligendi unite se habet ad scientem, non ad ignorantem, cum ex phantasmatibus eius intelligat, ita quod unus homo est

sciens et alius ignorans, non quia phantasmari unius plus sit intelligere quam alterius; nec quia species intelligibilis sit in corpore unius plus quam in corpore alterius, cum esse abstractum habeat; nec quia diversis intellectibus utantur intelligendo, ut dicet positionem defendens; sed quia intelligere sit secundum intellectum unitum corpori unius in operando et non alterius [199].

[It was therefore stated previously how man has intellection - or intellection is attributed to a human being itself - because, so to speak, the operation of the operator united to matter is attributed to the whole composite being. The intellect however in the work of intellection is related by union with the knower and not to a non-knower, since it has intellection arising from his phantasms. The reason, that one human being does know in such a way while another does not, is not because the mental imaging of one is more intellective than the second. Since the intelligible species has an abstract existence, it is not because the former is in the body of one human being more than it is in the body of a second. It is not because they use different intellects in intellection, as someone defending the position may say. It is, however, because intellection is according to an intellect which is united in its operation to the body of one and not of the second.]

Nevertheless, we will not be surprised to discover that he renews yet again, at the end of this chapter, his longtime recognition of the difficulty of determining this issue and of the ultimate primacy of supernatural revelation over natural reason:

Et ideo dico propter difficultatem praemissorum et quorumdam aliorum, quod mihi dubium fuit a longo tempore quid via rationis naturalis in praedicto problemate sit tenendum, et quid senserit Philosophus de dicta quaestione; et in tali dubio fidei adhaerendum est, quae omnem rationem humanam superat [200].

276

[And therefore I state that, on account of the difficulty involved in the premises and a number of other points, I have for a long time been uncertain what should be held by the path of natural reason and what Aristotle felt about the question. So, in such a matter of doubt, we should adhere to faith which supercedes all human reason.]

Such a conclusion contrasts abruptly with the more typical style of the determination of a "quaestio", as almost always presented elsewhere by Siger.

It seems almost irrelevant - let alone inaccurate - for authors such as Van Steenberghen [201] or Caparello [202] to be discussing whether or not Siger is still adhering to or has "given up" Averroism or Averroistic views! His concern is that colleagues do not make inaccurate or unsustainable claims on a philosophical level and that therefore his and their views remain subject to professional scrutiny on that level. No less would be demanded of and by a scientist today.

The eighth chapter provides another declaration that the intellective power cannot belong to the same substantial form as the vegetative and sensitive powers:

> Sentit ergo Philosophus intellectivum seu potentiam intelligendi non pertinere ad eamdem formam ad quam pertinet potentia vegetandi et sentiendi [203].

[Therefore Aristotle feels that the intellective or the faculty of intellection does not belong to the same form as that to which the vegetative and sentient faculty belongs.]

The ninth and final chapter is particularly interesting for showing that Siger has turned here not to his more customary Arab and Islamic sources to interpret Aristotle but to Moses Maimonides. It is, he says, the act of intellection that is the very substance of the intellect:

Non habet igitur (intellectus) ante intelligere nisi naturam in potentia. Intelligere igitur est eius substantia, sicut et expresse dicit Rabbi Moyses [204].

[The intellect only therefore previously has intellection as a natural potentiality. It follows that intellection is its substance as Rabbi Moses (Maimonides) explicitly states.]

In a section, reminiscent of Boethius of Dacia's thoughts in his De Bono Supremo on the inestimable value of philosophy, in which the latter praises study and learning while despising an anti-intellectual lifestyle, the chapter and book then conclude with a notable exhortation to Siger's readers:

Sed qualiter tunc debeat intelligi quod scientia est qualitas de prima specie qualitatis in praedicamentis, vigiles et studeas atque legas, ut ex hoc dubio tibi remanente exciteris ad studendum et legendum, cum vivere sine litteris mors sit et vilis hominis sepultura [205].

[But may you take care, study and read how it ought then to be understood that knowledge is a quality regarding the first species of quality in predications. Thus, from this remaining doubt of yours, may you be enthusiastic about studying and reading, since to live unlettered is death and the common burial of the human being.]

6.10.   Quaestiones Naturales (Lisbon).

The third of the "quaestiones", contained in the Lisbon Version of Siger's "Quaestiones Naturales", does very briefly throw some more light on that position which we have seen determined in the final chapter of De Anima Intellectiva. Here he declares that he disagrees with Ibn Rushd's view that the passive and agent intellects are two separate substances, contained within a permanent union. He prefers to follow what he believes to be Aristotle's view that the agent intellect is merely the potential (or receptive) intellect in the act of knowing, but that the latter has no reality before receiving the species from the phantasm in the imagination. In other words, the reality of the agent intellect lies in the very operation of the act of intellection:

> (Aristoteles) ... dicit quod intellectus agens est scientia secundum actum, hoc est sciens in actu. Dicit etiam ipsum esse substantiam in actu [206].

[Aristotle says that the agent intellect is knowledge according to act, that is the knower in act. He also says that this same is substance in act.]

6.11.   Quaestiones super Librum de Causis.

It is when we come to look at this book, almost certainly the last extant work of Siger's thought and probably derived from his lectures of the 1275-1276 academic year, that we really do appear to see a major change in his position. Van Steenberghen believes that this work, as a result of Siger's submission to the rigorous arguments of Thomas Aquinas against monopsychism, reflects his consideration of the intellective soul from this new perspective [207]. Our two most relevant "quaestiones" are 26 and 27. Indeed, in the former, we do see that he is apparently keeping Thomas' De Unitate Intellectus contra Averroistas in mind, because, in presenting his solution, he begins by declaring that:

> Solutio. Quidam volunt quod substantia animae intellectivae sit hominis forma, potentia tamen animae intellectivae sit separata non materiae perfectio nec organum habens [208].

[The answer is that certain people claim that the substance of the intellective soul is the form of man, while the faculty of the intellective soul is not a separated perfection of matter and it does not possess an organ.]

Then, from the plural form "quidam volunt" which would appear to indicate a number of such proponents, Siger now switches to the singular form "sic ponens" in the very next line with almost certainly a direct reference to Thomas' position in the De Unitate Intellectus contra Averroistas when he had said:

... unde remanet quod anima quantum ad intellectivam potentiam, sit immaterialis, et immaterialiter recipiens, et se ipsam intelligens (209).

[... therefore it remains that the soul, in its relationship to its intellective faculty, is immaterial, is receptive in an immaterial manner and has intellection of itself.]

Lest anyone should think that the above also sums up his own position, Siger immediately declares that this is not the case:

Sed haec positio stare non potest. Cum enim intellectiva anima sit hominis forma et perfectio, sicut rei veritas est, non potest esse potentia et operatio separata (210).

[But this position cannot be upheld. Since the intellective soul is the form and perfection of man, as is indeed the true case in reality, it follows that it cannot be a separate faculty and operation.]

So Siger is claiming that it is inconsistent of Thomas to maintain that the intellective soul is the form of man, but that its operative power or capacity is not. We have already seen earlier how Thomas was apparently insistent on the axiom that "agere sequitur esse" [operation follows existence] (211). Siger is indeed prepared here to revise to some extent his own position, as presented in De Anima Intellectiva, but is still adamant that he was right to voice his concerns that Thomas' position did not hold water. No wonder, perhaps he is implying, that he could not take it lock, stock and barrel before! As it is, Siger has had to think it all through and to try to resolve some of the problems for himself. This interpretation of what has been going on is probably a much closer reflection of the historical and intellectual realities than Van Steenberghen's claim that Siger was merely trying to save face in view of Thomas' success in convincing him of his own inconsistency [212].

Siger himself does seem nevertheless to have revised somewhat his own position, for the intellective soul is not just united to the composite soul through its operative power, but he is also emphasizing that Aristotle believed that the intellective soul is the form of man and has now implied, in language closer to that of Thomas, that it is of the substance of man:

> Vult Aristoteles quod anima universaliter est actus corporis et substantia secundum rationem [213].

[Aristotle claims that the soul taken in general is the act of a body, and is a substance by definition.]

However, from this "quaestio", his fundamental stance still remains that the union is such that the body remains the object rather than the subject in intellection:

> Aristoteles ... non arguit ipsum intelligere esse commune ex hoc modo quo intelligere egeat corpore sicut subiecto in quo sit intelligere, sed tantum sicut obiecto, cum phantasmata comparentur ad intellectum sicut sensibilia ad sensum [214].

[It is not Aristotle's case that intellection itself is common as a result of the way in which intellection requires a body as a subject in which it may be intellection, but ony as an object, when phantasms are united to the intellect like sense experiences are to a sense.]

Indeed, he still argues that we can only know the soul's substance and form from its potentiality and operation:

Substantia enim et forma non innotescit nisi ex potentia et opere (215).

[For knowledge of substance and form only arises from potentiality and operation.]

There is of course a critical difference between the way in which the intellective soul informs the body, and the way in which the vegetative-sensitive soul does so:

Sed est attendendum quod anima intellectiva est corporis perfectio et forma, non tamen sicut vegetativa et sensitiva. Anima enim intellectiva sic corpus perficit quod et per se subsistit in suo esse non dependens a materia, de potentia materiae non educta (216).

[But it should be expected that the intellective soul is the perfection and form of the body but in a different way from the vegetative and sensitive soul. This is because the intellective soul perfects the body in such a way that it also subsists of itself independently of matter without having originated from the potentiality of matter.]

Hence, on completing a reading of this "quaestio", it will be seen that Siger still continues to maintain that the union in the human being can only be known through its operation and that he is not here suggesting a separate soul that can subsist after death. This latter interpretation appears to be confirmed by his earlier consideration of this question in Quaestio 18, where he had declared that, philosophically speaking, it does not seem possible to have it both ways:

... dicendum quod anima intellectiva si esset perfectio et forma corporis et materiae ... non posset aliquando perficere materiam et aliquando separari ab eadem (217).

[... it should be stated that the intellective soul if it were the perfection and form of the body and of matter ... could not sometimes perfect matter and at other times be separated from the same.]

Quaestio 27 is even more fascinating in so far as it now tackles the issue as to whether each body has a different individual intellect or whether there is one universal intellect. Here, it does seem at first as if Siger has weighed up carefully the cogency of Thomas' psychological call to self-awareness and to diversity of knowledge in different individuals, e.g.:

> Sed intellectus est hominis forma.   Ergo plurium et diversorum hominum erunt intellectus diversi [218].

[The intellect however is the form of man and hence there will be different intellects for the multiplicity and diversity of human beings.]

> ... non erit scientia Socratis differens a scientia Platonis...[219].

[(In such a scenario) the knowledge of Socrates will be no different from the knowledge of Plato.]

Nevertheless, it must be noted that in his solution, he begins by stating what he sees to be the position of Ibn Rushd:

> Posuit etiam Commentator quod intelligere Socratis et intelligere Platonis secundum quod intelligunt eamdem naturam et simul, ut naturam lapidis, non est intelligere diversum secundum subiectum ipsius intelligere, nec est diversum secundum ipsam formam intelligibilem absolute, sed posuit ipsum intelligere Socratis et Platonis secundum quod intelligunt eamdem naturam simul, diversum diversitate speciei intelligibilis non absoluta sed respectiva [220].

[Ibn Rushd also posited that the intellection of Socrates and the intellection of Plato in the respect in which they have intellection of the same essence at the same time, such as the nature of a stone, is not different intellection in respect of the subject of the very act of intellection; neither is it different in respect of the very intelligible form in an absolute sense. He rather posited the very acts of intellection of Socrates and of Plato, in the respect in which they have intellection of the same essence at the same time, to be different as a result of the diversity of the intelligible species. This however is not in an absolute but in a relative sense.]

He does repeat that Ibn Rushd had posited the union of the intellect with the body, as an object, rather than as subject, in order to try overcome the basic difficulty:

> Averroes enim non posuit corpus communicare in hoc quod
> est intelligere ita quod esset subiectum eius, nec intelligendo
> intellectum egere corpore ut corpore subiecto, sed magis sicut
> obiecto, cui naturaliter intellectus unitur [221].

[Ibn Rushd did not indeed posit that the body communicates in the act of intellection in such a way that it would be the subject of it, nor that the intellect needs the body with the latter as the subject in the act of intellect, but it is rather as the object to which the intellect is naturally united.]

However, the critical and significant difference here is that he now declares this position to be not only heretical, but also that philosophical evidence points in the opposite direction:

> Sed ista positio in fide nostra haeretica, et irrationalis etiam sic
> apparet [222].

[That position however is heretical in our faith and also is apparently irrational.]

How then does this fit in with what has just been considered in the previous quaestio [223]?   In that context, in fact, Siger had purported to present Aristotle's teaching without further comment.   Here, he is presenting this view as a teaching of Ibn Rushd, implying that Aristotle's need to see the intellect as a form of the body would require multiplication of intellects and so would rule it out as untenable:

> Intellectus est unitus corpori hoc modo quod intellectus non intelligit sine phantasmate, ita quod in eius operatione communicat cum corpore.   Intellectus autem multa simul intelligere non potest, immo transmutatur de intelligibili ad intelligibile secundum quod diversa vult intelligere [224].

[The intellect is united to the body in this way because the intellect has no intellection without a phantasm.   Thus, it communicates in its operation with the body.   The intellect however cannot have intellection of many things at the same time.   On the other hand, it is changed from one intelligible to another in so far as it wants to have intellection of different ones.]

Indeed it is only, he now says, such multiplicity of intellectual activity that can explain diversity of understanding in different individuals:

> Nunc autem contingit in diversis hominibus vires sensitivas subministrantes intellectui de diversis cogitare, memorare et imaginari, ex quo et contingit homines diversos diversa simul intelligere, ut dum unus intelligat unum alius aliud [225].

[It does happen however that, in different human beings, the powers of sensation which service the intellect think, recall and imagine different things.   It follows from this that different human beings have intellection of different things at the same time so that, while one does so of one thing, another does so of something else.]

285

Siger, somewhat surprisingly, goes on to use some of Thomas' arguments, albeit in slightly different words. He even takes up the latter's example of how a body lighter than air will not rise if it is so prevented from doing by an intermediate object. Thomas had used this as an analogy to explain how he believed that the actual corruption of the body is the reason that prevents the soul from remaining in union with it, so obliging it to survive on its own:

> ... sicut levi quantum est de natura sua semper esse sursum convenit, licet per accidens impeditum possit non esse sursum ... similiter intellectus quilibet quantum est ex natura sua semper actus et perfectio corporis est, sed impeditur ab hoc sibi naturali [(226)].

[... just as it is always natural for something light to rise, although it can happen that something can prevent it from rising ... any intellect is like this in so far as it is always natural to be the act and perfection of the body but is prevented from what is natural for itself.]

He continues in this quaestio to suggest that, whether or not there can be infinite spiritual beings is a question that cannot be solved on a philosophical level alone, despite what Aristotle had to say:

> Si enim in separatis entibus, cuiusmodi sunt intellectus separati, sit infinitum, ad altiorem scientiam quam naturalem pertinet ... Et adhuc si sit inconveniens, contradicitur Aristoteles qui generationem hominum posuit perpetuam [(227)].

[If indeed it be infinite in separated beings, including separated intellects, it pertains to a knowledge on a higher level than that of nature ... If this now is unsuitable, it is in opposition to Aristotle who posited the perpetual generation of human beings.]

He is also prepared to state now that Ibn Rushd's interpretation of Aristotle, regarding the unicity of the intellect, is not the only possible one and may well be wrong:

> ... si forte quaereretur quid sentit Aristoteles si intellectus sit unus omnium hominum sicut et suus Expositor, non est bene certum ex verbis suis [228].

[... if perhaps it is sought whether Aristotle feels that there is one intellect for all human beings, as Ibn Rushd does, it is far from certain from the former's words.]

What is more, says Siger, Aristotle himself is indeed fallible over this matter, in a way that our faith cannot be:

> Qualitercumque autem senserit, homo fuit et errare potuit: firmiter tenendum quod hominum multiplicatione multiplicatur [229].

[Whatever he may however have felt, he was a human being and has been able to be wrong. It should be firmly upheld that it (the intellect) is multiplied with the multiplication of human beings.]

Has Siger then really decided that the thesis over the unicity of the intellective soul is no longer valid? He presents it now as if the issue is far from straightforward. In fact, we have already seen how he admitted longstanding doubts of his own in Chapter Seven of De Anima Intellectiva [230]. Perhaps it is simply that he feels the problem is better handled if greater account is taken of Thomas' psychological perspective. This may be reflected in the fact that, in this quaestio especially, Siger tends frequently now to use the term "intellectus" [intellect] rather than the more metaphysical "anima intellectiva" [intellective soul].

On the other hand, there have been crises at the University, in which Siger has been involved [231]. Does he believe that he needs to acknowledge the existence of multiple individual intellects in order to stave off further and greater trouble, whether for himself personally, for his circle of colleagues or even of the Faculty as a whole? He may even feel more vulnerable, precisely because of the recent death of Thomas.   However, perhaps, it would not be surprising if some ambivalence remained in Siger's heart and in his head.   Certainly, it is a very strange quaestio in that the Resolution, first presented as being that of Ibn Rushd, is then described as heretical as well as wrong [232].   It is again a highly unusual magisterial determination.

Was the fact that the Liber de Causis is not a genuine work of Aristotle but that of the Neoplatonist Proclus a factor? It is just possible but probably unlikely. Another more plausible explanation is that Siger was now truly maturing as a scholar and did not feel strongly enough either way.   Therefore, when lecturing to young students as in this commentary - perhaps with the closing words of Thomas' De Unitate Intellectus contra Averroistas ringing in his ears [233] - he may well have felt it best to try to come to some accommodation with the theologians and with the magisterium.   This would seem particularly essential if the Faculty of Arts was to be permitted to maintain its independence and if Aristotle's writings were to continue to have pre-eminence - above all, in these years following the death of Aristotle's greatest advocate among the theologians.

Finally, it is worthy of note that Siger is also prepared later in this commentary to understand the intellective soul in man now as being a substance that does not, as he has stated earlier, derive its existence only through its act of operation. He implies that it can exist on its own without the latter:

> Solutio.   Dicendum est quod natura quae est intellectualis operationis principium est forma per se subsistens, ita quod non tantum ipsa est qua aliquid est, sed est per se ens non egens in esse suo materiali subiecto quamquam etiam egeret in operatione [234].

[The answer is that it should be stated that the essence which is the principle of intellectual operation is a self-subsistent form.   This is such a way that

288

not only is it that by which something exists, but is a being of itself which does not have need of its material subject to be in existence, although it might have need of it in operation.]

It is interesting, though, that this does still have hints of the soul as acting on the body:

> ...immo magis proprie homo intelligit, non per unionem quam habeat ad corpus in ipso intelligere sicut ad subiectum ipsius intelligere, egens corpore tanquam fundamento materiali in quo sit intelligere: ... sed dicitur homo, non anima, intelligere eo quod in ipso intelligere corpore egeat sicut obiecto cui naturaliter unitur, cum commune sit intelligere ex modo quo intellectus nihil intelligit sine phantasmate [235].

[... it would rather be more proper (to say) that the human being has intellection, not through the union which it has to the body in the very act of intellection as though to the subject of the intellection itself, needing the body as a material base in which the act of intellection exists. ... but it is stated that the human being, not the soul, needs the body for intellection as an object to which it is naturally united, since intellection normally arises from the way in which the intellect only understands by means of a phantasm.]

Is this still a union of interaction, as was seen in the third chapter of De Anima Intellectiva, rather than a union of identity? Perhaps, if a parallel is drawn with the Christian idea of God's immanent presence in the world, then we have an analogy with that common thread which can be traced through all the stages of the development of Siger's ideas on the intellect and the intellective soul.

6.12.   Siger's Legacy on This Issue.

It seems appropriate to summarize briefly the contribution and the context of Siger's teaching on the intellective soul in relationship to medieval thought and to reflect a little on its possible contribution or relevance to contemporary thought.

We have seen that, despite past claims by scholars to the contrary, there was probably little change or development between his early teaching in the Quaestiones in Tertium de Anima and his later treatise De Anima Intellectiva, that cannot be explained by the different nature of the medium of teaching. Certainly, following Thomas' arguments in his De Unitate Intellectus contra Averroistas, there is some clarification of his views in the latter work, so as to avoid apparent ambiguity. Nevertheless, he does seem to believe that it is his theory that is still the more feasible of the two from a metaphysical point of view. To whatever extent he is or is not prepared to flirt with the notion of a substantial or a 'per se' union between the intellective soul and the composite body/vegetative-sensitive soul entity, he still remains insistent that it is only the process of operative activity that can bring this about.

It is possible that the anonymous "Ignoti Auctoris Quaestiones in Aristotelis Libros I et II de Anima", edited by Giele, may also reflect some teaching from the lectures of Siger. Van Steenberghen [236] follows Giele [237] and Kuksewicz [238] in considering that the teaching here is more extreme than that of Siger and therefore cannot belong to him. Such a blanket assertion should not go completely unchallenged. In particular, they all claim that Siger never declares in any of his texts that "quod homo proprio sermone intelligit non concedo" [I do not concede that one can strictly speak of the human being as having intellection] [239]. However, is this really the case, when we look beneath the surface of what he has been saying? Certainly, we have seen that in the late Quaestiones super Librum de Causis he does try to reconcile the psychological perspective with the metaphysical one, but earlier he maintains that the union of the body with the vegetative-sensitive soul is only the object, not the subject, of the intellect, in its intellective operation. It would thus be at least arguable to deduce from this that it is not man in his substance that strictly speaking is the subject of intellectual activity.   Similar expressions to those seen earlier in this chapter can indeed be found on a number of occasions in Giele's Anonymous Commentary, e.g.:

> ... intelligere proprium est animae et non corpori sicut subiecto, sed non aliter (240).

[... intellection is proper to the soul and not to the body as subject, but not the other way round.]

> Sed anima indiget in intelligere corpore sicut obiecto, non sicut subiecto (241).

[The soul in intellection needs however the body as object not as subject.]

Indeed, over the nature of the intellective soul, this author's ideas and language are quite reminiscent of Siger (242), as can be seen in the following text:

> Et est intelligendum adhuc, quamquam anima intellectiva sit separata sive separatum esse habens a corpore ... tamen, quantum [ad] operationes quas habet, non est separata, sed corpori communicat quantum ad suas operationes quas habet nonnisi mediante corpore (243).

[It should also be understood at this point that, although the intellective soul may be separated or have separate existence from the body, ... however, with regard to the operations which it has, it is not separate but communicates to the body with regard to the operations which it only has through the mediation of the body.]

Of course, this does not prove that Siger's lectures were the origin of this particular Commentary.   In both sets of writings, it is clear that reference is being made to Ibn Rushd and indeed we do know of course that this was very much an issue with which he was grappling [(244)].   Of course, the explanation could simply be that two different teachers in the Faculty of Arts were each poring over the latter's writings; certainly quite a number of references can be found to Ibn Rushd's own Commentary on the Third Book of De Anima, especially qu. 5, in Siger's writings as well as here in this anonymous Commentary on the two earlier books.

Eto, a Japanese historian, has however maintained that he can identify Siger as the latter's author [(245)]. It may be that the other forementioned scholars have over-reacted in rejecting out-of-hand the possibility that this Eastern scholar could be right.   Furthermore, we must recall that it is quite probable that lecturers would have repeated the gist of their lectures from year to year, as still happens in many universities today!   We have already seen that Siger developed from delivering fairly neutral expositions on Aristotle in his earlier Commentaries to becoming more critical, and how he became more prepared to assert his own independent views over the course of the decade or so of his active teaching. Besides, in these relatively early years of the University of Paris, the actual role and context of all the teaching in the Faculty of Arts was still of course a very long way from being definitively determined.   Hence, it could be that Siger is the same author and that some development in the latter's thoughts and maturity of expression might account for the points made by Kuksewicz to demonstrate the contrary [(246)]. This might also explain how Giles of Rome could have recalled, from his own days as a young student probably around 1265, that:

> Nos cum adhuc essemus bacchalaureus, vidimus quemdam magistrum magnum, in philosophia maiorem, qui tunc esset Parisiis, volentem tenere opinionem Commentatoris, concedentem quod homo non intelligit, nisi sicut caelum intelligit quia intelligit motor caeli; sic et homo intelligit quia intelligit ille intellectus separatus [(247)].

[When we were still of Bachelor status, we saw a certain great Master, eminent in philosophy, who was then in Paris.   He wanted to uphold the opinion of Ibn Rushd and conceded that the human being does not have intellection, save in the sense that heaven has intellection of heaven because the mover of heaven does so; likewise a man has intellection because that separated intellect does so.]

Certainly, there could not have been many Masters other than Siger that could have been so described. Writing some twenty-five years or so after the event, Giles' recall may or may not be totally accurate or uninfluenced by subsequent events. However, the actual resolution of the question of the identity of the author of Giele's Commentary is ultimately not of too great importance to this investigative study, since enough can be discerned from those works whose attribution to Siger is not in doubt.

It certainly does appear then that Thomas did help him to focus further on the difficulties posed in trying to reconcile Aristotle's psychology with his metaphysics. Yet again, his approach seems very reminiscent of that of a modern scientist trying to reconcile two different sets of empirical evidence that do not quite appear to fit together with each other, as might a student of quantum physics when he observes sub-atomic elements, simultaneously appearing to perform in one respect as if they are particles and in another respect as if they are waves [248]. In the same way, Thomas, while not succeeding in undermining Siger's basic metaphysical contentions, has made him reflect and re-assess to some extent. This, again, is not too dissimilar to the process whereby many scientists have had to retreat somewhat from the more traditional reductionist and mechanistic views of nature, so as to take on board recent discoveries regarding, for example, the roles of the left and right hemispheres of the brain, of consciousness and of the intangible and ephemeral properties of the originally so-called "physical" universe.

Certainly, as a result of writers such as Ryle [249], in rejecting the stark dualism of Descartes, it became fashionable to reject any idea of "spiritual" substance. However, in recalling Ryle's rejection of what he called the "ghost in the machine", we need to ask, in view of modern Quantum Physics, whether in fact the inaccuracy might not rather lie in speaking of the "machine" rather than just the "ghost"! Kenny has indicated how in "putting Aquinas' doctrine in modern terms, we might say that our thoughts have the sense they have because of the universal forms in which we think; they have the reference they have to individuals because of the sensory context in which they occur" [250]. This, as Kenny points out later [251], cannot be an entirely satisfactory answer. In his own way, Siger, as a non-theologian, saw the metaphysical difficulty and felt that his solution could better account for what happens. Of course, modern philosophers have built on what medieval and more recent ones have suggested. Hence, Lonergan explains that what he calls the "intentionality" in knowledge is cast, when expressed by Thomas, in metaphysical terms and is primarily concerned with the meaning of our thoughts and ideas [252], while, as Kenny indicates, Wittgenstein and the logical positivists look at this same intentionality in terms of the reference of our thoughts [253]. These should be seen, Kenny says, as complementary rather than contradictory.

It will be recalled that Siger managed, in a way that Thomas was unable to do despite his assertions to the contrary, to avoid bringing too much theological and religious baggage to his philosophical reflection. It can thus be understood why Siger had felt obliged to insist on the notion of the union between the intellective soul and the human individual as being an operative one. It is tempting to suggest that such a view could also offer a potential explanation of some psychical phenomena claimed today, such as telepathy, precognition and even Sheldrake's theories of "formative causation" [254]. If the brain is seen, as William James suggested [255], as the transmitter of thought, rather than the producer of thought, then Siger's phraseology in terms of the object, rather than the subject, of thought, may be interesting to re-consider in the light of this. Likewise, Jung, with, for example, his theory of "archetypes", may have a similarly interesting perspective to offer [256].

Furthermore, as we have already seen, it is no longer possible, except on the level of everyday colloquial speech, to talk of reality as something determined and definitive in this post-Einsteinian age. Teichman points out how, according to the Theory of Relativity, we would at least be aware that there are different subjective perspectives [257]. However, even that underlying objective reality, which was implied thereby, is now in some respects questionable. Hence, perhaps, we should rather speak of the material universe itself as being more "spiritual" and less definitive than most scientists have done until fairly recently.

It is clear therefore that both Siger and Thomas were aware of the problem from their own thirteenth century vantage points. Each listened to the other and perhaps each took on board for himself some of what the other was saying. However, since even now over seven hundred years later, we are still poring over the problems of consciousness, knowledge, brain and the mind - not to speak of the identity of the individual - we should not be too surprised that neither capitulated to the other.

We have again seen Siger immersed in his struggle on behalf of the Arts Faculty for the right to academic independence. It is understandable that earlier writers have however tended to miss this to a large extent in their enthusiasm to highlight the acknowledged differences between the content of the teaching of the two scholars. Indeed, it is over this issue, more than any other, that the latter show clear disagreement - save perhaps towards the very end of Siger"s career. Nevertheless, as Sánchez Sorondo suggests, we can perhaps see Siger as playing the role of Hegel, while Thomas, with his all-pervading Christianity, takes that of Kierkegaard [258]. Their great relevance lies precisely in the fact that they both saw the problem, asked appropriate questions and that each came up with different attempts to solve it, which can be paralleled in similar modern approaches today, even if the context of the theoretical solutions has moved on.

CHAPTER SEVEN

SIGER'S VIEWS ON DETERMINISM AND FREEWILL

7.0.   Introduction.

        This chapter will begin by considering the historical and theological context of the topic of determinism and freewill at the time of Siger's teaching and offer a brief review of research of earlier writers into his views.   There then follows an in-depth examination of his writings, where relevant to this issue, most especially in the fifth of the Impossibilia, in De Necessitate et Contingentia Causarum, in two of the Quaestiones in Metaphysicam and in one of the Quaestiones super Librum de Causis.   The chapter will concentrate in particular on whether Siger could be fairly accused of holding any of the positions affirmed in the three Articles of 1270 relevant to this matter and whether he was to amend his teaching at all following their promulgation.   It concludes with a survey of the implications of his position on freewill.

296

7.1. Historical Context of Issue.

The third of the four groups into which the thirteen propositions condemned on 10 December 1270 can be easily categorized is that concerned with determinism and freewill.

Thus we see the following statements falling under censure:

Article 3. Quod voluntas hominis ex necessitate vult vel eligit.

[That the human will desires or chooses out of necessity.]

Article 4. Quod omnia quae hic in inferioribus aguntur subsunt necessitati corporum caelestium.

[That all things which come to pass here in the lower worlds are subject to the necessity of the heavenly bodies.]

Article 9. Quod liberum arbitrium est potentia passiva, non activa; et quod necessitate movetur ab appetibili [1].

[That freewill is a passive, not an active, faculty and that it is moved necessarily by the object which is to be sought.]

At the heart of this issue is the question as to whether all the actions that we take are predetermined, whether by God, by the stars or by any other created beings. The Christian tradition declares that the freedom of each of our wills demands that we must accept responsibility for our deeds, if we are to speak of moral good and moral evil in any meaningful way.

Of course, the Fourth Lateran Council had determined the need for annual confession as the essential sacrament required to remove effectively guilt for sins committed subsequent to baptism [2]. It may be recalled that the thirteenth century marked the peak time for discussing and resolving the issue of the nature and the number of the sacraments. This theology implied the need for men and women to seek help through the Church so as to be able to fulfil adequately their Christian duties in the areas of morality and of avoidance of sin. The sacramental question was soon to be officially determined at the Council of Lyons in 1274 [3]. Hence, it can readily be seen how the theologians would have been particularly wary about any hint or suggestion that any of the above three propositions should have been taught anywhere, but most especially in the academic atmosphere of the University of Paris.

It is also advisable to note how there were Christian groups such as the Cathars, who resisted to some extent the dependence on the institutional Church which this sacramental theology demanded. Furthermore, there had been a number of Cathar voices, such as those of Alan of Lille and even John of Lugio, who explicitly denied the doctrine of freewill [4]. Likewise others, such as the Fraticelli, in so far as they preached from the middle of this century against the luxurious lifestyle of some of the Popes and of other prelates, also posed some threat. Thus, there can be little surprise that Tempier and the conservative theologians would want to ensure that there were no further threats, whether overt or subversive, from the Faculty of Arts, arising from an excessively intellectual adherence to what was perceived to be a pagan philosophy. The 1277 Decree of Tempier was to be the climax of this counter-movement and some twenty or so of the theses then condemned refer to this topic [5].

7.2.   Previous Scholarship Regarding Siger on This Issue.

As has been shown earlier [6], Mandonnet was the first scholar to make an in-depth survey of Siger's works and teachings. He was convinced that he could clearly find a denial of the existence of freewill within both of the relevant works that were known at that time, namely the De Necessitate et Contingentia Causarum and the fifth of the Impossibilia [7]. It will be recalled that the nature of the latter work was much misunderstood during the early years of the modern rediscovery of Siger [8]. This was matched by the weight of the vast majority of later writers in adopting, quite understandably, the same stance as a result of following the well-merited reputation of Mandonnet's scholarship. Hence, even Leff, as recently as 1958, was still asserting that Siger was a determinist over the matter of human freewill [9].

However, Lottin had asserted that he had detected in Siger's later writings some shift from an earlier position [10]. The great irony here, however, is that Lottin was basing this novel interpretation on an analysis of two texts which we now know cannot be classed as authentic Sigerian works. In fact, this mistake acted as the great breakthrough, for later he was also to come to the opposite conclusion to Mandonnet on the two writings that the latter had analysed [11].

Van Steenberghen, in his classic work of 1977, follows a similar pattern in his conclusions, while re-asserting some evolution in Siger's thought [12]. By then, of course, the Cambridge and Vienna versions of his Commentarium in Metaphysicam had been authenticated and were available for scholars, although not yet published. Furthermore, three years earlier, Van Steenberghen himself had written the preface to the edition of the Quaestiones super Librum de Causis. All three works contained material relevant to enable some elucidation of Siger's position, now that the two earlier falsely attributed Commentaries on sections of Aristotle's De Anima and In Physicam could no longer influence scholarly investigations.

Nevertheless, it has to be stated that Van Steenberghen only devotes five pages in this major work to the topic of freewill and that the best recent analysis is in fact to be found in an article of Ryan, published in 1983 [13].

7.3.   Impossibilia V.

In this sophistic disputation, Siger sets out to consider the proposal:

Quod in humanis actibus non esset actus malus, propter quam
malitiam actus ille deberet prohiberi vel aliquis ex eo puniri
(14).

[That among the activities of human beings there exists no evil act as a
result of whose wickedness that act should be forbidden or someone be punished
for it.]

It will be seen therefore that, although it is not explicitly concerned
with the question of freewill, that issue cannot be avoided, at least implicitly, in so
far as the existence of moral acts and the consideration of appropriateness of
punishment for failures to perform right deeds are examined.

It is interesting that even God's providence is cited as a possible
difficulty with regard to the validity of punishment:

Sed actus humani omnes, etiam mali, proveniunt ex ordine
Primi Provisoris prudentissimi (15).

[But all human acts, even evil ones, are ordained by the most wise First
Provident Being.]

However, the principal objection that Siger looks at involves what
some people, he says, consider to be the inevitable implications of the teaching and
principle of Ibn Sina concerning the necessary link between cause and effect:

Sed quaecumque vult homo et facit, necessario vult et facit,
quia nullus effectus evenit nisi a causa, respectu cuius suum
esse necessarium est, sicut et dicit Avicenna (16).

[However, whatsoever a human being wills and does, he wills and does of necessity, because no effect occurs save from a cause in respect of which its existence is necessary - so states Ibn Sina.]

Although Siger is not quoting Ibn Sina directly, this general principle is indeed to be found in the latter's writings [17]. In fact, Siger's solution to the difficulty that this poses for divine providence looks at the need for legislative punishment from a community or civic angle, rather than concentrating on any desirability or moral responsibility from the perspective of the individual:

> Solutio. In actibus humanis sunt actus qui simpliciter sunt mali naturae speciei et debent prohiberi, et homines etiam pro illis puniri; et punitionem etiam habent ordinatam a Primo Provisore, cum secundum ordinem Primi Provisoris sit quod legislatores malos puniunt [18].

[The answer is that among human acts there are some which in all respects are inimical to the nature of the species. These ought to be forbidden and human beings ought even to be punished for them. Furthermore, they even have punishment ordained by the First Provident Being, since the latter has ordained that lawmakers should punish evil people.]

Despite this mention of Providence, it can be seen that this is a philosophical argument, albeit concerned with those crimes that a theologian might describe as sins against the human race. It can be seen thus that this social justification of punishment is not based on mere pragmatic grounds but on highly principled non-theological criteria. Such an interpretation and understanding of this text is confirmed by the subsequent mention of the implied need for employing right reason to determine the morality of an act:

> ... actus humanus dicitur malus, qui fit extra rectam rationem, sicut et bonus, qui fit secundum ordinem rectae rationis [19].

[... a human act is called evil if it is done outside right reason, just as it is called good if it is done according to the domain of right reason.]

This might well cause us to reflect on many of the reasons produced in recent times by doctors and others for members of society to alter their behaviour in the light of the spread of the HIV virus and to make a comparison with that approach. Indeed, in many countries, there have been official educational efforts and campaigns directed at both adults and children with the aim of developing a more socially responsible approach over such matters [20].

Siger now goes on to assert that the privative aspect of evil acts comes, not from defects within a Provident God, but from within the human reason and human will:

> ... actus mali ordinati sunt a Primo Provisore, non tamen contingentes per eius defectum, sed propter defectum rationis et voluntatis [21].

[... evil acts are ordained by the First Provident Being, not however as depending on some defect of his but as a result of a defect of reason and of will.]

His approach, again as a metaphysician, asserts that punishment comes from God, as a First Cause:

> ... punitio illorum a Primo Principio est ordinata [22].

[... punishment for them is ordained by the First Principle.]

The language again is not theological but is looking for justification of what Siger sees as an authentic resolution of the dilemma, almost of that more rational kind which a modern scientist might use to solve a problem.

Likewise, he goes on once more to justify sanctions on the grounds of civil legislative desirability, but stating that it is the First Cause which provides the ultimate justification for their employment and validity:

> ... punitiones, quibus legislatores malos puniunt, ex ordine Primi contingunt [23].

[... punishments, with which lawmakers punish evil people derive from the ordination of the First Being.]

Despite this rationalism, it is however clear in his solution that Siger does genuinely accept the ethical difference between acts undertaken freely and those undertaken under duress. We may speak in ordinary parlance of the latter as being necessary, but this is quite a different use of the word from that employed to demonstrate the metaphysical link between cause and effect that we find in all our actions:

> ... necessarium coactionis ... non potest cadere in voluntate, quia voluntas in volendo cogi non potest [24].

[... necessary by compulsion ... cannot fall under the will because the will in willing cannot be compelled.]

He then goes on to consider the hypothesis of the situation where the will is involved but is unable to avoid its action. Here again, punishment would be inappropriate:

> ... si nostrae voluntates et actiones fierent ex causis non natis impediri, otiose legislatores punitiones ordinarent [25].

[... if our wills and actions derive from causes which are incapable of being prevented, it would be useless for lawmakers to ordain punishments.]

Siger proceeds further to distinguish this sense of necessity from that true nature of necessity in the moral forum, which, as declared above, he believes to lie in the metaphysical link between cause and effect. This can easily be reconciled with preserving the position that human beings are essentially free:

> Sed ex hoc non sequitur quod tales effectus a sua causa per se
> de necessitate eveniant, quia ipsa absentia impedimenti non est
> causa effectus per se, sed tantum sicut removens prohibens;
> et ideo, cum consideraveris illud quod fuit causa per se ad
> effectum, invenies effectum ex illo non semper evenire [26].

[Nevertheless it does not follow from this that such effects come from a cause out of intrinsic necessity. This is because the very absence of an impediment is not an intrinsic cause of an effect but only in so far as it removes a barrier. Hence, when you come to have considered what was the intrinsic cause for the effect, you will find that the effect does not always derive from it.]

Thus, he has believed himself able to maintain Ibn Sina's interpretation of the necessity of that metaphysical link without being compelled to deny freewill. He draws the analogy with how medicine can intervene to prevent the death of a patient which would otherwise be inevitable [27]. In such a situation, one cause can override another to prevent the original effect that would otherwise normally have occurred. This is a quite different situation from one where death cannot be avoided and will always be a consequence:

> Sed una istarum causarum non nata est impediri, et ideo
> semper effectum inducit [28].

[But one of those causes is not inherently preventable and therefore it invariably induces the effect.]

Siger does seem therefore quite explicitly to be asserting here, despite the interpretations of Mandonnet and other earlier writers, that we do really possess freewill. In this sophism he continues to tackle the opposing difficulties by determining the nature of the exercise of the will in a relatively negative, rather than a positive and straightforward, way:

> Absentia enim impedimenti nihil facit ad hoc ut sit effectus, nisi tantum removendo aliquid quod prohiberet ab effectu illud quod est causa per se effectus [29].

[The absence indeed of an impediment does not contribute to the existence of an effect, save only by the removal of something which would prevent the effect coming from what is its intrinsic efficient cause.]

The expression which he has used to describe this is "necessarium ex conditione" (conditional necessity) [30].

As Ryan well illustrates [31], Siger envisages that the human role in the use of freewill is to be found in the ability to remove anything which might act as an impediment to action. By this passive notion of freewill, he believes that he can maintain Ibn Sina's interpretation of Aristotle's need for the necessary metaphysical link between cause and effect. Without such a notion, he argues, sanctions for wrongdoing would be ineffective:

> ... hoc enim esset otiosum [32].

[... for this would be useless.]

Has he then avoided determinism or not? Even if we prescind from the sophistic nature of this kind of disputation with a determination in the Faculty of Arts based upon the perceived understanding of Aristotle's meaning, it can be seen that Siger's intentions, clearly illustrated by the distinction which we have already examined, are to do so. This indicates of course that he really did desire to uphold freewill. Of course, he does not explicitly mention freewill as such, but we should recall that the actual subject of the sophism is the appropriateness or otherwise of the use of punishment for wrongdoing. As we have seen, he does not consider this from the individual perspective of conscience or of its relationship to revealed moral law, as a theologian might have done, but from that of civic need and utility. Without denying the existence of either God or providence, which he does implicitly allow anyway in his consideration of objections, he wants to argue solely on rational and secular grounds.

It would seem therefore that Van Steenberghen is probably wrong in claiming that Siger remains here rooted in determinism. The former is attempting to put a psychological interpretation on a metaphysical argument, while denying the implications of the actual stated position of Siger over a topic that in any case is only being indirectly examined.

7.4.   De Necessitate et Contingentia Causarum.

In the first part of the actual determination of this "quaestio", which had earlier been described as both "difficilis" [difficult] [33] and "non immerito dubitabilis" [with good reason to cause doubt] [34], there can be found no less than five instances of "dico" [I state] in less than twenty lines [35]. This, allied to his declaration of intent to proceed "secundum intentionem philosophorum" [according to the intention of philosophers] [36], indicates his personal aim of searching on a rational level for a solution to the question regarding the necessity and contingent preventability of causes acting on effects.

In metaphysical terms, he does explain how he opposes the more extreme position of absolute determinism, when this arises from an understanding of the nature of the First Cause. Any of his colleagues who advocate this - and of course this is quite possible and may explain some of the strictures of the later 1277 Condemnation over this position - are, he believes, being unfaithful to authentic Aristotelian teaching:

> Et hoc fuit quod movit quosdam Parisienses doctores contra
> doctrinam magistri sui Aristoteles dicentes ... : licet, dicunt,
> quaelibet futura, quae diximus contingentia comparatione ad
> quasdam causas eorum ... relata tamen huiusmodi futura in

306

Causam Primam ... necessarium fore ex existentia Causae
Primae [37].

[And it was this which influenced certain teachers in Paris to speak out
against the teaching of Master Aristotle ... : although, they state, any future things,
which we have described as contingent by reference to their particular causes ...
are, however, in their relationship to the First Cause ... necessary by virtue of the
existence of the First Cause.]

It is the third section of this "Quaestio" which is the most interesting
and most relevant from the viewpoint of freewill. Here, he tackles the heart of the
issue and identifies what he sees as the respective errors of others in their own
attempts to solve the problem. Hence, he begins by being more specific regarding
the point mentioned above regarding the First Cause. Of course nothing can
prevent the latter from actually being the First Cause as such. However, it can
sometimes permit an intervening, but contingent, cause to act as an intermediary,
so that the effect will therefore not necessarily have to follow:

Licet ergo Causa Prima non sit impedibilis, producit tamen
effectum per causam impedibilem [38].

[Although therefore the First Cause is not able to be impeded, it does
however produce an effect through a cause which is capable of being impeded.]

This therefore appears to point a way through the difficulty, by
declaring, in other words, a metaphysical, but not a physical, necessity. The
Creator or First Cause can permit such intermediaries without compromising either
omnipotence or omniscience:

Ex Causa etiam Prima non evenit illud futurum necessario,
quia quamquam de eventu illius futuri non sit possibile aliter
evenire quam secundum ordinem Causae Primae eo quod non
est causa impedibilis, quia tamen sub eius ordine non tantum
cadit illud futurum sed et possibile oppositum, ideo nec

respectu Causae Primae est eventus illius futuri necessarius (39).

[For that to happen in the future does not arise of necessity from the First Cause. This is the case, although it is not possible for the circumstances of that future event to turn out otherwise than according to the ordination of the First Cause in that the latter is not a cause capable of being impeded. This does follow however from the fact that not only does what will happen in the future fall under its aegis but that a possible opposite does too. Hence, the occurrence of that future is not necessary by virtue of the First Cause.]

Siger now proceeds to examine Ibn Sina's notion of the necessity of cause and effect as such - it will be recalled that this work is of a similar period to the Impossibilia considered in the previous section - by invoking Aristotle's use of the principle of contradiction:

... ille qui sedet, dum sedet, habet potentiam ad standum. Sed qui sedet, dum sedet, non habet potentiam ad standum dum sedet (40).

[... the person who is sitting, while he is sitting has the potentiality to stand. However, the person who is sitting, while he is sitting, does not have the potentiality to stand and sit at the same time.]

The kind of necessity that Ibn Sina has in mind, he declares, is not however an absolute necessity:

Et hanc necessitatem intellexit Avicenna quando dixit quod omnis effectus respectu suae causae est necessarius. Ista tamen non est necessitas simpliciter ... (41).

[And Ibn Sina understood this necessity when he stated that every effect in respect of its cause is necessary. That is not however a necessity in every respect...]

The general point which Siger is making in his interpretation of Ibn Sina's principle is that, unless a nonimpeded cause normally does operate, then nothing would ever happen:

> Sic etiam causa ut in pluribus non impedita, etiam quando non est impedita, possibile est ut non eveniat ab ea effectus, licet non sit possibile quod a causa non impedita, non eveniat effectus, quando non impedita [42].

[Thus it is possible in the case of a cause which is usually non-impeded that, even when it is not impeded, the effect will not be brought about by it. On the other hand, it is not possible for an effect to fail to be brought about by a non-impeded cause, when it is not impeded.]

By steering the middle course, Siger believes that he has succeeded in avoiding the twin pitfalls of either upholding determinism or denying any universality about the link between cause and effect:

> Quidam enim, attendentes quod causa, non impedita et universaliter existens in dispositione in qua habet causare effectum, ... dixerunt omnia necessario evenire ... Alii autem, ut vitarent hunc errorem, inciderunt in alium dicentes quod causa ... nullo modo esset ad effectum necessaria, quia tunc tolleretur consilium et liberum arbitrium. Distinctio autem praedicta necessarii solvit hanc ipsorum ignorantiam [43].

[Some people indeed, concentrating on the fact that a cause, when it is not impeded and universally exists in a situation in which it is disposed to cause an effect, ... have stated that all things happen of necessity ... Others however, in order to avoid this error have fallen into another one by stating that a cause ... should in no way be necessary for an effect, because then freedom of decision and choice would be removed. The foresaid distinction of necessary does however solve this ignorance regarding these very matters.]

While the second extreme might appear to provide some attractive potential for a philosopher like David Hume, it is on the first group that Siger concentrates his efforts. Their position would provide a ridiculous kind of fatalistic determinism that cannot be considered tenable:

> ... otiosum esset consilium ad impediendum quosdam effectus futuros, ut si comestio veneni esset causa mortis non impedibilis, otiosum esset quaerere consilium medicinae [44].

[(In such a scenario) a decision to impede certain future effects would be useless so that, if the consumption of a poison were a cause of death that could not be impeded, it would be useless to seek medical attention.]

Besides, he argues, in a way that was only implicit in the fifth of the Impossibilia, we would be denying both freewill and also that it would be possible for us to resist anything to which we are attracted or tempted:

> Hoc etiam ipsum quod est: ipsam causam, producentem effectum, esse causam non impedibilem et necessariam, tolleret arbitrii libertatem, quia tunc omne velle nostrum causaretur a causa cui non posset resistere voluntas [45].

[The fact is that a cause which itself produces an effect, if it is a necessary cause that is not capable of being impeded, would remove freedom of decision. This is because in that case everything willed by us would be caused by a cause which the will is unable to resist.]

On the other hand, of course, the human will is not so absolute a master of its operations that we can understand its function without some awareness of the fact that the object of its desire is perceived as something attractive enough to be worth achieving:

Unde considerandum quod libertas voluntatis in suis operibus
non sic est intelligenda, quod voluntas sit prima causa sui velle
et sui operari potens se movere ad opposita, ab aliquo priori
non mota.   Voluntas enim non movetur ad volendum nisi ex
aliqua apprehensione [46].

[It should therefore be considered that the freedom of the will in its
deeds should not be understood as meaning that the will is the first cause of its
willing and of its operating and that it is able to move itself to opposites, when it
has not been moved by something earlier.   This is because the will is only moved
to willing as a result of some act of apprehending.]

Hereabouts, Siger in fact refers explicitly in the space of twenty four
lines to human freedom on no less than five occasions [47].   There can be no doubt
that he himself desires and intends to uphold it, even if it had been less obviously
the case at first glance in Impossibilia where the fifth "quaestio" had not been
directly concerned with it.

He proceeds to describe the manner in which the will can intervene to
prevent an effect from being the consequence:

... talis est natura voluntatis quod quodlibet eorum, quae
habent movere voluntatem, valeat a suo motu impediri [48].

[... the nature of the will is such that whatever there
might be to move the will, it is capable of being impeded by its own movement.]

B.F. Skinner [49] and other Behaviourists would of course disagree
with Siger's stark contrast between the will and the sense-appetite:

... voluntas vult ex iudicio rationis, appetitus autem sensualis
appetit ex iudicio sensus.   Nunc ita est nos nascimur cum
determinato iudicio sensus ...   Propter quod autem appetitus
sensualis non libere quaecumque appetit vel refugit.   Non sic

nascimur cum determinato iudicio circa bona et mala, sed possibile alterutrum; propter quod et in voluntate [50].

[... the will wills as a result of rational judgment, while the sense-appetite functions as a result of sense-judgment. The situation is that we are born with a determined sense-judgment ... Consequently the sense-appetite is not free to seek or to deter anything at all. We are not born like this with a fixed judgment regarding good and evil things but alternatives are possible so that such is the case in the will.]

Mandonnet had used this text to claim that Siger's reasoning was to provide a comparison rather than a contrast and that Siger was upholding a kind of psychological determinism by which the will could not help but follow what the intellect had apprehended [51]. However, the very phrase "possibile alterutrum" would definitely seem to imply that the operation of the will cannot be purely automatic. This is a difference from the instinctive knowledge of the senses and demonstrates the genuine distinctive freedom of the human will.

Although, at this point of his career, Siger does not clarify too completely the process by which the will exercises its freedom when attraction is taking place, it is certainly clear that he intends to maintain that it does so in a specifically human way. It is worth noting that he seems, in the process, to uphold the individuality of each person, in so far as he or she is human, and one ought to recall the heartsearching over the issue of the individuality of the intellect and of the intellective soul in the previous chapter.

While the views certainly do not conflict with the currently developing theological theories of grace and of the sacraments and would leave room for the doctrine of original sin, we can certainly see again how Siger's process has of course completely prescinded from such theological and religious considerations. His approach here too, is developing along the rational lines of a modern scientist, particularly in this case of a psychologist.

7.5.   Quaestiones in Metaphysicam.

There are four major examples here in which Siger expressly discusses the question of freewill - Book V Quaestio 37 (Cambridge), Book V Quaestio 8 (Vienna), Book VI Quaestio 9 (Cambridge) and Book VII Quaestio 1 (Vienna). In fact, they should really be considered in pairs, since the first two consider broadly similar material as do the latter two "quaestiones", despite the enumeration. The definitive publication of these texts was in fact only carried out in 1983 (Cambridge) and 1981 (Vienna). However, since the Vienna version, as we have already seen in Chapter 4 [52], does appear to reflect a later series of lectures than the Cambridge version, it does seem best to consider the Cambridge texts in the first instance. It should also be noted that Ryan, possibly because his article was being submitted around the same time, is mistaken in his numeration of the first of the above "quaestiones" [53]. Furthermore, in the case of Book VI Quaestio 9, he is forced to use the annotation of Duin [1954] rather than that of Maurer's more recent edition [1983].

It should also be noted of course that scholars, even as recently as Van Steenberghen in his 1977 work, do not refer to these texts in their consideration of Siger's views on freewill and determinism. Although they did not have the benefit of easy access to these texts, nevertheless greater account should probably have been taken, especially of the Cambridge version. It had been discovered in 1899 [54] and Duin, in particular, in his 1954 work had drawn much greater attention to it [55]. Certainly, as will be seen shortly, a greater examination of these texts would surely have been able to clear up much earlier any doubts as to whether Siger accepted freewill or not.

[a]   In fact, even Ryan ignores the context of the preceding "quaestio" to Book V Qu. 37 (Cambridge) in so far as Siger starkly outlines the similarities and the differences between the role of the sensual appetite in animals (and, by implication, in human beings too) and the role of the intellect:

Dico ad hoc quod appetitus humanus statim insurgit ex
cognitione alicuius sub ratione boni.   Sicut enim appetitus
animalis, statim cum sentit hoc delectabile et illud triste, hoc
appetit, illud autem fugit, ita, cum intellectus iudicat hoc esse
bonum et illud esse malum, statim hoc appetit et illud fugit
(56).

[I state in this regard that the human appetite immediately develops
from the cognition of something under the dimension of good.   For just as the
animal appetite, when it immediately senses this to give pleasure and that to give
pain, seeks the former and rejects the latter, so, when the intellect judges this to be
good and that to be evil, it immediately seeks the former and rejects the latter.]

It certainly might seem possible to interpret this text as it stands in a
determinist way, as if to indicate that Siger is making the point that the intellect
simply functions automatically.   However, it is fascinating to discover that, in the
Vienna version, he adds on an extra section which provides the same clarification
as has already been noted in examining De Necessitate et Contingentia Causarum:

Unum est quod a natura non sumus determinati ad esse bonos
vel malos, quia si sic, in nobis non esset [voluntas nostra].
Aliud est quod ex operibus voluntariis, non involuntariis,
fimus boni vel mali, ita quod habitus causantur ex operibus
quae sunt in voluntate nostra.   Et quia voluntas est in nobis,
et sic operari est in nobis, ideo in nobis est bonos esse vel
malos (57).

[It is one thing that we are not determined by nature to be good or evil,
because, if this were the case, our will would not exist within us.   It is something
else that we become good or evil from voluntary, not involuntary, acts so that
habits are developed as a result of deeds which are in our will.   Moreover, because
the will is in us and it is operational in us, it is therefore within us to be good or
evil.]

In any event, the possible confusion of interpretation in the Cambridge version is clarified in Quaestio 37, where the contrast between the animal appetite and the intellectual appetite is spelt out:

> Dico ad hoc quod in hominibus est libertas appetitus, quamvis de appetitu brutorum non sit hoc verum, eo quod ipsa nascuntur cum iudicio determinato a natura. Propter autem oppositam causam est libertas appetitus in hominibus. Homo enim non nascitur cum iudicio determinato de bonis et malis, sed cum iudicio possibili ad utrumque oppositorum [58].

[I state in this regard that there is freedom of desire in human beings, although this is not true about brute animal desire in that the latter are born with a judgment determined by nature. It is however for the opposite reason that there is freedom of desire in human beings. Moreover, the human being is not born with a fixed judgment with regard to good and evil deeds but with a judgment that is capable for both of the opposites.]

Indeed, Siger then goes on to explain how both habits and learning in our upbringing can influence our freewill to alter what we might naturally be otherwise inclined to decide:

> Quamvis enim quidam homines magis sint apti nati ad iudicandum quam alii, non tamen habent a natura determinatum iudicium quin per assuefactionem vel doctrinam possint induci ad iudicandum oppositum illius ad quod sunt apti nati [59].

[Indeed, although certain human beings are born more suited to making judgments than others, they do not however have a judgment fixed by nature. There is the possibility of their being influenced by means of the acquisition of habits or by teaching to make the opposite judgment of that to which they are born suited.]

In this, he seems to imply that some people are more inclined initially to choose good (or evil) than others - and perhaps also that there is something absolute about goodness anyway. Certainly, his contemporaries, such as Thomas Aquinas, would have seen this to lie in the Absolute Goodness of God. Indeed, the latter implies this in the Fourth of his Five Ways [60]. To this extent, the situation-ethics of Fletcher [61] and others would have seemed strange at first sight, even to Siger.

For example, the way in which people can be influenced for evil is highlighted in the Vienna version:

> ... poterant deduci per pravas consuetudines et operationes et
> iudicia prava, ita quod mali efficerentur [62].

[... they could be so directed, by means of wicked habits and activities and wicked judgments, that they became evil.]

The crucial difference lies in the self-control and responsibility for our actions that we, in contrast to animals, possess. This is indicated by the contrast between the active and the passive voices of the verb "agere" [to act] in both versions, e.g.:

> (Bruta) magis aguntur quam agant ad finem ... Homo autem
> liberum appetitum habet et non determinatum a natura,
> propter quod magis dicitur agere ad finem quam agi, cum non
> sit actus a natura [63].

[Brutes are more acted upon than active agents towards an end ... The human being however possesses a free appetite, which is also not determined by nature. For this reason (s)he is said to be more of an agent towards an end than to be acted upon, since (s)he is not driven by nature.]

Brute animals, it seems to Siger, are indeed led by animal instincts which are natural to them. The implication is clear that, while there is a basic determinacy and lack of freedom for animals, the freedom within human beings means that the determinacy of our free actions is obtained through the independent operations of the will.

Again, this clearly highlights - in contrast to that definitive determinism which Behaviourism bases on instinct and drives - what he sees as the higher level of human nature as compared with mere animal nature. Moreover, his suggestion that teaching and practice can influence the judgment of the will for the future anticipates in simple everyday terms much of the scientific approach of psychologists in the twentieth century.

[b] Book VI Quaestio 9 [Cambridge Version] - and its equivalent Book VII Quaestio 1 [Vienna Version] - directly focuses on the issue as to whether all events are pre-determined by necessity.

Siger produces a similar series of objections to his thesis in both versions, though it is worthy of note that, while the Cambridge version includes a threefold reference to the First Cause [64], this has nevertheless disappeared in the same argument in the Vienna version [65].

He roots the argument against determinism in what he perceives as its clear rejection by both Ibn Rushd and Aristotle [66]. In fact, in the Cambridge version, he clearly states that such a position would be untenable for rational reasons in so far as it militates against freewill and the justification of the use of punishment and reward. Furthermore, he declares determinism to be opposed not only to the Catholic faith but also to the authentic implied understanding of Aristotle's meaning too:

> Item, omnes effectus de necessitate evenire tollit arbitrii libertatem, tollit punitiones actuum malorum debere fieri, retrahit etiam ab actibus bonis. Quod si haec omnia catholicae fidei contradicunt, et cum hoc intentioni Aristotelis, non est ponendum omnia de necessitate evenire [67].

[Furthermore, for all effects to happen of necessity removes freedom of decision, removes the duty of punishment of evil acts and even deters from good acts. If all the above are opposed to the Catholic faith, along with the meaning of Aristotle, then it must not be claimed that everything happens of necessity.]

In fact, Siger notes again the universal validity of Ibn Sina's principle and employs once more the example of a medicine that can intervene to prevent death by poisoning [68]. He then takes Aristotle's argument from motion [69] to demonstrate that the fact that a cause will normally be certain to produce an effect, unless something intervenes to prevent it, does not mean that it is completely immovable in respect of that motion:

> Sed causa ut in pluribus, accepta ut sub defectu impedimenti, quamvis non impediatur, non tamen est immobilis illo mota [70].

[But a cause which normally operates, if we take it as lacking an impediment, is not incapable of being altered if it is affected by an impediment, even if it is not in fact being impeded.]

It is, again using the same distinction, a question of contingent, rather than absolute, necessity:

> Dico ad hoc quod ex ista immobilitate huius causae ad effectum non dicimus absolute quod effectus eius necessario futurus est, sed quod necessario futurum et contingenter ... Necessitas enim consistit in hoc quod causa non impedita semper producit effectum... Contingentia autem in hoc consistit, quod causa ista sic se habens semper impedibilis est [71].

[I state in this regard that we are not saying that, as a result of that inability for change in the relationship between a particular cause and an effect, its

318

effect will happen of absolute necessity but that it will happen of contingent necessity... After all, necessity consists in this that a cause which is not impeded always produces an effect... Contingency however consists in this that the latter cause is such that it is always capable of being impeded.]

In the Cambridge version, the application of this principle of contingent necessity through secondary causes is thus used to uphold freewill, punishment of evil acts and indeed the very opportunity to receive help and to conduct business:

> Unde, si omnes effectus provenirent a causis non impedibilibus, tolleretur libertas arbitrii et punitiones malorum actuum, et nihil valeret auxiliari neque negotiari [72].

[Hence, if all effects derived from causes which were not capable of being impeded, the freedom to take decisions would be removed, along with punishment of evil acts, and there would be no point in granting help or making deals.]

On the other hand, by the time of the Vienna version, Siger also uses this to explain the nature of divine providence:

> Nam et haec est providentia divina. Sic enim Deus providit talibus effectibus ut sic ex suis causis provenirent: quibusdam ut absolute ex suis causis necessario provenirent, quia causae eorum impedibiles non sunt, quibusdam autem sic quod provenirent ex suis causis, non simpliciter ex necessitate, sed contingenter, ut quia causae eorum impedibiles sunt [73].

[This indeed is divine providence. This is because God so oversees such effects that they derive causally from him in such a way that some have a causal origin in him of absolute necessity because their causes are incapable of being impeded. On the other hand, others have a causal origin in him in a way which is not necessary in every respect, but is of a contingent necessity in that their causes are capable of being impeded.]

This addition may well be in response to queries about his position, as almost certainly too is the clarification found in the Vienna version regarding the analogous use of necessity, which contingency must imply:

> ... si necessitas potest dici quod proprius dicitur contingentia ... (74).

> [... if what is strictly called contingency can be called necessity...]

> ... si necessitas potest dici ... (75).

> [... if it can be called necessity ...]

In both versions, his philosophical approach is as similar to that adopted by the modern empirical scientist as it is to that of a philosopher, but this is especially noticeable if the Vienna version is indeed seen as the later one, responding to points that have been made against the position which he has already described earlier.

He is adamant in his opposition to absolute determinism and quite scornful in dismissing those who feel obliged to uphold it:

> Ista obviatio fatua est et hominis non intelligentis (76).

> [That objection is wrong and is made by an unintelligent person.]

In fact, in this Quaestio - even in the Cambridge version - he makes it clear that the ability to intervene to prevent what would otherwise occur actually comes from the human will:

... voluntas, si ex causa aliqua moveatur ad volendum aliquid
et causa illa non impedibilis sit, idem necessario volet et
resistere non poterit; non habebit igitur arbitrium liberum [77].

[... the will, if it were to be moved by some cause and that cause were
not capable of being impeded, it wills the same necessarily and will not be able to
resist it; it will not therefore have freedom to take decisions.]

It is incidentally interesting to observe, in view of the impression
conveyed that Siger frequently seems to be repeating what he has more or less
already said earlier, that, in the Vienna version, he does actually acknowledge that
he is going back over the ground of the previous day's lecture for his students:

Ulterius intelligendum, sicut tangebatur heri [78].

[It needs to be further understood, just as it was touched upon
yesterday.]

It will be noted that this text strongly stresses the independence of the
human will, as compared with the more general phrases found in the De
Necessitate et Contingentia Causarum, which seemed rather to emphasize that a
number of external factors could impede the will [79].

He again repeats in the Cambridge version that denial of freewill
contradicts the teaching of both Christianity and Aristotle:

Et ex hoc patet quod istud tolleret punitiones fieri debere, et
retraheret ab actibus bonis; quae omnia sunt contra fidei
veritatem et contra Aristotelis intentionem [80].

[It is also clear from this that the latter (determinism) would remove
the duty for punishments to be carried out and it would take away from good acts.
All of these are against the truth of the faith and against the meaning of Aristotle.]

His metaphysical principles do not permit him to deny the basic universality of the principle of cause and effect, as some people - he says - mistakenly do, preferring to support unpredictability and variability instead. This is clearly unacceptable for Siger:

> Et dicebant quod non est vera; immo, quamquam nunc sic posita causet effectum, alias tamen posita eodem modo non necesse est quod causet effectum [81].

[And what they were saying is not true. That is to say that, although what is now so posited may cause the effect, if it were posited elsewhere in the same way it is not necessary for the effect to be caused.]

Indeed, by the Vienna version, he does feel confident enough also to attack more severely those on the other extreme who see providence as demanding that the irreversibility of predetermination is required by the necessity of cause and effect on the grounds that it would be against the Catholic faith:

> Alii autem, videntes primam propositionem esse veram et necessariam, inciderunt in alium errorem, scilicet quia, credentes ex veritate primae propositionis aliquid esse contra fidem catholicam, posuerunt quod omnia quae eveniunt de necessitate eveniunt, sic quod non oportet negotiari etc. [82].

[Others, who see the first proposition to be true and necessary, fall however into a different error. This lies in the fact that, because they believe as a result of the first proposition that something is against the Catholic faith, they have posited that all events happen of necessity. Consequently there is not need to make deals and so forth.]

He seems to hint that such a conclusion borders on superstition. Indeed, it is divine providence itself that has provided an explanation of the possibility for us to take advice and to make plans:

Non enim consiliamur, nec etiam negotiamur de aliquibus
futuris effectibus et quia velimus impedire providentiam
divinam, sed potius explere; nec etiam ut velimus impedire
connexionem causarum ad effectum.   Nam et hanc etiam
impedire non possumus, sic enim eam ordinavit providentia
divina [83].

[For we are not advised nor even persuaded about any future effects
because we might want to impede divine providence but rather to ensure the latter.
It is not even because we might want to impede the connection between causes and
effect.   Furthermore we cannot even impede this for it is what divine providence
has ordained.]

In the Vienna version - presumably again in a professional response to
objections that were being made in the Paris milieu - Siger explores further a
deeper understanding of what it means to speak of the freedom of the will:

Voluntas enim qualiter dicitur libera? ...Planum enim est quod
oportet, antequam voluntas velit aliquid vel non velit, quod
ipsa moveatur ab aliquo vel ex apprehensione alicuius, et ita,
ut ipsa moveatur, vel velit, vel non velit.   Quandocumque vult
sine aliqua apprehensione praecedente, in hoc voluntas non est
libera.   Sed cum iam mota est apprehendendo aliquid, libera
est ut velit vel non velit illud; ita quod libertas eius non esset si
nulla causa esset impedibilis, sed quia aliquae causae sunt
impedibiles, ideo, etc. [84].

[In what way can the will be said to be free? ... For it is plain that,
prior to its willing or not willing something, the will needs to be moved by
something, or in other words by the apprehension of something, so that, as it is
moved, it either does will or does not will.   Whenever it wills without any previous
apprehension, the will is not free in this.   However, when it has already been
moved by apprehending something, it is free to will or not to will the latter.   This
is such that freedom would not exist for it if there were no cause capable of being

impeded. However, because some causes are capable of being impeded, the rest follows.]

Certainly, as we saw in considering De Necessitate et Contingentia Causarum, this could give the impression at first sight of over-emphasizing the involvement of the reason in exercising free choice. Nevertheless, it appears from this and from other contexts that we should rather see it as implying that sometimes we react instinctively, rather like animals do, but that this does not derive from the freewill of the rational human being as such. In fact, the key answer to the problem of how divine providence can be reconciled with human freewill lies in the distinction that God, unlike us, has foreknowledge as to how we are going to use our freedom:

> Cuius ratio est quia praescientia hominis non potest esse nisi alicuius futuri necessarii; tale autem necessario eveniet. Praescientia autem Dei est et futurorum contingentium et necessariorum [85].

[The reason for this is that the foreknowledge of the human being can only be of some future necessary event. Such however will happen of necessity. The foreknowledge of God, however, is both of future contingent and necessary events.]

The fact that, in both the versions of the Quaestiones in Metaphysicam relevant here, Siger explicitly mentions God and the demands of the teachings of faith may indicate a considered reaction to the 1270 Condemnations. However, his approach remains of course totally prescinded from any theological arguments, while again he shows his scientific-style singleminded approach of which he is so great a proponent.

324

7.6.   Quaestiones super Librum de Causis.

In Siger's commentary on this work of Proclus, there can be found another explicit reference to the question of freewill, though it is not as detailed as might have been wished.   In Quaestio 25, Siger considers whether "higher heavenly souls" can make any impression on our human intellective souls in this world.   He then goes on to argue that the need to find a sufficient cause to justify all change would demand that, even in the context of willing and of intellection, there is a universal cause and mover of this world.

It is, incidentally, interesting in passing to note that he speaks of the author of the "Liber de Causis" [86] as being right in contrast to one of the Aristotelian texts [87], although he does employ Aristotle in his own support later on [88].   This would certainly suggest his awareness, following the recent discovery of this fact by Thomas Aquinas not long before his death [89], that this book was not written by Aristotle.   Since 1255, however, it had been required reading within the Faculty of Arts for seven weeks each year [90].

What is of importance here, however, is to discover that Siger twice accepts both that the will is free and that it possesses responsibility for its operations:

Voluntas enim libera est in volendo et sui actus domina [91].

[For the will is free in willing and mistress of its own action.]

...voluntas dicitur libera et sui actus domina, non quia sit primum principium ex quo ipsa agitur ad volendum, sed quia valet ad contraria sine organo existens nec obligata ad alterum propter materiam et corporis dispositionem sicut appetitus sensualis [92].

[... the will is called free and mistress of its own action, not because it is the first principle from which it is activated to willing, but because it is capable of being activated to opposites, as it exists without an (physical) organ and it is not obliged to either as a result of matter and bodily disposition, like the sense-appetite.]

The very phrase "valet ad contraria" demonstrates how this text, not known to most earlier writers, confirms that Siger intends to uphold the reality of genuine freewill. Again, he is using the contrast here with sense-appetite of the body, as a result of which the feeling of hunger, for example, cannot be avoided if no food has been taken for some time.

He has earlier made it clear that the will itself does not depend on any other will but is activated by its apprehension of something as good.   This then enables it to be an immediate agent for action:

> ... vult voluntas non ex alia voluntate sed ex apprehensione
> eius sub ratione boni; hoc est immediate agens ... [93].

[... the will wills not from another will but from the apprehension of it (the object willed) under the domain of good.   This is immediate activation.]

He is stressing that this reference to the First Cause and the will's ability to act immediately does not imply that the First Cause is its immediate agent.   Likewise, he certainly does not intend to be introducing any explanation of what he calls the miraculous or the extraordinary kind, set up by God:

> Quod autem dicimus omnia quae fiunt hic inferius reduci in
> causam primam et nihil esse novum nec in anima nec in
> voluntate nec in aliis a causa prima immediate, intelligendum
> est secundum communem usum et naturale fieri factionis
> ipsarum rerum, non intendente miracula et prodigia Dei
> omnipotentis immediate a Deo causata [94].

[We state that all things which are made in this lower world lead back to the First Cause and that nothing is new and immediate from the First Cause, either in the soul or in the will or in other things. This statement should be understood according to common usage and the natural development of the above and no reference is implied to miracles and wonders of the omnipotent God immediately caused by Him.]

This text is clearly determined to demonstrate that the human being possesses freewill and is truly committed to opposing any form of determinism, even that rooted in God as First Cause. Ryan claims nevertheless that it is not compatible with an active, positive and independent concept of freewill [95]. However, his argument that such an interpretation is required by the phrases "non ex alia voluntate sed ex apprehensione eius sub ratione boni" [not from another will but from the apprehension of the object under the domain of good] does not necessarily stand up to deep scrutiny. This text may well be asserting the independence of the human will, even from the control of God. Besides, it surely makes more sense to demand some prior intellectual apprehension of an object as good, if the will is ever to be able to respond to it in genuine freedom. Perhaps, however, it is partly a case of Ryan interpreting phrases in a psychological sense, while Siger may, according to his more usual philosophical practice, have been speaking on the metaphysical level.

Nevertheless, at the very least, as Ryan concedes, Siger is still maintaining a passive understanding of freedom of the will. Throughout, Siger seems to be trying to reason through his thought on a rational level and to be responding to the evidence of the arguments of others, again in a manner somewhat akin to that of a modern scientist faced with re-examining his own theory and of responding to those of others.

7.7.   Implications of Siger's Position.

It does seem therefore that, whatever Articles 3, 4 and 9 of the 1270 Condemnations had in mind, Siger did not intend to deny freedom of the will. Granted that he reacts, in good scholarly fashion, to the comments and criticisms of others, he does clarify his position somewhat with the passage of years. The

<u>Quaestiones super Librum de Causis</u> makes clear that he does not at the time of lecturing on that book - and probably never did - subscribe to what is stated in Article 4. Furthermore, while Article 9 may quite probably have had his teaching in mind, in so far as it speaks of a passive, rather than an active, potency of the will, with his references, which we have seen above, to the need for the will to be attracted, this is for him a metaphysical requirement that does not invalidate his upholding of its freedom. The difference, for Siger, in practical terms of the functioning of the will is not much more than a semantic one, in the same way as two scientific theories may both be attempting to describe and explain an empirically observable event in two apparently different ways.

We have already seen several times in this study how words taken out of context or misunderstandings of what Siger was probably intending to say can lead to misinterpretations by others. Indeed, it could well be that even Siger himself is occasionally guilty of the same fault, as when he speaks of those who deny Ibn Sina's fundamental principle [96]:

> Quidam enim credentes omnium causarum ad suos effectus
> esse consimilem necessitatem, ne viderentur tollere libertatem
> arbitrii, ... negaverunt hanc propositionem [97].

[For some people, believing there to be a similar necessity in the relationship of all causes with their effects, in order to avoid the impression of removing freedom of decision ... have denied this proposition.]

As Ryan points out [98], it is hard to find anyone who really would have held such an extreme position at that time, although Henry of Ghent does try to stress the autonomy of the will so much that the role of the intellect is quite dramatically diminished:

> ... bonum autem apprehensum sub ratione veri nullo modo
> potest ex ratione boni cogniti necessitare voluntatem in
> appetendo [99].

[...however, when good is apprehended qua (under the aspect of) true, it in no way is able, qua known good, to necessitate the will in seeking.]

In fact, it does seem that many modern psychologists would well understand the reasons why Siger would adhere to the idea of the importance of the role of reason as a pre-requirement of the will making a real choice. Otherwise, we would be speaking about completely random selection - if that is the right word! - of actions, much as a Lottery Computer selects the prizewinners. This would not of course be genuine freewill. Today, when people discuss the relative balance between the influences of genetic background and social environment on the development of personality and of inclination to make certain choices rather than others [100], we nevertheless are aware that people can sometimes react out of character or even through stubbornness or sheer bloodymindedness.

Even the claims by Dr. Dean Hamer and his team in Maryland in July 1993, regarding their discovery of a linkage between DNA markers on the X chromosome and male sexual orientation, stress that this does not even mean the existence of a definite predetermination towards homosexuality, but, at most, a genetically inherited trait that might predispose towards it [101]. Hence, we can perhaps begin to be more sympathetic to Siger's initial idea of how freedom of the will is best represented as a passive influence rather then an active one. We can also well understand how he sought to maintain his unique position when challenged, in the manner of any practitioner of psychology today if encountering a similar onslaught of academic criticism. Indeed, whether it is Marx exhorting the workers to throw off their chains, Christians preaching the need to overcome original sin or Freud referring to our unconscious drives, we can see how the same basic issue has been tackled in recent times too.

Furthermore, if we look at the second of Siger's <u>Quaestiones Morales,</u> we see the practical application of the above for he speaks of the need to develop good moral practices and habits, which can only be so rated if they are in accordance with reason:

Et hoc apparet ad sensum: consuetudo enim in operibus
inducit habitum qui est perseverantia in illis, ut patet ad
sensum, ita quod virtus moralis nihil aliud est quam habitus in
modum naturae, consentaneus rationi [102].

[This is indeed clear to see. It is because regularity in deeds induces a
habit of perseverance in them, as is quite clear, so that moral virtue is nothing other
than natural development of a habit which is consonant with reason.]

The practice of good habits requires, however, an act of the will that is
much more than mere discussion of moral rights and wrongs. It needs application
to actual choices and deeds although, once again Siger says, this should be in
accordance with right reason:

Frequenter audire loqui de virtutibus et earum actibus non
sufficit ad generandum virtutem, nisi homo manum apponat ad
opus. Cuius ratio est: si enim aliquis qui haberet rectam
rationem de agendis esset facilis ad ebriandum, deberet
quaerere remedia contra hoc, aliter saepe inebriaretur et
amitteret usum rationis: ebrius enim usum rationis non habet.
Sic etiam quantumcumque aliquis habeat rectam rationem, nisi
habeat appetitum ordinatum, recta ratio per passionem
corrumpetur multotiens. Et hoc patet ad sensum. Haec
enim est via determinata sine qua non pervenitur ad virtutem
[103].

[Listening to talk about the virtues and their acts is not enough to
generate virtue without the human being putting his hand to the task for the
following reason. If someone who had the correct judgment about what ought to
be done was easily inebriated, he ought to be seeking ways of curing this.
Otherwise, he would become inebriated frequently and would lose the use of
reason, since an inebriated person does not have the use of reason. So too,
however correct someone's judgment might be, the latter, unless he has a

controlled appetite, may be corrupted through passions on many occasions. This is quite clear for this is the definite way without which virtue will not be attained.]

Yet again, these two quotations, especially with the phrases "hoc apparet (patet) ad sensum" [(literally) this is clear to the sense(s)] demonstrate the methodology of the modern empirical scientist in Siger's approach to these topics. Indeed, it has been seen how he prescinds from Christian revelation over moral issues, in a way that one would not normally expect Thomas Aquinas, Bonaventure and others to do, even if it is not so consciously severe a decision as that of Margaret Knight when she began to advocate her religion-free morality in the tradition of Stuart Mill and the Utilitarians [104].

Nevertheless, it is again this independent approach which suggests that we can identify Siger as the first scholar to assert so positively his claim to be preserved from direct clerical interference in his philosophical investigations.

CHAPTER EIGHT

SIGER'S VIEWS ON DIVINE PROVIDENCE

8.0.   Introduction.

This chapter will consider the historical context of approaches to the topic of divine providence and foreknowledge of contingent events before offering a brief examination of some interpretations by earlier writers about Siger's teaching on this.

There follows an examination of the range of his writings to determine clearly not only what he taught but also its intellectual context and foundations for him, along with some consideration as to whether it is possible to detect any changes of emphasis or even of fact in this teaching. Subsequently a judgment will be made as to whether he really should be considered heretical over this issue and attempts will be made to analyse what lies behind his approach and what are the consequent implications for the relationship between philosophy and theology.

8.1.   Historical Context of Issue.

The fourth and last of the groups into which the thirteen propositions condemned on 10 December 1270 can be easily categorized is indeed that of divine providence.

In modern religious parlance, the notion of providence has often come to signify some general benevolent caring and love for the human race and of its individual members by the Almighty.   Its more strict and more exact medieval meaning - as its Latin etymology makes clear - refers rather to the possibility and nature of God's knowledge of created effects and its corollary regarding the relationship between this prior knowledge and the freedom of the human being to make genuine choices on which some acts and events are truly contingent.

Thus, we shall examine in this chapter a number of Sigerian texts relevant to an examination of the following three propositions:

Article 10. Quod Deus non cognoscit singularia.   [That God does not know individual things.]

Article 11. Quod Deus non cognoscit alia a se.   [That   God does not know things other than himself.]

Article 12. Quod humani actus non reguntur providentia Dei [1].   [That human acts are not governed by divine providence.]

Similar statements are also to come under scrutiny in fact by Tempier's Theological Commission in 1277, namely:

12.   Quod alius est intellectus in ratione secundum quod Deus intelligit se et alia. - Error quia, licet sit alia ratio intelligendi, non tamen alius intellectus secundum rationem.

13. Quod Deus non cognoscit alia a se.

14. Quod Deus non potest immediate cognoscere contingentia nisi per particularem causam et primam.

15. Quod Causa Prima non habet scientiam futurorum contingentium. Etc. (2)

[12. That there is a different intellect for reasoning, depending on whether God has knowledge of himself or of other things. - This is wrong because, although it is a different dimension of knowledge, it is not however a different intellect as regards reasoning.

13. That God does not know things other than himself.

14. That God can only know contingent things through a particular and first cause.

15. That the First Cause does not have knowledge of future contingent things. Etc.]

There had also been a requirement since 1208 that Waldensians returning to the mainstream fold should make a profession of faith that included a statement of belief in a God who was not only creator of the world but also "gubernatorem et (loco congruo et tempore) dispositorem omnium corporalium at spiritualium" ["who governed and (at a suitable place and time) disposed of all corporal and spiritual things"] (3). Hence, there was a general awareness among theologians that orthodoxy needed to be maintained in this matter. There had also of course been the problem of the Cathars in parts of France and elsewhere, as we saw in the last chapter. Thus there was a range of teachings on good and evil and on God's relationship and knowledge of free human acts which, from the perspective of the theologians and champions of orthodoxy, needed careful watching and scrutiny.

Certainly, the latter would not be wanting a challenge to this to come from the philosophers in the Faculty of Arts. This chapter will therefore consider whether these fears were justified.

We can indeed see the relationship of this issue to that of freewill. If some human acts are not predetermined by God, how can we speak of the First Cause as being aware of which choices will in fact be made in the future? On the other hand, of course, if God's omniscience and omnipotence are to be upheld, how can the dualism and semi-fatalism of the Cathars in fact be avoided? Hence, this opens up the further issue of the relationship between God existing in his eternity and his human creatures within time. Finally, the theological and philosophical point arises as to whether, on the hypothesis already considered in Chapter Five that the universe itself is eternal, this eternity as a created object is different from the eternal timelessness of the Creator.

8.2.   Previous Scholarship Regarding Siger on This Issue.

Mandonnet of course had taken for granted, just as he had done with the three issues examined in Chapters Five, Six and Seven, that Siger must have been guilty of teaching heresy. We have seen that Mandonnet simply assumed that all the propositions named in Tempier's 1270 decree must have been taught by Siger [4]. As Duin points out [5], this is not a good professional approach for an objective historian. Indeed, Van Steenberghen makes it clear that he does not accept that Siger did anything other than truly affirm God's providence [6]. Even the early Van Steenberghen had come to this conclusion [7].

Duin's (1954) book concentrates on the issue of providence, but, while many points which he makes are still valid, it is of very limited worth today, since he was very restricted by those texts available for him to examine at that time. As for Mandonnet himself, such a restriction of course particularly applies to the later works of Siger.

Van Steenberghen finds the topic of limited interest, as compared with the others already considered in this study and, even in his great work of 1977, he devotes very little space to its consideration. Perhaps, in the full context of all Siger's writings, this is justified.

8.3.   Quaestiones in Tertium de Anima.

In those works of Siger that can be dated as probably prior to 1270, we do not find much direct reference to the issue of providence. In this Commentary, however, Quaestio 17 does examine the general question as to whether one Intelligence is actually capable of understanding another. This problem arises from the nature of such spiritual, non-material beings, when the contrast is made with the whole process of abstraction from sense-phenomena undertaken by the human intellect, as seen in Chapter Six.

Siger simply offers his interpretation of Aristotle's position - as so often appears to be his practice in his earlier years - but then goes on to examine the latter's views regarding the identity between the subject and the object of knowledge in non-material beings, in so far as these will also apply to the First Cause itself:

> ... dicendum quod intelligentia quidquid intelligit, intelligit per rationem intelligendi suam substantiam.   Et hoc sentit Aristotelis in hoc tertio, cum dicit: in separatis a materia, idem est sciens et scitum, et in undecimo Metaphysicae, ubi dicit: Prima Causa aliud a se non intelligit [8].

[... it must be said that whatever it is that an intelligence understands, it understands by reason of understanding its own substance. Aristotle has this view, both in this Third Book, when he says 'in those things which are separated from matter there is identity between subject and object of knowledge', and also, in the Eleventh Book of the Metaphysics, where he says 'the First Cause has no knowledge of anything other than itself'.]

In such a being, knowledge comes then from some self-consideration of its own substance and its causal relationship to others:

> Unde dico quod intelligentia solum intelligit aliud secundum habitudinem suae substantiae ad aliud, scilicet in hoc quod ipsa se habet in ratione causae ad aliud vel in ratione causati (9).

[Thus I say that an Intelligence only understands something else according to the relationship of its substance to something else, that is to say in its relationship to something else by reason of being its cause or by reason of being that which has been caused.]

He explains that this is ultimately only possible through the Creature-Creator relationship:

> Unde ... dico quod una intelligentia aliam non intelligit sub habitudine causae, immo omnes ex aequo respiciunt Primam Causam sicut causam earum (10).

[... I therefore state that one Intelligence does not have knowledge of another one by a causal relationship but rather all equally regard the First Cause as their cause.]

He has no time for any theory of emanations in this respect, even for human knowledge of the Creator, which is direct:

> Similiter noster intellectus immediate respicit Primam Causam tamquam suam causam et non per intelligentias medias (11).

[Likewise, our intellect regards the First Cause as its own cause directly and not through intermediary Intelligences.]

Such a background is useful for understanding how, in explaining Aristotle's teaching, Siger endeavours not to take this particular issue out of the broader context of the relationship between cause and effect, regarding Creator and creature.

8.4.   Quaestiones in Physicam.

Quaestio 9 of Book II of this Commentary, which can possibly be dated very slightly later than the Quaestiones in Tertium de Anima [12], examines the nature of what we call Chance.   Siger discusses how chance, by its very definition, cannot be described as a "per se" [intrinsic] cause since it is not something that comes to pass by strict necessity.   He even employs, most unusually for him, the vernacular (though archaic and classical for us today) French phrase "de aventure" with his obvious etymological roots to indicate this:

> Et quod fortuna sit causa per accidens, hoc sonat nomen fortunae gallice: [de aventure] accidit aliquid, eo quod accidenter adveniebat, et proprie dictum est.   Quia si per se fuisset causa, ipso posito semper vel frequenter sequeretur effectus talis [13].

[And that chance ia a 'per accidens' cause is indicated by the French word for chance: it is rightly said that something happens by chance, in that it comes to pass by accident.   If there had been a 'per se' cause, once that was in place, such an effect would always or frequently follow.]

For a metaphysician of course, causality always requires a necessary binding link between cause and effect. The difference lies in the nature of this necessity:

> ... sciendum quod differt necessitatem simpliciter et necessarium ex suppositione [14].

[... it should be known that there is a difference between what is necessity in every respect and what is necessary as a result of a supposition.]

Thus, Siger, with his customary scientific-style rigour, has no time for the ancient view of those who attributed chance to some divine influence:

> Et hoc somniabant Antiqui dicentes quod fortuna est quid divinum. Sed quia vocaverunt fortunam causam ordinantem, male dixerunt [15].

[And thinkers in antiquity were dreaming to say that chance is something divine. Indeed, they spoke evil, in calling Chance a governing cause.]

He has already somewhat cynically, with perhaps a touch of humour, suggested that a chance concurrence of common interest may often lead to the striking of a bargain between two parties:

> ...quando creditor indiguit blado, tunc debitor indiguit vino [16].

[... when the creditor has need of some corn, then the debtor has need of some wine!]

However, we need also to beware lest we even describe the First Cause itself as a "per accidens" cause. This would logically imply two first causes and two gods. It will be noted how dualist elements of Manichaeanism had infiltrated into the teaching of Cathar groups in the thirteenth century, much to the concern of the mainstream Church [17]. Siger recognizes such a position to be heretical:

Et qui dicit Causam Primam esse causam alicuius per
accidens, ponit quod Prima Causa non est omnium causa,
immo ponit duas primas causas.   Et hoc est haeresis, quia
faciunt duos deos qui sic dicunt [18].

[And to say that the First Cause is a 'per accidens' cause of
something, is to affirm that the First Cause is not the cause of everything but
rather to affirm two first causes.   This, moreover, is heresy, because those
who state this set up two gods.]

The solution is that the distinction between necessity and
contingency arises from the nature of those causes which are closest to, not
those which are the most distant from, the effects:

Ulterius sciendum quod effectus non sortitur necessitatem nec
contingentiam ex causis remotis, sed ex propinquis [19].

[It should further be known that an effect does not derive from
either necessity or contingence as a result of remote causes, but of proximate
ones.]

At the conclusion of this Quaestio, Siger sums up - in a
thoroughly orthodox manner - how God's foreknowledge can and does
include knowledge not only of all that will happen, but also whether or not
this is contingent on a range of variable circumstances:

Dicamus nos sic: Praevisum vel provisum a Deo oportet quod
eveniat.   Sed hoc potest esse contingenter vel de necessitate.
Exponatur praevisio Dei: Deus non tantum scit quod futurum
eveniet, sed qualiter.   Deus ergo scit quod contingens eveniet
et quod contingenter eveniet.   Si autem scit aliquid provisum
ex necessitate evenire, necessario eveniet.   Nam ex causis
proximis dicuntur effectus necessarii vel contingentes [20].

[Let us say this: something foreseen by God must happen. However, this can be contingently or of necessity. Let us explain God's foreknowledge. He not only knows what is going to happen in the future but how. God therefore knows that a contingent thing will happen and that it will happen contingently. If however he knows that something he has foreseen will happen of necessity, it will necessarily happen. The reason is that it is as a result of proximate causes that we talk of necessary or contingent effects.]

It is not possible to determine whether Siger is considering this from the perspective of explaining and determining the limits of our own human knowledge when he speaks of chance contingent events, or whether he is simply looking explicitly at those human acts which derive from the nature of freewill. However, the basic principle concerning providence remains the same.

8.5.   De Intellectu.

There is also another occasion, apart from that mentioned above in the Quaestiones de Anima [21], when Siger does cite Aristotle's famous dictum that the First Cause can only know itself [22].

We come across this in Nifo's reference to what he calls the De Intellectu, describing it as Siger's initial response to Thomas' De Unitate Intellectus contra Averroistas. In the context of explaining how the Intelligences are apparently unable to know one another as such, he states that the First Cause "nihil intelligit extra se" [has no knowledge of anything outside of itself] [23]. Clearly this text can superficially be interpreted as suggesting that Siger subscribes to the condemned Article 11 of 1270. However, quite apart from the need to discover its genuineness, since this is a citation by Nifo rather than an original reference by Siger or one of his students, we should be a little wary of the context in which Siger may have been writing. Perhaps, he was simply trying at this stage to explain what he believed the Aristotelian original to mean, or even Ibn Rushd's interpretation of the latter:

> Hoc dicit Subgerius in tractatu suo de intellectu ... qui fuit missus Thomae, pro responsione ad tractatum suum contra Averroym [24].

> [Siger says this in his tract on the Intellect, which was sent to Thomas as a reply to his anti-Averroist tract.]

We cannot be sure what is the truth from this oblique reference alone. However, there is no reason to suppose that Siger is deviating at all from that earlier position in the Quaestiones de Anima, noted at the beginning of this section.

8.6.   De Necessitate et Contingentia Causarum.

It is worth noting that Mandonnet only had access to Godfrey of Fontaines' version of this work (Paris 16297). This will excuse to some extent his presumption that Siger is denying providence in it, since that former version does not include two references, at the very beginning of the actual presentation of his solution, to the fact that he is speaking and offering his interpretation of the problem "secundum intentionem philosophorum" [according to the intention of the philosophers.] [25]. It is of course possible that he has simply become more worldly-wise and more conscious that such a disclaimer, in the post-1270 atmosphere, is desirable, if not necessary, to preserve his own teaching position and to avoid further controversy.

In any case, Mandonnet does seem, as we have already noted, to have fallen into the trap of trying to prove a case that he has already predetermined 'a priori' and which is not justified elsewhere by the text. For example, Siger demonstrates his commitment to the reality of providence, that

342

it does not infringe human freedom and that it can be presented as God's practical knowledge of events:

> ... nec etiam necesse est evenire futura contingentia respectu providentiae divinae, quia visum est ex ordine et connexione causarum et habitudine praesentium non necesse evenire multa quae fient; quare nec ex ratione et intellectu huius ordinis et connexionis causarum ad causata. Providentia autem divina nihil aliud est quam ratio dicti ordinis et dictae connexionis practica (26).

[... from the point of view of divine providence, it is not necessary that future contingents come about, because we have already seen that, because of the relationship and connection of causes and the disposition of the present states of affairs, it is not necessary that many things which do come about should come about; hence neither (does any necessity follow) from the rational understanding of this order and the connection of causes to their effects. Divine providence, however, is nothing more than practical reason applied to the aforesaid relationship and connection.]

Providence, as a practical aspect of divine reason, comes from the very nature of the chain of causality:

> Providentia enim divina necessitatem rebus non imponit; quod sic apparet. Providentia divina nihil aliud est quam ratio practica seu intellectus connexionis et ordinis causarum ad sua causata (27).

[So it is clear that divine providence does not impose any necessity on things. Divine providence is nothing other than the grasp in practice or understanding of the connection and relationship of causes to those things they have themselves caused.]

He explains that God does not know future contingents in themselves, but through his own substance:

Nullum enim intellectum habent praedicta in Deo, nisi intellectum qui est sui ipsius et eius substantia [28].

[Things foretold are known in God only by that understanding, which God has of himself, and which is identical with his substance in God.]

He goes on to repeat this statement with irony directed at anyone who might misinterpret the implications, but also adds the extra claim that it does not in any way infringe contingency in the world:

Aut si graviter sonat in auribus aliquorum, quod non sit hoc praeintellectum a Deo, tunc dicendum, sicut prius dictum est, quod, cum hoc ipsum, quod est A fore, in Deo non habeat intellectum, nisi qui est ipsius substantiae divinae et ipsa substantia divina, etiam talis intellectus ipsius A quod fiet, qui est eius in alio quodam immutatibili, quamquam quod A fiet sit mutabile, nullam imponit necessitatem ipsi A ad eventum [29].

[Or, if it sounds serious to the ears of some people that this is not known in advance by God, then it should be said, as has been stated above, that the very proposition 'A will come about' is known in God only by that understanding which God has of his own divine substance; so even such an understanding of A, that it will come about, which is an understanding of A in another being who is immutable despite the fact that the coming about of A can be prevented, does not impose any necessity on A's coming about.]

He proceeds to answer three objections. Here again, his position is made perfectly clear; for example, with regard to the first of these, he declares:

In intellectu enim divino mutabilia habent scientiam immutabilem et futura etiam fallibilia praescientiam et providentiam infallibilem [30].

[For in the divine intellect there is an unchangeable knowledge of changeable things and an infallible foreknowledge and providence even of future fallible things.]

The same point is made twice more in the references to each of the other objections, immediately before he concludes this work [31].

It seems impossible, therefore, to support not only the position of Mandonnet but also that of the much more recent writer Hissette, who asserts that it is too farfetched for Duin [32] to argue that in the following text Siger is only opposing the objections of those who argue that God knows other effects in themselves rather than through his own substance, although this would seem to compromise their contingency:

... ita quod dicendum est de aliquo futuro contingenti, quod non est provisum et praeintellectum a Deo ipsum fore, cum nihil sit provisum a Deo et praeintellectum nisi quod est verum [33].

[... in such a way that it should be stated about any future contingent, which is neither foreseen nor foreknown by God as going to exist, since there is nothing foreseen nor foreknown by God unless it is true.]

For Hissette, this text must indicate that at least once in this work Siger must have opposed the existence of divine providence and foreknowledge [34]. Whatever we might think of Hissette's interpretation of Duin, it seems probable anyway that this text is asserting no more than that providence can only, in a strictly accurate sense, have knowledge of those contingent things which really are going to occur eventually. If they are not going to do so, God does not know them as such, since they will never actually exist.

This whole argument of Hissette seems especially weak here, when we consider how it is only four lines after this citation that Siger offers his comment and explanation noted above, beginning: "Aut si graviter sonat in auribus aliquorum ..." [Or if it sounds serious to the ears of some people...] (35).

8.7.   Quaestiones in Metaphysicam.

We do receive a little more elucidation by examining a number of relevant texts within some of Siger's Quaestiones in Metaphysicam, since the issue of providence is linked to metaphysical questions regarding causality and God as the First Cause.

We recall that he clearly asserts the existence of divine providence and describes it as deriving from the very nature of causality as regards both necessary and contingent effects:

> Nam et haec est providentia divina.   Sic enim Deus providit
> talibus effectibus ut sic ex suis causis provenirent: quibusdam
> ut absolute ex suis causis necessario provenirent, quia causae
> eorum impedibiles non sunt, quibusdam autem sic quod
> provenirent ex suis causis, non simpliciter ex necessitate, sed
> contingenter, ut quia causae eorum impedibiles sunt (36).

[This indeed is divine providence.   This is because God so exercises providence over such effects that they issue from their causes in the following way: some of them issue from their causes with absolute necessity because their causes cannot be impeded, while others issue from their causes not with unqualified necessity, but contingently, in that their causes can be impeded.]

346

Indeed, it will be recalled from the previous chapter how he also comes to acknowledge very promptly that it is only possible to speak of necessity in an analogous way as regards cause and effect in the so-called contingent cases:

> ... si necessitas potest dici quod proprius dicitur contingentia (37).

> [... if what is strictly called contingency can be called necessity ...]

> ... si necessitas potest dici (38).

> [... if it can be called necessity...]

Siger has already explained in the previous book of this Commentary how a being which has come into existence "per accidens" must itself have a proximate cause of that nature for it to be possible for it to exist:

> Et sic apparet quod ens per accidens non habet causam per se, scilicet propinquam (39).

> [And so it is clear that a 'per accidens' being does not have a 'per se' cause, needless to say a proximate one.]

Elsewhere, in another quaestio concerned with the nature of chance, which is found in the Paris Version of the Commentary, a further point in this context is clarified regarding the distinction between a "per accidens" cause and a "per accidens" being:

> Differt autem causa per accidens et ens per accidens. Ens enim per accidens in solo concursu attenditur: ut album est musicum per accidens, quia nullus ordo causalitatis est unius super alterum. Sed ubi est causa per accidens, ibi oportet

esse concursum et etiam ordinem, ita quod pro quanto est ibi
ordo, pro tanto est ibi causa [40].

[There is indeed a difference between a 'per accidens' cause and a
'per accidens' being.   After all, a 'per accidens' being is obtained by a mere
coming together, (such as for a white man who happens 'per accidens' to be a
musician), because there is no relationship of causality between one and the
other.   However, where there is a 'per accidens' cause, then there must be a
coming together and also a relationship, which will be proportionate in extent
to that of the cause.]

He then goes on to explain again how chance can only be
influenced by proximate causes, not by the First Cause, as this would imply
that the latter can be changed as the passive element in an act of causality:

... non dicitur casualis respectu huius suae causae, quia nihil
accidit Primae Causae: sed effectus raro eveniens a causa
proxima dicitur casualis [41].

[... it is not called chance with respect to this cause of it, because
nothing happens to the First Cause, but an effect rarely occurring is called
chance in so far as it comes from a proximate cause.]

We also recall that, as an exponent of Aristotle, Siger was averse
to the Neoplatonic idea of intermediaries and that, while particular perfections
may only be described of both creatures and of God by analogy, nevertheless
all these perfections must indeed be found in the First Principle, as, he says,
can be ascertained through an analysis of the nature of causality:

Estne ergo Primum perfectum sic quod in eo sint perfectiones
inventae in quolibet genere?   Dico quod sic et probatio huius
est ista: effectus enim omnis est in sua causa aut secundum
eandem rationem aut secundum aliam et nobiliorem....   Cum
ergo Primum Principium sit omnium aliorum entium

effectivum primum, sequitur quod in eo sit omnis perfectio, ut bonitas, essentia, vita etc., et omne quod in aliis entibus reperitur [42].

[Is the First Being perfect in the sense that it contains the perfections found in any genus whatsoever? I say that this is the case and here is the proof: any effect is present in its cause, either under the same or under some other higher description... Since therefore the First Principle is the first efficient cause of all other beings, it follows that it contains every perfection, such as goodness, essence, life, etc., in short, everything which is found in other beings.]

Thus, an understanding of this metaphysical link between the First Cause and any created effect, necessary or contingent, provides the basis for us to understand how God can know everything that is coming to pass through his providence.

8.8.   Quaestiones super Librum de Causis.

It has already been pointed out how Siger has noted well that God, as First Cause, must have foreknowledge of the whole of creation since it all depends on him for its existence.   However, one of the problems surrounding the issue of providence is how God as an eternal being can have knowledge of contingent effects, since the latter apparently do not depend on him as effects.   Links with the previous chapter of this study will be apparent since this would seem to be the case, for example, with those effects which are the result of the free choices of human beings if we are indeed to maintain that the latter are truly free.

Relatively near the beginning of this very late Commentary of his, Siger looks at the nature of eternity.   In Quaestio 10, we may begin to see how he discerns the concept of possible everlasting time, according to the hypothesis of an eternal world, as being very different from the nature of eternity outside time:

> ... aeternitas differt a tempore in hoc quod tota simul est aeternitas, tempus autem non, ita quod etiam secundum ponentes tempus esse aeternum, sine principio, sine fine, nihilominus praedicta differentia differt tempus ab aeternitate (43).

[... eternity differs from time in that eternity is an entire simultaneity while time is not, so that, even according to those who claim that time is eternal without a beginning or an end, time is nevertheless different from eternity by this forementioned difference.]

He goes on to assert that time and eternity are of quite different natures and therefore can co-exist:

> Diversae tamen mensurae durationis quae non sunt eiusdem rationis et generis et naturae, sicut sunt tempus et aeternitas, nihil prohibet simul esse (44).

[There is nothing to prevent different measures of duration, which are not of the same dimension, genus and nature, such as time and eternity, co-existing at the same time.]

Such a view of course begins to provide the ingredients of a possible resolution of the problem regarding God's foreknowledge of free human acts, as outlined above.

Later in the book, Siger returns to the question as to whether the First Cause knows anything apart from Himself. Siger declares that he must do so, although this cannot be a form of knowledge that would imply any potentiality and hence any imperfection within God:

350

Solutio. Dicendum est quod causa prima [alia] a se universa intelligit. Sed intelligere alia a se duobus modis est ... Primo modo causa prima non intelligit alia a se, nam tunc intellectus eius esset in potentia et esset suum intelligere cum passione et receptione et sequerentur multa alia quae arguta sunt in obiectis. Secundo tamen modo causa prima intelligit alia a se, ea intelligens non in seipsis sed in quodam altero ab eis ut intellectu essentiae suae et per speciem intelligibilem quae est ipsius intelligentis essentia et natura. Primum enim ens cum sit causa omnium entium, non contingit ipsum sciri et ignorari alia, sicut qui cognoscit primum calidum non ignorat alia calida (45).

[Here is the resolution of the 'quaestio'. It must be said that the First Cause does understand all things other than himself. Nevertheless, to understand things other than oneself is twofold ... In the first way, the First Cause does not understand things other than himself, for in such a case his intellect would be in potentiality and his process of understanding would be passive and receptive and there would be many other consequences which have been argued in the objections. However, in the second way, the First Cause does understand things other than himself, understanding them not in themselves but in something different from them, namely in understanding of his own essence and by the intelligible species which is identical with the essence and nature of the Knower. For since the first being is the cause of all beings, it is not viable for him to know himself but not to know other things, just as the person who knows the first warm object cannot fail to know other warm things.]

On concluding his answers to the objections, he even declares that the opposite view, that the First Intellect knows other things in themselves, independently of his own essence, is a reprehensible heresy:

... hoc enim ponere de intellectu primo nefas est et haereticum (46).

[... for to claim this about the first intellect is reprehensible and heretical.]

In the following quaestio, Siger delineates more precisely the metaphysical link between causality and knowledge regarding God and other things, in so far as it is not only applicable to them in their universality but also in their singularity and particularity:

> ... sicut causa prima principium est universalis naturae in qua entia conveniunt, sic et causa est propriae naturae cuiuslibet et ideo cognitione suiipsius non tantum cognoscit entia in universali et quantum ad naturam entis in qua conveniunt, sed et cognoscit proprias naturas eorum [47].

[... just as the First Cause is the principle of the universal nature in which beings come together, so he is the cause of any particular nature whatsoever. Thus, by self-knowledge, not only does he know beings in their universal form and in so far as they come together to form the nature of being, but he also knows their particular natures.]

Siger asks for it to be noted that, in reality, the knowledge of Himself and the knowledge of other things, which the First Cause possesses, are not two quite different processes but only happen to appear to us to be so:

> Sed est advertendum ... quod in causa prima cum sit cognitio suiipsius et cognitio aliorum ab ipsa, non sunt istae duae cognitiones realiter differentes, sed secundum quod [per] nostram considerationem distinguuntur [48].

[But it should be noted ... that in the first cause, since there is cognition of himself and cognition of things other than himself, those are not two cognitions different in reality but they are distinguished by the way in which we look at them.]

Finally, he reminds us that their very difference comes from the different ways in which they participate in God's essence:

> Tamen eis adaequatur nihilominus cum cognoscit alia a se per rationem eorum unumquodque eorum excellentem, ut per essentiam suam, quae scilicet diversimode ab unoquoque est imitabilis, eorum tamen uniuscuiusque propria ratio [49].

> [It (the First Cause) is however proportioned to them when it nevertheless knows things other than itself, by means of the reason for their existence and of each of their perfections, i.e. through his own essence, which of course can be imitated by each in various ways, each of which is the proper definition of individual things.]

8.9.   Summary and Assessment of Siger's Position.

We have already noted in Section 8.2 that Mandonnet started from the assumption that Siger was indeed guilty of denying providence. Not surprisingly, in view of his preeminence at that time regarding research into Siger, this view was repeated, over the next forty years or so, in a number of other books on medieval thought.   However, quite apart from this questionable approach of making an "a priori" assumption, he has no evidence to support this case other than one or possibly two texts taken out of context. In Mandonnet's defence, it could be added that a number of texts were not available to him at the turn of the last century.

There is indeed no sense in which, on the evidence of the texts which we now possess, we could even begin to make such a claim. Likewise, there is no basis for anyone to suggest that Siger was guilty of equivocation or even holding through the "double truth" theory that, while we should acknowledge providence through theology and religion, we should deny it at the same time on philosophical grounds.

Certainly, he does tend generally, especially in his earlier writings, to use philosophical language, in employing phrases such as "Causa Prima" [First Cause], although we do also find him on other occasions speaking explicitly of "God". In fact, his position is very close to that of Thomas Aquinas, as delineated in the Summa Theologiae. For example, Thomas produces a very similar argument when he maintains God's knowledge of future contingents through his providence:

> Unde manifestum est quod contingentia et infallibiliter a Deo cognoscuntur, inquantum subduntur divino conspectui secundum suam praesentialitatem: et tamen sunt futura contingentia, suis causis comparata [50].

[Thus it is clear both that contingent things are known infallibly by God, in so far as they are subordinate to the divine perspective of them as existing in the present, and yet they are contingent future things if viewed by comparison to their causes.]

This argument was to be developed much later in the sixteenth century by the Spanish Jesuit Luis Molina with his theory of "middle-knowledge", based on divine knowledge of future possibilities by means of logical succession of causes, which has been well outlined in a recent book by Lane Craig [51].

Thomas also asserts, like Siger, that God's knowledge of other beings comes through their very relationship to Himself in so far as they are reflected in his essence:

> Alia autem a se videt non in ipsis, sed in seipso, inquantum essentia sua continet similitudinem aliorum ab ipso [52].

[However, he sees things other than himself, not in themselves, but in himself, in so far as his essence contains the likeness of things other than himself.]

Thomas further declares that this knowledge is of them in their very singularity and particularity:

> Cum enim sciat alia a se per essentiam suam, inquantum est similitudo rerum velut principium activum earum, necesse est quod essentia sua sit principium sufficiens cognoscendi omnia quae per ipsum fiunt, non solum in universali, sed etiam in singulari (53).

[For since he knows things other than himself through his own essence, in so far as it is a likeness of things as their first active principle, it is necessary that his essence should be the sufficient principle of knowing all things which are made through him, not only in universal form but also in singular form.]

This foreknowledge by means of causality enables some events to happen through necessity, while others are contingent as a result of their relationship not to God but to more proximate causes:

> Non igitur divina providentia necessitatem rebus imponit, contingentiam excludens ... Et ideo quibusdam effectibus praeparavit causas necessarias, ut necessario evenirent; quibusdam vero causas contingentes, ut evenirent contingenter, secundum conditionem proximarum causarum (54).

[Divine providence does not therefore impose necessity on things to the exclusion of contingence ... And thus he prepared necessary causes for certain effects, so they would happen necessarily, and contingent causes for certain others, so that they would happen contingently, depending on the proximate causes.]

So, if Siger were to be accused of heresy in this regard, then Thomas seems to be equally guilty! Even a cursory examination of Siger's writings would show that there is not the slightest evidence that Siger could be accused of upholding the three Articles condemned by Tempier in 1270.

Van Steenberghen [55] does hint that it is possible that some such evidence might be found in some undiscovered work, but this seems highly unlikely, save possibly one dating from the very early years of Siger's career, when, as we have seen over other issues in earlier chapters, he tended merely to deliver and explain Aristotle's own teaching as he saw it. Certainly, Aristotle taught that Pure Act could not know the inferior world [56]. However, it could well be that the influence of Neoplatonism with the idea of emanations may have contributed just as much to this idea. It is possible that some other Master or Masters in the Faculty of Arts may have been guilty in this respect. Perhaps it is more likely that in 1270 the theologians, themselves once trained in philosophy, included this issue so as to fire a warning shot across the bows of the teachers of the Faculty of Arts that they should be careful not to mislead nor to sow any confusion in the minds and the hearts of their students.

On the other hand, we can with confidence state that Siger, just as he did regarding those topics which we have examined in earlier chapters, investigates the nature of God's foreknowledge of created effects and providence of necessary and created occurrences from a non-theological perspective. Again, there is no reference made to Scripture, not to mention Peter Lombard's Sentences, nor to revelation as expressed in the magisterium of the Church, as the theologians would have done. His approach certainly can yet again be seen as very much akin to that which, in this more modern era, has been described as a scientific-style methodology.

CHAPTER NINE

THE LIFE OF SIGER OF BRABANT AFTER 1276

9.0.   Introduction.

This study has rightly been predominantly concerned with examining the teaching career of Siger in Paris from around 1265 to his flight from Paris in 1276.   It has been assumed by earlier writers, as a result of probable references to his death in Orvieto by Dante Alighieri and others - as noted in Chapter Two - that he had probably been imprisoned in one way or another in Italy until his subsequent murder.

This chapter, however, breaks fresh ground by examining the historical circumstances that would have surrounded these years in the Papal States and speculates as to their possible effects on Siger.   It then concludes by explaining how the Florentine scholar might well have been prompted to include his paean of praise for Siger in his great drama La Divina Commedia.

9.1.   Direct Evidence from Medieval Sources.

It will be recalled from Chapter Three that Siger's active teaching in the Faculty of Arts at Paris was to come to an abrupt end when, together with Goswin of La Chapelle and Bernier of Nivelles, he was summoned by a decree dated 23 November 1276 and issued by Simon du Val, the French Inquisitor at that time, to appear before him on 18 January 1277 at Saint-Quentin [1].   There are also four further known sources of direct evidence about Siger's final years and about his death, which should be examined first of all.

Reference has already been made in Section 2.1 to those six fascinating verses, referring to Siger, which can be found in <u>La Commedia Divina</u> of Dante Alighieri:-

> Questi onde a me ritorna il tuo riguardo
> E il lume d'uno spirto, che in pensieri
> Gravi, a morir gli parve venir tardo.
> Essa è la luce eterna di Sigieri
> Che, leggendo nel vico degli strami,
> Sillogizzò invidiosi veri.
> Paradiso, Canto X, lines 133-138).

[This, from whom your glance returns to me, is the light of a spirit, in serious thoughts, to whom dying appears to come slowly.   It is the everlasting light of Siger, who, when teaching in the Street of Straw, did not escape envy in pronouncing true arguments.]

We recall that what makes these verses especially interesting is not only the implied praise in the expression referring to the "eternal light of Siger", but also the additional fact that these laudatory words were not merely left as personal thoughts of the poet himself but were actually placed in the mouth of none other than Dante's hero Thomas Aquinas himself.

Dante suggests indeed in the third of those lines above that Siger may have suffered a long and lingering death. Furthermore, he describes his philosophical teaching as including "invidiosi veri". Why should his teaching be apparently true and praiseworthy to Dante, yet be a cause of envy to others? Thus, it seems to indicate that, as a loyal and devoted Christian, Dante must have felt that Siger was either acquitted of heresy or, at the very least, have actually been innocent of such a charge. This view would seem to be confirmed by the fact that Siger is placed in heaven, where no heretics or non-Christians are otherwise placed, however meritorious their lives may have been. Even Virgil, Dante's companion during the journeys through Hell and Purgatory, is unable to accompany him through Paradise. Of course, contemporary Church teaching and theology would have permitted nothing else. Since we know that Dante was in far from full agreement with the actions of his contemporary Church authorities in many ways, the second of the two interpretations referred to above is very possible. Dante may well have been a strong believer in Siger's innocence, even if he had been pronounced guilty. However, this scenario is the less likely, because, unless the individual was willing to renounce any heresy for which he was convicted within a determined period of time, he was to be put to death [2].

We may further recall that Thomas Aquinas, Dante's great hero who speaks the very paean in praise of Siger, himself declared that a person was bound to speak the truth, even if it were to lead to that person's own death or even the death of another [3]. Dante's words indicate that Thomas accepted the fundamental orthodoxy of Siger and that his death was certainly not the result of a judicial condemnation. Needless to say, the possibility that the verse implies that Dante subscribed to the "double-truth" theory can be discounted and this has never been seriously suggested.

We also noted that the French scholar Castets had provided a second poetic source with interesting information about the death of Siger [4]. He had concluded that the author of an Italian poem, 232 sonnets long, which he discovered in the faculty of Medicine at Montpellier, who uses the nom-de-plume Durante, was none other than Dante Alighieri himself [5]. This poem Il Fiore, which was based on an earlier French work of Jehan de Meung, entitled Roman de la Rose, has three particularly relevant lines, from our point of view, in Sonnet 92. They are put into the mouth of Faux-Semblant, who represents Hypocrisy (somewhat in the manner of Bunyan's Pilgrim's Progress). They are especially fascinating since they do not occur in the original French poem and therefore almost certainly represent the personal work of Durante:-

> Mastro Sighier non andò guai lieto,
> A ghiado il fe' morire a gran dolore,
> Nella corte di Roma, ad Orbivieto [6].

[Master Siger ended up far from happy. I made him die by the sword in great pain in the Papal court at Orvieto.]

Hence, we have an apparent conflict with the implication in Paradiso X, 136, of a slow and lingering death. However, could the latter expression be used in a metaphorical sense to refer, either to some form of imprisonment or even to a kind of cruel restriction from teaching that a formerly active teacher like Siger might have felt most acutely?

We do, however, learn more about his possible fate, as a result of the third piece of evidence provided by a letter addressed to Oxford University by John Peckham, the then Archbishop of Canterbury:

> Nec eam (opinionem) credimus a religiosis personis, sed saecularibus quibusdam duxisse originem, cuius duo praecipui defensores vel forsitan inventores miserabiliter dicuntur conclusisse dies suos in partibus transalpinis, cum tamen non essent de illis partibus oriundi [7].

[We believe this opinion did not originate from religious but from certain secular persons. Its two principal defenders or perhaps inventors are said to have ended their days in pitiable fashion on the far side of the Alps, although they did not derive from those parts.]

There seems little doubt that one of these must have been Siger, whose death therefore must have occurred some little while before 10 November 1284, the date of this letter.

The fourth item to assist us in clearing up some of the confusion and ambiguities seen above is to be found in a piece of information, gleaned by Paget Toynbee from the "Martini Continuatio Brabantina" [8]:

> Albertus de ordine Praedicatorum, doctrina et scientia mirabilis magistrum Sygerum in scriptis suis multum redarguit. Qui Sygerus, natione Brabantinus, eo quod quasdam opiniones contra fidem tenuerat, Parisius subsistere non valens, Romanam curiam adiit ibique post parvum tempus a clerico suo quasi dementi perfossus periit [9].

[Albert, from the Order of Preachers, distinguished for his teaching and knowledge rebuked Master Siger a great deal in his writings. This Siger, a Brabantine by birth, as a consequence of holding certain opinions against the faith, was no longer able to remain in Paris, and went to the Roman court, where after a short while he died of stabbing by his half-mad secretary.]

This reference, from what is often known as the Brabantine Chronicle, then claims that Siger had been an opponent of Albert the Great, confirming that he had been forced to leave Paris and had gone to the Roman Court, where some while later he was to be stabbed by a demented secretary.

Thus, to aid us in our task of trying to unravel the truth about Siger's last years involving his exile and death, we have possessed for some time four potentially informative sources: La Commedia Divina, Il Fiore, John Peckham's letter and the Brabantine Chronicle. We know with virtual certainty therefore that he must have left Paris around the end of 1276 and must have died in exile some time before November 1284.

In trying to piece together what might have happened during these years, it is necessary to rely on what can be no more than intelligent speculation and to research into indirect sources. Certainly, it seems highly feasible that Siger may have felt that a direct appeal to the Roman Curia would offer him a better hearing than the French Inquisitor's Court, especially since, as we shall see, he must have made quite a number of enemies within the confines of both the City and the University in Paris. This would have happened, not only because of his academic teaching, but also because of his involvement in various conflicts there. No doubt, he may even have received early warning of Simon du Val's intentions as Inquisitor in France, of the attitude of Stephen Tempier, the Archbishop of Paris, and so on.

Gauthier has suggested that the three Masters of Arts cited in the summons of 23 November 1276 had fled to Liège, since Saint-Quentin, where they were called upon to appear, is about halfway between Paris and Liège [10]. While this is obviously possible, his opinion that Siger was then acquitted there and went on to pursue a clerical career as Canon in Liège, until he had to go to the Roman Curia in Orvieto on some matter of chapter business really does seem too incredible and far-fetched to be tenable [11]. The traditional view that he went to Rome sometime around the end of 1276 or the beginning of 1277 does appear far more probable, whether this journey was made direct from Paris or from Liège.

Incidentally, although a fair number of the Articles contained in the Syllabus do seem to be directed against Boethius of Dacia and indeed some texts explicitly name him [12], his omission from the Summons of the Inquisitor would strongly suggest that he was no longer involved in teaching in the Faculty of Arts. The Danish scholar Pinborg, who contributed much to the series containing most of the published texts of Boethius [13] has argued strongly that the latter probably ceased to teach philosophy in Paris around 1272-1273 [14]. We have already considered in the second chapter the strong possibility that he may have become a Dominican and was to attain respectability [15].

9.2.   Pope John XXI in Viterbo.

It is possible that Siger may even have felt or been persuaded that he would have a fairer and less prejudiced hearing at the Papal Court of Pope John XXI; such an assumption may seem particularly well founded when we learn of the latter's own admission that his interests in matters academic had been fostered in his youth in Paris itself:

> Ab annis teneris diucius observati variis scienciis inibi (Paris) studiose vacavimus, et per annos plurimos secus decursus sedentes ipsius, sapidissima eorum libamina gustavimus [16].

[From my youthful years we stayed in Paris studying various sciences, while for very many years besides we sat at this very fountain tasting their most delightful offerings.]

There is of course another possibility too that has never seriously been considered.   This is that Simon du Val, at the time of the actual decree of summons in November 1276, may have personally, or through an intermediary, persuaded Siger and a companion to have gone voluntarily to the Papal Court to try to explain their side of the story before the date at which they would have had to answer the charges from Paris.

In any event, it does seem an unusual coincidence that the Pope should send a formal letter to Tempier on 18 January 1277, the very date of the projected court appearance, instructing him, as a result of reports he has received in Italy, to investigate affairs at the University [17].   Whether or not Siger left Paris, voluntarily or involuntarily, on the advice of someone or for whatever reason, it does subsequently appear that the Pope is concerned about the state of affairs.   Is that the reason for his dating of his letter to Tempier to be identical with that day which the latter had fixed for the actual hearing, now to be superseded by more recent events?   Had Siger and his companion(s) already arrived at the Papal Court in Viterbo or had perhaps the Pope received some intimation to expect him very soon?

Whatever may have been the precise course of events, it seems unlikely that Siger and his companion - probably Goswin of La Chapelle, if we accept the evidence that Bernier of Nivelles, the third man cited by the Inquisition, is to be found after 1280, safely lecturing in Theology at the Sorbonne College [18] - were found guilty of persisting in heresy in Italy, for death was, as we have seen, the punishment for an unrepentant heretic. Even Thomas Aquinas himself, despite his earlier remarks on the need for personal integrity, had supported the death-sentence, in order to uphold the wider and more longterm good of the Church as a whole, as the best means of dealing with a persistent heretic [19].

Besides, it is more than possible that the Pope was either just making a general enquiry as a result of information received, or even had become somewhat concerned to hear about attempts to justify scandalous or immoral behaviour. Examples of condemnations of this latter were indeed to be found in a number of the Condemnations of 7 March 1277, such as n.205-208. Furthermore, even before this, there had come yet another intervention by Simon of Brion, the Papal Legate, on 6 December 1276, very soon after the departure of Siger and his colleagues, to condemn a whole range of excesses:

> Fertur enim quod modernis temporibus,.... commessationibus, potationibus aliisque reprobandis actibus intendentes, choreasque et alia nephanda exercere ludibria .... et armati incedunt nocturno tempore catervatim .... non sine gravi laicorum scandalo.... Et quod gravius est ferendum .... etiam super sacris altaribus .... non sine nota heretice pravitatis ad taxillos ludere non verentur [20].

[There are indeed reports these days of people getting involved in feasts, drinking sessions and other reprehensible deeds, of taking part in dance-tunes and other wanton and base activities and of armed gangs at large during the night-time. These cause serious scandal to laypeople. Furthermore there are more serious reports still that they have no qualms about playing dice in clearly depraved and heretical fashion even upon consecrated altars.]

Indeed, the <u>Chartularium Universitatis Parisiensis</u> refers to the fact that there had been a number of such occurrences for some time. A year earlier, the Masters of the Faculty of Arts had unanimously forbidden any involvement by members of the Faculty in activities such as dancing in the streets "non de die nec de nocte, cum torticiis, vel sine..." [neither by day nor at night. whether with or without small torches] [21].

In fact, it seems far more likely that Siger and his colleagues received a sympathetic and understanding hearing from the Pope. Peter of Spain had been somewhat unexpectedly chosen to succeed the brief pontificate of the uncrowned Hadrian V who had died without even being ordained priest, although his uncle Innocent IV had earlier bestowed on him many benefices and ecclesiastical honours [22]. Dante's view of all this can be seen in his placing of Hadrian in the fifth circle of Purgatory [23].

This one and only Portuguese Pope, who took the name John XXI, was clearly chosen as a healing candidate in so far as he belonged to neither the French nor the Italian partisan groups. He had not only acquired a reputation as an academic in the area of philosophy, especially of logic, but also as the chief physician to Gregory X [24] and indeed both his reputation and his general intellectual interests stretched much further than this. His premature death was to occur as a result of the collapse of the roof in a new extension added to the papal palace in Viterbo, designed for him to carry out astronomical observations. (The visitor can still see traces of this observatory in the grounds of the present episcopal palace).

Thus, we can understand quite easily how someone like Siger might well receive a much more favourable hearing in this kind of atmosphere than he would have done in the hotbed of intrigue that Paris had become. It will be recalled that the Pope sent the Bull <u>Flumen Aquae Vivae</u> to Tempier on 28 April 1277, instructing him to investigate further "tam in artibus quam in theologia" [in Arts and Theology alike] [25], despite the latter's solemn pronouncement of his Syllabus of 219 Errors a few weeks earlier on 7 March. We can only speculate as to why he thought this to be necessary. It could even be that he was far from happy with the way that the attack on Siger, Boethius and Thomas Aquinas had been carried out by the Theological Commission of Tempier.

It is interesting to discover that on 21 April 1277, only one week before this Bull was issued, the Pope had given orders that twelve Canons of "Saint-Materne" and twelve Canons of the Church popularly known as "Petit-Table" should take up residence in their city of Liège no later than one year from receiving their stipends [26]. It seems a strange coincidence, although it does not directly affect Siger. Was it an attempt to prevent further such problems? Was it a superficial gesture in the context of the politics of the major problem in Paris to appear evenhanded? We can only speculate.

Nevertheless, a relatively optimistic interpretation regarding the nature of Siger's reception in Italy seems to be clinched by the fact that John XXI is the only Pope whom Dante places in Paradise [27]. Considering that John's pontificate only lasted less than nine months, we might well wonder why he should take this step. Could it have been because Dante saw him as not being dishonest or avaricious in political and ecclesiastical wheelings and dealings - the accusation which he so often levels against other Popes of this period? Or was it even the fact that he may have treated Siger (of whom we have already seen that Dante shows such positive approval) with some real understanding and sympathy that might have been a factor in influencing this judgment?

In any event, when people did have the courage - and the finances - to appeal directly to the Papal Court, there is evidence that they seem to have been acquitted quite frequently since their readiness to submit to Papal judgment was seen in itself as strong presumptive evidence in favour of their innocence [28]. Assuming this to be close to what really happened, it seems certain in any case that Siger would not have been in a position to return to his teaching in Paris. Perhaps Van Steenberghen is right to think that there was some form of house-arrest, although even this may not have been continuous [29]. It is certainly more than probable that he remained in some way under the jurisdiction of the Curia.

9.3.   Pope Nicholas III and the Curia in Viterbo.

On 25 November 1277, more than six months after the death of John XXI, the Cardinals chose as his successor Giovanni Gaetani Orsini, who had long been prominent as the leading-figure of the anti-French element in the Curia. Since he came from a family already well used to providing Church leaders such as Celestine III, many may well have felt that someone of his stature was needed to challenge the Angevin influence of Charles of Anjou.   No doubt, Dante's comment on the nepotism of this Pope, who took the name Nicholas III, which is illustrated by the pun on the Italian word for 'bear' in the use of the phrase "avanzar gli orsatti" - and whom he also accused of simony too - would have been strongly influenced by his later experience of yet another Orsini Pope, the terrible Boniface VIII:

> E veramente fui figliuol de l'Orsa,
> Cupido si per avanzar li Orsatti,
> Che su l'avere, e qui me misi in borsa [30].

[And I really was son of the She-Bear, so anxious to promote the Orsini cubs, and having done so up above has caused me to be shut up down here.]

Nicholas' brother Orso, as Podestà of Viterbo, had been largely responsible for the security of the conclave at which he had been elected [31].   His brother Matteo was already Cardinal and he was himself to add another brother Giordano, as well as Latino Malabranca his sister's son, to the ranks of the Princes of the Church, whose numbers during this period rarely rose above about a dozen or so.   Matteo moreover was then appointed as Acting Senator of Rome, a position which the Pope had already taken over from Charles of Anjou in September 1278 and had conferred upon himself for life [32].

Even doubters in his family, such as two of his nephews, were told to be ultra-loyal to the interests of the Orsini family and numerous appointments, civil (in the context of the Papal States) and ecclesiastical, were made in the power-struggle against the French Angevins, the rival Roman family of the Colonnas and, of course, against the Ghibelline groups.

In fact, on his election, the citizens of Viterbo, no doubt with a view to their pecuniary and other self-interest, managed to tempt Nicholas to bring the Papal Court back from Rome, where he had been crowned with great splendour on 26 December 1277 - the first Roman Pope for sixty years or so.

One of the interesting offers incorporated in this deal was that they should allow the Papal Inquisitors to proceed against heretics and their supporters and would, furthermore, inscribe within their city statutes and laws any decrees against heretics that the Pope might issue:

> Quodque statuta summi pontificis et alia edita contra hereticos
> et alios praedictos ad mandatum dictorum inquisitorum in
> eiusdem Comunis Capitularibus conscribentur [33].

[And so the statutes of the Supreme Pontiff and other decrees against heretics and other people summoned by the said inquisitors are enrolled in the chapters of the same commune.]

It is perhaps especially interesting that this was an offer that needed to be made, since it indicates that, prior to this time, Viterbo, despite the presence of the Papal Court, had largely kept its civil and juridical independence.   A later section of the same document makes the interesting offer that the city would agree to refuse citizenship to any member of the curia or to any foreigner, for as long as the court should remain in Viterbo:

> Quamdiu ibi fuerit curia dominae papae, aliquem curiatem vel
> advenam in eorum civem aliquatenus non admictent [34].

[For as long as the court of his lordship the Pope should remain there, they will in no way grant their citizenship to any curial official or foreigner.]

These texts, then, offer further indication that Siger would almost certainly have been able at that time to have acquired some degree of freedom here, although clearly he would have had no opportunity of resuming his teaching post in Paris. Perhaps it may be a little too fanciful to suggest however that the case of someone like Siger may have been behind this proposed statute!

The Inquisition indeed was to prove an essential tool in the growth of the wealth of the Orsini family, for half of the value of confiscated wealth of those found guilty usually went into the Papal Treasury [35]. Thus, the Pope set the process in motion locally by instructing his local Inquisitor in the following way:

> Dilecto filio fratri Sinibaldo de Lacu ordinis fratrum Minorum, inquisitori hereticae pravitatis in Romana provincia in sede apostolica deputato salutem. Supra absolutione infamiae Viterbiensis super crimine hereseos dummodo in brevi ad hoc bene se cooptent [36].

[To my beloved son, Brother Sinibaldus de Lacu, of the the Order of Friars Minor, duly appointed Inquisitor into the depravity of heresy in the Province of Rome within the patrimony of the Apostle (i.e. Papal Territory), I send greeting and good wishes. Absolution from the infamous crime of heresy should be granted to the citizens of Viterbo, as long as they speedily and properly cooperate in this matter.]

We see further confirmation of this process in a register produced by a notary in 1279 recording the granting of privileges to the citizens of Viterbo whom the Pope is thanking for their recent inquisition into heresy [37]. His deeper intentions regarding this process are then revealed in his additional orders to his Franciscan protégé to give these local heretics three months to admit their guilt of heresy, which would deprive them of many rights anyway, or else to suffer the major financial penalties for their families:

> ... nec ad manus tuas vel cuiuscumque inquisitoris deveniat, sed libere ad mandatum nostrum possit haberi, cum nostrae

intentionis existat, quod eadem pecunia in pios usus et pietatis opera in eadem civitate vel eius districtu, sicut et quando expedire viderimus, convertatur [38].

[...it must not end up in your hands nor in those of any Inquisitor whomsoever but may be freely passed to our possession. This is because it is our intention to convert the same money to pious uses and for works of piety in the same city or its district, however and whenever it seems fit.]

Thus, Nicholas III was to acquire a fine country house at Soriano near Viterbo, from where he was to send out all his decrees in the last few months of his life and, furthermore, was eventually to die [39]. Pinzi comments in his study of the history of Viterbo that, following the most recent Ghibelline reverses, the issue was as much political as religious [40]. In any event, before the Pope was to die, he was to ensure, despite the scandal that this was naturally to create, that the much developed and rebuilt estate should be passed to the same brother Orso [41].

The penalties at this time, even when the accusation of heresy was openly conceded (it will be recalled that conviction without this admission meant execution after a period of time allowed for so-called repentance), involved imprisonment, very heavy fines and the obligation of wearing the two dreaded yellow crosses on one's clothes [42]. We will not be surprised therefore at Dante's vigorous attack on this papacy. In contrast, Joachim of Fiore can be seen portrayed in the Commedia Divina as a great prophet rewarded in Paradise [43]. Furthermore, it might have seemed worthy of criticism that, even just before the events of 1277, it had suited the Papal Curia to be pragmatic in preventing the legal expulsion of Jewish financiers because of its undoubted fears of the development of rival economic brokers in Perugia, who would not have been under its control [44].

Consequently, Dante's advocacy of the separation of the roles and much of the jurisdiction of each of the spiritual and temporal powers, as can be found in his Monarchia, is not surprising [45]. He argues in the Third Book that the authority of the Emperor derives immediately from God, without the need for any consent or appointment by the Pope. This challenges the Church's claim to perpetual and total authority in civil, as much as religious, jurisidiction as deriving in perpetuity from the so-called Donation of Constantine [46]. It is of course in complete contrast to the argument of those theologians such as Giles of Rome, who argues in his De Ecclesiastica Potestate that all earthly powers should be subject to the spiritual power of the Papacy [47]. Indeed, there was a lot of diplomatic strife, military action and revenge attacks between various Guelf and Ghibelline groups during this pontificate in many areas of Northern Italy. However, while Dante accepts that much of Nicholas' avarice, leading to the accusation of simony, was prompted by his politickings against Charles of Anjou, nevertheless Nicholas is shown accepting the justice of his punishment in Hell, where he is found with his legs protruding from two holes in a rock with the soles of his feet on fire [48].

At this point, it might well be wondered what Siger himself would have made of all these happenings. Whatever state of imprisonment or freedom he may have found himself in at this time, there can be little doubt that he would have been well aware of these unsavoury events. When we remember the circumstances under which he had himself been forced to leave Paris, as an academic with a strong zeal in his search for truth and for what he believed to be right, can we doubt that his agile and talented mind would not have been working on these matters? Pierre Dubois, who had been a student under Siger in Paris, declares that he had heard him commentate on Aristotle's Politics:

> Ad hac facit id quod super Polytica Aristotelis determinavit praecellentissimus doctor philosophiae, cujus eram tunc discipulus, magister Segerus de Brabantia, videlicet quod longe melius est civitatem regi legibus rectis quam probis viris, quoniam non sunt, nec esse possunt aliqui viri tam probi quin possibile sit eos corrumpi passionibus odii, amoris, timoris, concupiscentiae [49].

[A very distinguished doctor of philosophy, Master Siger of Brabant, of whom I was at that time a pupil, taught to this effect; that is to say, that it is considerably better for a city to be ruled by just laws than by upright men. This is because there are not, nor can there be, any men so honest that they cannot be corrupted by feelings of hatred, love, fear or desire.]

This thesis, adapted from a section towards the end of Aristotle's Third Book [50], might have given much food for thought to Siger during these years when he apparently remained in Viterbo.

9.4.   Pope Martin IV and the Curia in Orvieto.

If, as seems likely, he had experienced at close quarters some awareness of these corrupt occurrences during the pontificate of Nicholas III, no doubt Siger would have speculated on the choice that the Cardinals might make as successor.

The Pope had died on 22 August 1280 at the residence of Castel Soriano, which he had managed to keep in the family by giving it to Orso.   The Conclave was to last for six months and indeed the election was only able to take place as a result of an attack on the palace in Viterbo by the local populace and by the kidnapping of Cardinal Matteo Rosso, now the leader of the Orsini faction [51]. This enabled Simon of Brion to be elected twenty days later on 22 February 1281 as Pope Martin IV [52].

It had of course been none other than the same Simon of Brion who had been appointed the Papal Legate to France in 1265.   In his decree of 27 August 1266, following those student riots that occurred as a reaction to the fact that Jean d'Ulliaco had been received into the French Nation instead of the more geographically and legally correct Picard Nation, he specifically cited Siger of Brabant as having been a leading troublemaker among all the accusations and counter-accusations [53].

Although he was recalled to the Curia in January 1269, he was re-appointed in August 1274 by Gregory X as Legate to France, fulfilling his role as Collector-General of Papal Taxes until recalled by Nicholas III [54].   On his election as Pope, he wasted no time in furthering French interests, in partnership with Charles of Anjou, to whom he gave power and patronage over the entire Papal States, despite the Ghibelline opposition of Guido de Montefeltro.

Following the unrest at the Conclave, he decided to move the court to Orvieto, although there was an attempted attack on his coronation ceremony there, while Charles of Anjou was in attendance, by Tancred of Bisenzo and some irate citizens of Viterbo.   However, Tancred was lynched by a mob in the Piazza, so that the ceremony itself had to be moved to the Gate of Sant'Andrea [55].

He brought a French garrison to Orvieto to protect the Papal Court, which was to remain there for the most part for the next three years, apart from summer vacations at his newly-built palace at Montefiascone [56].   The presence of Charles of Anjou no doubt caused feelings of unrest and indeed there is evidence of a minor disturbance in the city at this time, in which the rioters were reported to be shouting "Death to the French" [57], about a year before the breaking out of the so-called "Sicilian Vespers", the major rebellion on that island which was to be exploited by Peter of Aragon as a movement of liberation from the hated French. That this riot was clearly put down with some brutality by the French garrison is illustrated by the fact that it only incurred one fatality, whereas the local population suffered many deaths and injuries.   This kind of inequality in the balance of casualties would seem to indicate that, like the experience of the Palestinian Intifada which began in 1989 in the territories occupied by Israel, there must have been a lot of frustration and bitterness seething under the surface, with very little real opportunity to get rid of the occupying force.

What was Siger doing during all this?   Naturally, as we have already seen, he was not free to return to active teaching in Paris.   Perhaps he was in a dungeon, taken from Viterbo to Orvieto, with the transfer of the Papal Court, but some kind of freedom or house-arrest, as we have seen, seems far more likely [58]. Indeed, the fact that we learn he was, according to the Brabantine Chronicle [59], to be stabbed by a clerical "secretary" might suggest - a point apparently missed by many earlier writers - that he was still able to write, or rather dictate, until his premature death.   This would all suggest that, if he had been sentenced by the

Inquisition to imprisonment, the latter would have been of the "murus largus" type modelled on the lifestyle of the monastery, rather than the maximum security dungeon-style of the "murus strictus" where prisoners were kept chained to the walls [60].

It does therefore seem impossible to imagine that he was not aware of these events happening around him. Indeed, he seems to be the sort of person who would have felt enraged by injustice. Furthermore, we will recall that he had already come into conflict with the new Pope some fifteen years earlier, when the latter had appeared to him to be unfairly advancing the French national interests at the expense of the Picards [61]. No doubt, he could now feel for the situation of the Italians. Was he perhaps, having already seen the greed and injustice of the Orsinis under Nicholas III, now formulating some of the ideas of the separation of the realms of the Church and of the Civil State, as Dante was to advocate to some extent in his Monarchia [62]?

Indeed, Martin IV was to put Venice, Perugia, Assisi, Spoleto and numerous other cities under an interdict for daring to oppose his political manoeuvrings at some time or another over the next two or three years. The outbreak of the Sicilian Vespers was matched on a smaller scale on the mainland by, for example, the massacre of two thousand French at Forli on 1 May 1282, following a cunning plan by Guido of Montefeltro [63]. Subsequently, indulgences, granted originally to Crusaders, were now made applicable to all those who fought for French interests in a Holy War against Peter of Aragon [64]. In fact, as early as October - less than three months after his election - Martin had also been offering special privileges and exemptions, along with material benefices, to bishops and priests among his fellow-countrymen [65].

Meanwhile, in Orvieto, there had been a considerable resurgence of popular feeling against the Angevin-Guelf axis, which, instead of taking the more traditional route of enlisting the support of the Ghibelline nobles, now involved the election by popular acclaim of Ranieri della Greca as Capitano del Popolo in 1280. He was replaced by two Guelfs in 1282 and 1283, after being forced to resign by the French, but regained this position by forging a new grouping which linked with the existing Ghibelline faction.   This was possible because the Filipeschi family saw a chance to overthrow their old city rivals and much more influential and powerful enemies the Monaldeschis, one of whose members was now the Capitano and another of whom was the Bishop of Orvieto from 1279 until 1295 [66].   The Filipeschis had indeed been sent into exile in 1283 but Simone dei Filipeschi surfaces as Ranieri della Greca's right hand man in the troubles of 1284 [67].   With all this unrest, which eventually was to lead to the flight of the two leaders mentioned above from the revenge of the Guelfs [68], Martin IV had thought it wise to leave Orvieto for Perugia, where he promptly removed the latter's interdict [69] and was to die in the following year, himself to be succeeded by a local citizen taking the name Honorius IV.

What again was Siger's reaction then to all these events?   We know that he was certainly dead, at the very latest, some weeks before Peckham writes his letter on 10 November 1284.   Had he died after getting caught up in all this unrest?   Had he perhaps reacted, as has already been suggested, to the lack of integrity displayed around the Papal Court?   Had he expressed himself verbally, or even in writing with the help of his cleric-secretary?   Was the latter a former colleague, as Van Steenberghen and most writers have assumed [70]?   Was he seconded to Siger by the Curia?   Was he a French speaker deputed to help in keeping an eye on him?   We do not know, nor can we do more than speculate as to whether, as we have seen the Brabantine Chronicle to indicate, the secretary was half-mad or whether he had become incensed with anti-Papal, anti-French or anti-Guelf views that Siger might have held.   Certainly, we can appreciate that this sensitive scholar, so adamant from his youth in the defence of what he saw to be right, fair and just, must have felt such incredible frustrations that Dante was able to speak of his "morir gli parve venir tardo" [death seeming to come slowly to him] [71].   We can but hope that it is coincidence that the Registers of Martin IV speak of the Pope's award on 11 December 1282 to one of his own chaplains of a benefice in the diocese of Liège, where Siger had for so long been a Canon [72].

We have already seen how Nicholas III had used the weapon of the legal sanctions and punishment of the Inquisition to increase his family prosperity, as well as the Papal possessions.   There had in fact been a lengthy series of trials against the Ghibelline families of Orvieto in 1268-1269, immediately after Charles of Anjou's first stay in the city, which came to an end in 1273 [73]. Later on, Nicholas III had appointed his nephew Berthold Orsini as Podestà in Orvieto, despite his holding similar positions either in person or by proxy in a whole string of towns and cities, as far afield as Bologna. Berthold indeed ordered a full census of the city [74]. Undoubtedly, this was with a view to raising further taxes and finance. Then, with the whole French experience, it is not surprising that the merchants of the city managed to foment a grassroots drive for a more independent Capitano del Popolo, such as Ranieri della Greca. Thus they were able to create a strategy of interests that they shared with the Ghibelline faction, which, although eventually to be defeated, was to cause the unrest which was to lead to the flight of Martin IV [75].

It would hardly be surprising if a man of the stature of Siger had been caught up behind the scenes in some small way with some of these events. The last five chapters have indicated how Siger was prepared to fight strongly for his belief that the Faculties of Arts and of Theology, at the very least, should be established as two separate fields of influence and that the former should have its general independence recognized and maintained. It seems highly likely that, at the very least, he would have had some very strong views about the general independent status of the civil authority from that of the Church. It may well be that these would have become better known in the surrounding areas after his death and so come to the notice of Dante. If so, this would also help to explain Dante's praise of him. It is quite possible that some of his ideas on Politics, or even in his De Felicitate, to which Nardi has found Agostino Nifo make reference over two hundred years later [76], might well have been developing along lines of practical application which, while obtaining interest and support from those critical of the secular influence of the Papacy, nevertheless would also have made enemies for him.

It is interesting to recall that it was his pupil Godfrey of Fontaines in Paris who gathered together that codex, which we know by the name Bibl. Nat. Lat. 16297 and which includes at least one of Siger's works and quite possibly more [77]. We know that Godfrey treated in the last decades of the thirteenth century a series of "Quodlibet" disputations on a number of political and current ethical issues. It would not be at all surprising if some of his ideas had developed out of what he had understood of Siger's views, even before his exile. Furthermore, some of Godfrey's views on the nature of the ecclesiastical and papal relationship to material goods were adopted by others, such as John of Paris in Chapters 6 and 7 of his De Potestate Regia et Papali issued around 1302 [78], and would almost certainly have then become well known to Dante Alighieri.

Moreover, further investigation of a text, held in the Stadsbibliotheek in Bruges, may well shed further light on this matter if it proves to be the missing text of Siger of Brabant's Commentary on the Politics of Aristotle [79]. It was once thought to be the work of Siger of Courtrai in Paris in the thirteenth century which we have already seen in the second chapter would be an anachronistic impossibility [80].

Likewise, we do not therefore need necessarily to accept Bykhovskii's suggestion that, as a young man, Dante might have met Siger in Orvieto [81]. We may well have already succeeded in rounding the circle and unearthing the direct link between Siger and Dante, which would further explain the high esteem held for the former by the latter.

CHAPTER TEN

SIGER'S PLACE AND SIGNIFICANCE IN HISTORY

10.0.   General Conclusions of Study.

This brief conclusion and assessment of Siger's place and significance in history will not attempt to re-present the many detailed points developed in the course of this book.

It begins with a re-affirmation of the injustice of the basic accusations that Siger is guilty of holding the "double-truth" doctrine and places the reasons for the assault on his teaching in its overall intellectual and historical context.   There follows a review and assessment of just what were the nature and significance of his basic intellectual stance as a Master of Arts at that time which leads to the description of him as the first anti-clerical intellectual of Europe and some indication of his place in history in this context.   A summary of his more specific positions, particularly over the four issues on which the 1270 Condemnations of Tempier had focused, is also explained in the practical context of Siger's lecturing and teaching in Paris and of the development and clarification of his views over these questions.

380

The chapter and book conclude with a very brief summary of how the positive legacy of his thought was perceived in subsequent years and can be so assessed today.

10.1.   The Attacks on Siger.

It will long since have become clear that there is no justification for suggesting that Siger was guilty of holding a position involving "double-truth" in its traditional understanding of the expression.   Although for a number of centuries, this was often implied by the use of the expression "Averroism", recent scholarship suggests that it is an unfair distortion of the facts to state that even Ibn Rushd can be justifiably accused of this [1].

Indeed, if we look more closely at the 1277 Decree itself - rather than concentrating on the comments and interpretations of later writers - it will be noted that even there Tempier inserts the word "quasi" (in effect).   This would seem to indicate that he is suggesting that the justification of this accusation is merely implied rather than actually explicit in the teaching of the Artists [2].   We have also seen that Boethius of Dacia - despite Sajo's earlier opinion [3] - certainly seems to be innocent of this too [4].   Indeed, there is every impression that the Church authorities and the theologians were trying to manoeuvre a situation in which some of the philosophers would be viewed as holding such a position.

Some research by Dales, published in 1984, in fact even suggests that the real origins of what later became described as the double-truth doctrine lie in Maimonides' attempt in his Dux Dubitantium to defend the Genesis Creation account.   Subsequently, this was to find its way into Christian thought, particularly through Alexander of Hales.   If this is the case, it is somewhat ironic that not only did Siger and his Artist colleagues not employ this doctrine in the way it has been classically understood and was claimed by Tempier and the Augustinian theologians, but that its origin is to be found in the highly respected Franciscan, holding a Chair in Theology in Paris just before Siger was born, who had himself began to develop the same subtle intellectual distinction about different domains or dimensions of learning as Siger [5]. In fact, even Mandonnet, when he comes to look at actual texts, is ambivalent about affirming Siger's position in this respect and tends rather to criticize him for freethinking and for excessive rationalism [6], while Gilson sees him as, in any event, attempting to remain on the right side of the Church's traditional faith and teaching [7].

Of course, over the most part of the last hundred years or so, many studies of the philosophical thought of the thirteenth century have been endowed with excessive respect - almost canonization - of the writings and thought of Thomas Aquinas. This is especially the case as a result of Leo XIII's nomination in 1878 of Thomas's teachings as the basic set of texts and the criterion for orthodoxy in Roman Catholic faculties of philosophy, particularly since medieval philosophy was rarely researched elsewhere [8]. This had the effect that even the editor of Bonaventure's writings tended to feel obliged to claim a considerable identity of his thought with that of Thomas [9]. Likewise, the understanding of many medieval writers in their own right was handicapped by the fact that, unless they were proclaimed saints or models for later generations of Christians on account of their spiritual way of life, little attempt was made to get behind the written page at their human personalities, problems, hopes, worries and so on. When occasionally this was done, it tended to be very perfunctory and to portray them in black-and-white fashion. As Bettoni points out [10], even Bonaventure himself suffered from this and there can be no doubt that there has been very little attempt to discover or to unravel the real Siger in this way.

It has become clear that the main impetus for the 1277 Condemnations came from the perceived danger to the monopoly of the teaching authority of the theologians from the more independent-minded members of the Faculty of Arts. This was further feared as a threat to the vital importance of maintaining the orthodoxy of the University, not only since Paris was twice as big in population with 100,000 inhabitants as the next largest city in Northern Europe [11], but also since it had become the training-ground of so many of the Church leaders of that time. Furthermore, it may well be the fact that many of the Franciscans, quite apart from Peckham, sometimes came to attack Thomas Aquinas's position by proxy, since his own basic theological orthodoxy and sanctity were beyond challenge. This could well have been the case with, for example, the question of the possibility of proving by reason the temporal nature of the creation of the world. The Franciscans of course mostly looked to Bonaventure rather than Thomas who, unlike the former, had been better able to read, research and reflect on the suitability and usefulness of Aristotelian thought and methodology for developing and presenting Christian ideas and theology. On the other hand, Bonaventure's academic career had been largely interrupted by his administrative responsibilities particularly as General of the Order [12]. Peckham had been an ardent disciple of the Augustinian tradition and was probably very influential while he was in the Curia too [13]. In fact, some of Peckham's letters of 1284 and 1285 were to indicate the extent of the rift and the rivalry between the two orders of Friars, in which even Thomas was criticized for alleged over-reliance on philosophy [14]. Quite apart from this, there is also evidence of very strong feeling against the increased study and status of philosophy in sermons such as that of William of Luxi which Bataillon cites as portraying "theologizing philosophers" and "philosophizing theologians" in the apocalyptic imagery of the Book of Revelation as frogs emanating from the mouths of the Dragon and the Beast [15].

It has proved important to distinguish between the 1270 Condemnations, of which Siger does seem to have taken account in developing his subsequent teaching, and the far more-reaching ones of 1277, by which time his philosophical positions, save perhaps over the unicity of the intellect, were not far from those of Thomas. Furthermore, despite the fact that many of Thomas' views are also condemned, it was the two Masters of Arts that were explicitly named in the preamble to the 1277 Condemnations. Nevertheless, we should note that the sanction , which in any case was localised to Paris appears to be less directed at them as personal individuals than at the dangers and threats to authority perceived from their teaching. This would also explain why even today it has proved impossible to find any writers or sources maintaining some of the views being condemned. Indeed, in some instances it seems extraordinary if not impossible to believe that any one could hold some of the opinions imputed. This all seems to confirm the point of view expressed in this study that it was for the most part the *process* of arguing for the independence of the Artists that created the problem rather than merely the *content* of his teaching. It was after all not too many years before John XXII was to canonise Thomas Aquinas in 1321. If Thomas' views, on for example, the inability to prove the temporal creation of the world, which were often so close to those of Siger, really were seen as quasi-heretical then the former would not have been possible so quickly.

In terms of assessing the way in which this challenge to the magisterium of the Church was perceived, it is likewise worth contrasting the reaction to the Cathars with that adopted towards the Waldensians. In the case of the former, they were hounded down because their criticism appeared to strike at the heart of the teaching authority of the Church, while the latter mostly escaped persecution during this period because their opposition was, up to this stage, mostly restricted to the tenet of the Donation of Constantine [16]. In the same way, the Joachimites had began with fairly mild criticism of the level of spirituality within the Church. Indeed, quite soon after the death of Siger, the College of Cardinals - albeit later to its considerable regret - was to elect the so-called Angelic Pope Celestine V, who was very much within this tradition.

This understanding that the key problem at this time was the threat to the traditional all-embracing authority of the Church leaders is also indicated by the fact that the disputations with the Jews in Paris and Barcelona appear not to have ended in any of the inquisitorial methods of later decades, when the aim of uniformity of faith and belief became a much greater priority. It should be noted that the Christian establishment did not take too kindly, however, to the idea propagated by Nahmanides and others that Judaism possessed a superior rationality to Christianity, particularly in the face of Christian remarks that not even the angels could understand the Trinity [17].

10.2.   Siger's Basic Intellectual Rationale as a Master of Arts.

It does seem clear, however, that Siger was not directly attempting to challenge the authority of the Christian message. Up to 1270, certainly, he appears to have been for the most part merely trying to commentate on Aristotle's works and to adjudicate between apparently conflicting texts when these arose [18].

This process was not dissimilar to the "Sic et Non" methodology of Peter Abelard. Furthermore, the textual commentary method was much as was employed by the theologians when using Peter Lombard's Sentences to lecture on the Scriptures and, in later centuries, the way that Thomas Aquinas's writings, especially the Summa Theologiae, were used to learn philosophy in Catholic universities.

After 1270, Siger seems to have reflected further on his teaching approach and the role and content of the Aristotelian tradition. Hence, it was during these next few years that he was to give every indication of possessing the potential to become a great thinker in his own right. He was willing to listen to Thomas, sometimes to agree [19] and sometimes to disagree [20]. We have seen a number of examples of how he clarified his teaching, particularly in the later versions of the Quaestiones in Metaphysicam [21] and in the Quaestiones in Librum de Causis [22]. Moreover, while he certainly held a number of views and ideas in common with colleagues such as Boethius of Dacia, he clearly demonstrates his own personal independence of position. Carol is right, in his unpublished thesis submitted in 1990, to assert that Siger appears to be first and foremost a metaphysician [23]. This study too has presented numerous further examples to confirm this and to show how it sometimes leads to apparent problems and controversy raised by his teaching, most notably over the nature of the intellect and of the intellective soul [24] and over the issues raised by the necessary link between cause and effect for human freewill [25].

He certainly does not follow Ibn Rushd slavishly and can by no stretch of the imagination be legitimately described as a Latin Averroist, while even Van Steenberghen's nomenclature of him as a Radical Aristotelian fails to do him justice. It has been seen that he develops his own distinctive thought, as a result of his own process of questioning and he has from this perspective been well described by Caparello as the "maestro del dubbio" [master of doubt] [26]. At the same time he makes it clear on numerous occasions that he does not wish to challenge the ambit of the theologians in their own area of teaching of revealed doctrines [27]. We have no way of knowing if this represents the perspective of a totally sincere and committed Christian believer in his private life or whether it is merely a politic gesture adopted to protect his professional position. The real situation may well have lain somewhere in between or have been a combination of both positions. However, it is maintained that this thesis has indicated that he is a philosopher of stature, worthy of full and independent consideration in his own right. Certainly, if his teaching career had not been so dramatically curtailed before he had reached middle-age and when it was barely half the length of that of Thomas Aquinas, there is little knowing how great a thinker of influence he might have become.

What is also quite clear is that his greatest concern was to preserve and to develop the independence of the Faculty of Arts, in so far as he saw the investigation of philosophy as being a discipline, not only distinct from theology and revelation, but also in its own right as on a different level from the presentation of revealed truth [28]. It is here that we can note the analogy - concerning which reference has been made on a number of occasions in the course of this study - to the situation of many religious believers, particularly Christian ones, working in the field of science today. Thus, it has been possible to demonstrate that Siger perceived the relationship between philosophy and theology in a similar way to that in which such a believer might now view the relationship between science and religious belief [29]. In this sense it has been argued that rather than science having taken over from theology in the modern world, it has been science that has taken over from philosophy if attention is paid to the examination of the process of knowledge rather than to mere content. Of course there are differences as we look at acquisition of content in so far as the philosophy of Siger and of his contemporaries started from an acceptance of basic metaphysical principles rather than the perceived empirical sense-experience of modern science. However, as has been indicated elsewhere in this thesis, the latter also assumes certain basic principles and tests hypotheses which it has itself postulated [30]. It was still in the future at that time for Masters of Arts such as John Buridan to move on from the use of philosophical disputation in general, and the use of "probable" arguments in particular, to a process which would later be called scientific enquiry [31].

While the rival group of the Faculty of Arts on 1 April 1272 had vowed not to touch upon any issue of theological import [32], Siger had no intention of discussing topics such as the Trinity and the Incarnation. The problem arose where issues such as creation, the intellective soul, freewill and divine foreknowledge were also capable of being examined from a purely philosophical perspective. Thus it was that he maintained the right to carry this out on that level as an academic without direct interference by other authorities. It was for this independence that he fought and struggled and which was undoubtedly seen as the real challenge to the theologians and to the magisterium [33]. It was this which was to result in the events of 1276 and 1277 and in his exile in Italy so that his teaching career came to an end, although his intellectual and rational reflections, as we have speculated in Chapter Nine, may very well not have done so.

On those occasions when he did touch upon issues of direct theological import, he insists that he is only speaking or considering them from a merely philosophical angle. These major topics have been considered in depth in Chapters 5 to 8 but, even where he discusses questions of more theological import such as whether the separated soul can suffer physical pains of fire, he is quick to acknowledge that this is "non multum philosophica" [not very philosophical] [34] and to restrict himself to a philosophical viewpoint. Despite this, Thomas was apparently to criticize him for getting involved in theological matters although it might not have been entirely fair [35]. Indeed, even Thomas seems to break his initial promise in De Unitate Intellectus contra Averroistas that he will concentrate on arguments of a philosophical nature [36], a claim asserted again at the end of that treatise [37].

The above may help to see how it was possible for Siger to be held in such high esteem by Dante Alighieri. However, it could not have been simply that Dante admired his relentless pursuit of rational investigation with the use of natural reason, since Ulysses is portrayed in the Commedia Divina as suffering in hell for this very vice [38]. On the other hand, Siger is placed in Heaven alongside Thomas Aquinas, indicating not only the author's respect for Siger but also his clear opinion that his much admired Thomas would not have found him worthy of consideration as a heretic but indeed with teaching to commend [39]. Dante's view of the relationship between religious authority and secular authority seems to parallel those of Siger on the role of supernatural theological beliefs and the independence of natural rational enquiry. Taken further, such proclamations of independence might well have been considered as having the potentiality to threaten those claims of clerical authority to have a monopoly over determining what should be permitted in intellectual discussion and teaching - a privileged position as jealously guarded and preserved by the Church as were its temporal claims.

It is for this reason that Siger can perhaps be described as the first real "anti-clerical" intellectual, on the lines of the recent definition of anti-clericalism adopted by the 1990 International Colloquium on Anticlericalism in Late Medieval and Early Modern Europe held at the University of Arizona. It was described as representing a challenge to this all-embracing set of claims to monitor and to supervise intellectual thought and to determine the lives of Christians in both the secular and the religious spheres [40]. Waldo of Lyons had offered a different kind of challenge and is unlikely to have even been a cleric in minor orders as virtually all intellectuals were at this time [41]. Certainly, there had been lay Franciscan movements beginning to be critical of the Papacy and of the magisterium while the Guelf-Ghibelline struggles, to which brief reference has been made in Chapter Nine, had taken up a similar approach on a more pragmatic level, which Dante himself was to verbalize more intellectually in his Monarchia [42].

However, while elements of Siger's teaching may have been found to have been taken up by Ferrand of Spain, a scholar discovered by Zimmermann [43], by John of Jandun and by others, it must be noted that this study has argued that it is his methodology and approach rather than its actual content that is of the most significance to us. This clear demarcation of intellectual investigation into truth on two different dimensions was to lead to Marsilius of Padua's Defensor Pacis, to Savonarola, to the Christian Humanism of Erasmus and eventually to the anticlericalism of Martin Luther and the Reformation. In another respect, it was to point the way towards Scotus, to the nominalism of William of Ockham, to the Enlightenment and to such philosophical movements as English Empiricism. As such apparent and real confrontations developed, so of course the mechanism of the Inquisition was to come into play to deal with the Poor Franciscans, the Joachimites, Meister Eckhardt, the Marranos and a host of others perceived to be threats.

10.3.   Intellectual Context and Content of Siger's Individual Philosophical Positions.

Mandonnet had simply assumed Siger's guilt in holding heretical positions over the four issues with which the 1270 decree had been concerned [44]. However, Chapters Five to Eight have demonstrated that the true situation was far more complicated.   It has been noted that the writings of Siger, prior to 1270, indicate some debt to John Sackville [45], Geoffrey of Haspall [46] and Adam of Buckfield [47] among others.   He owes most of course to Aristotle and Ibn Rushd, but much also to Proclus as the author of the Liber de Causis - an identification of which Siger was probably aware since this had been made in the last years before his death by Thomas following the translation of the work into Latin by William of Moerbeke in 1268 [48] - while the influence of Thomas and Albert, acknowledged and admired as "viri praecipui in philosophia" [eminent men in philosophy] [49], must also be noted.   However, it has been important to recall that, subsequent to 1270, during that very period following his unusual decision not to move on to another Faculty, Siger demonstrates his intellectual maturity and scholarship and develops ideas and interpretations of his own.   Of course, these are, for the most part, not hatched in a vacuum and we can see influences and reactions to other contemporary writers.   However, he really does stand out as a distinctive figure in so far as he, unlike Ferrand of Spain for example, does not remain solely an interpreter of Aristotle, of Ibn Rushd and of other authoritative philosophers [50].

This confirms his distinctive methodology in stressing the two levels of learning and of approaching the one single nature of truth, as described in Chapter Four.   For all of these reasons, he certainly should be viewed - despite being so often underestimated in the past - as a figure of enormous stature in the context of the development of intellectual thought in the Middle Ages.   Siger thus is trying to break away from merely commentating on highly-esteemed predecessors. It is of course no coincidence that the Latin words "auctor" [author] and "auctoritas" [authority] have the same root. This is, as we have seen, particularly demonstrated in the methodology of teaching and lecturing of that time, whether, for example, on Peter Lombard's Sentences commentating on the Bible or on Ibn Rushd's commentaries on Aristotelian writings. It is even demonstrated in the fact that, at a time when Siger's works remained under official disapproval, the marginal attribution to him in one of the manuscripts of his writings has been put into code, while in at least one other his name has been concealed and replaced by another more acceptable writer [51]. It seemed better indeed to have a falsely attributed work than one attributed to someone who had fallen under sanction. That is why some writers tried to reinterpret a pagan writer's intentions so as to reconcile it to the apparent Christian position [52]. It was also the reason why the hierarchical idea of authority, much more prevalent in the thirteenth century, seemed to some to be under threat when Albert the Great and Thomas Aquinas started to reappraise the significance of Peter Lombard and of Aristotle and to develop their own distinctive theologies [53].

Of course medieval theologians, even when they started to develop their own theologies independently of Peter Lombard in such ways, still saw the Bible as the Word of God and hence the ultimate criterion and bearer of revealed truth. Hence, their status as scholars derived from this [54], though clearly they had to take account of General Council Definitions in the manner that was later to be described by Karl Rahner and others as "Denzingertheologie". As we have seen, there is clear evidence that Siger did not view the teachings of Ibn Rushd, or even Aristotle, in this kind of light. Nevertheless, we should keep in mind that, particularly in the first half of the thirteenth century, it had been a much greater aim and preoccupation of the Masters to present a solid teaching rather than to explore debatable, albeit original, views and theories [55]. It is in this context therefore that we can come to assess more fairly Siger's overall importance as a thinker of the period.

It is incidentally interesting to note how Dante, in his relatively early Convivio, sees ancient Rome as the paradigm for justice, law and order - albeit that of the Republican rather the actual Imperial era! - and consequently as the best model for a new Imperial Order [56]. Likewise, Siger becomes more critical and selective in his stance regarding his esteem for his predecessors as he develops greater intellectual maturity and sense of balance. It is tempting furthermore to see a parallel between Siger's respect for Greek philosophy and that of Dante for Roman administration and law, each advocating in his own way some separation of domains of responsibility of theology and the Church from those of secular intellectual thought and secular power.

Certainly, the context and the content of Siger's later teaching, where he shows plenty of evidence of reflection and development, is highly significant. Thus, he had, like Thomas himself, stressed the impossibility of proving the temporality of creation by reason alone [57] and had fought very hard to develop a way of dealing with the apparent non-multiplicity of the spiritual and therefore of the intellect and its consequent implications for the intellectual soul [58]. He clearly affirmed the freedom of the will in human beings [59] and assessed the relationship of this to divine providence [60]. However, it is for his determination in preserving the autonomy of natural reason and investigation that he deserves to be highlighted by history. Hissette [61] underestimates this when he opposes Flasch's description of the years between 1270 and 1277 as being a kind of enlightenment [62].

Siger is certainly far from being the first to make the distinction between revelation and natural knowledge, between theology and philosophy. It is ironic in fact that Ibn Rushd, despite Siger's debt to him, does not perceive the distinctiveness in the same way. For him, the sublunar world here perfectly reflects, and depends in its activities on, the movement of the heavenly bodies which are themselves of course dependent on God. Thus, Ibn Rushd uses the Aristotelian framework, albeit retaining some real dependence on the Neoplatonic view of creation [63]. Certainly, most earlier writers seem to have thought of reason and revelation as being two sources of knowledge, rather like two different sense-faculties.

Thomas develops his thought on the lines of grace building on nature and on the impossibility of there being a contradiction between reason and divine revelation, so that the latter is seen simply as being more reliable but the former as being an invaluable tool to understanding. Siger fights for the autonomy of reason in a way that would be abhorrent to a Peckham or to a Bonaventure. Indeed, the latter states that philosophy should be seen as a way to other sciences and that anyone who does not progress further beyond it will remain unenlightened and in darkness [64]. While we have seen examples where Siger declares the ultimate authority and reliability of revelation [65], he nevertheless does seem to affirm the impossibility of reason itself ever actually being in conflict with what revelation tells us [66]. He acknowledges that sometimes we may be mistaken and that we know that all thinkers, however great they are, are sometimes in error [67]. It is indeed - he argues elsewhere [68] - the exciting task of the philosopher to search out mistakes, to correct and to improve what is claimed to be rationally true. Nevertheless, it has been possible to see how this statement of professional autonomy, whereby the members of the two faculties should not interfere gratuitously in one another's spheres, is preserved throughout Siger's career.

10.4.   The Legacy of Siger.

It is interesting that it was to be in Italian universities, where theology had little influence, that Siger's ideas were to be further developed and even perhaps adulterated by the so-called Italian Averroists. Nevertheless, even John of Jandun did not really begin to get into trouble until he allied himself with Marsilius of Padua in political opposition to Pope John XXII. It is worth considering that this academic atmosphere, with some debt to Siger's influence in its methodology and general ethos, may have contributed to the fact that Christian humanism was born and first flourished in Italy [69].

Although there is very little extant to ascertain Siger's views on moral questions and indeed he may not have taught very much in the area of ethics, nevertheless some farseeing members of the Church may well have grasped that here also there would develop a considerable threat to its monopoly of authority, if people were in practice allowed to develop independently rational thinking of their own. Siger may well have been viewed - justifiably or not - as being somewhat arrogant and certainly there is no doubt that he was dedicated to his teaching and learning. He even advocated the single, rather than the married, state as the ideal one for the philosopher, if he were to avoid family distractions [70]. This example incidentally also provides an instance of how Siger - over an issue about which he felt himself highly qualified and had strong views of his own - is quite prepared to oppose the position of Aristotle [71]. Perhaps more relevantly to such a view of his character is the fact that he was also to challenge the view that humility as such was in every respect to be considered a virtue [72], as had often been stated in forming a profile of the ideal teacher [73]. Perhaps his wish to work independently of ecclesiastical and clerical censure within his own faculty marks one of, if not the very first, bids for the right to scholarly neutrality and independence, as upheld in universities today. It may seem ironic that not so very much later it was indeed to be discussed whether Tempier himself might well have even exceeded his authority in 1277, in so far as one of the Disputationes Quodlibetales of Godfrey of Fontaines nearly twenty years later did consider whether his successor as Bishop of Paris might not have even sinned in failing to revoke Tempier's earlier Condemnation [74].

Thus, a clear picture has emerged of a strong independent thinker fighting for the independence of philosophical and rational investigation but who was also to be silenced fairly early in a career that might have become subsequently judged by history to be pivotal to the development of modern thought. The fundamental issues which he raised were not to disappear but were to become more acute with Erasmus, Galileo and so many others. In the present age, most Christians have gained the psychological benefit and spiritual security of accepting that scientific enquiry and theological reflection on revealed matters need not cause panic, conflict or fear. Siger did not have this luxury and had to grapple with all of this in a situation fraught with enormous problems. Admittedly, he was less directly concerned than many other thinkers such as Roger Bacon with the content of what we would today call science and physics, on which Oxford even at this time had much greater such emphasis than Paris. Nevertheless, we can see that the thesis can be proved that it is the contemporary relationship between science and theology that has replaced that between philosophy and theology.   Hence, Siger's stress on the two dimensions of knowledge can be better grasped today, although Thomas Aquinas with his own ideas of the relationship between grace and nature would certainly have understood what Siger was suggesting.

It is probably Siger's view of the application of metaphysical regularity, as for example in the relationship between cause and effect [75], that influenced him into defending philosophy so strongly - again as a modern scientist might do with his particular discipline - against what he considered to be unjustified interference by the religious authorities [76].   Thus, he can be truly described as the first anti-clerical intellectual.

Of course, modern philosophy does retain some links and continuity with medieval philosophy and, as we saw in Chapter Four, may even sometimes speak the same or a similar language.   This can even be sufficient to suggest that present-day philosophers could understand the questions being asked by the earlier ones six centuries or so ago.   However, much of the content of medieval philosophy has of course now become detached from philosophy and is now to be found in other areas such as psychology, astronomy, geometry and physics, while, as Ryle and Ayer affirm, the function of modern philosophy has often become "to solve puzzles rather than to discover truths" [77].   However, while the methodology of modern science begins from empirical observation and investigation, Popper has shown how trial and error is the process by which subsequent theorizing is tested [78].   While at first sight this may seem a long way from the study of Aristotle and other such writers, nevertheless there is a sense in which their texts were almost viewed as apparent empirical evidence - then to be investigated, challenged and so on, particularly by the later Siger.

If his career had been permitted to continue for another twenty years or so, there is no knowing how significant his influence and stature might have become.   Whether or not Thomas himself was appreciably influenced by Siger to amend his own views and teaching remains somewhat debatable [79].   However it is surely no understatement of Siger's ability, achievement and influence to assert that his was the most impressive and acute rational mind with which Thomas came into contact.   The latter's intellectual respect for Siger is quite evident in his discussions with him, especially in the <u>De Unitate Intellectus contra Averroistas</u> [80].   This would certainly explain fully why Dante links these two great intellectuals together in his <u>Paradiso</u>.

Certainly, we have come a long way in our assessment of Siger's importance, since Le Clerc in 1847 could say of him that it was Dante's poem that makes Siger famous rather than his actual works [81].   Indeed, in this respect, it would be hard to acknowledge sufficiently the debt owed to the great Sigerian scholars Mandonnet and Van Steenberghen, whose works certainly represent the pinnacle of research of their own periods.   It is believed that this work has been able to take such research an important stage further and that it provides greater light and deeper insights regarding the Brabantine scholar's contribution to medieval thought and to his major role in the history of ideas.   It is highly probable that future scholarship will continue this process in years to come.

APPENDIX A

WORKS OF SIGER OF BRABANT

The following constitutes a reasonable estimation for the dating of the various extant works which are generally now accepted as being genuine, although in most cases they may well be a year or two later (occasionally earlier) and it must of course be noted that the date given will usually refer to the beginning of the relevant academic year.

Compendium super De Generatione et Corruptione	1267
[Bazán 1974]	
Sententia super quartum Librum Meteorum	1267
[unedited but confer Dondaine & Bataillon 1966]	
Quaestio utrum haec sit vera: Homo est Animal,	1267
Nullo Homine Existente	
[Bazán 1974]	
Sophisma: Omnis Homo de Necessitate est Animal	1268
[Bazán 1974]	

Quaestiones Naturales [Lisbon] [Bazán 1974]	1274
Quaestiones Morales [Bazán 1974]	1274
Quaestiones in Metaphysicam [Vienna] [Dunphy 1981]	1274
Quaestiones super Librum De Causis [Marlasca 1972]	1275

BOOKS

BAZÁN B.   Siger de Brabant.   Quaestiones in tertium de Anima, De Anima Intellectiva, De Aeternitate Mundi. Philosophes Médiévaux XIII. Louvain: Publications Universitaires, 1972.

BAZÁN B.   Écrits de Logique, de Morale et de Physique. Philosophes Médiévaux XIV. Louvain: Publications Universitaires, 1974.

DUIN J.   La Doctrine de la Providence dans les Écrits de Siger de Brabant. Philosophes Médiévaux III.   Louvain: Editions de l'Institut Supérieur de Philosophie, 1954.

DUNPHY W.   Siger de Brabant.   Quaestiones in Metaphysicam.   Philosophes Médiévaux XXIV.   Louvain-la-Neuve: Éditions de l'Institut Supérieur de Philosophie, 1981.

MARLASCA A.   Les Quaestiones super Librum de Causis de Siger de Brabant. Philosophes   Médiévaux   XII.   Louvain: Publications Universitaires, 1972.

MAURER A.   Siger de Brabant.   Quaestiones in Metaphysicam.   Philosophes
              Médiévaux XXV.   Louvain-la-Neuve: Éditions de l'Institut
              Supérieur, 1983.

ARTICLE

DONDAINE A. & BATAILLON L. "Le Manuscrit Vindob. lat. 2330 et Siger de
              Brabant." Archivum Fratrum Praedicatorum 36 (1966) 153-261.

        i.   There are also three isolated "quaestiones" edited by Vennebusch in
1966 which can be found in ms.16133 [Latin] of the Paris National Library [1].
They basically follow the ideas already known to us from two "quaestiones" in the
Introduction and one in the Seventh Book of Siger's Quaestiones in Metaphysicam.
Ermatinger has recently discovered in 1980 another copy in Paris of the last of
these, whose attribution to James of Douai he believes to be wrong and hence not
to invalidate the case of Vennebusch that the three "quaestiones" belong to Siger
[2].   There is too little evidence to make a serious attempt at dating them and
indeed Vennebusch suggests that they may have been deliberately extracted from
Siger's lectures for publication [3].

        ii. Note has also been made (in Section 2.3) of the existence of two other
writings referred to by Nifo, namely the De Intellectu and the De Felicitate.   It has
been speculated that the former may in fact be one of the other writings on the
intellective soul [4] that we do possess but this is far from proven.   However, it
could well be that the latter constitutes part of the De Intellectu.   The latter seems
to date from around 1271-2 if it is indeed Siger's first response to Thomas Aquinas'
De Unitate Intellectus contra Averroistas.

        iii. Pierre Dubois refers to a Commentary on Aristotle's Politics [5].   This
thesis speculates that it may be the text, to which reference is made in Section 9.4,
contained in the Stadsbibliotheek in Bruges.   Duin expressed very serious doubts
in 1954 [6] but Van Steenberghen in his 1977 work seems to think it to be more
than possible [7].   Further research needs to be done to investigate this.

iv. There are two other texts attributed to Siger within the Vienna manuscript [Latin 2330]. However, Dondaine and Bataillon (in their 1966 article) do argue quite cogently that the <u>Sententia super Librum De Longitudine et Brevitate Vitae</u> and the <u>Sententia super Librum de Somno et Vigilia</u> both have very close kinship to known texts of Adam of Buckfield [8]. Since the latter was almost certainly a teacher of the young Siger and we have other examples where Siger seems to have followed his teaching quite closely, this does not in itself prove conclusive evidence against Sigerian authorship. However, enough doubts remain for these works to have been ignored for the purposes of this study.

v. In Section 6.12, it is speculated that the <u>Quaestiones in Libros I et II De Anima</u>, edited by Giele, may also reflect the teaching of Siger but again this cannot yet be proven satisfactorily.

vi. Zimmermann has also published in 1968 a number of <u>Quaestiones super I, IV et VIII Libros Physicorum</u> which were anonymous in the collection of Godfrey of Fontaines, but which he concluded could probably be attributed to Siger, though this still remains far from certain [9].

1. J. Vennebusch, "Die Quaestiones Metaphysice Tres des Siger von Brabant", Archiv. für Geschichte der Philosophie 48 (1966) 163-189

2. C. Ermatinger, "Another Copy of a Recently Discovered Sigerian Work," Manuscripta 24 (1980) 51-57

3. Vennebusch 165-166

4. See Section 6.8 note 140

5. See Section 9.3 note 49

6. Duin 253-254

400

7.   F. Van Steenberghen, Maître Siger de Brabant (Louvain: Publications Universitaires, 1977) 189 note 13

8.   Dondaine & Bataillon (1966) 184-196

9.   A. Zimmermann, Ein Kommentar zur Physik des Aristoteles aus der Pariser Artistenfakultät um 1273, Quellen und Studien zur Geschichte der Philosophie 11 (Berlin: de Gruyter, 1968)

APPENDIX B

A CHRONOLOGICAL OUTLINE OF RELEVANT EVENTS

1198   Death of Ibn Rushd.

1200   Most works of Aristotle translated into Latin.

            Masters and Students granted special juridical privileges by King
            Philip Augustus II.

1208   Pope Innocent III summons crusade against Albigensians.

1210   First ban on teachings of Aristotle in Paris by Council of Sens.

1215   Publication of statutes of University by Robert de Courçon
            following Bull of Pope Innocent III.

            Teaching of Aristotle's works forbidden save for those on Logic.

            Fourth Lateran Council condemns Joachim of Fiore.

1225   Alexander of Hales becomes Master in Paris (?).

1228	Renewal of ban on Aristotle's works.
1229	Founding of University of Toulouse in wake of Albigensian crusades. No ban on Aristotle.
1231	Pope Gregory IX permits use of edited version of Aristotle's Physics in Paris.
1240	Birth of Siger of Brabant (?).
	Peter of Spain Master of Arts in Paris (?).
	Major public disputation with Jewish Rabbis in Paris.
1243.	Adam of Buckfield Master of Arts in Paris (?).
	Roger Bacon Master of Arts in Paris (?).
1247	Roger Bacon leaves Paris.
1252.	Pope Innocent IV limits religious orders to only one Chair of Theology each.
	[September] Thomas Aquinas arrives in Paris to lecture in theology.
1253.	Strike by Secular Masters and students against alleged violence of Royal police. Dominicans and Franciscans ignore it and continue lectures.
1254.	Pope Alexander IV reinstates all privileges of Mendicant Orders.
1255	[19 March] Official statutes require compulsory study of all works of Aristotle in Faculty of Arts.

1256   John of Sackville elected Rector in Paris.

              Thomas Aquinas appointed Professor of Theology in Paris.

              Siger arrives in Paris as student in Arts (?).

1257.   [2 February] Bonaventure elected General of Franciscans.

              Founding of Sorbonne for Secular students of Theology.

              Roger Bacon returns to Paris.

1258-64   Thomas Aquinas writes <u>Summa contra Gentiles</u>.

1259.   Thomas Aquinas joins Albert the Great in Cologne.

1262.   Siger graduates as Bachelor of Arts (?).

1263.   Stephen Tempier appointed Master and Chancellor of University of
              Paris.

              Major public disputation with Jewish rabbis in Barcelona.

              John Sackville's <u>De Principiis Naturae</u> (?).

1264   Siger graduates as Master of Arts (?).

1265   Start of Siger's Magisterial Career.

              Birth of Dante Alighieri.

1266   [27 August] Siger first cited in decree of Simon of Brion.

404

1266-73	Thomas Aquinas writes <u>Summa Theologiae</u>.
1267	Bonaventure's Lenten Conferences - <u>De Decem Praeceptis</u>.
	William of Baglione, holder of Franciscan Chair, attacks controversial teachings in Faculty of Arts.
1268	Bonaventure's Lenten Conferences - <u>De Septem Donis</u>.
	[7 October] Stephen Tempier appointed Bishop of Paris.
1269	[January] Simon of Brion appointed to Roman Court.
	[February?] Thomas Aquinas returns to Paris.
1269-71	John Peckham teaches in Paris, before moving to Oxford.
1270	Giles of Rome writes <u>De Erroribus Philosophorum</u>.
	Thomas Aquinas writes <u>De Unitate Intellectus contra Averroistas</u>.
	[10 December] Tempier's first Decree condemning 13 alleged errors in teaching of Faculty of Arts.
	[Christmas] Election of Alberic of Reims as Rector creates unrest.
1271	A number of theologians expelled from Paris for alleged homosexual activities (?).
	[1 September] Election of Pope Gregory X.
1272	[25 March] Full-scale schism develops within Faculty of Arts.

[1 April] "Loyalist" group vow not to discuss so-called theological issues.

[After May] Thomas Aquinas leaves Paris for Italy.

1273   Bonaventure's Lenten Conferences - In Hexaemeron.

1274   [7 March] Death of Thomas Aquinas at Fossanuova.

[7 May] Opening of Council of Lyons.

[15 July] Death of Bonaventure in Lyons.

[August] Simon of Brion re-appointed Papal Legate to France.

Letter of Giles of Lessines to Albert the Great (?).

1275   [7 May] Simon of Brion determines end of schism in Faculty of Arts and appoints Peter of Auvergne as new Rector.

1276   [10 January] Death of Pope Gregory X.

[21 January] Election of Peter of Tarantaise as Pope Innocent V.

[22 June] Death of Pope Innocent V.

[11 July] Election of Pope Hadrian V.

[18 August] Death of Pope Hadrian V.

[2 September] Decree forbidding private teaching of all except logic and grammar.

[8 September] Election of Peter of Spain as Pope John XXI.

[23 November] Simon du Val, Inquisitor General of France summons Siger and two colleagues to appear before him on 18 January next.

1277   [18 January] Letter of Pope John XXI to Tempier.

[7 March] Tempier's second decree condemning 219 alleged errors.

[18 March] Robert Kilwardby, Archbishop of Canterbury, issues condemnation of Aristotelianism at Oxford.

[21 April] Pope John XXI orders 24 stipendiary Canons of Liege to take up residence.

[28 April] Flumen Aquae Vivae issued by Pope John XXI instructing Tempier to investigate Philosophy and Theology faculties in Paris.

[20 May] Death of Pope John XXI in Viterbo.

[25 November] Giovanni Orsini eventually elected as Pope Nicholas III after long deadlock in conclave.

1279   [28 January] John Peckham appointed Archbishop of Canterbury.

1280   [22 August] Death of Pope Nicholas III.

1281   [22 February] Eventual election of Simon of Brion as Pope Martin IV, who moves the Papal Court to Orvieto.

[Spring] Anti-French rioting in Orvieto ends in massacre of many local inhabitants by French garrison.

1282	[31 March] "Sicilian Vespers" begins.

[1 May] Massacre of 2000 French at Forli leads to award of indulgences by Pope to those fighting for French interests against Peter of Aragon for helping continuation of Sicilian revolt.

[18 November] Peter of Aragon excommunicated by Pope.

1282-4   Murder of Siger.

1284   [Summer] Following opposition of Ranieri della Greca as re-elected Capitano del Popolo in Orvieto, Pope transfers Papal Court to Perugia where interdict had just been removed following agreement to fine of 40000 florins.

[10 November] Letter of John Peckham with reference to death of Siger.

1299-1314   Dante Alighieri writes the <u>Divina Commedia</u>.

1302   [10 March] Dante Alighieri flees from Rome on being condemned to death.

1304-07   Dante Alighieri writes <u>Convivio</u>.

1313   Dante Alighieri writes <u>Monarchia</u>.

REFERENCES AND NOTES

IMPORTANT

Where a reference to a book or article is made for the first time in each chapter, the full details will normally be given. Subsequently, only sufficient detail will be given later in the same chapter as required to identify that particular work.

The major exception to this is the actual published editions of the works of Siger of Brabant which have been given in full in Appendix A. Generally, references will be made to the title of the actual Sigerian work in full, although abbreviations will be offered for the details regarding the particular edition involved. The date of publication will however also be included in the case of those works edited by Bazan to distinguish the two relevant volumes, e.g. Bazan (1972). Where reference is made to the introductions of the editors of any of these books, this will be indicated in the notes in a similar way.

Unlike the main body of this study, translations will not normally be offered where Latin texts are included in this section for the benefit of the reader.

NOTES TO PREFACE

1.   E. Gilson, Le Philosophe et la Théologie (Paris: 1960) 14-17 and E. Gilson, Introduction à la Philosophie Chrétienne (Paris: Vrin 1960) passim

2.   E. Gilson, The Christian Philosophy of St. Thomas Aquinas (New York: Random House 1956) passim

3.   F. Van Steenberghen, Maître Siger de Brabant (Louvain: Publications Universitaires 1977) 79

4.   F. Van Steenberghen, Introduction à l'Étude de la Philosophie Médiévale (Louvain: Publications Universitaires 1974) 95

5.   F. Van Steenberghen, "Philosophie et Christianisme," Revue Philosophique de Louvain 86 (1988) 187

6.   A. Kenny, Aquinas (Oxford: University Press 1980) 1-31

7.   A. Kenny, Wyclif (Oxford: University Press 1985) 5-8

8.   J. Marenbon, Later Medieval Philosophy 1150-1350 (London: Routledge and Kegan Paul 1987) 88

9.   N. Smart, The Phenomenon of Religion (London: Macmillan 1973) 53-78

10.   B. Lonergan, Insight: a Study of Human Understanding (London: Longmans, Green & Co. 1957) 415

11.   E. Renan, Averroes et l'Averroisme (Paris: Calmann-Lévy 1852) 318

12.   H. Denifle & A. Chatelain, eds., Chartularium Universitatis Parisiensis, vol. I (Paris: Delalain 1889) n.473 - 543-555

NOTES TO CHAPTER ONE

1. For an excellent list of these new translations, cf. M. De Wulf, Histoire de la Philosophie Médiévale, vol. II, 6th. ed., (Louvain: Institut Supérieur de Philosophie 1936) 25-58

2. H. Rashdall, The Universities of Europe in the Middle Ages, vol. I (Oxford: Clarendon Press 1895) 273-296; also, ed. F.M. Powicke & A.B. Emden, (Oxford: Clarendon Press 1936; reprint London, 1942-1958; reprint Oxford 1988) 271-294

3. A. Kenny & J. Pinborg, "Medieval Philosophical Literature," The Cambridge History of Later Medieval Philosophy, ed. N. Kretzmann et al. (Cambridge: University Press 1982) 11-13

4. L. Halphen, "Les Origines de l'Université de Paris,"Aspects de l'Université de Paris, ed. J. Calvet (Paris: Éditions Albin Michel 1949) 14

5. C. Thurot, De l'Organisation de l'Enseignement dans l'Université de Paris au Moyen Age (Paris: 1850; reprint Frankfurt am Main, Minerva Press 1967) 23

6. M. Deanesly, A History of the Medieval Church 590-1500 (London: Methuen 1925; reprint Cambridge: University Press 1969-1978) 114

7. C. Morris, The Papal Monarchy: the Western Church from 1050 to 1250 (Oxford: Clarendon Press 1991) 568

8. E. Gilson, A History of Christian Philosophy in the Middle Ages (London: Sheed & Ward 1955) 244

9. D. Knowles, The Evolution of Medieval Thought (London: Longman 1988) 149

10. J. Verger, "Patterns," A History of the University in Europe, vol. I, ed. H. de Ridder-Symeons (Cambridge: University Press 1992) 36

11. P. Nardi, "Relations with Authority," de Ridder-Symeons 91

12. Knowles 145

412

13. Thurot 23

14. H. Denifle & A. Chatelain, eds., <u>Chartularium Universitatis Parisiensis</u>, vol. I (Paris: Delalain 1889) n.409 - 451

15. Thurot 23

16. R.C. Dales, <u>The Intellectual Life of Western Europe in the Middle Ages</u> (Leiden: Brill 1992) 220

17. H. de Ridder-Symeons, "Mobility," de Ridder-Symeons 284

18. A. Maurer, <u>Medieval Philosophy</u> (Toronto: Pontifical Institute of Medieval Studies 1982) 110

19. Denifle & Chatelain n.201, 202 - 227-232

20. G. Leff, "The Faculty of Arts: the Trivium and the Three Philosophies," de Ridder-Symeons 326-328

21. Kenny & Pinborg 14

22. G. Leff, <u>Medieval Thought from Augustine to Ockham</u> (1958; London: Merlin Press 1980) 50

23. Kenny & Pinborg 15

24. Gilson 317

25. Denifle & Chatelain n.11 - 70

26. Denifle & Chatelain n.20 - 78-79

27. H. Küng, <u>The Council and Reunion</u>, trans. C. Hastings (London: Sheed & Ward 1961)

28. Denifle & Chatelain n.59 - 114-116

29. Denifle & Chatelain n.72 - 129-131

30. Denifle & Chatelain n.79 - 136-139

31. Gilson 245

32. Denifle & Chatelain n.86 - 143

33. Denifle & Chatelain n.59 - 116

34. M. Asztalos, "The Faculty of Theology," de Ridder-Symeons 413

35. G. Walker, The Growing Storm (London: Paternoster Press 1961) 202

36. F. Van Steenberghen, La Philosophie au XIIIe Siècle (Louvain: Publications Universitaires 1966) 119-132

37. Van Steenberghen (1966) 125

38. Leff, de Ridder-Symeons, 309

39. Leff, Medieval 169

40. Knowles 208

41. O. Lewry, ed., Robert Kilwardby O.P.: On Time and Imagination (Oxford: University Press 1987) xiii-xv

42. See note 19 above

43. Denifle & Chatelain n.246 - 277-279

44. Leff, Medieval 169

45. M. Cruz Hernandez, Vida, Obra, Pensamiento, Influencia Ibn Rusd (Cordoba: Publicaciones de Monte de Piedad y Caja de Ahorros de Cordoba 1986) 271

46. R.-M. Giguère, ed., Jean de Sècheville: De Principiis Naturae (Montreal: Publications de l'Institut d'Études Médiévales 1956) 16-27

47. F. Copleston, A History of Medieval Philosophy (London: Methuen 1972) 200

48. Gilson 327

49. A. Tuilier, ed., La Vie Universitaire Parisienne au XIIIe Siècle (Paris: Chapelle de la Sorbonne 1974) 25-26

50.   Leff, Medieval 207

51.   See notes 32 and 33 above

52.   E. Moody, "William of Auvergne and his Treatise De Anima (1933)," Studies in Medieval Philosophy, Science and Logic (Berkeley: University of California Press 1975) 2-3

53.   Asztalos, de Ridder-Symeons, 413

54.   Denifle & Chatelain n.27 - 85

55.   Denifle & Chatelain n.5 - 65

56.   M. Reeves, Joachim of Fiore and the Prophetic Future (London: SPCK 1976) 37-38

57.   Bonaventure, In Hexaemeron Collatio XXII, 21 - Omnia Opera, vol V (Florence: Quaracchi 1891) 440

58.   R. Seltzer, Jewish People, Jewish Thought (New York: Macmillan 1980) 360

59.   P. Mandonnet, Siger de Brabant et l'Averroisme Latin au XIIIe Siècle (Fribourg: Université 1899) 113

60.   H. Denzinger & A, Schönmetzer, eds., Enchiridion Symbolorum Definitionum et Declarationum de Rebus Fidei et Morum, 32nd ed. (Barcelona: Herder 1963) n.873-875/469 - 280-281

61.   J. Brewer, ed., Fr. Rogeri Bacon Opera Quaedam hactenus Inedita, (London: Longmans 1859) 428-429

62.   Thurot 203

63.   Thurot 160

64.   Denzinger & Schönmetzer n.3135-3140 - 610-612

NOTES TO CHAPTER TWO

1.   F. Cary, The Vision (or Hell, Purgatory and Paradise) of Dante Alighieri, vol. III (London: 1831) 212 - reprinted as Dante: the Divine Comedy (London: Bibliophile 1988) 377

2.   Peter Alighieri, (ed. Vernon), Super Dantis ipsius Genitoris Comediam Commentarium (Florence: Nannucci 1845) 623

3.   B. Nardi, Sigieri di Brabante nel Pensiero del Rinascimento Italiano (Rome: Edizioni Italiane 1945) 94-100

4.   A. Zimmermann, "Ein Averroist des Späten 13. Jahrhunderts: Ferrandus de Hispania," Archiv für Geschichte der Philosophie 50 (1968) 164

5.   O. Leaman, Averroes and His Philosophy (Oxford: Clarendon Press 1988) 167

6.   M. De Wulf, History of Mediaeval Philosophy, vol. II, trans. E. Messenger (London: Longmans, Green & Co 1926) 232

7.   M. Cruz Hernandez, Vida, Obra, Pensamiento, Influencia Ibn Rusd (Cordoba: Publicaciones del Monte de Piedad y Caja de Ahorros de Cordoba 1986) 280

8.   E. Gilson, Études de Philosophie Médiévale (Strasbourg: Faculté des Lettres de l'Université de Strasbourg 1921) 72

9.   S. MacClintock, Perversity and Error: Studies on the"Averroist" John of Jandun (Bloomington, Indiana: University Press 1956) 94

10.   Nardi, Sigieri 101

11.   John of Jandun, Super Libros Aristotelis de Anima III qu. 5 (Venice: 1587; reprinted Frankfurt am Main: Minerva 1966) 245

12.   Nardi, Sigieri 166

13.   E. Renan, Averroes et l'Averroisme (1852; 3rd. ed., Paris: Calmann-Lévy 1867) 39-40

416

14.   Nardi, <u>Sigieri</u> 131

15.   John of Baconthorp, <u>Quodlibeta</u> (Cremona: 1618; reprinted
        Farnborough: Gregg International 1969) I, qu. I, art. I, n.III - 586-588

16.   See note 14 above

17.   Nardi, <u>Sigieri</u> 140

18.   De Wulf, vol. II (1926) 272

19.   Nardi, <u>Sigieri</u> 152-155

20.   Nardi, <u>Sigieri</u> 160

21.   Nardi, <u>Sigieri</u> 170

22.   Nardi, <u>Sigieri</u> 13

23.   B. Nardi, <u>Saggi sull'Aristotelismo Padovano dal Secolo XIV al XVI</u>
        (Florence: Università degli Studi di Padova 1958) 314-319

24.   F. Van Steenberghen, <u>Maître Siger de Brabant</u> (Louvain: Publications
        Universitaires 1977) 415

25.   V. Le Clerc, <u>Histoire Littéraire de la France</u>, vol. XXI (Paris: Didot,
        Treuttel & Wurtz 1847) 96-127

26.   P. Venturi ed. <u>Dante</u>, vol. V (Florence: 1774) 203 - cited in Le Clerc
        98

27.   M. Biagioli, <u>La Commedia Divina di Dante Alighieri</u> vol. III (Rome:
        1815-1817) 167 - cited in Le Clerc 98

28.   Le Clerc vii

29.   Le Clerc 100

30.   Le Clerc 103

31.   William Tocco, <u>Acta Sanctorum</u>, trans. I. Martii (Anvers: 1668) 666
        n.20- cited in Van Steenberghen, <u>Maître</u> 12

32.   See Section 1.9

33.   H. Denifle & A. Chatelain, eds., Chartularium Universitatis Parisiensis, vol. I (Paris: Delalain 1889) n.354 - 402-403

34.   J. Quétif & J. Échard, Scriptores Ordinis Praedicatorum vol. I (Paris: 1719 - reprinted New York: Burt Franklin 1959) 295

35.   Quétif & Échard 395

36.   Le Clerc 105

37.   Van Steenberghen, Maître 14

38.   Pierre Dubois (ed. C. Langlois), De Recuperatione Terrae Sanctae (Paris: 1891) 121-122; (trans. and ed. W. Brandt) The Recovery of the Holy Land (New York: Columbia University Press 1956) 189-190 - also see Le Clerc (1847) 106

39.   Le Clerc 107

40.   Mss. de la Bibliothèque Royale, Fonds de Sorbonne, n.525, 543, 550 - cited in Le Clerc 111

41.   Mss. de la Bibliothèque Royale, Supp. Français, n.269, fol. 120 - cited in Le Clerc 113-114

42.   Le Clerc 120

43.   Le Clerc 125-126

44.   Renan 267-278

45.   Renan 276

46.   Renan 277-278

47.   C. Baeumker, Die Impossibilia des Siger von Brabant: eine Philosophische Streitschrift aus dem XIII.Jahrhundert, Beiträge zur Geschichte der Philosophie des Mittelalters Band II Heft VI (Münster: Aschendorffschen 1898)

48.   A. Potvin, "Siger de Brabant," <u>Bulletin de l'Académie Royale de Belgique</u>, 45 (1878) 330-357 - cited in Van Steenberghen, <u>Maître</u> 19

49.   B. Hauréau, <u>Notices et Extraits de Quelques Manuscripts Latins de la Bibliothèque Nationale</u> (Paris: 1892) 88-98 - cited in Van Steenberghen, <u>Maître</u> 19

50.   Baeumker (1898) 56

51.   Baeumker (1898) 58-61

52.   Baeumker (1898) 76-77

53.   C. Cipolla, "Sigieri nella Divina Commedia," <u>Giornale Storico della Letteratura Italiana</u>, VIII (1886) 53-139 - cited in Baeumker (1898) 90-95

54.   Baeumker (1898) 65-67

55.   F. Castets, <u>Il Fiore, Poème Italien du XIIIe Siècle en CCXXXII Sonnets, Imité du Roman de la Rose par Durante</u> (Montpellier and Paris: 1881) - cited in Baeumker (1898) 79

56.   Castets 47 - cited in Baeumker (1898) 81

57.   Baeumker (1898) 114

58.   See note 42 above

59.   B. Hauréau, "Boetius, Maître ès Arts à Paris," <u>Histoire Littéraire de la France</u>, vol. XXX (Paris: Imprimerie Nationale 1888) 270-279

     Also see Baeumker (1898) 107-109

60.   C. Baeumker, "Zur Beurteilung Sigers von Brabant," <u>Philosophisches Jahrbuch</u> 24 (1911) 183-188

61.   Baeumker (1898) 108

62.   P. Mandonnet, <u>Siger de Brabant et L'Averroisme Latin au XIIIe Siècle</u> (Fribourg: Université 1899) 82

63.   Mandonnet (1899) 88-90

64.   Mandonnet (1899) 282

65.   P. Mandonnet, "Autour de Siger de Brabant," Revue Thomiste 19 (1911) 314-337; 476-502

66.   Mandonnet (1899) 142; and Mandonnet, 2nd.ed., vol. I, Les Philosophes Belges VI (Louvain: 1911) 121

67.   C. Baeumker, Beiträge zur Geschichte der Philosophie des Mittelalters, vol. VI (1907) cahier 3, 118, n.1 - cited in Mandonnet (Revue Thomiste 1911) 318

68.   Mandonnet (Revue Thomiste 1911) 319-322

69.   Mandonnet (Revue Thomiste 1911) 330

70.   M. Grabmann, Neu aufgefundene Werke des Siger von Brabant und Boetius von Dacien, Sitzungsberichte der Bayerischen Akademie der Wissenschaften 1924, 2 (Munich: 1924) 108

71.   F. Van Steenberghen, Siger de Brabant d'après ses Oeuvres Inédits, vol. I, Les Philosophes Belges XII (Louvain: Éditions de l'Institut Supérieur de Philosophie 1931) 17

72.   J. Duin, La Doctrine de la Providence dans les Écrits de Siger de Brabant (Louvain: Editions de l'Institut Supérieur de Philosophie 1954) 171-175

73.   G. Sajó, "Boèce de Dacie et les Commentaires Anonymes Inédits de Munich sur la Physique et sur la Génération attribués à Siger de Brabant," Archives d'Histoire Doctrinale et Littéraire du Moyen Age 25 (1958) 21-58

74.   Van Steenberghen, Maître 135 & 198

75.   G. Meersemann ed., Laurentii Pignon Catalogi et Chronica accedunt Catalogi Stamsensis et Upsalensis Scriptorum O.P., Monumenta Ordinis Fratrum Praedicatorum Historica, 16 (Rome: 1936) 64-65 n.63

76.   F. Stegmüller, "Neugefundene Quaestiones des Siger von Brabant," Recherches de Théologie Ancienne et Médiévale 3 (1931) 158-182

77. P. Glorieux, "Un Recueil Scolaire de Godefroid de Fontaines," Recherches de Théologie Ancienne et Médiévale 3 (1931) 37-53

78. P. Mandonnet, Siger de Brabant et l'Averroisme Latin au XIIIe Siècle, 2nd. ed., Les Philosophes Belges VI-VII (Louvain: 1911-1908)

79. A. Maier, "Nouvelles Questions de Siger de Brabant sur la Physique d'Aristote," Revue Philosophique de Louvain 44 (1946) 497-513

80. A. Zimmermann, Die Quaestionen des Siger von Brabant zur Physik des Aristoteles (Cologne: De Gruyter 1956)

81. W. Dunphy, "The Similarity between Certain Questions of Peter of Auvergne's Commentary on the Metaphysics and the Anonymous Commentary on the Physics Attributed to Siger of Brabant," Medieval Studies 15 (1953) 159-168

82. A. Dondaine and L.J. Bataillon, "Le Manuscrit Vindob. lat. 2330 et Siger de Brabant," Archivum Fratrum Praedicatorum 36 (1966) 153-261

83. Dondaine & Bataillon 154-160

84. Dondaine & Bataillon 182-196

85. A. Otto & H. Roos, eds., and later J. Pinborg ed., Corpus Philosophorum Danicorum Medii Aevi, IV, V, VI, VIII, IX, (Copenhagen: Det danske Sprog- og Litteraturselskab udgaver 1969-1979)

86. F. Van Steenberghen, Les Oeuvres et la Doctrine de Siger de Brabant (Brussels: Académie Royale de Belgique 1938)

87. F. Van Steenberghen, Maître Siger de Brabant, Philosophes Médiévaux XXI (Louvain: Publications Universitaires 1977)

88. J. Vennebusch, "Die Questiones Metaphysice Tres des Siger von Brabant," Archiv für Geschichte der Philosophie 48 (1966) 163-189

89. A. Caparello, La 'Perspectiva' in Sigieri di Brabante (Rome: Pontificia Accademia di S. Tommaso e di Religione Cattolica 1987)

90. R. Dales, The Intellectual Life of Western Europe in the Middle Ages (Leiden: Brill 1992) 279

91. A. Carol, La Distinción entre "Esse" y "Essentia" en Siger de Brabant (Pamplona: Universidad de Navarra 1991)

92. R. Sanfilippo, La Composizione dell'Ente Finito in Sigieri di Brabante (Pamplona: Universidad de Navarra 1992)

93. W.-U. Klünker & B. Sandkühler, Menschliche Seele und Kosmischer Geist (Stuttgart: Verlag Freies Geistesleben 1988) 92-97

94. Klünker & Sandkühler 127-130

NOTES TO CHAPTER THREE

1. A. Dondaine, "Le Manuel de l'Inquisiteur (1230-1330)," <u>Archivum Fratrum Praedicatorum</u> 17 (1947) 191-192

2. F. Sassen, "Siger van Brabant," <u>Algemeen Nederlands Tijdschrift voor Wijsbegeerte en Psychologie</u> 35 (1942) n.1, 2

3. F. Van Steenberghen, <u>Maître Siger de Brabant</u> (Louvain: Publications Universitaires 1977) 28

4. H. Denifle & A. Chatelain, eds., <u>Chartularium Universitatis Parisiensis,</u> vol. I (Paris: Delalain 1889) n.409 - 449-457

5. D. Herlihy, <u>Medieval Households</u> (Cambridge, Massachusetts & London: Harvard University Press 1985) 87, 97

6. R. Schwinges, "Student Education, Student Life," <u>A History of the University in Europe</u>, vol. I, ed. H. de Ridder-Symeons (Cambridge: University Press 1992) 196

7. Schwinges, de Ridder-Symeons, 240

8. Van Steenberghen, <u>Maître</u> 30

9. J. Verger, "Patterns," de Ridder-Symeons 151

10. P. Mandonnet, <u>Siger de Brabant et l'Averroisme Latin au XIIIe Siècle,</u> 2nd. ed., vol. I (Louvain: 1911) 83

11. Van Steenberghen, <u>Maître</u> 29

12. Denifle & Chatelain n.405 - 445

13. Denifle & Chatelain n.409 - 449

14. Denifle & Chatelain n.409 - 450

15. Denifle & Chatelain n.409 - 451

16. Van Steenberghen, <u>Maître</u> 33

17.   Van Steenberghen, Maître 30

18.   R. Gauthier, "Notes sur Siger de Brabant I," Revue des Sciences
        Philosophiques et Théologiques 67 (1983) 204-206

19.   I. Brady, "Background of the Condemnation of 1270: Master William
        of Baglione O.F.M.," Franciscan Studies 30 (1970) 5-48

20.   Van Steenberghen, Maître 34

21.   See Section 1.8

22.   J. Russell, Dictionary of Writers of Thirteenth Century in England
        (London: Longman, Green & Co. 1936) 3

23.   Bonaventure, De Decem Praeceptis Collatio II, 25 - Omnia Opera vol.
        V (Florence: Quaracchi 1891) 514

24.   Bonaventure, De Septem Donis Spiritus Sancti Collatio VIII, 16 -
        Omnia Opera vol. V, 497

25.   Bonaventure, De Septem Donis Spiritus Sancti Collatio IV, 12 -
        Omnia Opera vol. V, 476

26.   J.-I. Sarayana, "Lo Statuto Epistemologico della Teologia
        nell'Università di Parigi (Secolo XIII)," Paper given at Conference
        entitled Autonomia delle Scienze e Unità del Sapere nelle Dispute
        Parigine del XIII Secolo, Storia e Attualità del Problema. Ateneo
        Romano della Santa Croce, Rome. 26 February 1993.

27.   B. Bazán, Siger de Brabant. Quaestiones in Tertium de Anima. De
        Anima Intellectiva. De Aeternitate Mundi (Louvain: Publications
        Universitaires 1972) 67*-74*, 78*

        B. Bazán, Siger de Brabant, Écrits de Logique, de Morale et de
        Physique (Louvain: Publications Universitaires 1974) 25, 38-39

28.   A. Dondaine and L. Bataillon, "Le Manuscrit Vindob. Lat. 2330 et
        Siger de Brabant," Archivum Fratrum Praedicatorum 36 (1966) 182-
        184

29.   Denifle & Chatelain n.432 - 486-487

424

30. Giles of Rome, ed. J. Koch, trans. J. Riedl, Errores Philosophorum (Milwaukee: University Press 1944)

31. M. Haren, Medieval Thought. The Western Intellectual Tradition from Antiquity to the Thirteenth Century. (Basingstoke: Macmillan 1985) 200

32. Denifle & Chatelain n. 460 - 521-522

33. Mandonnet (1911) 200

34. Van Steenberghen, Maître 83

35. Denifle & Chatelain n.441 - 499-500

36. Denifle & Chatelain n.460 - 523, 527

37. Van Steenberghen, Maître 83

38. R. Gauthier, "Notes sur Siger de Brabant II. Siger en 1272-1275: Aubry de Reims et la Scission des Normands," Revue des Sciences Philosophiques et Théologiques 68 (1984) 20-25

39. J. Brewer, ed., Fr. Rogeri Bacon Opera Quaedam hactenus Inedita (London: Longmans 1859) 412

40. F. Delorme, ed., S. Bonaventurae Collationes in Hexaemeron (Florence: Quaracchi 1934) Visio I, Collatio I, s.2, 59

41. Albertus Magnus, De Quindecim Problematibus - B. Geyer, ed., Alberti Magni Omnia Opera XVII part I (Cologne: Aschendorff 1975) 31-44

42. Denifle & Chatelain n.460 - 521-530

43. H. Mann & J. Hollsteiner, The Lives of the Popes in the Middle Ages vol. XVI (London: Kegan Paul, Trench, Trubner 1932) 179

44. Dondaine, Archivum Fratrum Praedicatorum 17 (1947) 191-192

    Also see note 1 above

45. Denifle & Chatelain n.468 - 538-539

46.   Denifle & Chatelain n.470 - 540-541

47   Denifle & Chatelain n.471 - 541

48.   A. Moreira de Sa, "Pedro Hispano e la Crise de 1277 da Universidade de Paris," Boletim da Biblioteca da Universidade de Coimbra 22 (1954) 237

49.   R. Hissette, Enquête sur les 219 Articles Condamnés à Paris le 7 mars 1277 (Louvain: Publications Universitaires 1977) 8

50.   R. Hissette, "Note sur le Syllabus 'Antirationaliste' du 7 mars 1277," Revue Philosophique de Louvain 88 (1990) 408

51.   J. Wippel, "The Condemnations of 1270 and 1277 at Paris," Journal of Medieval and Renaissance Studies 7 (1977) 186

52.   Denifle & Chatelain n.473 - 543-555

        Also see Preface note 12.

NOTES TO CHAPTER FOUR

1.   A. Kenny, Reason and Religion, (Oxford: Blackwell 1987) 8

2.   B. Russell, Logic and Knowledge, ed. R.C. Marsh, (London: 1956) 192-193

3.   L. Wittgenstein, Tractatus Logico-Philosophicus, trans. D. Pears and B. McGuinness (1922; London: Routledge & Kegan Paul 1961) ref.2.01

4.   Wittgenstein, Tractatus ref. 2.0272

5.   A.J. Ayer, Language, Truth and Logic, (1936; rev. ed. 1946; London: Penguin 1980) 41

6.   Ayer, Language 103

7.   Ayer, Language 114

8.   Ayer, Language 117

9.   Ayer, Language 124

10.   Ayer, Language 145

11.   Ayer, Language 153

12.   A.J. Ayer, The Problem of Knowledge (1956; London: Penguin 1969) 71-75

13.   L. Wittgenstein, Philosophical Investigations, trans. G. Anscombe (Oxford: Blackwell 1963) 23-24, 11e-12e

14.   R.B. Braithwaite, "An Empiricist's View of Religious Belief," Christian Ethics and Contemporary Philosophy, ed. I.T. Ramsey (London: S.C.M. 1966) 53-73

15.   P. van Buren, The Secular Meaning of the Gospel (London: S.C.M. 1963) 134

16.   G. Warnock, English Philosophy since 1900 (1958; Oxford: University Press 1969) 96

17.   J. Wisdom, Philosophy and Psychoanalysis (Oxford: Blackwell 1953) 245

18.   Wittgenstein, Tractatus ref. 6.54

19.   A.J. Ayer, Logical Positivism (London: Allen & Unwin 1959) 15

20.   Wittgenstein, Philosophical 273-278, 95e-96e and 398, 120e-121e

21.   K. Popper, Conjectures and Refutations (London: Routledge & Kegan Paul 1963) passim

        C. Simkin, Popper's Views on Natural and Social Science (Leiden: Brill 1993) 54-57

22.   A. Kenny, The Legacy of Wittgenstein (Oxford: Blackwell 1984) xi

23.   L. Wittgenstein, On Certainty, ed. G. Anscombe and G. von Wright, trans. D. Paul & G. Anscombe (Oxford: Blackwell 1979) 87e-90e

24.   I. Ramsey, Religious Language (London: S.C.M. 1957) 49-89

25.   J. Macquarrie, God-Talk (London: S.C.M. 1967) 238-248

26.   J. Hick, Philosophy of Religion (Englewood Cliffs: Prentice-Hall 1963) 90-92

27.   John XXIII, Opening Address to Second Vatican Council [11 October 1962], The Documents of Vatican II, ed. W.M. Abbott (London: Geoffrey Chapman 1966) 715

28.   William of Ockham, Scriptum in Librum Primum Sententiarum, ed. S. Brown & G. Gal, Opera Philosophica et Theologica, Opera Theologica II (New York: St. Bonaventure's College 1970) 252 lines 1-3

29.   G. Leff, William of Ockham (Manchester: University Press 1975) 1-6

30.   G. Leff, Medieval Thought from Augustine to Ockham, (London: Merlin Press 1980) 111

428

31.   W. James, <u>Principles of Psychology</u>, vol. I (1890; Mineola, N.Y.: Dover 1950) 266-269

32.   Thomas Aquinas, <u>Tractatus de Unitate Intellectus contra Averroistas</u>, ed. L.W. Keeler, (Rome: Pontifical Gregorian University 1936) para. 124 lines 33-35 - 80

33.   See Section 2.7

34.   <u>Quaestiones in Metaphysicam</u> (Munich) Book IV Commentum before qu. 6 lines 14-16 - Dunphy 180-181

35.   Ayer, <u>Problem</u> 105-113

    Also see note 9 above

36.   <u>Impossibilia</u> II lines 80-82 - Bazán (1974) 76

37.   <u>Impossibilia</u> II lines 90-94 - Bazán (1974) 76

38.   <u>Impossibilia</u> II lines 98-101 - Bazán (1974) 76

39.   <u>Impossibilia</u> II lines 43-45 - Bazán (1974) 74-75

40.   <u>Impossibilia</u> II lines 55-56 - Bazán (1974) 75

41.   <u>Impossibilia</u> II lines 69-72 - Bazán (1974) 75-76

42.   F. Van Steenberghen, <u>Maître Siger de Brabant</u> (Louvain: Publications Universitaires 1977) 274-275

43.   B. Lonergan, <u>Method in Theology</u> (London: Darton, Longman & Todd 1972) 13-20

44.   <u>Quaestiones in Metaphysicam</u> (Munich) Book II qu.1 lines 12-13 - Dunphy 51

45.   <u>Quaestiones in Metaphysicam</u> (Munich) Book II qu.2 lines 9-10 - Dunphy 52

46.   <u>Quaestiones in Metaphysicam</u> (Munich) Book II qu.9 lines 18-21 - Dunphy 63

47.   Thomas Aquinas, Summa Theologiae Book I qu.16 art.1 - [Madrid vol. I: 136]; and Book I qu.21 art.2 - [Madrid vol. I: 179]

48.   Dunphy [Introduction] 20-25

49.   Quaestiones in Metaphysicam (Cambridge) Book II qu.9 lines 13-24 - Maurer 51-52

50.   Quaestiones in Metaphysicam (Munich) Book II qu.18 lines 6-7 - Dunphy 83

51.   Quaestiones in Metaphysicam (Munich) Book IV qu.34 lines 105-111 - Dunphy 230-231

52.   Quaestiones in Metaphysicam (Munich) Book II qu.1 lines 28-29 - Dunphy 52

53.   Quaestiones in Metaphysicam (Munich) Book IV qu.32 lines 28-30 - Dunphy 226

54.   Bazán (1974) [Introduction] 29-30

55.   Quaestiones Morales qu.4 lines 20-21 - Bazán (1974) 102

56.   cited in R.C. Dales The Intellectual Life of Western Europe in the Middle Ages (Leiden: Brill 1992) 190

57.   Quaestiones in Metaphysicam (Cambridge) Book IV qu.33 lines 23-26 - Maurer 179-180

58.   Quaestiones in Metaphysicam (Munich) Book IV qu.32 lines 23-24 - Dunphy 226

59.   Quaestiones in Metaphysicam (Munich) Book IV qu.34 lines 134-139 - Dunphy 231

60.   Quaestiones in Metaphysicam (Munich) Book II qu.17 lines 21-28 - Dunphy 81-82

61.   Quaestiones in Metaphysicam (Munich) Book II qu.19 lines 27-34 - Dunphy 84

62.   Van Steenberghen, Maître 272

430

63.   Quaestiones in Metaphysicam (Munich) Book IV qu.34 lines 35-36 - Dunphy 229

64.   Quaestiones in Metaphysicam (Munich) Book IV qu.34 lines 80-81 - Dunphy 230

65.   See note 21 above

66.   Quaestiones in Metaphysicam (Cambridge) Book IV qu.34-35 lines 76-79 - Maurer 182

67.   St. Anselm, Proslogion, ed. M. Charlesworth (Oxford: University Press 1965) ch. 2-5

68.   Quaestiones super Librum de Causis Proemium lines 12-14 - Marlasca 35

69.   Quaestiones super Librum de Causis lines 19-20 - Marlasca 35

70.   J. Marenbon, Later Medieval Philosophy 1150-1350 (London: Routledge and Kegan Paul 1987) 16-20

71.   Ayer, Problem 20

72.   Ayer, Language 21

73.   Ayer, Language 100-103

74.   Quaestiones in Metaphysicam (Cambridge) Book IV qu.8 lines 12-13 - Maurer 146

75.   Ayer, Problem 43

76.   Impossibilia VI lines 59-60 - Bazán (1974) 94

77.   Impossibilia VI lines 29-32 - Bazán (1974) 93

78.   Quaestiones in Metaphysicam (Cambridge) Book IV qu.13 lines 11-16 - Maurer 152

79.   Impossibilia VI lines 117-145 - Bazán (1974) 96-97

80. Quaestio utrum haec sit vera: Homo Est Animal, Nullo Homine Existente lines 20-34 - Bazán (1974) 53-54

81. Quaestiones in Metaphysicam (Munich) Book IV Commentum before qu.7 lines 21-23 - Dunphy 185

82. Quaestiones in Metaphysicam (Munich) Book IV qu.7 lines 13-14 - Dunphy 185

83. Quaestiones in Metaphysicam (Cambridge) Book IV qu.9 line 13 - Maurer 148

84. B. Bazán, "La Signification des Termes Communs et la Doctrine de la Supposition chez Maître Siger de Brabant," Revue Philosophique de Louvain 77 (1979) 349

85. Quaestiones in Metaphysicam (Cambridge) Book IV qu.15 line 22 - Maurer 155

86. Quaestiones in Metaphysicam (Munich) Book IV qu.14 lines 9-19 - Dunphy 195-196

Quaestiones in Metaphysicam (Cambridge) Book IV qu.16 lines 10-15 - Maurer 155

87. Quaestiones in Metaphysicam (Cambridge) Book IV qu.18 lines 27-28 - Maurer 157

88. Quaestiones in Metaphysicam (Cambridge) Book IV qu.17 lines 12-14 - Maurer 156

89. Quaestiones Logicales lines 82-86 - Bazán (1974) 62

90. See note 47 above

91. De Aeternitate Mundi ch. 3 lines 33-37 - Bazán (1972) 122

92. Omnis Homo de Necessitate est Animal lines 85-88 - Bazán (1974) 45

93. Quaestiones in Metaphysicam (Cambridge) Book IV qu.22/23 lines 62-64 - Maurer 161

94. Van Steenberghen, Maître 389

95.   Quaestiones in Metaphysicam (Paris) Book III qu.5 lines 43-44 -
        Maurer 412

96.   De Aeternitate Mundi ch.4 lines 85-86 - Bazán (1972) 132

97.   De Anima Intellectiva ch.3 lines 79-80 - Bazán (1972) 81

98.   "Die Quaestiones Metaphysice Tres des Siger von Brabant," ed. J.
        Vennebusch, Archivium für Geschichte der Philosophie 48 (1966) 179
        - qu.1 lines 110-111

99.   Vennebusch 164-166

100.   Van Steenberghen, Maître 396

        Vennebusch 168-169

101.   Quaestiones in Metaphysicam (Munich) Book III Commentum before
        qu.16 lines 87-88 - Dunphy 132

102.   Quaestiones in Metaphysicam (Cambridge) Book III qu.15 lines 81-83
        - Maurer 110

103.   A. Minnis, Medieval Theory of Authorship (London: Scolar 1984)
        157-158

104.   Quaestiones in Metaphysicam (Paris) Book IV qu.21 lines 3-5 -
        Maurer 428-429

105.   H. Mann & J. Hollsteiner, The Lives of the Popes in the Middle Ages,
        vol. XVI (London: Kegan Paul, Trench, Trubner & Co. 1932) 32-33

106.   J. Mullally, ed., The Summae Logicales of Peter of Spain (South Bend:
        Notre Dame 1945) xxii-xxiii

107.   N. Kretzmann, ed. & trans., William of Sherwood's Introduction to
        Logic (Minneapolis: University of Minnesota 1966) 4-5

108.   William of Sherwood, Introduction to Logic ch.3 qu.2.5 - Kretzmann
        ed. (1966) 159-162

109. E. Moody, "The Medieval Contribution to Logic (1966)" Studies in Medieval Philosophy, Science and Logic (Berkeley: University of California Press 1975) 379

110. Quaestiones in Metaphysicam (Cambridge) Book II qu.23 lines 27-30 - Maurer 71

111. A. Maurer, "Siger of Brabant on Fables and Falsehoods in Religion," Medieval Studies 43 (1981) 519

112. Quaestiones in Metaphysicam (Munich) Book III Commentum before qu.17 - Dunphy 137-138

113. Quaestiones in Metaphysicam (Cambridge) Book III qu.17 - Maurer 116

114. Quaestiones in Metaphysicam (Cambridge) Book III qu.17 lines 9-12 - Maurer 116

115. Quaestiones in Metaphysicam (Cambridge) Book III qu.17 line 30 - Maurer 117

116. Quaestiones in Metaphysicam (Cambridge) Book III qu.17 lines 30-34 - Maurer 117

117. Moses Maimonides, The Thirteen Principles of Faith, trans. & ed. A. Kaplan (New York: National Conference of Synagogue Youth 1984) 27-28

118. Ibn Rushd, Averroes' On the Harmony of Religion and Philosophy, trans. G. Hourani (London: Luzac 1961) c.2, 8 lines 4-9 - 51

119. I. Bello, The Medieval Islamic Controversy between Philosophy and Theology (Leiden: Brill 1989) 17-25

120. R. Markus, Saeculum: History and Society in the Theology of St. Augustine (Cambridge: University Press 1970) 193

121. Maurer, Medieval Studies 43 (1981) 521

122. Quaestiones in Metaphysicam (Cambridge) Book V qu. 41 line 128 - Maurer 282

434

123. Quaestiones in Metaphysicam (Cambridge) Book V qu. 41 lines 158-162 - Maurer 283

124. Quaestiones in Metaphysicam (Vienna) Book VI Commentum I lines 17-25 - Dunphy 359-360

125. Quaestiones in Metaphysicam (Vienna) Book VI Commentum I lines 88-90 - Dunphy 361

126. P. Teilhard de Chardin, The Phenomenon of Man (London: Collins 1959) 318

NOTES TO CHAPTER FIVE

1. H. Denifle & A. Chatelain, eds. Chartularium Universitatis Parisiensis, vol. 1 (Paris: Delalain 1889) n.473 - 543

2. Denifle & Chatelain n.473 - 543-555

> 39. Quod omnia separata coaeterna sunt Primo Principio.
>
> 80. Quod ratio Philosophi demonstrans motum caeli esse aeternum non est sophistica; et mirum quod homines profundi hoc non vident.
>
> 83. Quod mundus, licet sit factus de nihilo, non tamen est factus de novo; et quamvis de non esse exierit in esse, tamen non esse non praecessit esse duratione, sed natura tantum.
>
> 84. Quod mundus est aeternus, quia quod habet naturam per quam possit esse in toto futuro, habet naturam per quam potuit esse in toto praeterito.
>
> 85. Quod mundus est aeternus, quantum ad omnes species in eo contentas; et quod tempus est aeternum, et motus et materia, et agens, et suscipiens; et quia est a potentia Dei infinita, et impossibile est innovationem esse in effectu sine innovatione in causa.
>
> 87. Quod nihil est aeternum a parte finis, quod non sit aeternum a parte principii.
>
> 88. Quod tempus est infinitum quantum ad utrumque extremum: licet enim impossibile sit infinita esse pertransita, quorum aliquid fuit pertranseundum, non tamen impossibile est infinita esse pertransita, quorum nullum fuit pertranseundum.

89.   Quod impossibile est solvere rationes Philosophi de aeternitate mundi, nisi dicamus voluntas Primi implicat incompossiblia.

90.   Quod universum non potest deficere, quia primum agens habet transmutare aeternaliter vicissim, nunc in istam formam, nunc ad illam, et similiter materia nata est transmutari.

138. Quod non fuit primus homo, nec erit ultimus, immo semper fuit et semper erit generatio hominis ex homine.

3.   Denifle & Chatelain n.432 - 486-487

5.   Quod mundus est aeternus.

6.   Quod nunquam fit primus homo.

4.   École Biblique de Jérusalem, La Sainte Bible (Paris: Éditions du Cerf 1956) 810

5.   Peter Lombard, Sententiae Book II Dist. 1a [Genesis 1:1] - J. Migne, ed., Patrologiae Cursus Completus, Series Latina, vol. 192 (Paris: 1880) 651

6.   Aristotle Physica 8.1 (251a8 - b28) - Aristoteles Latinus VII i Physica, ed. F. Bossier & J. Broms (Leiden: Brill 1990) 278-281

7.   Thomas Aquinas, Summa Theologiae, Ia, qu. 45, art. 2 ad 1 - [Madrid vol I: 339]

8.   D. Hume, Dialogues Concerning Natural Religion, ed. N. Kemp Smith (Indianapolis: Bobbs-Merrill 1980), Part VIII, 182-187, esp. 184

9.   Origen, De Principiis, 1. 4. 3 - G. Butterworth, trans., Origen on First Principles (London: SPCK 1936) 42: [It follows plainly from this that at no time whatever was God not Creator nor benefactor nor providence.]

10.   G. Verbeke, "The Bible's First Sentence in Gregory of Nyssa's View," A Straight Path: Studies in Medieval Philosophy and Culture ed. R.

Link-Salinger (Washington D.C.: Catholic University of America Press 1988) 238-239

11.   Justin, Apologia I, ch. 59 - T. Falls, ed., Writings of Saint Justin Martyr, (1948; Washington D.C.: Catholic University of America 1967) 97

12.   Philo, De Opificio Mundi 46, 69, 134 - R. Arnaldez, ed., Les Oeuvres de Philon d'Alexandre, vol. 1 (Paris: Editions du Cerf 1961) 171, 187, 231

13.   G. May, trans. A. Worrall, Creatio ex Nihilo: The Doctrine of 'Creation out of Nothing' in Early Christian Thought (Edinburgh: T.& T. Clark 1994) 62-84;   148-163

14.   R. Sorabji, Time, Creation and the Continuum (London: Duckworth 1983) 194-199

15.   Augustine, De Civitate Dei Book I ch. 12 lines 17-19 - J. Welldon ed., St. Augustine vol. I (London: SPCK 1924) 24;

       also Augustine, Confessiones xii 12 - J. Migne ed., Patrologiae Cursus Completus, Series Latina, vol. 32 (Paris: 1877) 834 and L. Vermeijen, ed., Sancti Augustini Opera: Confessiones Libri XIII, Corpus Christianorum Series Latina XXVII (Turnholt: Brepols 1981) 222

16.   H. Denzinger & A. Schönmetzer, Enchiridion Symbolorum Definitionum et Declarationum de Rebus Fidei et Morum, 32nd ed. (Barcelona: Herder 1963) n 800/428 - 259

17.   E. Le Roy Ladurie, Montaillou: Cathars and Catholics in a French Village, trans. B. Bray (London: Penguin 1980) 240

18.   Denzinger & Schönmetzer n.951-953/501-503 - 291-292

                       Here, the following three statements are condemned, as extracted from Eckhardt as a result of a confession at the hands of the Inquisition of the Archbishop of Cologne:

                       951.   Quam cito Deus fuit, tam cito mundum creavit.

                       952.   Item concedi potest mundum fuisse ab aeterno.

953.   Item semel et semel, quando Deus fuit, quando Filium sibi coaeternum per omnia coaequalem Deum genuit, etiam mundum creavit.

19.   Denzinger & Schönmetzer n.3002/1783 - 587

20.   Denzinger & Schönmetzer n.3890/2317 - 777

Negatur mundum initium habuisse, atque contenditur creationem mundi necessariam esse, cum ex necessaria liberalitate divini amoris procedat; aeterna et infallibilis liberarum actionum hominum praescientia Deo item denegatur; quae quidem Vaticani Concilii declarationibus adversantur.

21.   Denzinger & Schönmetzer n.2901/1701 - 577

We can see the background to this controversy clearly in the Holy Office Decree of 18 September 1861, where censure is demanded for the proposition that "res creatae sunt in Deo tamquam pars in toto, non quidem in toto formali, sed in toto infinito, simplicissimo, quod suas quasi partes absque ulla sui divisione et diminutione extra se ponit" (Denzinger & Schönmetzer n.2846/1664 - 567).

Likewise, over five centuries earlier, John XXII's condemnation of Meister Eckhardt quoted above (note 18: Denzinger & Schönmetzer n.952/502 - 292) must be seen from the same perspective, in so far as it viewed Eckhardt's spirituality in a very literal way, so interpreting it to imply pantheism and identity between the world and God.   In this way the statement is used to buttress the general censure rather as the condemnation of a specific tenet in itself.   In recent years, of course, the spirituality and views of Meister Eckhardt have been to some extent rehabilitated.

22.   Denzinger & Schönmetzer n.3897/2328 -780

Cum vero de alia conjecturali opinione agitur, videlicet de polygenismo ... nequaquam appareat quomodo huiusmodi sententia componi queat cum iis quae fontes revelatae veritatis et acta Magisterii Ecclesiae proponunt de peccato originali ....

23.   Denzinger & Schönmetzer n.1333/706 - 338

Firmissime credit ... Deum ... esse omnium visibilium et invisiblium creatorem: qui quando voluit, bonitate sua universas, tam spiritales quam corporales, condidit creaturas.

24.   C. Vollert et al., ed. and trans., St. Thomas Aquinas, Siger of Brabant and St. Bonaventure on the Eternity of the World (Milwaukee: Marquette University Press 1964) 4

25.   D. Cupitt, The Worlds of Science and Religion (London: Sheldon 1980) 9

26.   P. Teilhard de Chardin, Christianity and Evolution trans. R. Hague (London: Collins 1971) 23

27.   Teilhard de Chardin 53

28.   R. Jolivet, The God of Reason (London: Burns & Oates 1958) 100

29.   Moses Maimonides, The Fundamentals of Jewish Faith, trans. & ed. A. Kaplan (New York: National Conference of Synagogue Youth / Union of Orthodox Jewish Congregations of America 1984) 13

cf. The First of Maimonides' Thirteen Principles of Faith, viz. "I believe with perfect faith that God is the Creator and ruler of all things. He alone had made, does make and will make all things".

30.   Moses Maimonides (trans. & ed. Kaplan) 71 - cf. The Ninth Principle: Commentary on Mishnah, viz. "The ninth principle involves permanence. The Torah is God's permanent word, and no one else can change it".

31.   ZOHAR -Be-ha' alotkha III 152a, quoted in: P.S. Alexander ed., Textual Sources for the Study of Judaism (Manchester: University Press 1984) 127

cf. " ... the Torah, which created the angels and all the worlds and through which all the worlds are sustained. When it descended into this world, it put on the garments of this world, otherwise the world could not have endured it".

The same text can be found in a different translation in: Zohar - The Book of Enlightenment, trans. D. Matt (New York: Paulist Press 1983) 43

32.   B. Kogan, "The Problem of Creation in Late Medieval Jewish Philosophy," ed. Link-Salinger 161-164

33.   Qu'ran: Sura 36: 81 - N. Dawood, trans., The Koran with Parallel Arabic Text (London: Penguin 1990) 444

34.   B. Kogan, Averroes and the Metaphysics of Causation (New York: State University 1985) 203-265

35.   L. Bianchi, L'Errore di Aristotele: La Polemica contro l'Eternità del Mondo nel XIII Secolo (Florence: Nuova Italia Editrice 1984) 20-24

       R.C. Dales, Medieval Discussions of the Eternity of the World (Leiden: Brill 1990) 84-85

36.   Bianchi, L'Errore 30-31

37.   P. Mandonnet, Siger de Brabant et l'Averroisme Latin au XIIIe Siècle (Fribourg: Université 1899) 181-183

38.   F. Van Steenberghen, Siger de Brabant d'après ses Oeuvres Inédits, vol. 2 (Louvain: Éditions de l'Institut Supérieur de Philosophie 1942) 610

39.   F. Van Steenberghen, Introduction à l'Étude de la Philosophie Médiévale (Louvain: Publications Universitaires 1974) 519-520

40.   F. Van Steenberghen, Maître Siger de Brabant (Louvain: Publications Universitaires 1977) 310-311

41.   J-P. Müller, "Philosophie et Foi chez Siger de Brabant," Miscellanea Philosophica ... J. Gredt O.S.B. Oblata (Rome: Studia Anselmiana 1938) 46-50

441

42. T. Bukowski, "The Eternity of the World according to Siger of Brabant," <u>Recherches de Théologie Ancienne et Médiévale</u> 36 (1969) 229

43. O. Argerami, "La Cuestion 'De Aeternitate Mundi': Posiciones Doctrinales," <u>Sapientia</u> 27 (1972) 313-334 and 28 (1973) 99-124 & 179-208, esp. 189, 205-207

44. G. Sajó, "Boece de Dacie et les Commentaires Anonymes Inédits de Munich sur la Physique et sur la Génération Attribués à Siger de Brabant," <u>Archives d'Histoire Doctrinale et Littéraire du Moyen Age</u> 25 (1958) 21-58

45. Van Steenberghen, <u>Maître</u> 311-312, n.62

46. L. Bianchi, "L'Evoluzione dell'Eternalismo di Sigeri di Brabante et la Condanna del 1270," <u>L'Homme et Son Univers au Moyen Age</u>, ed. C.Wenin, vol. II (Louvain-la-Neuve: Éditions de l'Institut Supérieur de Philosophie 1986) 903-910

    Also see Bianchi, <u>L'Errore</u> 81-91

47. Dales, <u>Discussions</u> 140-145

48. <u>Quaestio utrum haec sit vera: Homo est Animal, Nullo Homine Existente</u> lines 131-132 - Bazán (1974) 57

49. <u>Q.U.H.S.V.</u> lines 150-198 - Bazán (1974) 57-59

50. <u>Q.U.H.S.V.</u> lines 208-210 - Bazán (1974) 59

51. Van Steenberghen, <u>Maître</u> 310

    Also see: F. Van Steenberghen, <u>Thomas Aquinas and Radical Aristotelianism</u> (Washington: Catholic University of America Press 1980) 6

    F. Van Steenberghen, "Le Débat du XIIIe Siècle sur le Passé de l'Univers," <u>Revue Philosophique de Louvain</u> 83 (1985) 233

52. Bazán (1974) [Introduction] 25

53.   Q.U.H.S.V. lines 216-221 - Bazán (1974) 59

54.   Bianchi, ed. Wenin, 904

55.   J. Duin, La Doctrine de la Providence dans les Écrits de Siger de Brabant (Louvain: Éditions de l'Institut Supérieur de Philosophie 1954) 215-223

       Also see Section 3.2

56.   See Section 2.9 note 84 and Section 3.2 note 28

57.   A. Dondaine & L. Bataillon, "Le Manuscrit Vindob. Lat. 2330 et Siger de Brabant," Archivum Fratrum Praedicatorum 36 (1966) 182-184

58.   Van Steenberghen, Maître 310

59.   Bianchi, ed. Wenin, 905

60.   In Tertium de Anima qu. 2 lines 24-31 - Bazán (1972) 5

61.   In Tertium de Anima qu. 2 lines 64-65 - Bazán (1972) 6

62.   In Tertium de Anima qu. 2 lines 69-70 - Bazán (1972) 7

63.   In Tertium de Anima qu. 2 lines 72-75 - Bazán (1972) 7

64.   Boethius of Dacia, Tractatus De Aeternitate Mundi, ed. G. Sajó (Budapest: Akadémiai Kiado 1954) 105 lines 612-626

65.   In Tertium de Anima qu. 2 lines 81-83 and 96-97 - Bazán (1972) 7-8

66.   In Tertium de Anima qu. 2 lines 98-99 - Bazán (1972) 8

67.   G. Da Palma, "L'Eternità dell'Intelletto in Aristotele secondo Sigieri di Brabante," Collectanea Franciscana 25 (1955) 410

68.   Van Steenberghen, Maître 247 - who refers to the research of G. De Mattos "L'Intellect Agent Personnel dans les Premiers Écrits d'Albert le Grand et de Thomas d'Aquin," Revue Neoscholastique de Philosophie 43 (1940) 157-158, where the latter explains how a typical remark at that time of Albert or Thomas can state, for example, that: "haec

opinio inter praedictas probabilior est: tamen omnes sunt falsae et haereticae".

69.   Impossibilia IV lines 59-60 - Bazán (1974) 81

70.   Van Steenberghen, Radical 8

71.   Bonaventure, Commentarium in II Sententiarum disp. XVIII, art. II qu. 3 - where he states that "animae non seminantur, sed, formatis corporibus, a Deo creantur et creando infunduntur et infundendo producuntur" - Omnia Opera, vol. II (Florence: Quaracchi 1885) 453

72.   O. Argerami, "Circa Petri de Tarantasia Quaestionem 'De Aeternitate Mundi'" Patristica et Mediaevalia 4 (1981) 81 lines 88-90

      Peter of Tarantaise, "Questio de Eternitate Mundi," Medieval Latin Texts on the Eternity of the World, ed. R. Dales & O. Argerami (Leiden: Brill 1991) 65 lines 7-8

73.   See Section 6.5

74.   In Tertium de Anima qu. 5 line 24 - Bazán (1972) 17

75.   Bazán (1972) 67*-74*

76.   A. Zimmermann, ed. "Les Quaestiones in Physicam de Siger de Brabant" - Bazán (1974) 145-147

77.   Quaestiones in Physicam Book II qu. 19 lines 4-5 - Zimmermann - Bazán (1974) 179

78.   Bonaventure, Commentarium in II Sententiarum disp. I p. I art. I qu. 2 - Omnia Opera, vol. II 19-24

79.   Quaestiones in Physicam Book II qu. 19 lines 41-42 - Zimmermann - Bazán (1974) 180

80.   Van Steenberghen (1977) 330

81.   Quaestiones in Physicam Book II qu. 20 lines 59-64 - Zimmermann - Bazán (1974) 182

444

82. <u>Quaestiones in Physicam</u> Book II qu. 22 lines 14-15 - Zimmermann - Bazán (1974) 183

83. <u>Impossibilia I</u> line 68 - Bazán (1974) 73

84. <u>Impossibilia I</u> lines 74-75 - Bazán (1974) 73

85. <u>Impossibilia III</u> - Bazán (1974) 77-79

86. Van Steenberghen, <u>Maître</u> 310

87. Bazán (1972) [Introduction] 77*-78*

Bazán (1974) [Introduction] 26-28

88. F. de Grijs "The Theological Character of Aquinas' De Aeternitate Mundi" and J. Aertsen "The Eternity of the World: the Believing and the Philosophical Thomas. Some Comments," <u>The Eternity of the World in the Thought of Thomas Aquinas and his Contemporaries</u>, ed. J. Wissink (Leiden: Brill 1990) 1-8 & 9-19

89. <u>De Aeternitate Mundi</u> Introd. lines 4-10 - Bazán (1972) 113

90. <u>De Aeternitate Mundi</u> Introd. lines 14-17 - Bazán (1972) 113

91. <u>De Aeternitate Mundi</u> Introd. lines 25-26 - Bazán (1972) 114

92. <u>De Aeternitate Mundi</u> ch. 1 lines 25-57 - Bazán (1972) 116-117

93. <u>De Aeternitate Mundi</u> ch. 3 - Bazán (1972) 120-127

94. <u>De Aeternitate Mundi</u> ch. 1 lines 36, 43, 48 - Bazán (1972) 116-117

95. <u>De Aeternitate Mundi</u> ch. 2 lines 24-27 - Bazán (1972) 118

96. <u>De Aeternitate Mundi</u> ch. 2 lines 30, 44 - Bazán (1972) 119

97. <u>De Aeternitate Mundi</u> ch. 2 lines 55-57 - Bazán (1972) 120

98. <u>De Aeternitate Mundi</u> ch. 2 lines 58-60 - Bazán (1972) 120

98. <u>De Aeternitate Mundi</u> ch. 4 lines 24-25 - Bazán (1972) 129

100.   De Aeternitate Mundi ch. 4 lines 44-46 - Bazán (1972) 130

101.   De Aeternitate Mundi ch. 4 lines 63-70 - Bazán (1972) 131

102.   John Peckham, ed. O. Argerami, "Quaestio Disputata 'De Aeternitate Mundi'," Patristica et Mediaevalia I (1975) 98 lines 389-394

        John Pecham, "Utrum Mundus Potuit ab Eterno Creari," Medieval Latin Texts on the Eternity of the World, ed. R. Dales & O. Argerami (Leiden: Brill 1991) 83

103.   De Aeternitate Mundi ch. 4 lines 80-85 - Bazán (1972) 132

104.   De Aeternitate Mundi ch. 4 lines 85-86 - Bazán (1972) 132

105.   De Aeternitate Mundi ch. 4 lines 121-122 - Bazán (1972) 134

106.   De Aeternitate Mundi ch. 4 lines 142-143 - Bazán (1972) 135

107.   De Aeternitate Mundi ch. 4 lines 179-183 - Bazán (1972) 136

108.   Van Steenberghen, Maître 90

109.   Boethius of Dacia, De Aeternitate Mundi - G. Sajó, ed. (Budapest: Akadémiai Kiado 1954) 99 lines 450-454

110.   Boethius of Dacia, De Aeternitate Mundi - Sajo 103 lines 559 sq. and 105 lines 606 sq.

111.   Dales (1990) 142

112.   See notes 44 & 45 above

113.   R. Dales, "Maimonides and Boethius of Dacia on the Eternity of the World," New Scholasticism 56 (1982) 306-319

114.   See notes 63 & 64 above

115.   Dales, New Scholasticism (1982) 307-308

116.   Van Steenberghen, Maître 218

117.   De Necessitate et Contingentia Causarum lines 3-8 - Duin 14

118.   De Necessitate et Contingentia Causarum lines 132 (twice), 135, 140, 150 - Duin 20

119.   De Necessitate et Contingentia Causarum line 132 - Duin 2O

120.   De Necessitate et Contingentia Causarum lines 267-275 - Duin 26

121.   De Necessitate et Contingentia Causarum lines 281-288 - Duin 26-27

122.   See notes 61 & 63 above

123.   De Necessitate et Contingentia Causarum lines 130-131 - Duin 20

124.   De Necessitate et Contingentia Causarum line 147 - Duin 20

125.   De Necessitate et Contingentia Causarum lines 141-144 - Duin 20

126.   Bazán (1972) [Introduction] 77*

    See note 87 above

127.   De Anima Intellectiva ch. 5 lines 3, 5, 7, 9, 12, 22, 31, 51, 53-54, 57-58 - Bazán (1972) 90-93

128.   De Anima Intellectiva Prologue lines 11-15 - Bazán (1972) 70

129.   De Anima Intellectiva ch. 5 lines 11-12 - Bazán (1972) 91

130.   De Anima Intellectiva ch. 4 lines 6-9 - Bazán (1972) 89

131.   De Anima Intellectiva ch. 5 lines 17-21 - Bazán (1972) 91

132.   De Anima Intellectiva ch. 5 lines 22-26 - Bazán (1972) 91

133.   De Anima Intellectiva ch. 5 lines 38-42 - Bazán (1972) 92

134.   De Anima Intellectiva ch. 5 lines 54-57 - Bazán (1972) 93

135.   De Anima Intellectiva ch. 5 lines 74-99 - Bazán (1972) 93-94

136.   De Anima Intellectiva ch. 5 lines 96-99 - Bazán (1972) 94

137.   J. Weisheipl, "The Date and Context of Aquinas' 'De Aeternitate Mundi'," Graceful Reason: Essays in Ancient and Medieval Philosophy Presented to Joseph Owens CSSR, ed. L. Gerson (Toronto: Pontifical Institute of Mediaeval Studies 1983) 254

138.   Van Steenberghen, Maître 310

139.   De Anima Intellectiva ch. 3 lines 144-148 - Bazán (1972) 83-84

140.   See note 128 above

141.   Dales, Discussions 144

142.   Quaestiones in Metaphysicam (Munich) Book III Commentum and qu. 16 - Dunphy 129-136

        Quaestiones in Metaphysicam (Cambridge) Book III Commentum I, qu. 15, Commentum II and qu. 16 - Maurer 107-115

143.   Quaestiones in Metaphysicam (Cambridge) Book III qu. 15 lines 95-105 - Duin 77

144.   Quaestiones in Metaphysicam (Munich) Book III Commentum before qu. 16 lines 87-88 - Dunphy 132

        Also see Section 4.12 note 101

145.   Quaestiones in Metaphysicam (Munich) Book III Commentum before qu. 16 lines 91-94 - Dunphy 132

146.   Quaestiones in Metaphysicam (Munich) Book III qu. 16 lines 86-91 - Dunphy 136

147.   Quaestiones in Metaphysicam (Cambridge) Book III qu. 15 lines 77-85 - Maurer 110

148.   Quaestiones in Metaphysicam (Munich) Book III qu. 19 lines 7-10 - Dunphy 144

149.   Quaestiones in Metaphysicam (Munich) Book III qu. 19 lines 18-19 - Dunphy 144

150. Quaestiones in Metaphysicam (Munich) Book III qu. 19 lines 21-24 - Dunphy 144

151. Quaestiones in Metaphysicam (Munich) Book III qu. 19 lines 30-34 - Dunphy 145

152. Quaestiones super Librum de Causis qu. 3 lines 95-97 - Marlasca 45

153. Quaestiones super Librum de Causis qu. 8 lines 7-8 - Marlasca 56

154. Quaestiones super Librum de Causis qu. 8 lines 17-19 - Marlasca 56

155. Quaestiones super Librum de Causis qu. 9 lines 14-16 - Marlasca 58

156. Quaestiones super Librum de Causis qu. 10 lines 18-21 - Marlasca 60

157. Quaestiones super Librum de Causis qu. 10 lines 21-25 - Marlasca 61

158. Quaestiones super Librum de Causis qu. 10 lines 43-45 - Marlasca 61

159. Quaestiones super Librum de Causis qu. 10 lines 50-53 - Marlasca 61

160. Robert Grosseteste, Hexaemeron I, VIII, lines 5-13 - R. Dales & S. Gieben ed. (Oxford: University Press 1982) 62

161. Quaestiones super Librum de Causis qu. 11 lines 31-33 - Marlasca 63

162. Quaestiones super Librum de Causis qu. 12 lines 74-77 - Marlasca 65

163. Quaestiones super Librum de Causis qu. 12 lines 83-85 - Marlasca 65

164. Quaestiones super Librum de Causis qu. 12 lines 108-111 - Marlasca 66

165. Quaestiones super Librum de Causis qu. 12 lines 89-92 - Marlasca 66

166. Quaestiones super Librum de Causis qu. 12 lines 119-120 - Marlasca 67

167. St. Augustine, De Civitate Dei Book XI ch. 4 lines 17-20- Welldon 465-467.

168. Sorabji 242

169.   Thomas Aquinas, <u>Summa Theologiae</u> I qu. 46 art. 1 ad 6 - [Madrid vol. I: 349]

170.   John Peckham, <u>De Aeternitate Mundi</u> - Argerami <u>Patristica et Mediaevalia</u> (1975) 95 lines 307-315; Dales & Argerami 81

171.   E. Bertola, "Tommaso d'Aquino e Il Problema dell'Eternità del Mondo," <u>Rivista di Filosofia Neo-Scolastica</u> 66 (1974) 348

172.   Thomas Aquinas, <u>Quaestiones Quodlibetales</u> 3 qu.2 art.1 - R. Spiazzi ed. (Turin: Marietti 1956) 41-42

173.   Dales, <u>Discussions</u> 133

174.   F. Van Steenberghen, <u>Introduction</u> 515-525

175.   L. Bianchi, <u>L'Errore</u> 167

176.   Thomas Aquinas, <u>De Aeternitate Mundi contra Murmurantes</u> - <u>Opuscula Omnia</u> vol. I, ed. P. Mandonnet (Paris: Leithielleux 1927) 22-27

177.   J. Wippel, "Did Thomas Aquinas Defend the Possibility of an Eternally Created World?" <u>Journal of History of Philosophy</u> 19 (1981) 21-37

178.   H. Davidson, <u>Proofs for Eternity, Creation and the Existence of God in Medieval Islamic and Jewish Philosophy</u> (Oxford: University Press 1987) 5

179.   Boethius of Dacia, <u>De Aeternitate Mundi</u> - Sajó 107 lines 671-675

180.   F. Van Steenberghen, "Le Mythe d'un Monde Éternel," <u>Revue Philosophique de Louvain</u> 76 (1978) 157-179, esp. 167-175

181.   See note 2 above

182.   See note 4 above

183.   See note 66 above

184.   See note 64 above

450

185.   See notes 165 & 166 above

186.   _Quaestiones in Tertium De Anima_ qu. 2 lines 90-92 - Bazán (1972) 7-8

187.   _De Anima Intellectiva_ ch. 5 lines 9-10 - Bazán (1972) 91

188.   _Quaestiones in Metaphysicam (Munich)_ Book III Commentum before qu. 16 lines 82-83 - Dunphy 132

189.   R. Hissette, _Enquête sur les 219 Articles Condamnés à Paris le 7 Mars 1277_ (Louvain: Publications Universitaires 1977) 150

190.   See note 129 above

191.   See note 144 above

192.   Hissette, _Enquête_ 154-155

193.   See notes 95 & 96 above

194.   _Quaestiones in Metaphysicam (Munich)_ Book III qu. 16 lines 53-56 - Dunphy 135

195.   See notes 146 & 147 above

196.   See note 81 above.

197.   _De Anima Intellectiva_ ch. 5 lines 5-7 - Bazán (1972) 90-91

198.   See notes 163 & 164 above

199.   See notes 48 & 50 above.

200.   See notes 94, 96 & 98 above

201.   Denifle & Chatelain n.473 - 543

202.   S. Mazierski, "Temps et Éternité," _L'Homme et Son Univers_ ed. C. Wenin, vol. II (Louvain-La-Neuve: Éditions de l'Institut Supérieur de Philosophie 1986) 878-879

203. P. Bergmann, "General Relativity and Our View of the Physical Universe," <u>Cosmology, History and Theology</u> ed. W. Yourgrau & A. Breck (New York: Plenum Press 1977) 25

204. A. Peacocke, <u>Creation and the World of Science</u> (Oxford: Clarendon Press 1979) 69

205. C. Misner, "Cosmology and Theology," Yourgrau & Breck 99

206. Peacocke 65

207. Peacocke 80

208. J. Moltmann, "Creation and Redemption," <u>Creation, Christ and Culture</u>, ed. R.W.A. McKinney (Edinburgh: T. & T. Clark 1976) 124

209. G.J. Whitrow, "On the Impossibility of an Infinite Past," and K. Popper, "A Reply to Whitrow," <u>British Journal of the Philosophy of Science</u> 29 (1978) 39-45 & 47-48 respectively

210. A. Kenny, <u>The God of the Philosophers</u> (Oxford: Clarendon Press 1979) 40

211. Peacocke 142-143

212. I.G. Barbour, <u>Religion in an Age of Science</u> (London: SCM 1990) 270

213. W.R. Lane, "The Initiation of Creation," <u>Vetus Testamentum</u> 13 (1963) 72

214. Denzinger & Schönmetzer (1963) n. 223, 231, 3897

215. K. Rahner, <u>Theological Investigations</u>, vol. I, trans. C. Ernst (1961; London: Darton, Longman & Todd 1965) 242

NOTES TO CHAPTER SIX

1.   H. Denifle & A. Chatelain, eds., <u>Chartularium Universitatis Parisiensis</u>, vol. I (Paris: Delalain 1889) n.432 - 486-487

2.   Denifle & Chatelain n.473 - 543-555

113.   Quod homo est homo praeter animam rationalem.

114.   Quod homo per nutritionem potest fieri alius numeraliter et individualiter.

115.   Quod Deus non posset facere plures animas in numero.

116.   Quod individua euisdem speciei differunt sola positione materiae, ut Socrates et Plato; et quod forma humana existente in utroque eadem numero, non est mirum, si idem numero est in diversis locis.

117.   Quod intellectus est unus numero; licet enim separetur a corpore hoc, non tamen ab omni.

118.   Quod intellectus agens est quaedam substantia separata superior ad intellectum possibilem; et quod secundum substantiam, potentiam et operationem est separatus a corpore, nec est forma corporis hominis.

119.   Quod motus caeli sunt propter animam intellectivam; et anima intellectiva sive intellectus non potest educi, nisi mediante corpore.

120.   Quod forma hominis non est ab extrinseco, sed educitur de potentia materiae, quia aliter non esset generatio univoca.

121.   Quod nulla forma ab extrinseco veniens potest facere unum cum materia. Quod enim

separabile est, cum eo quod est corruptibile unum non facit.

122. Quod ex sensitivo et intellectivo in homine non fit unum per essentiam, nisi sicut ex intelligentia et orbe, hoc est, unum per operationem.

123. Quod intellectus non est forma corporis nisi sicut nauta navis, nec est perfectio essentialia hominis.

124. Quod humanitas non est forma rei, sed rationis.

125. Quod operatio intellectus non uniti copulatur corpori, ita quod operatio est rei non habentis formam, qua operatur. - Error, quia ponit quod intellectus non sit forma hominis.

126. Quod intellectus, qui est ultima hominis perfectio, est penitus abstractus.

127. Quod anima humana nullo modo est mobilis secundum locum, nec per se, nec per accidens; et si ponatur alicubi per substantiam suam, numquam movebitur de ubi ad ubi.

128. Quod anima numquam moveretur, nisi corpus moveretur, sicut grave vel leve numquam moveretur, nisi aer moveretur.

129. Quod substantia animae est aeterna; et quod intellectus agens et possibilis sunt aeterni.

130. Quod intellectus humanus est aeternus, quia est a causa eodem modo semper se habente, et quia non habet materiam per quam prius sit in potentia quam in actu.

131. Quod intellectus speculativus simpliciter est aeternus et incorruptibilis; respectu vero huius hominis corrumpitur corruptis phantasmatibus in eo.

132.   Quod intellectus quando vult, dimittit corpus, et quando vult, induit.

133.   Quod anima est inseparabilis a corpore; et quod ad corruptionem harmoniae corporis, corrumpitur anima.

134.   Quod anima rationalis, quando recedit ab animali, adhuc remanet animal vivum.

135.   Quod anima separata non est alterabilis secundum philosophiam, licet secundum fidem alteretur.

136.   Quod intellectus potest transire de corpore in corpus, ita quod sit successive motor diversorum corporum.

137.   Quod generatio hominis est circularis, eo quod forma hominis redit pluries super eandem partem materiae.

138.   Quod non fuit primus homo, nec erit ultimus, immo semper fuit et semper erit generatio hominis ex homine.

139.   Quod quamvis generatio hominum possit deficere, virtute Primi tamen non deficiet; quia orbis primus non solum movet ad generationem elementorum, sed etiam hominum.

140.   Quod intellectus agens non copulatur nostro possibili, et quod intellectus possibilis non unitur nobiscum secundum substantiam. Et si uniretur nobis ut forma, esset inseparabilis.

141.   Quod intellectus possibilis nihil est in actu antequam intelligat, quia in natura intelligibili esse aliquid in actu est esse actu intelligens.

142. Quod intellectus possibilis est inseparabilis a corpore simpliciter quantum ad hunc actum qui est specierum receptio, et quantum ad iudicium, quod fit per simplicem specierum adeptionem, vel intelligibilium compositionem. - Error, si intelligatur de omnimoda receptione.

143. Quod homo pro tanto dicitur intelligere, pro quanto caelum dicitur ex se intelligere, vel vivere, vel moveri, id est, quia agens istas actiones est ei unitum ut motor mobili, et non substantialiter.

144. Quod ex intelligente et intellecto fit una substantia, eo quod intellectus sit ipsa intellecta formaliter.

145. Quod anima intellectiva cognoscendo se cognoscit omnia alia. Species enim omnium rerum sunt sibi concreatae. Sed haec cognitio non debetur intellectui nostro, secundum quod noster est, sed secundum quod est intellectus separatus.

146. Quod nos peius aut melius intelligimus, hoc provenit ab intellectu passivo, quem dicit esse potentiam sensitivam. - Error, quia hoc ponit unum intellectum in omnibus, aut aequalitatem in omnibus animabus.

147. Quod inconveniens est ponere aliquos intellectus nobiliores aliis, quia, cum ista diversitas non possit esse a parte corporum, oportet quod sit a parte intelligentiarum; et sic animae nobiles et ignobiles essent necessario diversarum specierum, sicut intelligentiae. - Error, quia sic anima Christi non esset nobilior anima Judae.

148. Quod scientia magistri et discipuli est una numero; ratio autem quod intellectus sit unus,

456

est quia forma non multiplicatur, nisi quia educitur de potentia materiae.

149.   Quod intellectus Socratis corrupti non habet scientiam eorum quorum habuit.

3.   C. Butterworth, "La Valeur Philosophique des Commentaires d'Averroes sur Aristote," Multiple Averroes, Actes du Colloque International organisé à l'occasion du 850e anniversaire de la naissance d'Averroes 20-23 septembre 1976 (Paris: Les Belles Lettres 1978) 117-126

4.   O. Mohammed, Averroes' Doctrine of Immortality: A Matter of Controversy (Waterloo, Ontario: Canadian Corporation for Studies in Religion 1984) 10-12

5.   A. Ivry, "Averroes and the West: the First Encounter/Nonencounter," A Straight Path: Studies in Medieval Philosophy and Culture, ed. R. Link-Salinger (Washington D.C.: Catholic University of America 1988) 143

6.   Aristotle, III De Anima 4, 429a, 15-17 - R. Hicks, ed. & trans., Aristotle de Anima (Cambridge: University Press 1907) 131

7.   Ibn Rushd, Averroes Cordubensis Commentarium Magnum In Aristotelis De Anima Libros, ed. F.S. Crawford (Cambridge, Massachusetts: Mediaeval Academy of America 1953) 411 - Book III ch. 5 lines 710-717

8.   Ibn Rushd, In III De Anima ch. 19 lines 35-46 - Crawford 441-442

9.   Ibn Rushd, In II De Anima ch. 63 lines 41-50 - Crawford 225

10.   Ibn Rushd, Averroes' Destructio Destructionum Philosophiae Algazalis in the Latin Version of Carlo Calonymos, ed. B.H. Zedler (Milwaukee: Marquette University Press 1961) - In Physicis Disputat. II a. - 435

11.   Ibn Rushd, Destructio Destructionum In Metaphysicis Disputat. I a. - Zedler 84

12.   Mohammed 133

13.   Ibn Rushd, <u>Destructio Destructionum</u> In Physicis Disputat. 4a. - Zedler 454

14.   <u>Qur'an</u> Sura 55: 54-60 - N.J. Dawood, ed., <u>The Koran with Parallel Arabic Text</u> (London: Penguin 1990) 532

15.   Ibn Rushd, <u>Averroes' On the Harmony of Religion and Philosophy</u>, ed., G.F. Hourani (London: Luzac & Co., 1961) n.68 - 51

16.   A. Nasri Nader, "La Doctrine des Deux Vérités Chez Ibn Rochd (Averroes) et les Averroistes Latins," <u>Actas del Vo Congreso Internacional de Filosofia Medieval</u>, vol. II (Madrid: Editora Nacional 1979) 1048-1049

17.   Ibn Rushd <u>On the Harmony of Religion and Philosophy</u> n.70 - Hourani 53

18.   <u>Qur'an</u> Sura 16: 125 - Dawood 280

19.   W. Montgomery Watt, <u>Bell's Introduction to the Qur'an</u> (Edinburgh: University Press 1970) 159-160

20.   <u>Qur'an</u> Sura 20: 55 - Dawood 314

21.   Bazán (1972) [Introduction] 74*

        Also see Section 3.2 note 27

22.   Bazán (1972) [Introduction] 67*

23.   <u>In Tertium de Anima</u> qu. 1 lines 58-64 - Bazán (1972) 3

24.   B. Nardi, <u>Studi di Filosofia Medievale</u> (Rome: Edizioni di Storia e Letteratura 1960) 157-159

25.   Albertus Magnus, <u>De Natura et Origine Animae</u> tr. I ch. 5 - <u>Opera Omnia</u>, vol. XII, ed. B. Geyer (Cologne: Aschendorff 1955) 14 lines 10-19

26.   <u>In Tertium de Anima</u> qu. 1 lines 65-68 - Bazán (1972) 3

27.   See Chapter 5.10 note 63

28.   <u>In Tertium de Anima</u> qu. 3 lines 46-49 - Bazán (1972) 10

29.   <u>In Tertium de Anima</u> qu. 1 lines 48-49 - Bazán (1972) 3

        <u>In Tertium de Anima</u> qu. 4 lines 59-60 - Bazán (1972) 12

30.   <u>In Tertium de Anima</u> qu. 4 lines 78-100 - Bazán (1972) 13

31.   <u>In Tertium de Anima</u> qu. 4 lines 76-77 - Bazán (1972) 13

32.   <u>In Tertium de Anima</u> qu. 4 lines 109-110 - Bazán (1972) 14

33.   <u>In Tertium de Anima</u> qu. 4 lines 178-182 - Bazán (1972) 16

34.   <u>In Tertium de Anima</u> qu. 5 lines 8, 12, 14, 19, 24 - Bazán (1972) 17

35.   <u>In Tertium de Anima</u> qu. 5 lines 12-16 - Bazán (1972) 17

36.   <u>In Tertium de Anima</u> qu. 5 lines 19-24 - Bazán (1972) 17

37.   <u>In Tertium de Anima</u> qu. 6 lines 62-63 - Bazán (1972) 20

38.   <u>In Tertium de Anima</u> qu. 9 lines 29-30 - Bazán (1972) 26

39.   <u>In Tertium de Anima</u> qu. 9 lines 36-37 - Bazán (1972) 27

40.   <u>In Tertium de Anima</u> qu. 9 lines 52-54 - Bazán (1972) 27

41.   <u>In Tertium de Anima</u> qu. 9 lines 49-52 - Bazán (1972) 27

42.   See Section 4.7 above

43.   <u>In Tertium de Anima</u> qu. 9 lines 64-67 - Bazán (1972) 28

44.   <u>In Tertium de Anima</u> qu. 7 lines 38-40 - Bazán (1972) 23

45.   <u>In Tertium de Anima</u> qu. 7 lines 52-55 - Bazán (1972) 24

46.   <u>In Tertium de Anima</u> qu. 8 lines 20-28 - Bazán (1972) 25

47.   e.g.<u>In Tertium de Anima</u> qu. 7 line 46 - Bazán (1972) 23
        <u>In Tertium de Anima</u> qu. 8 line 19 - Bazán (1972) 25

48.   Albertus Magnus, In III De Anima, tr. 2, ch. 12 - Opera Omnia, vol.VII part I, ed. C. Stroick (Cologne: Aschendorff 1968) 193 lines 53-55

49.   See note 25 above in this Section

50.   See Section 6.7 below

51.   F. Van Steenberghen, Maître Siger de Brabant (Louvain: Publications Universitaires 1977) 51-53

52.   In Tertium de Anima qu. 7 lines 59-60 - Bazán (1972) 24

53.   In Tertium de Anima qu. 7 lines 12-14 - Bazán (1972) 22

54.   A. Caparello, "La Prima Apparizione dell'Anima 'Composita' in Sigieri di Brabante," Studi Filosofici 4 (1981) 69

55.   In Tertium de Anima qu. 9 lines 89-92 - Bazán (1972) 29

56.   Mohammed 128-130

57.   Ibn Rushd, III De Anima ch. 20 lines 124-155 - Crawford 447-449

58.   Ibn Rushd, III De Anima ch. 20 lines 213-219 - Crawford 450-451

59.   In Tertium de Anima qu. 15 lines 142-143 - Bazán (1972) 58

60.   In Tertium de Anima qu. 10 lines 27-29 - Bazán (1972) 31

61.   In Tertium de Anima qu. 12 lines 147-148 - Bazán (1972) 41

62.   In Tertium de Anima qu. 12 lines 114-117 - Bazán (1972) 40

63.   In Tertium de Anima qu. 12 lines 206-209 - Bazán (1972) 43

64.   In Tertium de Anima qu. 13 lines 77-80 - Bazán (1972) 46

65.   In Tertium de Anima qu. 14 lines 64-66 - Bazán (1972) 48

66.   In Tertium de Anima qu. 14 lines 83-100 - Bazán (1972) 49-50

67.   In Tertium De Anima qu. 14 lines 101-106 - Bazán (1972) 50

460

68.   In Tertium de Anima qu. 14 lines 8-9 - Bazán (1972) 46

69.   In Tertium de Anima qu. 14 lines 179-182 - Bazán (1972) 52

70.   In Tertium de Anima qu. 14 lines 201-202 - Bazán (1972) 53

71.   In Tertium de Anima qu. 14 lines 118-121, 124-126, 137-139 - Bazán (1972) 57-58

72.   In Tertium de Anima qu. 17 lines 95-97 - Bazán (1972) 64

73.   In Tertium de Anima qu. 18 lines 55-60 - Bazán (1972) 66

74.   In Tertium de Anima qu. 18 lines 70-74 - Bazán (1972) 67

75.   In Tertium de Anima qu. 10 lines 27-29 - Bazán (1972) 31

76.   In Tertium de Anima qu. 11 lines 10-13 - Bazán (1972) 31

77.   In Tertium de Anima qu. 11 lines 92-96 - Bazán (1972) 34

78.   In Tertium de Anima qu. 11 lines 106-112 - Bazán (1972) 35

79.   In Tertium de Anima qu. 11 lines 54-69 - Bazán (1972) 33

80.   In Tertium de Anima qu. 11 lines 29-31 - Bazán (1972) 32

81.   Van Steenberghen, Maître 52-53

82.   Van Steenberghen, Maître 37-39

83.   In Tertium de Anima qu. 2 lines 72-75 - Bazán (1972) 7

84.   D. Salman, rev. of Les Oeuvres et la Doctrine de Siger de Brabant, by F. Van Steenberghen, Bulletin Thomiste 10 (1939) 654-672

85.   Caparello, Studi Filosofici 4 (1981) 81

86.   In Tertium de Anima qu. 9 lines 84-85 - Bazán (1972) 28

87.   Thomas Aquinas, Tractatus De Unitate Intellectus Contra Averroistas, ed. L.W. Keeler (Rome: Pontificia Universitas Gregoriana 1936) xviii

88.   Bonaventure, <u>De Septem Donis Spiritus Sancti</u> Collatio VIII, 16 - <u>Opera Omnia</u> vol. V (Florence: Quaracchi 1891) 497-498

89.   Bonaventure, <u>De Septem Donis Spiritus Sancti</u> Collatio IV, 12 - <u>Opera Omnia</u> vol. V, 476

90.   E.-H. Wéber, <u>L'Homme en Discussion à l'Université de Paris en 1270. La Controverse de 1270 à l'Université de Paris et son Retentissement sur la Pensée de S. Thomas d'Aquin</u> (Paris: Librairie Philosophique J. Vrin 1970) 18

91.   Van Steenberghen, <u>Maître</u> 43

92.   J. D'Albi, <u>S. Bonaventure et les Luttes Doctrinales de 1267-1277</u> (Paris: Giraudon 1923) 219

93.   I. Brady, "Background to the Condemnation of 1270: Master William of Baglione O.F.M.," <u>Franciscan Studies</u> 30 (1970) 6

     R.-A. Gauthier, "Quelques Questions à propos du Commentaire de S. Thomas sur le De Anima" <u>Angelicum</u> 51 (1974) 438-442

94.   Thomas Aquinas, <u>De Unitate Intellectus</u> para. 2, lines 23-26 - Keeler 2

95.   Thomas Aquinas, <u>De Unitate Intellectus</u> para. 10 lines 85-90 - Keeler 8-9

96.   Thomas Aquinas, <u>De Unitate Intellectus</u> para. 8 line 69 - Keeler 7
     <u>De Unitate Intellectus</u> para.14 lines 27-28 - Keeler 10-11

97.   Thomas Aquinas, <u>De Unitate Intellectus</u> para. 26 lines 121-123 - Keeler 18

98.   Thomas Aquinas, <u>De Unitate Intellectus</u> para. 56 lines 71-72 - Keeler 35

99.   Thomas Aquinas, <u>De Unitate Intellectus</u> para. 59 lines 37-39 - Keeler 38

100.   Thomas Aquinas, <u>De Unitate Intellectus</u> para. 62 lines 21-23 - Keeler 39

462

101.   C. Genequand, Ibn Rushd's Metaphysics (Leiden: Brill 1984) 50

102.   Thomas Aquinas, De Unitate Intellectus para. 63-66 - Keeler 40-42

103.   Thomas Aquinas, De Unitate Intellectus para. 70 lines 44-47 - Keeler 45

104.   Thomas Aquinas, De Unitate Intellectus para. 83 line 3 - Keeler 52

105.   Thomas Aquinas, De Unitate Intellectus para. 84 lines 20-21 - Keeler 53

106.   Thomas Aquinas, De Unitate Intellectus para. 86 lines 1-16- Keeler 54-55

107.   Thomas Aquinas, De Unitate Intellectus para. 89 lines 62-65 - Keeler 57

108.   Thomas Aquinas, De Unitate Intellectus para. 103 lines 53-59 - Keeler 66-67

109.   Thomas Aquinas, De Unitate Intellectus para. 105 lines 88-90 - Keeler 68

110.   Thomas Aquinas, De Unitate Intellectus para. 116 lines 27-30 - Keeler 75

111.   Thomas Aquinas, De Unitate Intellectus para. 121 lines 37-41 - Keeler 78

112.   Thomas Aquinas, De Unitate Intellectus para. 122 lines 1-10 - Keeler 78-79

113.   Thomas Aquinas, De Unitate Intellectus para. 122-123 lines 10-17 - Keeler 79

114.   Thomas Aquinas, De Unitate Intellectus para. 123 lines 23-28 - Keeler 79-80

115.   Thomas Aquinas, De Unitate Intellectus para. 124 lines 29-31 - Keeler 80

116.   Thomas Aquinas, <u>De Unitate Intellectus</u> para. 124 lines 33-35 - Keeler 80

117.   F. Van Steenberghen, <u>Thomas Aquinas and Radical Aristotelianism</u> (Washington D.C.: Catholic University of Washington 1980) 59

119.   Thomas Aquinas, <u>De Unitate Intellectus</u> para. 114, 117 - Keeler 73-75

120.   Van Steenberghen, <u>Maître</u> 356-357

121.   Thomas Aquinas, <u>De Unitate Intellectus</u> para. 43 lines 138-140 - Keeler 28

122.   Van Steenberghen, <u>Maître</u> 354

123.   B. Bazán, "Le Dialogue Philosophique entre Siger de Brabant et Thomas d'Aquin. À Propos d'un Ouvrage Récent de E.H.Wéber O.P.," <u>Revue Philosophique de Louvain</u> 72 (1974) 53-155

124.   C.H. Lefevre, "Siger de Brabant a-t-il Influencé Saint Thomas? Propos sur la Cohérence de l'Anthropologie Thomiste," rev. of <u>L'Homme en Discussion à l'Université de Paris en 1270. La Controverse de 1270 à l'Université de Paris et son Retentissement sur la Pensée de S. Thomas d'Aquin</u>, by E.-H. Wéber. <u>Mélanges de Science Religieuse</u> 31 (1974) 203-215

125.   Van Steenberghen, <u>Maître</u> 358-360

126.   E.-H. Wéber, "Les Discussions de 1270 à l'Université de Paris et leur Influence sur la Pensée Philosophique de S. Thomas d'Aquin," <u>Miscellanea Mediaevalia</u> 10 (1976) 285-316

127.   Van Steenberghen, <u>Maître</u> 359

128.   Weber, <u>L'Homme</u> 271-276; 313-314

129.   Van Steenberghen, <u>Maître</u> 360

130.   B. Nardi, <u>Sigieri di Brabante nel Pensiero del Rinascimento Italiano</u> (Rome: Edizioni Italiane 1945) 23

131.   A. Nifo, <u>De Intellectu</u> (Venice: 1503) II tr. 2 c. 39 - cited in Nardi, <u>Sigieri</u> 18

464

132. loc. cit.

133. loc. cit.

134. A. Nifo, De Intellectu I tr. 3 c. 26 - cited in Nardi, Sigieri 20

135. Nardi, Sigieri 22

136. A. Nifo, De Intellectu II tr. 2 c. 1 - cited in Nardi, Sigieri 24

137. F. Van Steenberghen, La Philosophie au XIIIe Siècle (Louvain: Publications Universitaires 1966) 444

      Van Steenberghen, Maître 360

138. Van Steenberghen, Maître 363

139. Van Steenberghen, Maître 63; 197-198

140. A. Pattin, "Notes Conçernant Quelques Écrits Attribués à Siger de Brabant," Bulletin de la Philosophie Médiévale 29 (1987) 176-177

141. Bazán (1972) [Introduction] 74*-77*

142. A. Caparello, "Il 'De Anima Intellectiva' di Sigieri di Brabante - Problemi Cronologici e Dottrinali," Sapienza 36 (1983) 450-457

143. De Anima Intellectiva Prologue lines 11-15 - Bazán (1972) 70

144. De Anima Intellectiva ch. 3 lines 79-80 - Bazán (1972) 81

145. De Anima Intellectiva Prologue lines 9-11 - Bazán (1972) 70

146. De Anima Intellectiva ch. 6 line 54 - Bazán (1972) 97

147. B. Bazán, "Intellectum Speculativum: Averroes, Thomas Aquinas and Siger of Brabant on the Intelligible Object," Journal of the History of Philosophy 19 (1981) 440

      Also see note 59 above

148. De Anima Intellectiva ch. 3 lines 67-74 - Bazán (1972) 80

149.   See Section 4.9

150.   <u>De Anima Intellectiva</u> ch. 3 lines 79-82 - Bazán (1972) 81

151.   <u>De Anima Intellectiva</u> ch. 3 lines 144-148 - Bazán (1972) 83-84

152.   <u>De Anima Intellectiva</u> ch. 3 lines 107-109 - Bazán (1972) 86

153.   Thomas Aquinas, <u>De Unitate Intellectus</u> para. 83-84 - Keeler 52-53

154.   <u>De Anima Intellectiva</u> ch. 3 lines 103-107 - Bazán (1972) 82

155.   <u>De Anima Intellectiva</u> ch. 3 line 160 - Bazán (1972) 84

156.   <u>De Anima Intellectiva</u> ch.3 lines 113-116 - Bazán (1972) 82

157.   <u>De Anima Intellectiva</u> ch.3 lines 169-172 - Bazán (1972) 85

158.   <u>De Anima Intellectiva</u> ch. 3 lines 165-167 - Bazán (1972) 84-85

159.   <u>De Anima Intellectiva</u> ch. 3 lines 180-181 - Bazán (1972) 85

160.   <u>De Anima Intellectiva</u> ch. 3 line 188 - Bazán (1972) 85
        ch. 3 line 231 - Bazán (1972) 87

161.   <u>In Tertium De Anima</u> qu. 8 lines 20-27 - Bazán (1972) 25

        Also see note 46 above

162.   M. Chossat, "Saint Thomas d'Aquin et Siger de Brabant," <u>Revue de Philosophie</u> 24 (1914) 562

163.   Van Steenberghen, <u>Maître</u> 369

164.   Caparello, <u>Sapienza</u> 36 (1983) 450-451

        Also see note 142 above

165.   <u>De Anima Intellectiva</u> ch. 3 lines 174-175 - Bazán (1972) 85

166.   <u>In Tertium De Anima</u> qu. 6 lines 104-108 - Bazán (1972) 21

167. <u>De Anima Intellectiva</u> ch. 3 lines 194-197 - Bazán (1972) 86

168. <u>De Anima Intellectiva</u> ch. 3 lines 176-177 - Bazán (1972) 85

169. <u>De Anima Intellectiva</u> ch. 3 lines 180-181 - Bazán (1972) 85

170. <u>De Anima Intellectiva</u> ch. 3 lines 179 - Bazán (1972) 85

171. Thomas Aquinas, <u>De Unitate Intellectus</u> para. 78 lines 57-58 - Keeler 49

172. <u>De Anima Intellectiva</u> ch. 3 lines 197-200 - Bazán (1972) 86

173. <u>De Anima Intellectiva</u> ch. 3 lines 201-206 - Bazán (1972) 86

174. H. Denzinger & A. Schönmetzer, <u>Enchiridion Symbolorum Definitionum et Declarationum de Rebus Fidei et Morum</u>, 32nd. ed. (Barcelona: Herder 1963) n.902/481 - 284

175. <u>De Anima Intellectiva</u> ch. 3 lines 250-253 - Bazán (1972) 88

176. See note 151 above

177. See Section 5.16 notes 165 & 166

178. Caparello, <u>Sapienza</u> 36 (1983) 456

179. R. Hissette, <u>Enquête sur les 219 Articles Condamnés à Paris le 7 Mars 1277</u> (Louvain: Publications Universitaires 1977) 199

180. See Section 5.14

181. <u>De Anima Intellectiva</u> ch. 4 lines 7-9 - Bazán (1972) 89

182. <u>De Anima Intellectiva</u> ch. 5 lines 19-21 - Bazán (1972) 91

183. Van Steenberghen, <u>Maître</u> 363

184. <u>De Anima Intellectiva</u> ch. 5 lines 54-56 - Bazán (1972) 93

185. <u>De Anima Intellectiva</u> ch. 5 lines 96-99 - Bazán (1972) 94

186. <u>De Anima Intellectiva</u> ch. 6 lines 46-49 - Bazán (1972) 97

187.   De Anima Intellectiva ch. 6 lines 57-60 - Bazán (1972) 98

188.   W.-U. Klünker & B. Sandkühler, Menschliche Seele und Kosmischer Geist (Stuttgart: Verlag Freies Geistesleben 1988) 95

189.   De Anima Intellectiva ch. 6 lines 78-83 - Bazán 99

190.   De Anima Intellectiva ch. 6 lines 95-106 - Bazán (1972) 99-100

191.   De Anima Intellectiva ch. 6 lines 113-119 - Bazán (1972) 100

192.   De Anima Intellectiva ch. 7 lines 5-12 - Bazán (1972) 101

193.   Van Steenberghen, Radical 80

194.   De Anima Intellectiva ch. 7 lines 48-49 - Bazán (1972) 103

        Also see note 100 above

195.   See note 164 above

196.   De Anima Intellectiva ch. 7 lines 111-115 - Bazán (1972) 105

197.   De Anima Intellectiva ch. 7 lines 142-144 - Bazán (1972) 107

198.   De Anima Intellectiva ch. 7 line 155 - Bazán (1972) 1O7

199.   De Anima Intellectiva ch. 7 lines 158-169 - Bazán (1972) 107-108

200.   De Anima Intellectiva ch. 7 lines 183-187 - Bazán (1972) 108

201.   Van Steenberghen, Maître 374

202.   Caparello, Sapienza 36 (1983) 473-474

203.   De Anima Intellectiva ch. 8 lines 30-32 - Bazán (1972) 110

204.   De Anima Intellectiva ch. 9 lines 14-16 - Bazán (1972) 112

205.   De Anima Intellectiva ch. 9 lines 21-24 - Bazán (1972) 112

206.   Quaestiones Naturales (Lisbon) qu. 3 lines 34-37 - Bazán (1974) 109

207.   Van Steenberghen, _Maître_ 377

208.   _Quaestiones super Librum de Causis_ qu. 26 lines 65-67 - Marlasca 105

209.   Thomas Aquinas, _De Unitate Intellectus_ para. 83 lines 14-16 - Keeler 52-53

210.   _Quaestiones super Librum de Causis_ qu. 26 lines 72-74 - Marlasca 105

211.   See note 127 above

212.   Van Steenberghen, _Maître_ 379

213.   _Quaestiones super Librum de Causis_ qu. 26 line 48 - Marlasca 104

214.   _Quaestiones super Librum de Causis_ qu. 26 lines 86-93 - Marlasca 105

215.   _Quaestiones super Librum de Causis_ qu. 26 lines 111-112 - Marlasca 106

216.   _Quaestiones super Librum de Causis_ qu. 26 lines 115-118 - Marlasca 106

217.   _Quaestiones super Librum de Causis_ qu. 18 lines 37-41 - Marlasca 81

218.   _Quaestiones super Librum de Causis_ qu. 27 lines 92-94 - Marlasca 110

219.   _Quaestiones super Librum de Causis_ qu. 27 line 104 - Marlasca 111

220.   _Quaestiones super Librum de Causis_ qu. 27 lines 121-128 - Marlasca 111-112

221.   _Quaestiones super Librum de Causis_ qu. 27 lines 136-139 - Marlasca 112

222.   _Quaestiones super Librum de Causis_ qu. 27 lines 147-148 - Marlasca 112

223.   See note 214 above

224.   _Quaestiones super Librum de Causis_ qu. 27 lines 162-166 - Marlasca 113

225. Quaestiones super Librum de Causis qu. 27 lines 174-177 - Marlasca 113

226. Quaestiones super Librum de Causis qu. 27 lines 188-193 - Marlasca 113-114

227. Quaestiones super Librum de Causis qu. 27 lines 242-246 - Marlasca 115

228. Quaestiones super Librum de Causis qu. 27 lines 246-248 - Marlasca 115

229. Quaestiones super Librum de Causis qu. 27 lines 250-252 - Marlasca 115

230. See note 200 above

231. See Section 3.3

232. See note 222 above

233. See note 116 above

234. Quaestiones super Librum de Causis qu. 52 lines 69-72 - Marlasca 179-180

235. Quaestiones super Librum de Causis qu. 52 lines 145-153 - Marlasca 182

236. Van Steenberghen, Maître 65-70

237. M. Giele ed., "Un Commentaire Averroiste sur les Livres I et II du Traité de l'Ame," Trois Commentaires Anonymes sur le Traité de l'Ame d'Aristote eds. M. Giele, F. Van Steenberghen, B. Bazán (Louvain: Publications Universitaires 1971) 17

238. Z. Kuksewicz, De Siger de Brabant à Jacques de Plaisance. La Théorie de l'Intellect chez les Averroistes Latins des XIIIe et XIVe Siècles (Wroclaw-Warsaw-Cracow: Institut de Philosophie et de Sociologie de l'Académie Polonaise des Sciences 1968) 67

239. Quaestiones de Anima Book II qu. 4 line 245 - Giele 75

470

240.   <u>Quaestiones de Anima</u> Book II qu. 4 lines 146-147 - Giele 72

241.   <u>Quaestiones de Anima</u> Book I qu. 6 lines 67-68 - Giele 39

242.   See notes 73, 166 and 224 above

243.   <u>Quaestiones de Anima</u> Book I qu. 3 lines 33-40 - Giele 26

244.   O. Leaman, <u>Averroes and His Philosophy</u> (Oxford: Clarendon Press 1988) 96-103

245.   T. Eto, "On the Author of a Commentary on De Anima (Merton College MS.275 f. 108-121): a Re-examination," <u>Studies in Medieval Thought</u> 11 (1969) [Précis of Japanese Article] 149-150

246.   Kuksewicz 66-68

247.   Giles of Rome, <u>In Secundum Sententiarum</u> disp. xvii, qu.2 a.1 (Venice: 1581), [vol. II part 2] 48 - cited in Van Steenberghen, <u>Maître</u> 67

248.   J. Polkinghorne, <u>Reason and Reality</u> (London: SPCK 1991) 87

249.   G. Ryle, <u>The Concept of Mind</u> (1949; London: Hutchinson 1967)

250.   A. Kenny, <u>The Legacy of Wittgenstein</u> (Oxford: Blackwell 1984) 71

251.   Kenny 75

252.   B. Lonergan, <u>Insight</u> (London: Longmans, Green & Co 1957) 369-372 & 407

         B. Lonergan, <u>Method in Theology</u> (London: Darton, Longman & Todd 1972) 7-17 & 73-74

253.   Kenny xii

254.   R. Sheldrake, <u>A New Science of Life</u> (London: Paladin 1987) 258-265

255.   W. James, <u>Some Problems of Philosophy: A Beginning of an Introduction to Philosophy</u> (New York: Longmans, Green & Co. 1916) 208-219

256. C. Jung, <u>Man and his Symbols</u> (1964; London: Aldus/Jupiter 1979) 67-69

257. J. Teichman, <u>Philosophy and the Mind</u> (Blackwell: Oxford 1988) 99

258. M. Sánchez Sorondo, "La Querella Antropologica del Siglo XIII (Sigerio y Santo Tomas)" <u>Sapientia</u> 35 (1980) 358

NOTES TO CHAPTER SEVEN

1. H. Denifle & A. Chatelain, eds., Chartularium Universitatis Parisiensis, vol. I (Paris: Delalain 1889) n.432 - 486-487

2. H. Denzinger & A. Schönmetzer, eds., Enchiridion Symbolorum Definitionum et Declarationum de Rebus Fidei et Morum, 32nd. ed. (Barcelona: Herder 1963) n.812/437 - 264

3. Denzinger & Schönmetzer n.860/465 - 277

4. J. Duvernoy, La Religion des Cathares (1976; Toulouse: Edouard Privat 1986) 69

5. Denifle & Chatelain n.473 - 543-555

    150.   Quod illud quod de sui natura non est determinatum ad esse vel non esse, non determinatur nisi per aliquid quod est necessarium respectu sui.

    151.   Quod anima nihil vult, nisi mota ab alio. Unde illud est falsum: anima seipsa vult. - Error si intelligatur mota ab alio, scilicet ab appetibili vel obiecto, ita quod appetibile vel obiectu sit tota ratio motus ipsius voluntatis.

    152.   Quod omnes motus voluntarii reducuntur in Motorem Primum. - Error, nisi intelligatur in Motorem Primum simpliciter, non creatum; et intelligendo de motu secundum substantiam, non secundum deformitatem.

    153.   Quod voluntas et intellectus non moventur in actu per se, sed per causam sempiternam, scilicet corpora caelestia.

    154.   Quod voluntas nostra subiacet potestati corporum caelestium.

    155.   Quod orbis est causa voluntatis medici ut sanet.

156.   Quod effectus stellarum super liberum arbitrium sunt occulti.

157.   Quod duobus bonis propositis, quod fortius est, fortius movet. - Error, nisi intelligatur quantum est ex parte boni moventis.

158.   Quod homo in omnibus actionibus suis sequitur appetitum, et semper maiorem. - Error, si intelligatur de maiori in movendo.

159.   Quod appetitus, cessantibus impedimentis, necessario moventur ab appetibili. - Error est de intellectivo.

160.   Quod voluntate existente in tali dispositione, in qua nata est moveri, et manente sic disposito quod natum est movere, impossibile est voluntate non velle.

161.   Quod voluntas secundum se est indeterminata ad opposita sicut materia; determinatur autem ab appetibili sicut materia ab agente.

162.   Quod scientia contrariorum solum est causa quare anima rationalis potest in opposita; et quod Potentia simpliciter una non potest in opposita, nisi per accidens et ratione alterius.

163.   Quod voluntas necessario prosequitur quod firmiter creditum est a ratione; et quod non potest abstinere ab eo quod ratio dictat. Haec autem necessitatio non est coactio, sed natura voluntatis.

164.   Quod voluntas hominis necessitatur per suam cognitionem, sicut appetitus bruti.

165.   Quod post conclusionem factam de aliquo faciendo, voluntas non manet libera, et quod poenae non adhibentur a lege nisi ad

ignorantiae correptionem et ut correptio sit aliis principium cognitionis.

166. Quod si ratio recta, et voluntas recta. - Error, quia contra glossa Augustini super illud Psalmi: "Concupivit anima desiderare" etc., et quia secundum hoc, ad rectitudinem voluntatis non esset necessaria gratia, sed scientia solum, quod est error Pelagii.

167. Quod non est possibile esse peccatum in potentiis animae superioribus. Et ita peccatum fit passione, non voluntate.

168. Quod homo agens ex passione coacte agit.

169. Quod voluntas, manente passione et scientia particulari in actu, non potest agere contra eam.

6.   See Section 2.7

7.   P. Mandonnet, Siger de Brabant et l'Averroisme Latin au XIIIe Siècle (Fribourg: Université 1899) 194-200

8.   See Sections 2.4 and 2.6

9.   G. Leff, Medieval Thought from Augustine to Ockham (1958; London: Merlin Press 1980) 228

10.   O. Lottin, "Liberté Humaine et Motion Divine," Recherches de Théologie Ancienne et Médiévale 7 (1935) 62

11.   O. Lottin, Psychologie et Morale aux XIIe et XIIIe Siècles (Gembloux: Ducelot 1942) 263-265

12.   F. Van Steenberghen, Maître Siger de Brabant, (Louvain: Publications Universitaires 1977) 383-388

13.   C. Ryan, "Man's Freewill in the Works of Siger of Brabant," Medieval Studies 45 (1983) 155-199

14. Impossibilia V lines 1-3 - Bazán (1974) 86

15. Impossibilia V lines 9-10 - Bazán (1974) 86

16. Impossibilia V lines 25-28 - Bazán (1974) 86-87

17. Ibn Sina, Avicenna Latinus: Liber de Prima Philosophia sive Scientia Divina, ed. S. Van Riet (Louvain: 1977) [In Metaph. 1.7] 46 - lines 69-71

18. Impossibilia V lines 32-36 - Bazán (1974) 87

19. Impossibilia V lines 37-39 - Bazán (1974) 87

20. National Curriculum Council, Curriculum Guide 5 - Health Education (York: N.C.C 1990) 2-4

21. Impossibilia V lines 67-69 - Bazán (1974) 88

22. Impossibilia V lines 69-70 - Bazán (1974) 88

23. Impossibilia V lines 80-81 - Bazán (1974) 89

24. Impossibilia V lines 108-110 - Bazán (1974) 89

25. Impossibilia V lines 122-123 - Bazán (1974) 90

26. Impossibilia V lines 152-156 - Bazán (1974) 91

27. Impossibilia V lines 161-167 - Bazán (1974) 91

28. Impossibilia V lines 131-132 - Bazán (1974) 90

29. Impossibilia V lines 172-174 - Bazán (1974) 91

30. Impossibilia V line 160 - Bazán (1974) 91

31. Ryan 169

32. Impossibilia V lines 170-171 - Bazán (1974) 91

33. De Necessitate et Contingentia Causarum line 3 - Duin 14

476

34.   <u>De Necessitate et Contingentia Causarum</u> line 5 - Duin 14

35.   <u>De Necessitate et Contingentia Causarum</u> lines 132-150 - Duin 20

36.   <u>De Necessitate et Contingentia Causarum</u> lines 132 - Duin 20

37.   <u>De Necessitate et Contingentia Causarum</u> lines 267-275 - Duin 26

38.   <u>De Necessitate et Contingentia Causarum</u> lines 287-288 - Duin 27

39.   <u>De Necessitate et Contingentia Causarum</u> lines 394-400 - Duin 31-32

40.   <u>De Necessitate et Contingentia Causarum</u> lines 402-404 - Duin 32

41.   <u>De Necessitate et Contingentia Causarum</u> lines 416-418 - Duin 32

42.   <u>De Necessitate et Contingentia Causarum</u> lines 406-409 - Duin 32

43.   <u>De Necessitate et Contingentia Causarum</u> lines 423-430 - Duin 33

44.   <u>De Necessitate et Contingentia Causarum</u> lines 433-435 - Duin 33

45.   <u>De Necessitate et Contingentia Causarum</u> lines 436-439 - Duin 34

46.   <u>De Necessitate et Contingentia Causarum</u> lines 450-455 - Duin 34

47.   <u>De Necessitate et Contingentia Causarum</u> lines 437, 448-449, 451, 455, 46O0 - Duin 33-34

48.   <u>De Necessitate et Contingentia Causarum</u> lines 462-464 - Duin 34-35

49.   B.F. Skinner, <u>Science and Human Behavior</u> (1953; New York: Macmillan 1966) 227-241

50.   <u>De Necessitate et Contingentia Causarum</u> lines 465-473 - Duin 35

51.   P. Mandonnet, <u>Siger de Brabant et l'Averroisme Latin au XIIIe Siècle</u>, 2nd. ed., vol. I (Louvain: 1911) 182-184

52.   See Section 4.6, esp. note 48

53.   Ryan 164 & 177

54.   Maurer [Introduction] 7

55.   Duin 137-139

56.   Quaestiones in Metaphysicam (Cambridge) Book V qu. 36 lines 21-25
        - Maurer 269

57.   Quaestiones in Metaphysicam (Vienna) Book V qu. 7 lines 44-49 -
        Dunphy 329

58.   Quaestiones in Metaphysicam (Cambridge) Book V qu. 37 lines 18-23
        - Maurer 271

59.   Quaestiones in Metaphysicam (Cambridge) Book V qu. 37 lines 23-26
        - Maurer 271

60.   Thomas Aquinas, Summa Theologica Book I qu. 2 art. 3 - [Madrid
        vol. I: 18-19]

61.   J. Fletcher, Situation Ethics (London: SCM 1966)

62.   Quaestiones in Metaphysicam (Vienna) Book V qu. 8 lines 50-51 -
        Dunphy 331

63.   Quaestiones in Metaphysicam (Vienna) Book V qu. 8 lines 29-32 -
        Dunphy 330

64.   Quaestiones in Metaphysicam (Cambridge) Book VI qu. 9 lines 12, 13,
        22, - Maurer 317

65.   Quaestiones in Metaphysicam (Vienna) Book VII qu. 1 lines 9-32 -
        Dunphy 374-375

66.   Quaestiones in Metaphysicam (Cambridge) Book VI qu. 9 lines 51-78
        - Maurer 318-319

67.   Quaestiones in Metaphysicam (Cambridge) Book VI qu. 9 lines 79-83
        - Maurer 319

68.   Quaestiones in Metaphysicam (Cambridge) Book VI qu. 9 lines 106-
        109 - Maurer 320

69.   Aristotle, Physica 8.1 (251b1-10) - Aristoteles Latinus VII i Physica, ed. F. Bossier & J. Broms (Leiden: Brill 1990) 280

        See Section 5.3 note 8

70.   Quaestiones in Metaphysicam (Cambridge) Book VI qu. 9 lines 129-131 - Maurer 321

71.   Quaestiones in Metaphysicam (Cambridge) Book VI qu. 9 lines 139-146 - Maurer 321

72.   Quaestiones in Metaphysicam (Cambridge) Book VI qu. 9 lines 157-159 - Maurer 321

73.   Quaestiones in Metaphysicam (Vienna) Book VII qu. 1 lines 207-211 - Dunphy 379

74.   Quaestiones in Metaphysicam (Vienna) Book VII qu. 1 line 230 - Dunphy 380

75.   Quaestiones in Metaphysicam (Vienna) Book VII qu. 1 line 267 - Dunphy 381

76.   Quaestiones in Metaphysicam (Vienna) Book VII qu. 1 line 400 - Dunphy 385

77.   Quaestiones in Metaphysicam (Cambridge) Book VI qu. 9 lines 272-275 - Maurer 325

78.   Quaestiones in Metaphysicam (Vienna) Book VII qu. 1 lines 413 - Dunphy 385

79.   See note 48 above

80.   Quaestiones in Metaphysicam (Cambridge) Book VI qu. 9 lines 278-281 - Maurer 325

81.   Quaestiones in Metaphysicam (Vienna) Book VII qu. 1 lines 416-418 - Dunphy 385

82.   Quaestiones in Metaphysicam (Vienna) Book VII qu. 1 lines 426-430 - Dunphy 385

83.   *Quaestiones in Metaphysicam* (Vienna) Book VII qu. 1 lines 432-436 - Dunphy 386

84.   *Quaestiones in Metaphysicam* (Vienna) Book VII qu. 1 lines 464-470 - Dunphy 386

85.   *Quaestiones in Metaphysicam* (Cambridge) Book VI qu. 9 lines 342-344 - Maurer 327

86.   *Quaestiones super Librum de Causis* qu. 25 line 15 - Marlasca 100

87.   *Quaestiones super Librum de Causis* qu. 25 lines 11-12 - Marlasca 100

88.   *Quaestiones super Librum de Causis* qu. 25 lines 17, 34 - Marlasca 101

89.   J. Aertsen, "Ontology and Henology in Medieval Philosophy (Thomas Aquinas, Master Eckhart and Berthold of Moosburg)," *On Proclus and his Influence on Medieval Philosophy*, eds. E. Bos and P. Meijer (Leiden: Brill 1992) 126

90.   Denifle & Chatelain n.246 - 278

       Also see Section 1.8 note 43

91.   *Quaestiones super Librum de Causis* qu. 25 lines 8-9 - Marlasca 100

92.   *Quaestiones super Librum de Causis* qu. 25 lines 61-62 - Marlasca 102

93.   *Quaestiones super Librum de Causis* qu. 25 lines 42-43 - Marlasca 101

94.   *Quaestiones super Librum de Causis* qu. 25 lines 56-61 - Marlasca 102

95.   Ryan 187

96.   See note 17 above

97.   *Quaestiones in Metaphysicam* (Cambridge) Book VI qu. 9 lines 167-170 - Maurer 322

98.   Ryan 196

99.   Henry of Ghent, *Quodlibet I* - *Opera Omnia* vol.V, ed. R.Macken (Louvain: University; Leiden: Brill 1979) 125 lines 30-32

480

100.   W. Kay, <u>Moral Development</u> (1968; London: George Allen 1972) 26-28

101.   T. Radford, "Your Mother Should Know," <u>Guardian Outlook</u> 17 July 1993: 23 [reference made to report in <u>Science</u> 16 July 1993]

102.   <u>Quaestiones Morales</u> II lines 10-13 - Bazán (1974) 100

103.   <u>Quaestiones Morales</u> II lines 19-27 - Bazán (1974) 100

104.   M. Knight, "Morality - Supernatural or Social?" <u>The Humanist Outlook</u>, ed. A.J. Ayer (London: Pemberton 1968) 47-64

NOTES TO CHAPTER EIGHT

1. H. Denifle & A. Chatelain, eds., <u>Chartularium Universitatis Parisiensis</u>, vol. I (Paris: Delalain 1889) n.432 - 486-487

2. Denifle & Chatelain, n.473 - 543-555

3. H. Denzinger & A. Schönmetzer, eds., <u>Enchiridion Symbolorum Definitionum et Declarationum de Rebus Fidei et Morum</u>, 32nd. ed. (Barcelona: Herder 1963) n.790/421 - 255

4. P. Mandonnet, <u>Siger de Brabant et l'Averroisme Latin au XIIIe Siècle</u> (Fribourg: Université 1899) 178 - 2nd. ed., vol. I (Louvain: les Philosophes Belges 1911) 165

5. J. Duin, <u>La Doctrine de la Providence dans les Écrits de Siger de Brabant</u> (Louvain: Éditions de l'Institut Supérieur de Philosophie 1954) 322-323

6. F. Van Steenberghen, <u>Maître Siger de Brabant</u> (Louvain: Publications Universitaires 1977) 77

7. F. Van Steenberghen, <u>Les Oeuvres et la Doctrine de Siger de Brabant</u> (Brussels: Académie Royale de Belgique 1938) 128

8. <u>Quaestiones in Tertium de Anima</u> qu. 17 lines 77-81 - Bazán (1972) 63

9. <u>Quaestiones in Tertium de Anima</u> qu. 17 lines 85-88 - Bazán (1972) 63

10. <u>Quaestiones in Tertium de Anima</u> qu. 17 lines 93-95 - Bazán (1972) 64

11. <u>Quaestiones in Tertium de Anima</u> qu. 17 lines 95-97 - Bazán (1972) 64

12. See Section 5.10 note 76

13. <u>Quaestiones in Physicam</u> Book II qu. 9 lines 74-78 - Zimmermann - Bazán (1974) 164

14. <u>Quaestiones in Physicam</u> Book II qu. 9 lines 83-84 - Zimmermann - Bazán (1974) 165

482

15.   *Quaestiones in Physicam* Book II qu. 9 lines 98-99 - Zimmermann - Bazán (1974) 165

16.   *Quaestiones in Physicam* Book II qu. 9 line 94 - Zimmermann - Bazán (1974) 165

17.   J. Duvernoy, *La Religion des Cathares* (1976; Toulouse: Edouard Privat 1986) 39-55

18.   *Quaestiones in Physicam* Book II qu. 9 lines 106-109) - Zimmermann - Bazán (1974) 165

19.   *Quaestiones in Physicam* Book II qu. 9 lines 110-111 - Zimmermann - Bazán (1974) 165

20.   *Quaestiones in Physicam* Book II qu. 9 lines 171-177 - Zimmermann - Bazán (1974) 167

21.   See note 8 above

22.   Aristotle, *Metaphysics* XII, 9, 1074 b 33-34 - *Aristoteles Latinus XXV 2 Metaphysica*, ed. G. Vuillemin-Diem (Leiden: Brill 1976) 220

23.   A. Nifo, De Intellectu (Venice: 1503) II tr. 2 c. 11 - quoted in B. Nardi, *Sigieri di Brabante nel Pensiero del Rinascimento Italiano* (Rome: Edizioni Italiane 1945) 22

24.   ibid.

25.   *De Necessitate et Contingentia Causarum* lines 128-129 & 132 - Duin 19 & 20

26.   *De Necessitate et Contingentia Causarum* lines 343-349 - Duin 29-30

27.   *De Necessitate et Contingentia Causarum* lines 544-547 - Duin 38-39

28.   *De Necessitate et Contingentia Causarum* lines 608-609 - Duin 41

29.   *De Necessitate et Contingentia Causarum* lines 618-625 - Duin 42

30.   *De Necessitate et Contingentia Causarum* lines 636-638 - Duin 43

31.   <u>De Necessitate et Contingentia Causarum</u> lines 646-648 & 654-658 - Duin 43 & 44

32.   Duin 334-339

33.   <u>De Necessitate et Contingentia Causarum</u> lines 611-614 - Duin 42

34.   R. Hissette, <u>Enquête sur les 219 Articles Condamnés à Paris le 7 mars 1277</u> (Louvain: Publications Universitaires 1977) 42-43

35.   See note 29 above

36.   <u>Quaestiones in Metaphysicam</u> (Vienna) Book VII qu. 1 lines 207-211 - Dunphy 379

    Also see Chapter 7 note 73

37.   <u>Quaestiones in Metaphysicam</u> (Vienna) Book VII qu. 1 line 230 - Dunphy 380

    Also see Chapter 7 note 74

38.   <u>Quaestiones in Metaphysicam</u> (Vienna) Book VII qu. 1 line 267 - Dunphy 381

    Also see Chapter 7 note 75

39.   <u>Quaestiones in Metaphysicam</u> (Vienna) Book VI qu. 5 lines 39-40 - Dunphy 369

40.   <u>Quaestiones in Metaphysicam</u> (Paris) Book V qu. 4 lines 5-9 - Maurer 435

41.   <u>Quaestiones in Metaphysicam</u> (Paris) Book V qu. 4 lines 19-20 - Maurer 435

42.   <u>Quaestiones in Metaphysicam</u> (Vienna) Book V qu. 12 lines 32-39 - Dunphy 348

43.   <u>Quaestiones super Librum de Causis</u> qu. 10 lines 17-21 - Marlasca 60

    Also see Section 5.17 note 156

484

44.   _Quaestiones super Librum de Causis_ qu. 10 lines 43-45 - Marlasca 61

        Also see Section 5.17 note 158

45.   _Quaestiones super Librum de Causis_ qu. 43 lines 56-72 - Marlasca 156

46.   _Quaestiones super Librum de Causis_ qu. 43 line 126 - Marlasca 158

47.   _Quaestiones super Librum de Causis_ qu. 44 lines 32-36 - Marlasca 160

48.   _Quaestiones super Librum de Causis_ qu. 44 lines 47-53 - Marlasca 160

49.   _Quaestiones super Librum de Causis_ qu. 44 lines 60-64 - Marlasca
        160-161

50.   Thomas Aquinas, _Summa Theologiae_ I qu. 14 art. 13 - [Madrid vol. I:
        125]

51.   W. Lane Craig, _Divine Foreknowledge and Human Freedom_ (Leiden:
        Brill 1991) 237-278

52.   Thomas Aquinas, _Summa Theologiae_ I qu. 14 art. 5 - [Madrid vol. I:
        114]

53.   Thomas Aquinas, _Summa Theologiae_ I qu. 14 art. 11 - [Madrid vol. I:
        122]

54.   Thomas Aquinas, _Summa Theologiae_ I qu. 22 art. 4 - [Madrid vol. I:
        187-188]

55.   Van Steenberghen, _Maître_ 78

56.   See note 22 above

NOTES TO CHAPTER NINE

1. A. Dondaine, "Le Manuel de l'Inquisiteur (1230-1330)," <u>Archivum Fratrum Praedicatorum</u> 17 (1947) 191-192

2. D. Meade, <u>The Medieval Church in England</u> (Worthing: Churchman 1988) 161

3. Thomas Aquinas, <u>Summa Theologiae</u> II 2, q. 110, art. 3, ad 4 - [Madrid vol. III: 724-725]

4. See Section 2.6

5. F. Castets, <u>Il Fiore, Poème Italien du XIIIe Siècle en CCXXXII Sonnets, Imité du Roman de la Rose par Durante</u> (Montpellier and Paris: 1881) - cited in F. Van Steenberghen, <u>Maître Siger de Brabant</u> (Louvain: Publications Universitaires 1977) 21

6. Castets, Sonnet 92, 47.

7. John Peckham, <u>Registrum Epistolarum Fratris Joannis Peckham</u>, vol. III, ed. C. Martin (London: Longman, Trubner & Co. 1885) 842.

8. P. Toynbee, <u>Dante Studies and Researches</u> (London: Methuen 1902) 314-319.

9. "Martini Continuatio Brabantina," <u>Monumenta Germaniae Historica, Scriptores</u>, vol. XXIV (Hannover: 1879) 263 lines 37-40

10. R. Gauthier, "Notes sur Siger de Brabant II. Siger en 1272-1275: Aubry de Reims et la Scission des Normands," <u>Revue de Sciences Philosophiques et Théologiques</u> 68 (1984): 26

11. Gauthier 27

12. R. Hissette, <u>Enquête sur les 219 Articles Condamnés à Paris le 7 mars 1277</u> (Louvain: Publications Universitaires 1977) 11-12

    Also see Section 3.3

13.   A. Otto and H. Roos (eds.), and later J. Pinborg (ed.) <u>Corpus Philosophorum Danicorum Medii Aevi</u> IV, V 1-2, VI 1-2, VIII, IX (Copenhagen: Det danske Sprog-og Litteraturselskab 1969-1979)

14.   J. Pinborg, "Zur Philosophie des Boethius de Dacia. Ein Uberblick," <u>Studia Mediewistcyzne</u> 15 (1974) 165

15.   See Section 2.8 note 75

16.   Ap. Dictamina Berardi, Cod. Vat. Lat., 3977, f. 170 - quoted in H. Mann & J. Hollsteiner, <u>The Lives of the Popes in the Middle Ages</u>, vol. XVI (London: Kegan Paul, Trench, Trubner & Co. 1932), 32

17.   H. Denifle and A. Chatelain, eds., <u>Chartularium Universitatis Parisiensis</u>, vol. I (Paris: Delalain 1889) n.471 - 541

18.   F. Van Steenberghen, <u>Maître Siger de Brabant</u> (Louvain: Publications Universitaires 1977) 144

19.   Thomas Aquinas, <u>Summa Theologiae</u> II 2, qu. 11, art. 3 - [Madrid vol. III: 88-89]

20.   Denifle & Chatelain n.470 - 540-541

21.   Denifle & Chatelain n.461 - 532

22.   Mann & Hollsteiner 23-25

23.   Dante Alighieri, <u>La Commedia Divina</u> Purgatorio, c. xix, v.85-145 - F. Chiappelli ed., <u>Tutte Le Opere di Dante</u> (Milan: Mursia 1965) 190-191

24.   Mann & Hollsteiner 38

25.   See Section 3.3 note 48

26.   <u>Cartulaire de l'Église Saint-Lambert de Liège</u>, vol II (Brussels: Hayez 1895) n.695-696 - 283-285

27.   Dante Alighieri, <u>La Commedia Divina</u> Paradiso, c. xii, v.134-135 - Chiappelli 287

28.   B. Hamilton, <u>The Medieval Inquisition</u> (London: Edward Arnold 1981) 49

29.   Van Steenberghen, <u>Maître</u> 164

30.   Dante Alighieri, <u>La Commedia Divina</u> Inferno, c. xix, v.70-72 - Chiappelli 66

31.   C. Pinzi, <u>Storia della Città di Viterbo</u>, vol. II (Rome: Camera dei Deputati 1889) 372

32.   H. Becket et al., <u>History of the Church</u>, vol IV - <u>From the High Middle Ages to the Reformation</u>, trans. A. Biggs (London: Burns & Oates 1980) 235

33.   Vatican Archives, Arm. XIII, Chap. 1 & 2, b.c. 231 - cited in Pinzi 360

34.   Ibidem - cited in Pinzi 362-363

35.   P. de Rosa, <u>Vicars of Christ</u> (1988; London: Corgi-Transworld 1989) 230

36.   <u>Registrum Nicolai III</u>, J. Gay & S. Vitte eds. (Paris: Boccrd 1898-1938) n.490 -185

37.   C. Vendittelli, <u>Liber Memorie Omnium Privilegiorum et Instrumentorum et Actorum Communis Viterbii (1283)</u> (Rome: Vallicelliana 1990) n.399 - 144

38.   <u>Registrum Nicolai III</u> n.490 - 186

39.   <u>Registrum Nicolai III</u> n.666-672 - 296-302 and n.836-861 - 382-390

40.   Pinzi 374

41.   Pinzi 377

42.   Pinzi 380

43.   Dante Alighieri, <u>La Commedia Divina</u> Paradiso c. xii, v. 140-141 - Chiappelli 287

44.   A. Toaff, <u>The Jews in Umbria</u>, vol. I (1245-1435), (Leiden: Brill 1993) xiii-xiv and 8-15

45.   B. Nardi, <u>Saggi di Filosofia Dantesca</u> (Florence: La Nuova Italia 1967) 309

46.   Dante Alighieri, <u>Monarchia</u> Book III - Chiappelli 820-838

47.   Giles of Rome, <u>De Ecclesiastica Potestate [On Ecclesiastical Power]</u>, part I qu. 1-3 and part II qu. 4-7, ed. & trans. R. Dyson, (Woodbridge: Boydell 1986) 1-7 & 43-69

48.   Dante Alighieri, <u>La Commedia Divina</u> Inferno, c. XIX, v.73-81 - Chiappelli 66

49.   Pierre Dubois, <u>De Recuperatione Terrae Sanctae,</u> ed. C. Langlois (Paris: Picard 1891) 121-122

      Also P. Dubois, <u>The Recovery of the Holy Land,</u> ed. and trans. W. Brandt (New York: Columbia University 1956) 189-190

      Also see Section 2.4

50.   Aristotle, <u>Politics</u> 3.11 (1282b1-3) - J. Welldon, ed. & trans., <u>The Politics of Aristotle</u> (London: Macmillan 1893) 133-134

51.   D. Waley, <u>The Papal State in the Thirteenth Century</u> (London: Macmillan 1961) 201

      Also see Pinzi 389

52.   Mann & Hollsteiner 174

53.   Denifle & Chatelain n.409 - 449-457

      Also see Section 3.2 notes 14 & 15

54.   Mann & Hollsteiner 202-203

55.   L. Fumi, ed., "Cronaca di Luca di Domenico Manenti (1174-1413)," <u>Ephemerides Urbevetanae dal Codice Vaticano Urbinate 1745</u>, vol. 1 (Città di Castello, Lapi 1920) 317

56.   Fumi, ed., "Annales Urbevetanae (1161-1332)," 133 lines 15-17

57. D. Waley, <u>Mediaeval Orvieto: the Political History of an Italian City-State 1157-1334</u> (Cambridge: University Press 1952) 49

58. See note 29 above

59. See note 9 above

60. Hamilton 52-53

61. See Section 3.2 and also Section 3.3 note 43

62. See note 46 above

63. Mann & Hollsteiner 232

64. Mann & Hollsteiner 263-264

65. <u>Registrum Martini IV 1281-1285</u> (Paris: Fontemoing 1914) n.47-53 - 23-25

66. M. Rossi Caponeri & L. Riccetti, "Archivio Vescovile," <u>Chiese e Conventi degli Ordini Mendicanti in Umbria nei Secoli XIII-XIV - Inventario delle Fonti Archivistiche e Catalogo delle Informazioni Documentarie</u> (Archivi di Orvieto: 1987) Codice A

67. Waley, <u>Mediaeval</u> 54

68. Fumi ed., "<u>Annales Urbevetane</u>," 160 lines 12-15

69. <u>Registrum Martini IV</u> n.492 - 218 and n.575 - 286-287

70. Van Steenberghen, <u>Maître</u> 27

71. Dante Alighieri, <u>La Commedia Divina</u> Paradiso c. X, v.135 - Chiappelli 280

    Also see Section 2.1

72. <u>Registrum Martini IV</u> n.201 - 73

73. E. Carpentier, <u>Orvieto à la Fin du XIIIe Siècle</u> (Paris: Centre National de la Recherche Scientifique 1986) 60

74.   Carpentier 60

75.   G. Ciacci, Gli Aldobrandeschi nella Storia e nella "Divina Commedia",
       vol. 1 (Rome: Biblioteca d'Arte Editrice 1935) 242

76.   J. Coleman, "Poverty, Property and Political Thought in Fourteenth
       Century Scholastic Philosophy," L'Homme et Son Univers au Moyen
       Age, ed. C. Wenin, vol. II (Louvain: Editions Peeters 1986) 846-847

77.   See Section 2.9 note 77

78.   John of Paris, On Royal and Papal Power, introd. & trans. J. Watt
       (Toronto: Institute of Mediaeval Studies 1971) 96-105

79.   Commentarium in Politica Aristotelis (MS 482 folios 1-38) - Bruges:
       Stadsbibliotheek

80.   See Section 2.7

81.   B. Bykhovskii, "Siger of Brabant - A Beam of Light in the Darkness of
       Scholasticism," Soviet Stud

NOTES TO CHAPTER TEN

1.   D. Urvoy, Ibn Rushd (Averroes) (London: Routledge 1991) 101

      A. Nasri Nader, "La Doctrine des Deux Vérités chez Ibn Rochd (Averroes) et les Averroistes Latins," Actas del Vo Congreso Internacional de Filosofia Medieval II (Madrid: Editora Nacional 1979) 1044-1048

2.   H. Denifle & A. Chatelain, Chartularium Universitatis Parisiensis, vol. I (Paris: Delalain 1889) n.473 - 543

      Also see Preface note 12

3.   G. Sajó, Un Traité Récemment Découvert de Boèce de Dacie. De Mundi Aeternitate (Budapest: Akadémiai Kiado 1954) 35-37 & 64-79

4.   See Section 5.17 note 179

5.   R. Dales, "The Origin of the Doctrine of the Double Truth," Viator 15 (1984) 172-173

6.   P. Mandonnet, Siger de Brabant et l'Averroisme Latin au XIIIe Siècle (Fribourg: Université 1899) 161-174

7.   E. Gilson, History of Christian Philosophy in the Middle Ages (London: Sheed & Ward 1955) 391-399

8.   H. Denzinger & A. Schönmetzer, eds. Enchiridion Symbolorum Definitionum et Declarationum de Rebus Fidei et Morum, 32nd. ed. (Barcelona: Herder 1963) n.3135-3140 [esp. n.3139-3140] - 610-612

9.   P.J. Fitzpatrick, "Neoscholasticism," The Cambridge History of Later Medieval Philosophy, eds. N. Kretzmann et al. (Cambridge: University Press 1982) 847

10.   E. Bettoni, Saint Bonaventure, trans. A. Gambatese (Westport: Greenwood Press 1981) 3

11.   J. Rossiaud, "The City-Dweller and Life in Cities and Towns," The Medieval World, ed. J. Le Goff (London: Collins & Brown 1990) 140

12.   Bettoni 8

13.   J. Russell, Dictionary of Writers of Thirteenth Century England (London: Longmans, Green & Co. 1936) 71

14.   Denifle & Chatelain n.517 & n.518 - 624-627

           M. Aztelos, "The Faculty of Theology," A History of the University in Europe, vol. I, ed. H. de Ridder-Symeons (Cambridge: University Press 1992) 429

15.   L. Bataillon, "Les Crises de l'Université de Paris d'après les Sermons Universitaires," Miscellanea Mediaevalia X (1976) 168

16.   G. Bouchard, "An Ancient and Undying Light," Christian History VIII (1989) 8-15, esp. 9-11

17.   H. Maccoby, Judaism on Trial (East Brunswick, London & Toronto: Associated University Presses 1982) 62-63

18.   See Sections 5.17 and 6.6

19.   See Section 5.12; also Section 6.11 note 226

20.   See Section 6.12

21.   See Section 4.9 notes 82 & 83; also Section 7.4 note 73

22.   See Section 6.11

23.   A. Carol, "Naturaleza de la Metafisica segun Siger de Brabant," unpublished doctoral thesis, University of Navarra, 1990, 291

24.   See Section 6.9 note 185; also Section 6.12

25.   See Sections 7.3 and 7.4

26.   A. Caparello, "Sigieri di Brabante: Maestro del Dubbio," Angelicum 67 (1985) 565-608

27.   See Section 5.9 note 63; also Section 6.9 note 143

28.   See Section 4.15 and passim

29.   See Section 4.15 and passim

30.   See Section 4.1 note 21

31.   M. McLoughlin, "Paris Masters of the Thirteenth and Fourteenth Centuries and Ideas of Intellectual Freedom," Church History 24 (1955) 200

32.   See Section 3.3 note 35

33.   See Section 6.6 note 83

34.   Quaestiones in Tertium de Anima qu. 11 line 4 - Bazán (1972) 31

       Also see Section 6.6

35.   See Section 6.7 note 114

36.   See Section 6.7 note 94

37.   See Section 6.7 note 115

38.   Dante Alighieri, La Commedia Divina Inferno, c.XXVI v.97-99 & 118-120 - F. Chiappelli ed., Tutte le Opere di Dante (Milan: Mursia 1965) 92

39.   Dante Alighieri, La Commedia Divina Paradiso, c.X v.133-138 - Chiappelli 280

40.   P. Dykema & H. Oberman eds., Anticlericalism in Late Medieval and Early Modern Europe (Leiden: Brill 1993) x

41.   "A Prophet without Honor," Christian History VIII (1989) 6-7

42.   See Section 9.3 note 46

43.   A. Zimmermann, "Ein Averroist des Späten 13. Jahrhunderts: Ferrandus de Hispania," Archiv für Geschichte der Philosophie 50 (1968) 145-164

44.   Mandonnet 177-179

494

45.   See Section 1.8 notes 45 and 46

46.   See Section 5.8 note 55

47.   See Section 3.2 note 28 and Section 5.8 note 56

48.   See Section 7.6 note 89

49.   <u>De Anima Intellectiva</u> ch. 3 lines 79-8O - Bazán (1972) 81

50.   F. Van Steenberghen, <u>Introduction à l'Etude de la Philosophie Médiévale</u> (Louvain: Publications Universitaires 1974) 564

51.   See Section 2.9 note 83

52.   A. Minnis, <u>Medieval Theory of Authorship</u> (London: Scolar Press 1984) 21

53.   Minnis 157

54.   B. Price, <u>Medieval Thought: An Introduction</u> (Oxford: Blackwell 1992) 90-91

55.   L. Bataillon, "Bulletin d'Histoire des Doctrines Médiévales," <u>Revue des Sciences Philosophiques et Théologiques</u> 73 (1989) 94

56.   Dante Alighieri, <u>Convivio</u> tr. IV, c. IV, 11-13 - Chiappelli 590-591

57.   See Chapter 5

58.   See Chapter 6

59.   See Chapter 7

60.   See Chapter 8

61.   R. Hissette, "Note sur le Syllabus Anti-Rationaliste du 7 mars 1277," <u>Revue Philosophique de Louvain</u> 88 (1990) 404-415, esp. 410-413

62.   K. Flasch, <u>Aufklärung im Mittelalter? Die Verurteilung von 1277. Das Dokument des Bischofs von Paris Ubersetzt und Erklärt</u> (Mainz: Dieterich'sche 1989) passim

63. C. Genequand, Ibn Rushd's Metaphysics (Leiden: Brill 1984) 57

64. See Section 6.7 note 89

65. See Section 5.16 note 165; also Section 6.9 notes 175, 189 and 200; also Section 6.11 note 229

66. See Section 6.9 notes 190 and 192; also Section 6.11 note 222

67. See Section 4.12 note 95

68. See Section 6.9 note 205

69. W. Ruegg, "The Rise of Humanism," de Ridder-Symeons 453

70. Quaestiones Morales qu. 4 - Bazán (1974) 102-103

71. Aristotle, Metaphysics 5.4 (1014b16-23) - Aristoteles Latinus XXV ii Metaphysica, ed. G. Vuillemin-Diem (Leiden: Brill 1976) 88

72. Quaestiones Morales qu. 1 - Bazán (1974) 98-99

73. J. Verger, "Teachers," de Ridder-Symeons 163

74. M.-H. Laurent, "Godefroy de Fontaines et la Condemnation de 1277," Revue Thomiste 35 (1930) 273-281

75. See Section 7.3 notes 24 and 26; also Section 8.4 note 14 and Section 8.6 note 27.

76. G. de Lagarde, La Naissance de l'Esprit Laïque au Déclin du Moyen Age II - Secteur Social de la Scholastique (Louvain: Nauwelaerts 1958) 66

77. A.J. Ayer, Language, Truth and Logic (1936; rev. ed. 1946; London: Penguin 1980) 34-35, n.27

78. See note 30 above

79. See Section 6.7 notes 123-126

80. E. Mahoney, "Saint Thomas and Siger of Brabant Revisited," Review of Metaphysics 27 (1974) 553

496

81.   V. Le Clerc, <u>Histoire Littéraire de la France</u>, vol. XXI (Paris: Didot, Treuttel & Wurtz 1847) 115

BIBLIOGRAPHY

EDITIONS OF MEDIEVAL SCHOLARLY TEXTS

ALBERTUS MAGNUS   Opera Omnia ad Fidem Codicum Manuscriptorum.   20 vols. Cologne: Aschendorff 1951-1987.

[ANONYMOUS]   Quaestiones in Libros I et II de Anima.   Ed. M. Giele. Philosophes   Médiévaux   XIII.   Louvain: Publications Universitaires, 1971.

ANSELM OF CANTERBURY   Proslogion. Ed. M. Charlesworth.   Oxford: University Press, 1965.

AUGUSTINE   Confessiones. Ed. J. Migne. Vol. 32 of Patrologiae Cursus Completus. Paris: 1877.

Sancti   Augustini   Opera: Confessiones   Libri XIII.   Ed. L. Vermeijen.   Corpus   Christianorum   Series   Latina   XXVII. Turnholt: Brepols, 1981.

De Civitate Dei. Ed. J. Welldon. Vol. I.   London: SPCK, 1924.

BOETHIUS OF DACIA   Sophisma: Omnis Homo de Necessitate est Animal. Ed. M. Grabmann.   "Die   Sophismaliteratur   des   12. und   13. Jahrhunderts mit Textausgabe eines Sophisma des Boetius von Dacien". Münster: Aschendorffsche Verlagsbüchandlung, 1940.

Quaestio Naturalis de Mundi Aeternitate.   Unedited Text. "Un Traité Récemment Découvert de Boèce de Dacie". Ed. G. Sajó. Budapest: Akadémiai Kiado, 1954. 81-119.

Modi Significandi sive Quaestiones super Priscianum Maiorem. Ed. J. Pinborg & H. Roos. Corpus Philosophorum Danicorum Medii Aevi IV. Copenhagen: Det danske Sprog- og Litteraturselskabs udgaver, 1969.

Quaestiones de Generatione et Corruptione. Ed. G. Sajó. Corpus Philosophorum Danicorum Medii Aevi V part 1. Copenhagen: Det danske Sprog- og Litteraturselskabs udgaver, 1972.

Quaestiones super Libros Physicorum. Ed. G. Sajó. Corpus Philosophorum Danicorum Medii Aevi V part 2. Copenhagen: DSL, 1974.

Quaestiones super Librum Topicorum. Ed. N. Green-Pedersen & J. Pinborg. Corpus Philosophorum Danicorum Medii Aevi VI part 1. Copenhagen: DSL, 1976.

Opuscula De Aeternitate Mundi. De Summo Bono. De Somniis. Ed. N. Green-Pedersen. Corpus Philosophorum Danicorum Medii Aevi VI part 2. Copenhagen: DSL, 1976.

On the Supreme Good; on the Eternity of the World; on Dreams. Ed. & trans. J. Wippel. Toronto: Pontifical Institute of Mediaeval Studies, 1987.

BONAVENTURE *Omnia Opera.* 11 vols. Florence: Quaracchi, 1882-1902.

Collationes in Hexaemeron. Ed. F. Delorme. Bibliotheca Franciscana Scholastica Medii Aevi VIII. Florence: Quaracchi 1934.

DANTE ALIGHIERI *Tutte le Opere.* Ed. F. Chiappelli. Milan: Mursia, 1965.

GILES OF ROME *Errores Philosophorum.* Ed. J. Koch. Trans. J. Riedl. Milwaukee: Marquette University Press, 1944.

De Ecclesiastica Potestate. Ed. & Trans. R. Dyson. Woodbridge: Boydell Press, 1986.

GODFREY OF FONTAINES *Les Quatre Premiers Quodlibets.* Ed. M. De Wulf & A. Pelzer. Les Philosophes Belges II. Louvain: 1904.

HENRY OF GHENT   Opera Omnia. Vol. V. Ed. R.Macken. Louvain:
        University Press; Leiden: Brill, 1979.

IBN RUSHD   Averroes Cordubenis Commentarium Magnum in Aristotelis De
        Anima Libros. Ed. F. Crawford. Corpus Commentarium
        Averrois in Aristotelem VI i. Cambridge, Massachusetts:
        Mediaeval Academy of America, 1953.

        Averroes' On the Harmony of Religion and Philosophy. Trans.
        G. Hourani. London: Luzac, 1961.

        Aristotelis Opera cum Averrois Commentariis. 9 vols. Venice:
        1562-1574. Reprinted Frankfurt am Main: Minerva, 1962.

        In Aristotelis Librum II Metaphysicorum Commentarius. Ed. G.
        Darms. Freiburg: Paulusverlag, 1966.

        Averroes' Destructio Destructionum Philosophiae Algazalis in
        the Latin Version of Carlo Calymnos. Ed. B. Zedler.
        Milwaukee: University Press, 1961.

IBN SINA   Avicenna Latinus. Eds. S. Van Riet & G. Verbeke. 7 vols. to
        date. Leiden: Brill, 1968- .

JOHN OF BACONTHORP   Quodlibeta. Cremona: 1618. Reprinted
        Farnborough: Gregg International 1969.

JOHN OF JANDUN   Super Libros Aristotelis de Anima. Venice: 1587.
        Reprinted Frankfurt am Main: Minerva 1966.

JOHN OF PARIS   De Potestate Regia et Papali. Introd. & trans. J. Watt.
        Toronto: Institute of Mediaeval Studies, 1971. 96-105.

JOHN PECKHAM   "De Aeternitate Mundi". Ed. O. Argerami. Patristica et
        Mediaevalia 1 (1975) 82-100   or

        Utrum Mundus Potuit ab Eterno Creari. Ed. R. Dales & O.
        Argerami. Medieval Latin Texts 69-87.

JOHN SACKVILLE   De Principiis Naturae. Ed. R.-M. Giguère. Montreal:
        Publications d'Études Médiévales, 1956.

MOSES MAIMONIDES The Fundamentals of Jewish Faith. Trans. & ed. A. Kaplan. 1975. New York: National Conference of Synagogue Youth / Union of Orthodox Jewish Congregations of America, 1984.

PETER ALIGHIERI Super Dantis ipsius Genitoris Comediam Commentarium. Ed. Vernon. Florence: Nannucci, 1845.

PETER LOMBARD Sententiarum Libri. Ed. J. Migne. Vol. 192 of Patrologiae Cursus Completus. Paris: 1880   or

Sententiarum Libri. Magistri Petri Lombardi Sententiae in IV Libris Distinctae. Specilegium Bonaventurianum 4-5. Grottaferrata: Collegii S. Bonaventurae, 1971-1981.

PETER OF TARANTAISE Quaestio De Aeternitate Mundi. Ed. O. Argerami. Patristica et Mediaevalia 4 (1981) 74-84   or

Questio de Eternitate Mundi. Ed. R. Dales & O. Argerami. Medieval Latin Texts 63-68.

PIERRE DUBOIS De Recuperatione Terrae Sanctae. Ed. C. Langlois. Paris: Picard, 1891.

QUR'AN The Koran with Parallel Arabic Text. Trans. N. Dawood. London: Penguin, 1986.

ROBERT GROSSETESTE Hexaemeron. Ed. R. Dales & S. Gieben. Auctores Britannici Medii Aevi VI. Oxford: University Press, 1982.

ROGER BACON Opera Quaedam hactenus Inedita. Ed. J. Brewer. London: Longmans, 1859.

THOMAS AQUINAS Tractatus De Aeternitate Mundi contra Murmurantes. Ed. P. Mandonnet. Vol. I of S. Thomae Aquinatis Opuscula Omnia. 5 vols. Paris: Lethielleux, 1927. 22-27.

Tractatus De Unitate Intellectus contra Averroistas. Ed. L. Keeler. Rome: Pontifical Gregorian University, 1936.

Quaestiones Quodlibetales. Ed. R. Spiazzi. Turin: Marietti, 1956.

Summa Theologiae 5 vols. Madrid: Biblioteca de Autores Cristianos, 1952-1958.

Quaestiones Disputatae. Turin: Marietti, 1964.

WILLIAM OF OCKHAM   Scriptum in Librum Primum Sententiarum.Ordinatio - Distinctiones 2-3. Ed. S. Brown & G. Gal. Opera Philosophica et Theologica.   Opera Theologica II.   New York: St. Bonaventure's College, 1970.

WILLIAM OF SHERWOOD Introduction to Logic. Ed. & trans. N. Kretzmann. Minneapolis: University of Minneapolis, 1966.

ZOHAR - The Book of Enlightenment. Trans. D. Matt. New York: Paulist Press, 1983.

502

BOOKS

ABBOTT W. ed. <u>The Documents of Vatican II</u>. London: Geoffrey Chapman, 1966.

<u>ACTAS DEL V CONGRESO INTERNACIONAL DE FILOSOFIA MEDIEVAL</u>. Asociacion Espanola de Filosofia Medieval Editorial Nacional. 2 Vols. Madrid: Editora Nacional, 1979.

ACTES DU COLLOQUE INTERNATIONAL ORGANISÉ À L'OCCASION DU 85e ANNIVERSAIRE DE LA NAISSANCE D'AVERROES 20-23 SEPTEMBRE 1976, <u>Multiple Averroes</u>. Paris: Les Belles Lettres 1978.

AERTSEN J.   "The Eternity of the World: the Believing and the Philosophical Thomas." Wissink 9-19.

"Ontology and Henology in Medieval Philosophy (Thomas Aquinas, Master Eckhart and Berthold of Moosburg)." Bos & Meijer 120-140.

ALEXANDER P. ed. <u>Textual Sources for the Study of Judaism</u>. Manchester: University Press, 1984.

APPLEYARD B. <u>Understanding the Present: Science and the Soul of Modern Man</u>. London: Picador, 1992.

ASZTALOS M. et al. ed. <u>Knowledge and the Sciences in Medieval Philosophy</u>. Proceedings of the Eighth International Congress of Medieval Philosophy (S.I.E.P.M.). Helsinki 24-29 August 1987. 2 Vols. Helsinki: Yliopistopaino, 1990.

"The Faculty of Theology." de Ridder-Symeons 409-441.

AYER A.J.   <u>Language, Truth and Logic</u>. 1936. Rev. Ed. London: Victor Gollancz 1946. London: Penguin, 1980.

<u>The Problem of Knowledge</u>. 1956. London: Penguin, 1969.

<u>Logical Positivism</u>. London: Allen & Unwin, 1959.

ed. <u>The Humanist Outlook</u>. London: Pemberton, 1968.

BACKHOUSE H. ed. Meister Eckhart. London: Hodder & Stoughton, 1992.

BAEUMKER C. Die Impossibilia des Siger von Brabant: Eine Philosophische Streitschrift aus dem XIII. Jahrhundert. Beiträge zur Geschichte der Philosophie des Mittelalters Band II Heft VI. Münster: Aschendorffschen 1898.

BARBOUR I. Religion in an Age of Science. The Gifford Lectures 1989-1991. Vol. I. London: SCM, 1990.

BAUMGARTH W. & REGAN R. eds. Saint Thomas Aquinas: on Law, Morality and Politics. Indianapolis: Hackett 1988.

BAZÁN B. ed. Siger de Brabant. Quaestiones in Tertium de Anima. De Anima Intellectiva. De Aeteritate Mundi. Philosophes Médiévaux XIII. Louvain: Publications Universitaires, 1972.

ed. Siger de Brabant. Écrits de Logique, de Morale et de Physique. Philosophes Médiévaux XIV. Louvain: Publications Universitaires, 1974.

"Averroes y Sigerio de Brabante: La Nocion de 'Intellectum Speculativum'." Actas del V Congreso Internacional de Filosofia Medieval vol. I 541-549.

BECKET H. et al. From the High Middle Ages to the Reformation. Vol. IV of History of the Church. Trans. A. Biggs. London: Burns & Oates, 1980.

BELLO I. The Medieval Islamic Controversy between Philosophy and Theology. Leiden: Brill, 1989.

BERGMANN P. "General Relativity and Our View of the Physical Universe." Yourgrau & Breck 23-28.

BERMAN L. "The Broken Mirror: Ibn Rushd and Ibn Rushd's Aristotle on Ethics." Wenin vol. I 763-768.

BETTONI E. Saint Bonaventure. Trans. A. Gambatese. Westport: Greenwood Press, 1981.

BIANCHI L. L'Errore di Aristotele: La Polemica contro l'Eternità del Mondo nel XIII Secolo. Florence: Nuova Italia Editrice, 1984.

504

"L'Evoluzione dell'Eternalismo di Sigeri [sic] di Brabante e la Condanna di 1270." Wenin vol. II 903-910.

BIFFI I.   "La Teologia in Sigieri di Brabante e Boezio di Dacia." Martínez 97-133.

BOKENKOTTER T. A Concise History of the Catholic Church. 1979. New York: Image Doubleday, 1990.

BOS E. & MEIJER P. eds. On Proclus and his Influence on Medieval Philosophy. Leiden: Brill, 1992.

BOSSIER F. & BROMS J. eds. Aristoteles Latinus VII i Physica. Leiden: Brill, 1990.

BRAITHWAITE R.B. "An Empiricist's View of Religious Belief." Ramsey, Christian Ethics 53-73.

BRANDT W. trans. & ed. Pierre Dubois's The Recovery of the Holy Land. New York: Columbia University Press, 1956.

BREWER J. ed. Fr. Rogeri Bacon Opera Quaedam hactenus Inedita. London: Longmans, 1859.

BROWN S. & GAL G. eds. Scriptum Guglielmi Ockham in Librum Primum Sententiarum. Ordinatio -Distinctiones 2-3. Opera Philosophica et Theologica.   Opera Theologica II.   New York: St. Bonaventure's College, 1970.

BURRELL D.   "Aquinas' Debt to Maimonides." Link-Salinger 37-48.

BUTTERWORTH C. "La Valeur Philosophique des Commentaires d'Averroes sur Aristote." Actes du Colloque International ... Anniversaire ... d'Averroes 117-126.

BUTTERWORTH G. trans. Origen on First Principles. London: SPCK, 1936.

CALVET J. ed. Aspects de l'Université de Paris. Paris: Editions Albin Michel, 1949.

CAPARELLO A. La "Perspectiva" in Sigieri di Brabante. Studi Tomistici 31. Rome: Pontificia Accademia di S. Tommaso e di Religione Cattolica, 1987.

CAROL A.   Naturaleza de la Metafisica segun Siger de Brabant. Unpublished Thesis: Universidad de Navarra, Pamplona, submitted 1990.

              La Distinción entre "Esse" y "Essentia" en Siger de Brabant. Pamplona: Universidad de Navarra, 1991.

CARPENTIER E.   Orvieto à la Fin du XIIIe Siècle. Paris: Centre National de la Recherche Scientifique, 1986.

CARRUTHERS P.   Introducing Persons: Theories and Arguments in the Philosophy of Mind. London: Routledge, 1989.

Cartulaire de l'Église Saint-Lambert de Liège. Vol. II. Brussels: Hayez 1895.

CARY F. ed. & trans. The Vision (or Hell, Purgatory and Paradise) of Dante Alighieri. Vol. III. London: 1831. Reprinted as Dante: the Divine Comedy. London: Bibliophile 1988.

CASTETS F.   Il Fiore, Poème Italien du XIIIe Siècle en CCXXXII Sonnets, Imité du Roman de la Rose par Durante. Montpellier & Paris: 1881.

CHARLESWORTH J. ed. Jews and Christians: Exploring the Past, Present and Future. New York: Crossroad, 1990.

CHARLESWORTH M. ed. St. Anselm: Proslogion. Oxford: University Press, 1965.

CHIAPPELLI F. ed. Dante Alighieri: Tutte le Opere. Milan: Mursia, 1965.

CIACCI G.   Gli Aldobrandeschi nella Storia e nella "Divina Commedia". Vol. 1. Rome: Biblioteca d'Arte Editrice, 1935.

COLEMAN J.   "Poverty, Property and Political Thought in Fourteenth Century Scholastic Philosophy." Wenin vol. II 845-855.

COPLESTON F.   Mediaeval Philosophy: Augustine to Scotus. London: Burns Oates/Search, 1950. Vol. II of IX. Series 1947-1975.

Aquinas. 1955. London: Penguin, 1986.

A History of Medieval Philosophy. London: Methuen, 1972.

CRAWFORD F. ed. Averroes' Commentarium Magnum in Aristotelis De Anima Libros. Cambridge, Massachusetts: Medieval Academy of America, 1953.

CROWE M. "Paradiso X: Siger of Brabant." Nolan 146-163.

CRUZ HERNANDEZ M. Vida, Obra, Pensamiento, Influencia Ibn Rusd. Cordoba: Publicaciones de Monte de Piedad y Caja de Ahorros de Cordoba, 1986.

CUPITT D. The Worlds of Science and Religion. London: Sheldon 1980.

DA CRUZ PONTES J.-M. "Astrologie et Apologetique au Moyen Age." Wenin vol. II 631-637.

D'ALBI J. S. Bonaventure et les Luttes Doctrinales de 1267-1277. Paris: Giraudon, 1923.

DALES R. Medieval Discussions of the Eternity of the World. Leiden: Brill, 1990.

The Intellectual Life of Western Europe in the Middle Ages. Leiden: Brill, 1992.

DALES R. & ARGERAMI O. eds. Medieval Latin Texts on the Eternity of the World. Leiden: Brill, 1991.

DAVIDSON H. Proofs for Eternity, Creation and the Existence of God in Medieval Islamic and Jewish Philosophy. Oxford: University Press, 1987.

DAWOOD N. ed. & trans. The Koran with Parallel Arabic Text. London: Penguin, 1990.

DEANESLY M. A History of the Medieval Church 590-1500. London: Methuen, 1925. Cambridge: University Press, 1969-1978.

DE GRIJS F. "The Theological Character of Aquinas' De Aeternitate Mundi." Wissink 1-8.

DE LAGARDE G. La Naissance de l'Esprit Laique au Declin du Moyen Age. Vol. II. Secteur Social de la Scholastique. Louvain: Éditions Nauwelaerts, 1958. 5 vols.

DELORME F. ed. S. Bonaventurae Collationes in Hexaemeron et Bonaventuriana Quaedam Selecta. Bibliotheca Franciscana Scholastica Medii Aevi VIII. Florence: Quaracchi, 1934.

DENIFLE H. & CHATELAIN A. eds. Chartularium Universitatis Parisiensis. Vol. I. Paris: Delalain, 1889. 4 vols. 1889-1897.

DENZINGER H. & SCHÖNMETZER A. eds. Enchiridion Symbolorum, Definitionum et Declarationum de Rebus Fidei et Morum. 32nd. ed. Barcelona: Herder, 1963.

DE RIDDER-SYMEONS H., ed. A History of the University in Europe. Vol. I. Cambridge: University Press, 1992. "Mobility" 280-306.

DE ROSA P. Vicars of Christ. 1988; London: Corgi-Transworld, 1989.

DE WULF M. Histoire de la Philosophie Médiévale. 3 vols. 6th. rev. ed. Louvain: Institut Supérieur de Philosophie, 1934-1936-1947.

History of Mediaeval Philosophy. 2 vols. Trans. E. Messenger (of original edition - 1924-1925). London: Longmans, Green & Co., 1926.

DOULL J. "Dante on Averroism." Actas del V Congreso Internacional de Filosofia Medieval vol. I 669-676.

DUIN J. La Doctrine de la Providence dans les Écrits de Siger de Brabant. Philosophes Médiévaux III. Louvain: Éditions de l'Institut Supérieur de Philosophie, 1954.

DUNPHY W. ed. Siger de Brabant. Quaestiones in Metaphysicam. Philosophes Médiévaux XXIV. Louvain: Éditions de l'Institut Supérieur de Philosophie, 1981.

"Maimonides and Aquinas on Creation: a Critique of their Historians." Gerson 361-379.

DUVERNOY J. La Religion des Cathares. 1976. Toulouse: Edouard Privat, 1986.

DYKEMA P. & OBERMAN H. eds. Anticlericalism in Late Medieval and Early Modern Europe. Leiden: Brill, 1993.

DYSON R. ed. & trans. Giles of Rome. On Ecclesiastical Power. Woodbridge: Boydell Press, 1986.

ÉCOLE BIBLIQUE DE JERUSALEM, La Sainte Bible. Paris: Éditions du Cerf, 1956.

ELDERS L. The Philosophical Theology of St. Thomas Aquinas. Leiden: Brill, 1990.

EVANS G. Philosophy and Theology in the Middle Ages. London: Routledge, 1993.

FAES DE MOTTONI B. "Un Aspetto dell'Universo Angelologico di Egidio Romano: Utrum sit unum aevum omnium aeviternorum." Wenin vol. II 911-920.

FAKHRY M. A History of Islamic Philosophy. 1970. London: Longman, 1983.

FALLS T. ed. Writings of Saint Justin Martyr. 1948; Washington D.C.: Catholic University of America, 1967. Vol. 6 of The Fathers of the Church. 1947- .

FITZPATRICK P. "Neoscholasticism." Kretzmann et al. 838-852.

FLASCH K. Aufklärung im Mittelalter? Die Verurteilung von 1277. Das Dokument des Bischofs von Paris Ubersetzt und Erklärt. Mainz: Dieterich'sche, 1989.

FLETCHER J. Situation Ethics. London: SCM, 1966.

FORTIN E. "Dante and Averroism." Actas del V Congreso Internacional de Filosofia Medieval vol. II 739-746.

FUMI L. ed. Ephemerides Urbevetanae dal Codice Vaticano Urbinate 1745. Vol. I. Città di Castello: Lapi, 1920.

GAY J. & VITTE S.eds. Registrum Nicolai III. Paris: Boccrd, 1898-1938.

GENEQUAND C. ed. & trans. Ibn Rushd's Metaphysics. Leiden: Brill, 1986.

GERSON L. ed. Graceful Reason: Essays in Ancient and Medieval Philosophy Presented to Joseph Owens CSSR. Toronto: Pontifical Institute of Medieval Studies, 1983.

GEYER B. ed. Alberti Magni Omnia Opera vol XVII. Cologne: Aschendorff, 1975.

GHISALBERTI A. "Boezio di Dacia e l'Averroismo Latino." Actas del V Congreso Internacional de Filosofia Internacional vol. II 765-773.

GIELE M., VAN STEENBERGHEN F. & BAZÁN B. Trois Commentaires Anonymes sur le Traité de l'Ame d'Aristote. Philosophes Médiévaux XIII. Louvain: Publications Universitaires, 1971.

GIGUÈRE R.-M. ed. Jean de Sècheville: De Principiis Naturae. Montreal: Publications de l'Institut d'Études Médiévales, 1956.

GILSON E. Études de Philosophie Médiévale. Strasbourg: Faculté des Lettres de l'Université de Strasbourg, 1921.

A History of Christian Philosophy in the Middle Ages. London: Sheed & Ward 1955.

The Christian Philosophy of St. Thomas Aquinas. New York: Random House, 1956.

Le Philosophe et la Théologie. Paris: 1960.

Introduction à la Philosophie Chrétienne. Paris: Vrin, 1960.

GLORIEUX P. La Faculté des Arts et ses Maîtres au XIIIe Siècle. Paris: Librairie Philosophique Vrin, 1971.

GRABMANN M. Neu aufgefundene Werke des Siger von Brabant und Boetius von Dacien. Sitzungsberichte der Bayerischen Akademie der Wissenschaften. Philosophischhistorische Abteilung 1924, 2. Munich: 1924.

GRAIFF C.   Siger de Brabant. Questions sur la Métaphysique. Philosophes Médiévaux I.   Louvain: Éditions de l'Institut Supérieur et Philosophie, 1948.

GREGORY J.   The Neoplatonists. London: Kyle Cathie, 1991.

GREGORY T.   "Forme di conoscenza e ideali di sapere nella cultura Mediévale." Aztalos vol. I 10-71.

GRIFFE E.   Le Languedoc Cathare et l'Inquisition.   Paris: Letouzey & Ane, 1980.

HACKETT J.   "Averroes and Roger Bacon on the Harmony of Religion and Philosophy." Link-Salinger 98-112.

HALPHEN L.   "Les Origines de l'Université de Paris."   Aspects de l'Université de Paris. Ed. J. Calvet. Paris: Éditions Albin Michel, 1949. 11-27

HAMILTON B.   The Medieval Inquisition. London: Edward Arnold, 1981.

HANA G.   "Comment Saint Thomas et Averroes ont-ils lu la Définition de l'Ame d'Aristote?"   Actas del V Congreso Internacional de Filosofia Medieval vol. II 817-824.

HAREN M.   Medieval Thought.   The Western Intellectual Tradition from Antiquity to the Thirteenth Century. Basingstoke: Macmillan, 1985.

HAURÉAU B.   "Boetius, Maître ès Arts à Paris." Histoire Littéraire de la France vol. XXX 270-279. Paris: Imprimerie Nationale, 1888.

Notices et Extraits de Quelques Manuscripts Latins de la Bibliothèque Nationale. 6 vols. Paris: 1890-1893.

HERLIHY D.   Medieval Households. Cambridge, Massachusetts & London: Harvard University Press, 1985.

HICK J.   Philosophy of Religion. Englewood Cliffs: Prentice-Hall, 1963.

HICKS R. ed. & trans. Aristotle de Anima. Cambridge: University Press, 1907.

HISSETTE R.   Enquête sur les 219 Articles Condamnés à Paris le 7 mars 1277.
                Philosophes Médiévaux XXII.   Louvain: Publications
                Universitaires, 1977.

HOEDL L.   "Die 'Averroistische' Unterscheidung zwischen Materie und
                Moeglichkeit in den Naturphilosophischen Schriften des Siger
                von Brabant." Actas del V Congreso Internacional de Filosofia
                Medieval vol. II 831-841.

HOLMES J. & BICKERS B.   A Short History of the Catholic Church.   Tunbridge
                Wells: Burns & Oates, 1983.

HOURANI G. ed. Averroes' On the Harmony of Religion and Philosophy.
                London: Luzac & Co., 1961.

HUME D.   Dialogues Concerning Natural Religion.   Ed. N. Kemp Smith.
                Indianapolis: Bobbs-Merrill,   1980.

IVRY A.   "Averroes and the West: The First Encounter/ Non-Encounter."
                Link-Salinger 142-158.

JAMES W.   Principles of Psychology. Vol. I. 1890.   Mineola, N.Y.: Dover,
                1950.

                Some Problems of Philosophy: A Beginning of an Introduction
                to Philosophy. New York: Longman, Green & Co., 1916.

JOHN XXIII [POPE] Address. Opening of Second Vatican Council.   St.
                Peter's Basilica, Rome. 11 October 1962. Abbott 710-719.

JOLIVET R.   The God of Reason. London: Burns & Oates, 1958.

JUNG C.   Man and His Symbols. 1964. London: Aldus/Jupiter, 1979.

KAPLAN A. ed. & trans. Maimonides' Principles: The Fundamentals of Jewish
                Faith.   1975.   New York: National Conference of Synagogue
                Youth / Union of Orthodox Jewish Congregations of America,
                1984.

KAY W.   Moral Development. 1968. London: George Allen, 1972.

KEELER L. ed.   Sancti Thomae Aquinatis Tractatus De Unitate Intellectus contra
                Averroistas. Rome: Pontifical Gregorian University, 1936.

512

KENNY A.   The God of the Philosophers. Oxford: Clarendon Press, 1979.

                  Aquinas. Oxford: University Press, 1980.

                  The Legacy of Wittgenstein. Oxford: Blackwell, 1984.

                  Wyclif. Oxford: University Press, 1985.

                  "Philosophy of Mind in the Thirteenth Century." Wenin vol.I 42-
                  55.

                  Reason and Religion. Oxford: Blackwell, 1987.

                  Aquinas on Mind. London: Routledge, 1993.

KENNY A. & PINBORG J. "Medieval Philosophical Literature." Kretzmann et
                  al. 11-42.

KLÜNKER W.-U. & SANDKÜHLER B. Menschliche Seele und Kosmischer
                  Geist. Stuttgart: Verlag Freies Geistesleben, 1988.

KNIGHT M.   "Morality - Supernatural or Social?" Ayer Humanist 47-64.

KNOWLES D.   The Evolution of Medieval Thought. 1962. London: Longman,
                  1988.

KOCH J. ed.   Giles of Rome.   Errores Philosophorum. Trans. J. Riedl.
                  Milwaukee: Marquette University Press, 1944.

KOGAN B.   Averroes and the Metaphysics of Causation.   New York: State
                  University, 1985.

                  "The Problem of Creation in Late Medieval Jewish Philosophy."
                  Link-Salinger 159-173.

KRETZMANN N. ed. & trans.   William of Sherwood's Introduction to Logic.
                  Minneapolis: University of Minnesota, 1966.

KRETZMANN N. KENNY A. & PINBORG J. eds.   The Cambridge History of
                  Later Medieval Philosophy: from the Rediscovery of Aristotle to
                  the Disintegration of Scholasticism 1100-1600.   Cambridge:
                  University Press, 1982.

KRISTELLER P. "Man and his Universe in Medieval and Renaissance Philosophy." Wenin vol. 1 77-91.

KROP H.   Siger van Brabant: De Dubbele Waarheid.   Rotterdam: Ambo/Baarn, 1992.

KUKSEWICZ Z. De Siger de Brabant à Jacques de Plaisance. La Théorie de l'Intellect chez les Averroistes Latins des XIIIe et XIVe Siècles. Wroclaw-Warsaw-Cracow: Institut de Philosophie et de Sociologie de l'Académie Polonaise des Sciences, 1968.

KUNG H.   The Council and Reunion. Trans. C. Hastings. London: Sheed and Ward 1961.

LANE CRAIG W. Divine Foreknowledge and Human Freedom. Leiden: Brill, 1991.

LANGLOIS C. ed. Pierre Dubois. De Recuperatione Terrae Sanctae. Paris: Picard, 1891.

LEAMAN O.   Averroes and His Philosophy. Oxford: Clarendon Press, 1988.

LE CLERC V.   "Siger de Brabant, Professeur aux Écoles de la Rue du Fouarre". Histoire Littéraire de la France vol. XXI 96-127. Paris: Didot, Treuttel & Wurtz 1847.

LEFF G.   William of Ockham. Manchester: University Press, 1975.

                Medieval Thought from Augustine to Ockham. 1958. London: Merlin Press, 1980.

                "The Faculty of Arts: the Trivium and the Three Philosophies." de Ridder-Symeons 307-336.

LE GOFF J. ed. The Medieval World. Trans. L. Cochrane. London: Collins & Brown, 1990.

LE ROY LADURIE E. Montaillou: Cathars and Catholics in a French Village 1294-1324. Trans. B. Bray. 1978. London: Penguin, 1990.

LEWRY O. ed.   Robert Kilwardby O.P.: On Time and Imagination. Oxford: University Press, 1987.

514

LINK-SALINGER R. ed. A Straight Path: Studies in Medieval Philosophy and Culture. Washington D.C.: Catholic University of America Press, 1988.

LONERGAN B. Insight: a Study of Human Understanding. London: Longmans, Green and Co., 1957.

Method in Theology. London: Darton, Longman & Todd, 1972.

LOTTIN O. Psychologie et Morale aux XIIe et XIIIe Siècles. Gembloux: Ducelot, 1942.

MacCLINTOCK S. Perversity and Error. Studies on the "Averroist" John of Jandun. Bloomington: Indiana University Press, 1956.

MACCOBY H. ed. & trans. Judaism on Trial. East Brunswick, London & Toronto: Associated University Presses, 1982.

MACQUARRIE J. God-Talk. London: S.C.M., 1967.

MAGEE B. Popper. 1973. London: Fontana/Collins, 1981.

MAHDI M. "Man and his Universe in Medieval Arabic Philosophy." Wenin vol. I 102-113.

MANDONNET P. Siger de Brabant et l'Averroisme Latin au XIIIe Siècle. Fribourg: Université, 1899. Second Ed., 2 vols. Louvain: les Philosophes Belges VI-VII, 1911-1908.

MANN H. & HOLLSTEINER J. The Lives of the Popes in the Middle Ages. Vol. XVI. The Popes at the Height of their Temporal Influence: Innocent II to Blessed Benedict XI 1130-1305. London: Kegan Paul, Trench, Trubner & Co., 1932.

MARENBON J. Later Medieval Philosophy 1150-1350. London: Routledge and Kegan Paul, 1987.

"The Theoretical and Practical Autonomy of Philosophy as a Discipline in the Middle Ages: Latin Philosophy, 1250-1350." Aztalos vol. I 262-274.

MARKUS R.   Saeculum: History and Society in the Theology of St. Augustine. Cambridge: University Press, 1970.

MARLASCA A. ed. Les Quaestiones super Librum De Causis de Siger de Brabant. Philosophes Médiévaux XII. Louvain: Publications Universitaires, 1972.

MARTIN C. ed. Chronicles and Memorials of Great Britain during the Middle Ages. Vol. III. London: Longman, Trubner & Co., 1885. 842. 3 vols. 1882-1885.

"Martini Continuatio Brabantina" [Brabantine Chronicle]. Monumenta Germaniae Historica, Scriptores. Vol. XXIV 259-265. Hannover: 1879.

MARTÍNEZ R. ed. Unità e Autonomia del Sapere: il Dibattito del XIII Secolo. Rome: Armando, 1994.

MAURER A.   Medieval Philosophy. Toronto: Pontifical Institute of Medieval Studies, 1982.

                     ed.   Siger de Brabant.   Quaestiones in Metaphysicam. Philosophes Médiévaux XXV.   Louvain: Éditions de l'Institut Supérieur de Philosophie, 1983.

MAY G.   Creatio ex Nihilo: The Doctrine of 'Creation out of Nothing" in Early Christian Thought.   Trans. A. Worrall.   Edinburgh: T. & T. Clark, 1994.

MAZIERSKI S. "Temps et Éternité." Wenin Vol.II 876-881.

McCREA W.   "Models, Laws and the Universe." Yourgrau & Breck 59-74.

McINERNEY R. "Aquinas on Divine Omnipotence." Wenin Vol.I 440-444.

McKINNEY R. ed. Creation, Christ and Culture.   Studies in Honour of T.F. Torrance. Edinburgh: T. & T. Clark, 1976.

MEADE D.   The Medieval Church in England. Worthing: Chapman, 1988.

MEERSSEMANN G. ed. Laurentii Pignon Catalogi et Chronica, accedunt Catalogi Stamensis et Upsalensis Scriptorum O.P. Monumenta Ordinis Fratrum Praedicatorum Historica, 16. Rome: 1936.

MIGNE J. ed. Patrologiae Cursus Completus. Series Graeca. 166 vols. Paris: Garnier, 1857-1904.

Patrologiae Cursus Completus. Series Latina. 221 vols. Paris: Garnier, 1844-1904.

MINNIS A. Medieval Theory of Authorship. London: Scolar, 1984.

MISNER C. "Cosmology and Theology." Yourgrau & Breck 75-100.

MOHAMMED O. Averroes' Doctrine of Immortality: a Matter of Controversy. Waterloo, Ontario: Canadian Corporation for Studies in Religion, 1984.

MOLTMANN J. "Creation and Redemption." McKinney 119-134.

MONTGOMERY WATT W. Bell's Introduction to the Qur'an. Edinburgh: University Press, 1970.

Islamic Philosophy and Theology. Edinburgh: University Pres, 1985.

MOODY E. Studies in Medieval Philosophy, Science and Logic. Berkeley: University of California Press, 1975.

MORRIS C. The Papal Monarchy: the Western Church from 1050 to 1250. Oxford History of the Christian Church. Eds. H. & O. Chadwick. Oxford: Clarendon Press, 1991.

MULLALLY J.P. ed. Introduction. The Summae Logicales of Peter of Spain. South Bend: Notre Dame, 1945.

MÜLLER J.-P. "Philosophie et Foi chez Siger de Brabant. La Théorie de la Double Vérité." Miscellanea Philosophica R.P. Josepho Gredt O.S.B. Completis LXXV Annis Oblata. Studia Anselmiana 7-8. Rome: 1938. 35-50.

NARDI B. Sigieri di Brabante nel Pensiero del Rinascimento Italiano. Rome: Edizioni Italiane, 1945.

Saggi sull'Aristotelismo Padovano dal Secolo XIV al XVI. Florence: Università degli Studi di Padova, 1958.

Saggi di Filosofia Dantesca. Florence: La Nuova Italia, 1967.

NARDI P.   "Relations with Authority." de Ridder-Symeons 77-107.

NASRI NADER A. "La Doctrine des Deux Vérités chez Ibn Rochd (Averroes) et les Averroistes Latins." Actas del V Congreso Internacional de Filosofia Medieval vol. II 1043-1050.

NATIONAL CURRICULUM COUNCIL Curriculum Guide 5 - Health Education. York: N.C.C., 1990.

NEDERMAN C. & FORHAN K. eds. Medieval Political Theory - a Reader. London: Routledge, 1993.

NOLAN D. ed. Dante Soundings. Dublin: Irish Academic Press, 1981.

PEACOCKE A. Creation and the World of Science. The Bampton Lectures, 1978. Oxford: Clarendon Press, 1979.

"Cosmos and Creation." Yourgrau & Breck 365-382.

PINZI C.   Storia della Città di Viterbo. Vol. II. Rome: Camera dei Deputati, 1889.

POLKINGHORNE J. Reason and Reality. London: SPCK, 1991.

POPPER K.   Conjectures and Refutations. London: Routledge & Kegan Paul, 1963.

PRIEST S.   Theories of the Mind. London: Penguin, 1991.

PRICE B.   Medieval Thought: An Introduction. Oxford: Blackwell, 1992.

QUÉTIF J. & ÉCHARD J. Scriptores Ordinis Praedicatorum. 2 vols. Paris: 1719. Reprinted New York: Burt Franklin 1959.

RAHNER K.   Theological Investigations. Vol. I. Trans. C. Ernst. 1961. London: Darton, Longman & Todd, 1965.

RAMSEY I. ed. Christian Ethics and Contemporary Philosophy. London: S.C.M., 1966.

Religious Language. London: S.C.M., 1957.

RASHDALL H. The Universities of Europe in the Middle Ages 3 vols. Oxford: Clarendon Press, 1895.   Republished, eds. F. Powicke and A. Emden, 1936. Reprint London: 1942-1958 and Oxford: 1988.

REEVES M. Joachim of Fiore and the Prophetic Future.   London: SPCK, 1976.

RENAN E. Averroes et l'Averroisme. Paris: Calmann-Lévy, 1852. 3rd ed. 1867.

RICHTER M. "Dante the Philosopher-Historian in the Monarchia." Nolan 164-187.

ROSSI CAPONERI M. & RICCETTI L. eds. Chiese e Conventi degli Ordini Mendicanti in Umbria nei Secoli XIII-XIV - Inventario delle Fonti Archivistiche e Catalogo dell Informazioni Documentarie. Archivi di Orvieto: 1987.

ROSSIAUD J. "The City-Dweller and Life in Cities and Towns." Le Goff 139-180.

RUEGG W. "The Rise of Humanism." de Ridder-Symeons 442-467

RUSSELL B. Logic and Knowledge. Ed. R. Marsh. London: Allen & Unwin, 1956.

RUSSELL J. Dictionary of Writers of Thirteenth Century England. London: Longmans, Green & Co.. 1936.

RYLE G. The Concept of Mind. London: Hutchinson, 1949.

SAJÓ G. Un Traité Récemment Découvert de Boèce de Dacie. De Mundi Aeternitate. Budapest: Akadémiai Kiado, 1954.

SANFILIPPO R. La Composizione dell'Ente Finito in Sigieri di Brabante. Pamplona: Universidad de Navarra, 1992.

SARANYANA J.-I. "Lo Satuto Epistemologico della Teologia nell'Università di Parigi (Secolo XIII)." Martínez 157-170.

SCHWINGES R. "Student Education, Student Life."   de Ridder-Symeons 195-243.

SELTZER R.   Jewish People, Jewish Thought. New York: Macmillan, 1980.

SIMKIN C.   Popper's Views on Natural and Social Science.   Leiden: Brill,
              1993.

SHELDRAKE R. A New Science of Life. London: Paladin, 1987.

SKINNER B.   Science and Human Behavior.   1953.   New York: Macmillan,
              1966.

SMALLEY B.   The Study of the Bible in the Middle Ages.   1952.   3rd. ed.
              Oxford: Blackwell, 1984.

SMART N.   The Phenomenon of Religion. London: Macmillan, 1973.

SORABJI R.   Time, Creation and the Continuum. London: Duckworth, 1983.

TEILHARD DE CHARDIN P. The Phenomenon of Man. London: Collins, 1959.

              Christianity and Evolution.   Trans. R. Hague.   London: Collins,
              1971.

TEICHMANN J. Philosophy and the Mind. Oxford: Blackwell, 1988.

THUROT C.   De l'Organisation de l'Enseignement dans l'Université de Paris au
              Moyen Age. Paris: 1850. Frankfurt am Main: Minerva, 1967.

TILBY A.   Science and the Soul. London: SPCK, 1992.

TOAFF A.   The Jews in Umbria. Vol. I (1245-1435).   Leiden: Brill, 1993.

TOYNBEE P.   Dante Studies and Researches. London: Methuen, 1902.

TUILIER A. ed. La Vie Universitaire Parisienne au XIIIe Siècle.   Paris: Chapelle
              de la Sorbonne, 1974.

URVOY D.   Ibn Rushd (Averroes). Trans. O. Stewart.   London: Routledge,
              1991.

VAN RIET S. ed. Avicenna Latinus: Liber de Prima Philosophia sive Scientia
              Divina. Leiden: Brill, 1977.

520

VAN STEENBERGHEN F. Siger de Brabant d'après ses Oeuvres Inédits. 2 vols. Les Philosophes Belges XII-XIII. Louvain: Éditions de l'Institut Supérieur de Philosophie 1931-1942.

Les Oeuvres et la Doctrine de Siger de Brabant. Brussels: Académie Royale de Belgique, Classe des Lettres et des Sciences Morales et Politiques, 1938.

La Philosophie au XIIIe Siècle. Philosophes Médiévaux IX. Louvain: Publications Universitaires, 1966.

Introduction à l'Étude de la Philosophie Médiévale. Philosophes Médiévaux XVIII. Louvain: Publications Universitaires, 1974.

La Bibliothèque du Philosophe Médiéviste. Philosophes Médiévaux XIX. Louvain: Publications Universitaires, 1974.

Maître Siger de Brabant. Philosophes Médiévaux XXI. Louvain: Publications Universitaires, 1977.

Thomas Aquinas and Radical Aristotelianism. Washington D.C.: Catholic University of America Press, 1980.

"Thomas d'Aquin et Siger de Brabant en Quête d'Arguments pour le Monothéisme." Gerson 381-400.

"Publications Récentes sur Siger de Brabant." Historia Philosophiae Medii Aevi. Eds. O. Mojisch et al. Amsterdam: Gruner, 1991. 1003-1111.

VAN VELDHUIJSEN P. "The Question on the Possibility of an Eternally Created World: Bonaventura and Thomas Aquinas." Wissink 20-38.

VENDITTELLI C. Liber Memorie Omnium Privilegiorum et Instrumentorum et Actorum Communis Viterbii (1283). Rome: Vallicelliana, 1990.

VERBEKE G. "Répertoires des Commentaires Latins Médiévaux sur Aristote." Wenin vol. I 142-154.

"The Bible's First Sentence in Gregory of Nyssa's View." Link-Salinger 230-243.

VERGER J. "Patterns." de Ridder-Symeons 35-76.

"Teachers." de Ridder-Symeons 144-168.

VOLLERT C. ed. & trans. Introduction. St. Thomas Aquinas, Siger of Brabant and St. Bonaventure on the Eternity of the World. Milwaukee: Marquette University Press, 1964.

VUILLEMIN-DIEM G. ed. Aristoteles Latinus XXV ii Metaphysica. Leiden: Brill, 1976.

WALKER G.   The Growing Storm. London: Paternoster Press, 1961.

WALEY D.   Mediaeval Orvieto: The Political History of an Italian City-State 1157-1334. Cambridge: University Press, 1952.

    The Papal State in the Thirteenth Century. London: Macmillan, 1961.

WARNOCK G.   English Philosophy since 1900. 1958. Oxford: University Press, 1969.

WATT J. introd. & trans. John of Paris. On Royal and Papal Power. Toronto: Institute of Mediaeval Studies, 1971. 96-105.

WÉBER E.-H.   L'Homme en Discussion à l'Université de Paris en 1270. La Controverse de 1270 à l'Université de Paris et son Retentissement sur la Pensée de S. Thomas d'Aquin. Paris: Librairie Philosophique J. Vrin, 1970.

WEISHEIPL J.   "The Date and Context of Aquinas' 'De Aeternitate Mundi'." Gerson 239-272.

WELLDON J. ed. & trans. The Politics of Aristotle. London: Macmillan, 1893.

    ed. & trans. Saint Augustine. Vol. I. London: SPCK, 1924.

WENIN C. ed.   L'Homme et Son Univers au Moyen Age. Actes du Septième Congrès International de Philosophie Médiévale. 30 August - 4 September 1982. 2 vols. Philosophes Médiévaux XXVI-XXVII. Louvain-la-Neuve: Éditions de l'Institut Supérieur de Philosophie, 1986.

WHITROW G.   "The Role of Time in Cosmology." Yourgrau & Breck 159-178.

The Natural Philosophy of Time. 1980. Oxford: University Press, 1990.

WIPPEL J. ed.   Boethius of Dacia: On the Supreme Good; On the Eternity of the World; On Dreams. Toronto: Pontifical Institute of Mediaeval Studies, 1987.

WISDOM J.   Philosophy and Psychoanalysis. Oxford: Blackwell, 1953.

WISSINK J. ed.   The Eternity of the World in the Thought of Thomas Aquinas and his Contemporaries. Studien und Texte zur Geistesgeschichte des Mittelalters XXVII. Leiden: Brill, 1990.

WITTGENSTEIN L. Tractatus Logico-Philosophicus. Trans. D. Pears & B. McGuinness. 1922. London: Routledge & Kegan Paul, 1961.

Philosophical Investigations. Trans. G. Anscombe. 1953. Oxford: Blackwell, 1963.

On Certainty. Ed. G. Anscombe & G. von Wright. Trans. D. Paul & G. Anscombe. 1969. Oxford: Blackwell, 1979.

YOURGRAU W. & BRECK A. eds. Cosmology, History and Theology. New York: Plenum Press, 1977.

ZEDLER B. ed.   Averroes' Destructio Destructionum Philosophiae Algazalis in the Latin Version of Carlo Calonymos. Milwaukee: University Press, 1961.

ZIMMERMANN A.   Ein Kommentar zur Physik des Aristoteles aus der Pariser Artistenfakultät um 1273. Quellen und Studien zur Geschichte der Philosophie 11. Berlin: De Gruyter, 1968.

ARTICLES

ARGERAMI O. "El Problema de la Contingencia en Siger de Brabante." <u>Revista de Filosofia</u> 20 (1968) 44-56.

"La Cuestion 'De Aeternitate Mundi': Posiciones Doctrinales." <u>Sapientia</u> 27 (1972) 313-334; 28 (1973) 99-124, 179-208.

"Johannis Peckham Quaestio Disputata 'De Aeternitate Mundi'." <u>Patristica et Mediaevalia</u> 1 (1975) 82-100.

"Circa Petri de Tarantasia Quaestionem 'De Aeternitate Mundi'." <u>Patristica et Mediaevalia</u> 4 (1981) 74-84.

"Aristoteles y las Disputas Escolasticos del Siglo XIII." <u>Sapientia</u> 36 (1981) 263-272.

BAEUMKER C. "Zur Beurteilung Sigers von Brabant." <u>Philosophisches Jahrbuch</u> 24 (1911) 177-202.

BATAILLON L. "Les Crises de l'Université de Paris d'après les Sermons Universitaires." <u>Miscellanea Mediaevalia</u> 10 (1976) 155-169.

"Bulletin d'Histoire des Doctrines Médiévaux: le Treizième Siècle (fin)." <u>Revue des Sciences Philosophiques et Théologiques</u> 65 (1981) 101-122.

"Bulletin d'Histoire des Doctrines Médiévales: le Treizième Siècle." <u>Revue des Sciences Philosophiques et Theologiques</u> 73 (1989) 87-103.

BAZÁN B. "La Eternidad y la Contingencia del Intelecto en Sigerio de Brabante." <u>Philosophia</u> 39 (1973) 63-84.

"Le Dialogue Philosophique entre Siger de Brabant et Thomas d'Aquin. A Propos d'un Ouvrage Récent de E.-H. Wéber O.P.," <u>Revue Philosophique de Louvain</u> 72 (1974) 53-155

"La Union entre el Intelecto Separado y los Individuos, segun Sigerio de Brabante." <u>Patristica et Mediaevalia</u> 1 (1975) 5-35.

524

"La Signification des Termes Communs et la Doctrine de la Supposition chez Maître Siger de Brabant." Revue Philosophique de Louvain 77 (1979) 345-372.

"La Réconciliation de la Foi et de la Raison était-elle possible pour les Aristotéliciens Radicaux?" Dialogue 19 (1980) 235-254.

"Intellectum Speculativum: Averroes, Thomas Aquinas and Siger of Brabant on the Intelligible Object." Journal of the History of Philosophy 19 (1981) 425-446.

BELTRAN M. & LLORENS J.-F. "Siger de Brabante sobre el Libre Arbitrio." Studia Lulliana 31 (1991) 167-178.

BERTOLA E. "Tommaso d'Aquino e il Problema dell'Eternità del Mondo." Rivista di Filosofia Neoscolastica 66 (1974) 312-355.

BIANCHI L. "'Velare Philosophiam non est Bonum': a Proposito della Nuova Edizione delle Quaestiones in Metaphysicam di Sigeri di Brabante." Rivista di Storia di Filosofia 40 (1985) 255-270.

BRADY I. "Background to the Condemnation of 1270: Master William of Baglione O.F.M." Franciscan Studies 30 (1970) 5-48.

BUKOWSKI T. "The Eternity of the World according to Siger of Brabant: Probable or Demonstrative?" Recherches de Théologie Ancienne et Mediévale 36 (1969) 225-229.

"J. Pecham, T. Aquinas et al. on the Eternity of the World." Recherches de Théologie Ancienne et Médiévale 46 (1979) 216-221.

"Siger of Brabant v. Thomas Aquinas on Theology." New Scholasticism 61 (1987) 25-32.

"Siger of Brabant, Anti-Theologian." Franciscan Studies 50 (1990) 57-82.

BYKHOVSKII B. "Siger of Brabant - A Beam of Light in the Darkness of Scholasticism." Soviet Studies in Philosophy (English Edition) 17 (1978) 80-98

CAPARELLO A. "La Prima Apparizione dell'Anima 'Composita' in Sigieri di Brabante - Problemi Cronologici e Dottrinali." Studi Filosofici 4 (1981) 55-94.

"Il 'De Anima Intellectiva' di Sigieri di Brabante." Sapienza 36 (1983) 441-474.

"Sigieri di Brabante: Maestro del Dubbio." Angelicum 67 (1985) 565-608.

CIPOLLA C. "Sigieri nella Divina Commedia." Giornale Storico della Letteratura Italiana VIII (1886) 53-139.

CRITTENDEN P. Arguments from Straw Street: Questions about Schillebeeckx's Account of the Resurrection." Colloquium 14 (1982) 25-35.

DALES R. "Maimonides and Boethius of Dacia on the Eternity of the World." New Scholasticism 56 (1982) 306-319.

"Discussions of the Eternity of the World during the First Half of the Twelfth Century." Speculum 57 (1982) 495-508.

"The Origin of the Doctrine of the Double Truth." Viator 15 (1984) 168-179.

DA PALMA G. "L'Eternità dell'Intelletto in Aristotele secondo Sigieri di Brabante." Collectanea Franciscana 25 (1955) 397-412.

DE MATTOS G. "L'Intellect Agent Personnel dans les Premiers Écrits d'Albert le Grand et de Thomas d'Aquin." Revue Neoscholastique de Philosophie 43 (1940) 145-161.

DONDAINE A. "Le Manuel de l'Inquisiteur (1230-1330)." Archivum Fratum Praedicatorum 17 (1947) 85-194.

DONDAINE A. & BATAILLON L. "Le Manuscrit Vindob. Lat. 2330 et Siger de Brabant." Archivum Fratrum Praedicatorum 36 (1966) 153-261.

DUNPHY W. "The Similarity between Certain Questions of Peter of Auvergne's Commentary on the Metaphysics and the Anonymous Commentary on the Physics Attributed to Siger of Brabant." Medieval Studies 15 (1953) 159-168.

ERMATINGER C.   "A Second Copy of a Commentary on Aristotle's Physics Attributed to Siger of Brabant."   Manuscripta 5 (1961) 41-49.

"Another Copy of a Recently Discovered Sigerian Work." Manuscripta 24 (1980) 51-57.

ETO T.   "Siger von Brabant und die Quaestiones in I und II De Anima. [Summary in German of Japanese article.]   Studies in Medieval Thought 1 (1958) 160-161.

"On the Author of a Commentary on De Anima.   [Summary in English of Japanese article.]   Studies in Medieval Thought 11 (1969) 149-150.

FIORAVANTI G.   "Il MS. 1386 Universitatsbibliothek Leipzig, Egidio Romano, Sigieri di Brabante e Boezio di Dacia."   Medioevo 10 (1984) 1-40.

GAUTHIER R.   "Notes sur Siger de Brabant I. Siger en 1265."   Revue des Sciences Philosophiques et Théologiques 67 (1983) 201-232.

"Notes sur Siger de Brabant II. Siger en 1272-1275: Aubry de Reims et la Scission des Normands."   Revue des Sciences Philosophiques et Théologiques 68 (1984) 3-49.

GIELE M.   "La Date d'un Commentaire Médiéval Anonyme et Inédit sur le Traité de l'Ame d'Aristote."   Revue Philosophique de Louvain 58 (1960) 529-556.

GILSON E.   "Boece de Dacie et la Double Vérité."   Archives d'Histoire Doctrinale et Littéraire du Moyen Age 20 (1955) 81-99.

GLORIEUX P.   "Un Recueil Scolaire de Godefroid de Fontaines."   Recherches de Théologie Ancienne et Médiévale 3 (1931) 37-53.

HISSETTE R.   "Substance et Création selon Siger de Brabant. À propos de l'Interpretation d'Étienne Gilson."   Recherches de Théologie Ancienne et Médiévale 46 (1979) 221-224.

"Etienne Tempier et ses Condemnations."   Recherches de Théologie Ancienne et Mediévale 47 (1980) 231-270.

"Albert le Grand et Thomas d'Aquin dans la Censure Parisienne du 7 mars 1277." <u>Miscellanea Mediaevalia</u> 15 (1982) 226-246.

"Note sur le Syllabus 'Antirationaliste' du 7 mars 1277." <u>Revue Philosophique de Louvain</u> 88 (1990) 404-416.

"L'Implication de Thomas d'Aquin dans les Censures Parisiennes de 1277." <u>Recherches de Théologie et Philosophie Médiévales</u> LXIV (1997) 3-31.

JENSEN S. SKOVGAARD "On the National Origin of the Philosopher Boetius de Dacia." <u>Classica et Mediaevalia</u> 24 (1963) 232-241

KOVACH F.   "The Question of the Eternity of the World in St. Bonaventure and St. Thomas - A Critical Analysis." <u>South Western Journal of Philosophy</u> July 1974: 141-172.

KUKSEWICZ Z. "Das 'Naturale' und das 'Supernaturale' in der Averroistischen Philosophie." <u>Miscellanea Mediaevalia</u> 21 (1991) 371-382.

LANE W.   "The Initiation of Creation." <u>Vetus Testamentum</u> 13 (1963) 63-73.

LAURENT M.-H. "Godefroy de Fontaines et la Condemnation de 1277." <u>Revue Thomiste</u> 35 (1930) 273-281.

LEFEVRE C.   "Siger de Brabant a-t-il Influencé Saint Thomas? Propos sur la Cohérence de l'Anthropologie Thomiste." Rev. of <u>L'Homme en Discussion à l'Université de Paris en 1270. La Controverse de 1270 à l'Université de Paris et son Retentissement sur la Pensée de S. Thomas d'Aquin</u>, by E.-H. Wéber. <u>Mélanges de Science Religieuse</u> 31 (1974) 203-215.

MAHONEY E. "Themistius and the Agent Intellect in James of Viterbo and other 13th Century Philosophers (Saint Thomas, Siger of Brabant and Henry Bate)." <u>Augustiniana</u> 23 (1973) 422-467.

"St. Thomas and Siger of Brabant Revisited." <u>Review of Metaphysics</u> March 1974: 531-553.

MAIER A.   "Nouvelles Questions de Siger de Brabant sur la Physique d'Aristote." <u>Revue Philosophique de Louvain</u> 44 (1946) 497-513.

MANDONNET P. "Autour Siger de Brabant." Revue Thomiste 19 (1911) 314-337; 476-502.

MARLASCA A. "La Antropologia Sigeriana en las 'Quaestiones super Librum de Causis'." Estudios Filosoficos 20 (1971) 3-37.

"De Nuevo, Tomas de Aquino y Siger de Brabante." Estudios Filosoficos 23 (1974) 431-439.

MAURER A. "Esse and Essentia in the Metaphysics of Siger of Brabant." Medieval Studies 8 (1946) 68-86.

"Another Redaction of the Metaphysics of Siger of Brabant?" Medieval Studies 11 (1949) 224-232.

"Siger of Brabant and an Averroistic Commentary on the Metaphysics in Cambridge, Peterhouse MS152." Medieval Studies 12 (1950) 233-235.

"Siger of Brabant's De Necessitate et Contingentia Causarum and MS Peterhouse 152." Medieval Studies 14 (1952) 48-60.

"Boethius of Dacia and the Double Truth." Medieval Studies 17 (1955) 235-239.

"Between Reason and Faith: Siger of Brabant and Pomponazzi on the Magic Arts." Medieval Studies 18 (1956) 1-18.

"Siger of Brabant on Fables and Falsehoods in Religion." Medieval Studies 43 (1981) 515-530.

"Siger of Brabant and Theology." Medieval Studies 50 (1988) 257-278.

McKEON R. "Philosophy and Theology, History and Science in the Thought of Bonaventura and Thomas Aquinas." Journal of Religion 58 (1978) S24-S51.

McLAUGHLIN M. "Paris Masters of the Thirteenth and Fourteenth Centuries and Ideas of Intellectual Freedom." Church History 24 (1955) 195-211.

MÍCHAS W. "Pour Préciser la Date de 'In III De Anima' de Siger de Brabant." Mediaevalia Philosophica Polonorum 26 (1982) 159-160.

MOREIRA DE SÀ A. "Pedro Hispano e la Crise de 1277 da Universidade de Paris." Boletim da Biblioteca da Universidade de Coimbra 22 (1954) 1-21

PATTIN A. "Notes Concernant Quelques Écrits Attribués à Siger de Brabant." Bulletin de la Philosophie Mediévale 29 (1987) 173-177.

PINBORG J. "Zur Philosophie des Boethius de Dacia." Studia Mediewistyczne 15 (1974) 165-185.

POPPER K. "On the Possibility of an Infinite Past: a Reply to Whitrow." British Journal of the Philosophy of Science 29 (1978) 47-48.

POTVIN A. "Siger de Brabant." Bulletin de l'Académie Royale de Belgique 45 (1978) 330-357.

"A Prophet without Honor." Christian History VIII (1989) 6-7

PUTALLAZ F.-X. "La Connaissance de Soi au Moyen Age: Siger de Brabant." Archives d'Histoire Doctrinale et Littéraire du Moyen Age 59 (1992) 89-157.

RYAN C. "Man's Freewill in the Works of Siger of Brabant." Medieval Studies 45 (1983) 155-199.

SAJÓ G. "Boèce de Dacie et les Commentaires Anonymes Inédits de Munich sur la Physique et sur la Génération Attribués à Siger de Brabant." Archives d'Histoire Doctrinale et Littéraire du Moyen Age 25 (1958) 21-58.

SALMAN D. Rev. of Les Oeuvres et la Doctrine de Siger de Brabant, by F. Van Steenberghen. Bulletin Thomiste 10 (1939) 654-672.

SÁNCHEZ SORONDO M. "La Querella Antropologica del Siglo XIII (Sigerio y Santo Tomas)." Sapientia 35 (1980) 325-358.

SARAYANA J.-I. "Lo Statuto Epistemologico della Teologia nell'Università di Parigi (secolo XIII)." Paper delivered at Conference on Autonomia delle Scienze e Unità del Sapere nelle Dispute Parigine del XIII Secolo, Storia e Attualità del Problema. Ateneo Romano della Santa Croce, Rome. 26 February 1993.

SASSEN F. "Siger de Brabant et la Doctrine de la Double Vérité." Revue Neoscolastique de Philosophie 33 (1931) 170-179.

"Siger van Brabant." Algemeen Nederlands Tijdschrift voor Wijsbegeerte en Psychologie 35 (1942) 1-11.

STEGMÜLLER F. "Neuaufgefundene Quaestiones des Siger von Brabant." Recherches de Théologie Ancienne et Médiévale 3 (1931) 158-182.

VAN STEENBERGHEN F. "Le Mythe d'un Monde Eternel." Revue Philosophique de Louvain 76 (1978) 157-179.

"Les Leçons de Siger sur la Métaphysique." Revue Philosophique de Louvain 81 (1983) 638-645.

"Le Débat du XIIIe Siècle sur le Passé de l'Univers." Revue Philosophique de Louvain 83 (1985) 231-238.

"Philosophie et Christianisme." Revue Philosophique de Louvain 86 (1988) 180-191.

VENNEBUSCH J. "Die Quaestiones Metaphysice Tres des Siger von Brabant." Archiv für Geschichte der Philosophie 48 (1966) 163-189.

WAGNER M. "Supposition Theory and the Problem of Universals." Franciscan Studies 41 (1981) 385-414.

WEBER E.-H. "Les Discussions de 1270 à l'Université de Paris et leur Influence sur la Pensée Philosophique de S. Thomas d'Aquin." Miscellanea Medievalia 10 (1976) 285-316.

WHITROW G. "On the Impossibility of an Infinite Past." British Journal of the Philosophy of Science 29 (1979) 39-45.

WIECOCKX R. "Le Manuscrit Paris Nat. lat. 16096 et la Condamnation du 7 mars 1277." Recherches de Théologie Ancienne et Médiévale 48 (1981) 227-237.

WILPERT P. "Boethius von Dacien - die Autonomie des Philosophen." Miscellanea Mediaevalia 3 (1964) 135-152.

WIPPEL J. "The Condemnations of 1270 and 1277 at Paris." Journal of Medieval and Renaissance Studies 7 (1977) 169-201.

"Did Thomas Aquinas Defend the Possibility of an Eternally Created World? [The De Aeternitate Mundi Revisited]." Journal of the History of Philosophy 19 (1981) 21-37.

"Possible Sources for Godfrey of Fontaines' Views on the Act-Potency 'Composition' of Simple Creatures." Medieval Studies 46 (1984) 222-244.

"Thomas Aquinas and the Condemnation of 1277." The Modern Schoolman 72 (1995) 233-272.

WÖHLER H.-U. "Humanismus und Rationalität im Werk des Siger von Brabant." Deutsche Zeitschrift für Philosophie 32 (NO DATE- after 1981) 558-562.

ZIMMERMANN A. "Dante hatte doch Recht. Neue Ergebnisse der Forschung über Siger von Brabant." Philosophisches Jahrbuch 75 (1967-1968) 206-217.

"Ein Averroist des Späten 13. Jahrhunderts: Ferrandus de Hispania." Archiv für Geschichte der Philosophie 50 (1968) 145-164.

INDEX